DATE DUE

~~DE 16~~			
~~DE 1 ? '00~~			
AP 23 '02			
~~JE 1 0 '02~~			
~~DE 19~~			

DEMCO 38-296

Marketing
the Menacing Fetus
in Japan

A

B O O K

The Philip E. Lilienthal imprint
honors special books
in commemoration of a man whose work
at the University of California Press from 1954 to 1979
was marked by dedication to young authors
and to high standards in the field of Asian Studies.
Friends, family, authors, and foundations have together
endowed the Lilienthal Fund, which enables the Press
to publish under this imprint selected books
in a way that reflects the taste and judgment
of a great and beloved editor.

Twentieth-Century Japan: The Emergence of a World Power

Irwin Scheiner, Editor

/2

Marketing the Menacing Fetus in Japan

Helen Hardacre

UNIVERSITY OF CALIFORNIA PRESS

Berkeley / Los Angeles / London

University of California Press
Berkeley and Los Angeles, California

University of California Press, Ltd.
London, England

© 1997 by
The Regents of the University of California

Library of Congress Cataloging-in-Publication Data

Hardacre, Helen, 1949–
    Marketing the menacing fetus in Japan / Helen Hardacre.
        p.   cm.
    "A Philip E. Lilienthal book."
    Includes bibliographical references and index.
    ISBN 0-520-20553-7 (alk. paper)
        1. Fetal propitiatory rites—Buddhism.   2. Fetal propitiatory
    rites—Japan.   3. Abortion—Religious aspects.   4. Abortion—
    Japan.   I. Title
    BQ5030.F47H37   1997
    291.3'8'0952—dc20   96-28732
                                                                   CIP

Unless otherwise attributed, illustrations and translations are by the
author.

The epigraph is from *The Witching Hour* by Anne Rice (New York:
Ballantine, 1990), pp. 64–65.

Printed in the United States of America
9   8   7   6   5   4   3   2   1

The paper used in this publication meets the minimum requirements of
American National Standard for Information Sciences—Permanence of
Paper for Printed Library Materials, ANSI Z39.48-1984.

Judith moved out while Michael was at work. The bill for the abortion—Boston hospital and doctor—came a week later. Michael sent his check to the appropriate address. He never saw Judith again.

And after that, for a long time Michael was a loner. Erotic contact had never been something he enjoyed with strangers. But now he had a fear of it, and chose his partners only very occasionally and with great discretion. He was careful to an extreme degree. He wanted no other lost children.

Also, he found himself unable to forget the dead baby, or the dead fetus more properly speaking. It wasn't that he meant to brood on the child—he had nicknamed it Little Chris, but nobody needed to know this—it was that he began to see images of fetuses in the movies he went to see, in the ads for movies which he saw in the papers.

As always movies loomed large in Michael's life. As always they were a major, ongoing part of his education. He fell into a trance in a darkened theater. He felt some visceral connection between what was happening on the screen and his own dreams and subconscious, and with his ongoing efforts to figure out the world in which he lived.

And now he saw this curious thing which no one else around him mentioned: did not the cinematic monsters of this time bear a remarkable resemblance to the children being aborted every day in the nation's clinics?

Take Ridley Scott's Alien *for instance, where the little monster is born right out of the chest of a man, a squealing fetus who then retains its curious shape, even as it grows large, gorging itself upon human victims.*

And what about Eraserhead, *where the ghastly fetal offspring born to the doomed couple cries continuously.*

Why, at one point it seemed to him there were too many horror films with fetuses in them to make a count. There was The Kindred *and* Ghoulies *and* Leviathan *and those writhing clones being born like fetuses out of the pods in* Invasion of the Body Snatchers. *He could hardly bear to watch that scene when he saw it again at the Castro. He got up and walked out of the theater.*

God only knew how many more fetus horror movies there were. Take the remake of The Fly. *Didn't the hero wind up looking like a fetus? And what about* Fly II, *with its images of birth and rebirth? The never-ending theme, he figured. And then came* Pumpkinhead, *where the great vengeful Appalachian demon grows out of a fetal corpse right before your eyes, and keeps its overblown fetal head throughout its hideous rampages.*

What must this mean, Michael tried to figure out. Not that we suffer guilt for what we do, for we believe it is morally right to control the birth of our young, but that we have uneasy dreams of all those little beings washed, unborn, into eternity? Or was it mere fear of the beings themselves who want to claim us—eternally free adolescents—and make us parents. Fetuses from Hell! He laughed bitterly at the whole idea in spite of himself.

Anne Rice, *The Witching Hour*

Contents

List of Illustrations

Plans

Maps

Figures

List of Tables

Acknowledgments

To study contemporary religious life in Japan is to see Japanese society from unsuspected angles, which frequently cut across the country's most cherished images and stereotypes about itself, especially one presenting it as a model of harmony and consensus in all things. To see from new vantage points is not, fundamentally, a question of exposing contradictions, but instead a matter of recognizing previously unnoticed connections and complexities within social life, the points at which, the issues over which, people draw on historical religious tradition to address problems in contemporary life. The study of contemporary religious life is necessarily an interdisciplinary endeavor, requiring techniques drawn from anthropology, sociology, and history, besides the ability to construct a historical context within Japanese religious history for the great variety of religious ideas, behavior, and aspirations in Japan today. The subject of religious ritual surrounding abortion in Japan has required me to reach into areas of inquiry that were new to me, and in the process I acquired new intellectual debts, which I am pleased to acknowledge here.

To Judith Allen, Director of Women's Studies at Indiana University, I owe a great deal for sustained encouragement and intellectual prodding over the course of research and writing. She constantly urged me to link my research to feminist investigations of abortion in contemporary Western countries and to studies of abortion's history in the West, to demonstrate the relevance of Japan's experience with abortion to a wider community of scholarship. She helped me especially to understand abortion's meanings in sexual negotiations between women and men, and to understand its different, often opposed, meanings for the sexes. We share an ongoing concern that scholarship showing how abortion can perpetuate women's disadvantaged positions in heterosexual practice not play into the hands of those who oppose abortion in the religious right. If this book holds any interest for scholars outside Japanese studies, the credit goes to Judith. I happily received from her frequent "tutorials" and much bibliographic advice, as well as support in the attempt to bring an analysis of popular media to my subject. Enduring dramatic readings of the whole manuscript, chapter by chapter, she gave me hope and determination to expand beyond my previous horizons.

The field research on which this book is based was carried out with Suemoto Yōko, longtime friend and research assistant, of Yokohama. During the summer of 1994, Japan's hottest summer in living memory, Yōko and I crisscrossed the country visiting the temples, shrines, new religions, and miscellaneous sites where *mizuko kuyō* is practiced, documenting the practices of more than two hundred of them with interviews, statistical calculations, maps and diagrams, photographs, and attendance at ritual performances. Having assisted me previously in studies of State Shintō and the new religion Kurozumikyō, and on the basis of her own experience as a parishioner of the Sōtō sect of Zen Buddhism, Yōko helped me see transsectarian connections in *mizuko kuyō*, the elements that have given rites for abortion a currency transcending any particular religious doctrinal or institutional framework. She helped me especially to understand the motivations of temple priests and parishioners in supporting—or tolerating—*mizuko kuyō* even if they have no particular experience of abortion or religious anxiety about it, attitudes which are a big part of the overall story of these rites. My research was greatly enriched by Yōko's insight, persistence, determination, and humor—one could find no better friend in life.

I am much indebted to Professor Tamamuro Fumio of Meiji University and to Tamamuro Eiko, whose house provided me with a base of operations and a place of much comfort and happiness between field trips. Professor and Mrs. Tamamuro encouraged me greatly during my fieldwork and provided valuable introductions to others knowledgeable about the practice of *mizuko kuyō* in particular locales. I am similarly indebted to Professor Miyata Noboru of Kanagawa University, from whose work on the history of abortion and related practices in Japan I continue to learn. Professor Morikuri Shigekazu of Osaka University of Foreign Studies shared valuable data and research materials with me, and I have profited greatly from reading his works on *mizuko kuyō*, cited in the bibliography. Dr. Kozy Kazuko Amemiya loaned me important materials and discussed Seichō no Ie with me extensively.

The complexity of abortion and *mizuko kuyō* in Japan today is brought home to the researcher by the utter sincerity and conviction of people on opposing sides of the issue. Two of the religionists whom I interviewed in depth on the topic provided special stimulus: Morita Guyō, priest at Jionji, a Tsuyama temple loosely affiliated with the Tendai school of Buddhism, and Takai Ryūichi, the priest of Daigiji, a Yukuhashi Sōtō temple. Morita feels that performing *mizuko kuyō* is a matter of her personal social and ethical responsibility, while the priest of Daigiji finds it exploitative and a distraction from the serious social problems that Buddhism should be addressing. This clash of views was enacted countless times during my fieldwork.

Discussing parts of this book with others has substantially helped to shape it. In particular, I would like to thank Tiana Norgren of Columbia University, who researched the history of the Eugenics Protection Law, for providing me with significant legal materials, bibliographic information, and journal literature. I am also grateful to the members of my 1994 seminar at Harvard, "Religion and Gender in Japanese History," especially Sarita Ellen Hudson, whose discussions of her activist work on abortion gave me many useful ideas. Harvard's Committee on the Study of Religion hosted discussions of my work on *mizuko kuyō*, which were very useful. Laurel Cornell of the Department of Sociology, Indiana University, frequently discussed with me dynamics surrounding abortion in the Edo period, and her graduate seminar afforded me the opportunity to learn the perspectives of historical demography on my subject.

My research received financial support from the Northeast Asia Council of the Association for Asian Studies, for which I am most grateful. I received related assistance in Japan from the International House of Japan. Margot Chamberlain of the Edwin O. Reischauer Institute of Japanese Studies, Harvard University, provided extensive assistance over two years in typing and revising this study.

Finally, I would like to thank Corday Productions, especially Vivian, Celeste, and Stephano, for daily amusement and serious insights into television and the tabloid media.

Preface

Rosalind Petchesky and Kristin Luker broke new ground in the study of abortion in the United States by shifting attention from demographers' statistical concern with "fertility control," and by treating abortion as a sexual practice instead. That is, Petchesky and Luker examined abortion not only as an outcome or result, but as a phenomenon that cannot be understood apart from the process and practice of sexual negotiations between women and men. In the postwar decades those negotiations have taken place over intercourse and contraception. Will a couple use contraception? Will it be used consistently? Will either or both parties make consistent contraceptive practice a precondition of intercourse? Which sex is responsible for procuring contraceptive devices? What division of labor is worked out between women and men over contraception, and with what consequences for their relationship, if they have sex continuingly? The answers to these questions depend on prior considerations, on the volatile and historically changing cultural constructions of intercourse, contraception, pregnancy, childbirth, and abortion. What range of meaning do the individual members of heterosexual couples attribute to each of them, and how do these meanings change, first, over the course of the relationship for each pair, and, second, over long periods of time for society? Petchesky, Luker, and researchers following in their footsteps have, in effect, brought the study of abortion into the realm of sexual culture.[1]

In a different framework, scholars troubled by political challenges to federal and state legislation in the United States guaranteeing women's right to abortion have embarked upon historical studies of abortion.

Sometimes the approach adopted has the clear intent to remind readers of the personal tragedies suffered by women seeking abortion before the historic *Roe v. Wade* decision of 1973, illustrating vividly the situation women would likely face again if that legislation were overturned. Challenges to *Roe v. Wade* sometimes invoke the notion that abortion is a very recent practice, powered by the so-called sexual revolution of youth in the 1960s, a time that antiabortion ideologues associate with promiscuity on an unprecedented scale and with permissiveness in many areas, with a consequent weakening of parental, especially patriarchal, authority. Once that authority is restored, according to some, the necessity for abortion will disappear. In this right-wing fantasy, abortion is persistently stigmatized as a form of licensed homicide for the convenience of irresponsible people engaged in illicit, nonmarital, nonreproductive sexual relations. To counter this, feminist historians have stressed abortion's history, its importance to married couples, and the way abortion regularly involves physicians—qualified medical personnel operating as ordinary practitioners who treat people for ordinary medical needs. While works by historians such as Rickie Solinger have focused on the twentieth century, others have discussed abortion in a longer historical time frame, examining its criminalization and state regulation in the nineteenth century, following a much longer period of its customary practice without systematic state regulation.[2] In *Sex and Secrets,* Judith Allen shows how unexceptional abortion was for much of Australian history.[3] Historical studies of abortion frequently show that in earlier times there existed no fetocentric discourse to shroud abortion in moral opprobrium. That is, people did not generally believe that human life is fully present from the moment of conception, but instead associated fetal life with "quickening," the time when perceptible movement of the fetus in the womb begins. Some scholars have identified fetal photography as a technology that makes it possible to imagine that the fetus has some independent agency of its own, apart from the mother, whose body is erased and made invisible by this photographic technique.

Thus, two traditions in scholarship on abortion have developed outside of demography, stressing abortion's nature as a sexual practice, embedded in a society's sexual culture, and showing that it is subject to historical change. This book attempts to unite the two approaches in a study of contemporary ritualization of abortion in Japan, and thereby to contribute to both lines of scholarship.

Abortion has been practiced for centuries in Japan, but it is only since the mid-1970s that religious rituals for aborted fetuses, rites called *mizuko kuyō*, have been commercialized on a large scale. While these rites enjoyed popularity for about two decades, they now appear to be in decline. This book links the contemporary practice of performing rites for aborted fetuses to a longer history of abortion's meanings in sexual culture, beginning in the seventeenth century. Much ritual surrounded a woman's first childbirth in premodern Japan, but there was virtually no ritualization of abortion. Abortion was culturally constructed along two axes: one had a tolerant attitude toward abortion when it was performed for reasons of economic hardship, and a second stigmatized it when it terminated pregnancies conceived in relationships regarded as illicit. In the latter case, the stereotyped image of the age involved a man with power and authority who sexually exploited a maidservant.

The meaning of pregnancy changed significantly when the state adopted national policies on population and public health after the Meiji Restoration of 1868. State regulation resulted in a deritualization of pregnancy and childbirth, which was compounded by a universalization of hospital birth after 1945. Reproductive life remained deritualized until the 1970s with the invention and marketing of *mizuko kuyō*, which recognized abortion as an experience that large numbers of Japanese women shared since its legalization under the 1948 Eugenics Protection Law, but for which they had no symbolic resolution. In the interval, however, popular culture, especially as seen in the personal advice columns of the national newspapers, had perpetuated the two constructions of abortion seen in the premodern era, adding new ideas and interpretations to them.

Mizuko kuyō was first popularized by religious entrepreneurs through a media campaign in Japan's tabloid newspapers and magazines. The campaign principally targeted young, unmarried women, frightening them with graphic images of menacing fetuses, a technique derived from the recent development of fetal photography, buttressing the visual message with spiritualists' dire predictions of fetal wrath and spirit attacks if proper rituals were not performed. The problems foretold for women who failed to perform *mizuko kuyō* are, in essence, a list of physical and emotional problems associated with menopause. Young women were not, however, the only ones to "get the message." Older women who had had abortions decades earlier found their unresolved feelings stirred again by the spiritualists, and many sought ritual atonement. The older generations more frequently sought such rites from the religions with which they were already affiliated, however, and many eschewed tawdry spiritualists in favor of a visit to the Buddhist parish priest. Women did not perform this ritual in shame or fear so often as they sought to give public recognition to an act that for them was both sorrowful and unavoidable. Making this recognition public meant involving men and Buddhist parish temples, as well as, occasionally, Shintō shrines, and the churches of numerous new religions. But while the spiritualists promoted *mizuko kuyō* as an unending ritual obligation, younger women did not uniformly accept this verdict of limitless guilt, and established religious institutions such as parish temples never propounded any such message. Hence, for most people who have ever paid to have a rite of *mizuko kuyō* performed, the rite was either a one-time venture from the start, or the rites were incorporated into a routinized ritual calendar in which the sexualized association of abortion was gradually lost. *Mizuko kuyō* is dying out as it fulfills the basic meaning women give to it: assuaging feelings of irresolution and ambivalence.

Mizuko kuyō is built upon a fetocentric discourse that so goes against the weight of Japanese historical tradition and public support for legalized abortion that it only ever found acceptance with a small minority of the people and their religious institutions. The degree to which fetocentrism found acceptance registers the international currency of a religious climate of anxiety at the end of the twentieth century, prompted and enabled by the intense competition surrounding the marketing of popular culture, including popular religion.

Introduction

While studying Kurozumikyō, a new Shintō religion, in the summer of 1981, I had my first opportunity to observe a ritual memorializing an aborted fetus. Mrs. Niguma, a longtime follower who was in her early sixties at the time, came to the female ministers of the rural Okayama Kurozumikyō church where I was working and told them she wanted to have a service performed. Kurozumikyō has no standard rites of this kind, nor does its doctrine mention abortion anywhere. Nevertheless, prevailed upon by this follower seeking their spiritual counsel, the two women ministers of the church created a rite adapted to the purpose. The rite relied, as do all Kurozumikyō rites, on the motif of purification. The soul of the fetus would become pure, allowing it to join the company of *kami*, the deities of Shintō, and Mrs. Niguma's state of mind would be purified, allowing her to return to Kurozumikyō's ideal condition of optimism and joy.[1]

Generally speaking, Shintō so idealizes purity that it would not ordinarily ritualize events involving blood and death, and while Kurozumikyō provides funerals for its followers, it shares this broad orientation idealizing physical and spiritual purity. Although I visited many other Kurozumikyō churches around Japan that summer (and since that time), I never again encountered ceremonies for aborted fetuses.

As a historian of the religions of Japan, I was aware that there was a growing enthusiasm for memorializing spirits of aborted fetuses, a practice called *mizuko kuyō*, but I assumed in 1981, on the basis of the little evidence available at the time, that these rites were Buddhist and centered in sectarian temples. I concluded that what I had seen in Kurozumikyō was a single follower's rather eccentric adaptation of a religious fad, of which there are many examples in Japan's religious history. I felt confirmed in that view when observation elsewhere turned up no further instances.

In fact, however, Mrs. Niguma's desire to recognize and commemorate a difficult and painful experience of thirty or forty years before exemplified a new kind of religious activity, one that had already crossed the sectarian bounds within Buddhism and was by the early 1980s taking shape in all the major institutional forms of religion in Japan: Shintō, Buddhism, Shugendō (a tradition centered on sacred mountains), new religions, and spiritualist forms. This activity was powered not primarily by the advocacy of religious leaders but by the initiative of laywomen. Thinking about Mrs. Niguma's purpose solely within the framework of the religious group within which I happened to meet her could never disclose to me the nature of the religious phenomenon in which she was participating.

The term *mizuko kuyō* literally means "rites" (*kuyō*) for *mizuko*. The word *mizuko,* literally "water children," had very limited use in premodern Japan and is absent from most lexicons of traditional folk religious life. Although it is used in a variety of religions today, it has no textual basis in any of them. The term *mizuko* is not found in Buddhist canons, in Shintō or Shugendō texts; nor is it prominent in the revelations to founders of Japan's major new religions. The absence of any textual "anchor" makes it possible for individual religionists to use the term as narrowly or as widely as they choose and as their clientele will accept. Virtually all known usages of the term include the spirits of aborted, miscarried, and stillborn fetuses, and wider uses of the term enlarge it to include the spirits of newborn infants and young children.

The ritual content of *mizuko kuyō* also varies widely but aims uniformly to comfort and honor these spirits. The motivation for such a ritual lies in the belief that misfortune will otherwise result. This is sometimes expressed as the idea that these spirits cause *tatari* (spirit attacks), sickness, accidents, loss of a husband's affections or children's obedience, or loss of economic resources. Further variation can be seen in terms of the categories of persons whom the *mizuko* are believed to "attack"; most practitioners agree that the wrathful *mizuko* certainly assaults its parents or would-be parents, especially the mother, and possibly its siblings or their children as well. Wider interpretations say that the *mizuko* can even target completely unrelated people, people who had nothing to do with their "deaths." By this interpretation, it is not possible to distinguish *mizuko* from ideas of the *muenbotoke,* the restless spirits with "no relations" (*muen*) to ritualize them properly.

Mizuko kuyō is a transsectarian ritual style that draws selectively upon historical religious tradition. At the same time, it departs strikingly from historical traditions of ritualizing reproductive life, for example, during the Edo period (1600–1868), especially from the ideas about the unity of mother and child upon which that ritualization was based. *Mizuko kuyō* is inconceivable apart from the dramatic speed of Japan's postwar demographic transition, which was made possible by the rapid and widespread introduction of legalized abortion. Abortion became a reproductive experience shared by large numbers of women, but one that was not ritualized significantly until the 1970s. In the 1970s, nonsectarian spiritualists originally promoted *mizuko kuyō,* primarily through the tabloid press, with an advertising campaign directed mainly to young women. Its message was that the spirits of aborted fetuses resent those women who "should have" carried them to term and become their mothers. Denied life by these selfish women, the spirit fetuses will menace and harm them if not properly ritualized. Tabloid accounts of "spirit attacks" by aborted fetuses gave visible shape to the idea of a vengeful fetus by using fetal photography, creating images of a scowling, full-term fetus turned head-up, hovering over young women cowering in their beds in terror. Since the same articles typically provided the addresses of spiritualists' temples, transportation directions, and a schedule of fees for different grades of ritual to assuage fetal wrath, it is little wonder that many young women, sometimes with boyfriend in tow, went in shame to a spiritualist with whom they were otherwise unacquainted to appease the *mizuko.* All indications are, however, that only a small minority of women who experience abortion are sufficiently convinced by fetocentric rhetoric to seek such rituals.

Fetocentric rhetoric asserts the idea of fetal personhood, the proposition that the fetus has the same moral value as a human being. It treats the fetus as a baby from the moment of conception and attributes to it the full spectrum of human rights. It further separates the "rights" of the fetus from those of the mother, positioning mother and fetus as antagonists. Frequently invoked in the United States antiabortion movement, fetocentric rhetoric draws on the emotionalism aroused by fetishized images of the fetus. Photographs of the fetus at various stages of development, shown as if the fetus existed outside the woman's body, help convince the viewer of the fetus's humanity. Clinical descriptions of fetal development, accompanied by images of recognizable features such as a beating heart, fingers, and toes, and combined with language referring to the fetus as a "baby," "child," or "unborn child," support the belief that the fetus is fully human from the moment of conception, and that any termination of pregnancy is an act of homicide for which the mother is to be blamed.[2]

Clearly, fetocentrism owes much to such medical technologies as fetal photography, sonar, and fetal monitoring. Nevertheless, the cultural interpretation of the images these technologies provide, and their fetishization, are separate phenomena. Fetocentric rhetoric claims that the only possible interpretation of such images is that the fetus is a "baby," who has an existence independent of its mother, and who is to be protected on the same terms as an adult human being. This interpretation leads to a different way of regarding abortion than has generally occurred in the past.

While abortion seems to have existed in virtually all societies worldwide, it has been regarded in various lights, as George Devereux's anthropological studies of 350 premodern societies have shown. The practice is universal, but attitudes toward it have varied widely, from resignation to abhorrence. Some accord the fetus the same funeral rites as adults, while others dispose of them with abbreviated rites or no ritual at all.[3] In premodern Japan, neither abortion nor infanticide was generally regarded as homicide, nor were they (or the related issue of child abandonment) considered primarily in a framework of human rights. The fetus was not conceptualized as existing apart from the mother's body, as chapter 1 will show.

Fetocentric rhetoric thus represents a significant departure from the bulk of historical tradition, as does the invoking of fetocentric rhetoric by contemporary United States opponents of abortion. Even those opposing abortion in the past did not necessarily base their arguments on fetocentric rhetoric, as Petchesky explains:

As a brief submitted by over four hundred professional historians in the *Webster* case (*Webster v. Reproductive Health Services*, July 1989) argued, never before in history has the fetus been the primary focus of campaigns to restrict abortion. In the mid-to-late nineteenth century in the United States, such campaigns had a variety of purposes all unrelated to 'protecting fetal life': the protection of women from harmful substances; the consolidation of physicians' authority over obstetrical practice; the 'enforcement of sharply differentiated concepts of [gender roles];' and the expression of 'ethnocentric fears about the relative birthrates of immigrants [especially Catholics] and Yankee Protestants'. Only in the last two decades, 'when traditional justifications for restricting access to abortion became culturally anachronistic or constitutionally impermissible,' has 'the moral value attached to the fetus [become] a central issue in American culture and law'.[4]

In Japan, fetocentric rhetoric was not marshaled in opposition to abortion in any systematic way before the postwar period, and the new religion Seichō no Ie is the single significant example of such an attempt since 1945. Drawing on the idea of fetal personhood, this religion opposed 1948 and 1949 amendments to the Eugenics Protection Law, which permitted abortion on grounds of economic hardship. The religion's opposition to legalized abortion was part of a larger platform, supporting a variety of issues, such as state funding for the Yasukuni Shrine for the war dead, rejection of Article 9 of the postwar constitution (the clause renouncing war), a return to prewar educational policy, abolition of teachers' unions, anticommunist measures, and other ultraconservative issues. Abortion opposition was but one element in a larger perspective opposing postwar progressive social change on many fronts, as is explained in chapter 2. In spite of a struggle lasting from 1960 to 1983, however, Seichō no Ie failed in efforts to repeal the economic hardship clause of the Eugenics Protection Law, and it also failed to persuade the government or the Japanese people as a whole of its notions of fetal personhood. Since the death of the religion's founder in 1985, Seichō no Ie has abandoned its antiabortion campaign entirely. The Ministry of Justice rejected Seichō no Ie's claims about fetal personhood in this 1970 statement before the National Diet: "We hold the position that the protection of human rights guaranteed in the Constitution . . . should be applied to a living, natural human being [*shizen-jin*] who, legally, is a person [*jinkakusha*]. A fetus is part of a mother's body until it is born, and is not by itself a person. Therefore, the fetus is not a legal subject of human rights under the Constitution."[5] This pronouncement rests on broad, popular support for legalized abortion in Japan, attitudes that are firmly established and unlikely to be shaken by the advocates of *mizuko kuyō*.

Mizuko kuyō, especially in its tabloid advertising campaigns, regularly invokes fetocentric rhetoric, framing abortion as a moral violation of the fetus's personhood and predicting that the wronged fetus will exact revenge on the mother. Given this pervasive tactic, it might be supposed that *mizuko kuyō* includes political action to oppose abortion or, like Seichō no Ie, a general philosophy about the fetus's rights. This is not, in fact, the case. *Mizuko kuyō* selectively applies fetocentric rhetoric, usually to young, unmarried women, using an ideology of motherhood to stigmatize nonreproductive sexual activity in them, but not their male partners, and casting much greater moral opprobrium upon single women than upon married women who have abortions. It seeks to motivate young, unmarried women to pay for rituals to appease wrathful fetuses. But young women are not the only patrons of *mizuko kuyō*.

The fetocentric discourse of *mizuko kuyō* takes on different meanings for women of different generations, and for many of those who actually sponsor *mizuko kuyō* in some form, it is not a recent abortion that they seek to commemorate. Instead, like Mrs. Niguma, they commemorate abortion decades after the fact, not necessarily from fear, but as a demonstration that they acted responsibly, often in the absence of any other choice. They do not necessarily sponsor *mizuko kuyō* in shame, nor do they always consider that ritualizing abortion is a matter that only concerns women. Where parish temples or new religions such as Kurozumikyō have instituted *mizuko kuyō*, it frequently takes forms sponsored by all parishioner household units, regardless of whether they have experienced abortion personally. For many older women, it makes sense to go for these rites to the religion from which they seek ongoing guidance, even if, like Kurozumikyō, the religion does not "advertise" or promote these rites. From the point of view of older generations of both sexes, it would be a bit sleazy to go to a spiritualist, though entrepreneurial religionists are easily found, even in rural Japan; older people prefer to consult the same minister or priest they would consult on any question of spiritual significance. To them, the idea of a religionist "specializing" in abortion is strange and has overtones of an illegitimate exploitation of fear and confusion. They feel that they should be able to rely on their usual priest or minister for all the spiritual guidance they require.

This study of *mizuko kuyō* attempts to depict contemporary religious life in Japan today both as actively adapting and transforming historic religious traditions and as immersing itself in vast industries of popular culture: print and broadcast media, popular literature and film. Moreover, because of Japanese religions' historic preoccupation with health and sexuality, they must now concern themselves with developments in medicine, medical ethics, and reproductive technologies, though many of their practitioners, especially Buddhist parish priests without guidance from their sectarian headquarters, are ill prepared to take on the task and frequently substitute the lore of popular culture for disciplined moral questioning. Other practitioners, spiritualists especially, have themselves created the popular culture surrounding religion in Japan today and its preoccupations with an "occult boom." This book seeks to interpret *mizuko kuyō* in both historical and contemporary frameworks, devoting its separate chapters to differing viewpoints on aspects of the problem.

This study of *mizuko kuyō* crosses all the institutional boundaries usually constraining religions. In addition to having Buddhist, Shintō, and Shugendō forms, *mizuko kuyō* is found within a wide range of new religious movements, and among independent, entrepreneurial religionists of a spiritualist, shamanistic character who are known by a variety of terms, such as *ogamiya* (prayer healer) and *uranaishi* (fortune-teller, diviner). *Mizuko kuyō* arose in the 1970s, flourished in the 1980s, and continues in the mid-1990s, though it is beginning to decline in some areas. As a cultural phenomenon, it is not an unmediated expression of collective sentiment but is instead unintelligible apart from the critique that has grown up against it, including its complete rejection by Jōdo Shinshū, Japan's largest Buddhist sect, as well as by many religionists and laypeople.

Mizuko kuyō has been remarkably little studied, but it has particularly attracted the attention of Western scholars, no doubt because of the association with abortion.[6] By contrast, it tends to fall between the disciplines in Japanese academe, not an obvious object of study for scholars of Buddhism, Shintō, Shugendō, or the new religions, not least because of the lack of any textual basis, as discussed above.[7] The few sociological surveys now available, however, provide much useful statistical information.[8] It seems a likely prospect for scholars of folklore, but at this writing only a few studies have been published.[9] Existing Western studies emphasize Buddhism's ritual addressing the feelings of women who, having experienced abortion, seek solace and the reassurance that the souls of the aborted will find peace.[10] While scholars in Japan focus primarily upon *mizuko kuyō*'s problematic aspects, Western writing to date has generally tended to pass over these in favor of lauding *mizuko kuyō* for providing rites to "help women deal with abortion." Western writers frequently create the impression that *mizuko kuyō* dates from time immemorial, that it exists only in a Buddhist form, that *mizuko* simply means the spirits of aborted fetuses, and that there is widespread social approbation of the ritual—that it is not the object of sophisticated critical discourse.[11] This study seeks to supplement existing research by correcting these mistaken impressions and by adding dimensions not previously addressed.

William LaFleur's *Liquid Life: Abortion and Buddhism in Japan* is a very insightful book that examines *mizuko kuyō* within the framework of Buddhist symbolism, thought, and ethics; it has provided a major inspiration for this study. It traces a continuing tradition of thought and liturgy in Japanese Buddhism surrounding abortion, culminating in contemporary *mizuko kuyō*. The book presents a detailed history of the deity Jizō, his connection with children, and his complex symbolism. Like the present study, *Liquid Life* examines contemporary rites as a reflection of broader issues in Japanese society. Moreover, it refers to Western debates on abortion, noncelibate clergy, and other issues to illuminate the full implications of *mizuko kuyō*.

This study of *mizuko kuyō* is in agreement with many of LaFleur's points and is mainly complementary to it, but also differs in significant respects. This study treats *mizuko kuyō* as a transsectarian practice that appears in the new religions, Shintō, Shugendō, and in the practice of contemporary religious entrepreneurs, as well as in Buddhism; LaFleur's overarching framework is Buddhist thought. This study is much concerned with variety within Buddhist practice, based on sectarian differences, region, and character of temple leadership. The fact that Japan's largest Buddhist sect, Jōdo Shinshū, explicitly rejects *mizuko kuyō* is a major object of attention for this study. By contrast, *Liquid Life* largely treats Japanese Buddhism as a unified phenomenon that bears a continuous cultural tradition.

This study sees a major discontinuity between contemporary *mizuko kuyō* and past Buddhist pronouncements on abortion. Whereas occasional Buddhist statements deploring abortion can be found in the past, they did not result in a transsectarian, highly commercialized, ritual form. These past pronouncements should be understood mainly as testaments to the continued, widespread practice of abortion, infanticide, and child abandonment, from which Buddhist rites were mostly absent. The intense commercialization of *mizuko kuyō* since the 1970s, its transmission through the media of popular culture, and its transsectarian character distinctly mark the contemporary character of *mizuko kuyō*.

This study is feminist in its investigation of gender conflict surrounding abortion and the practice of *mizuko kuyō*. It looks to Edo-period attitudes toward childbirth and motherhood, rather than to religious tradition, to understand the roles of abortion, infanticide, and child abandonment in that era; religious institutions did not, as a general rule or in any systematic way, concern themselves with these issues. This book examines the uncharacteristic involvement of one Buddhist figure, Saint Yūten, in questions of abortion, infanticide, and child abandonment to illustrate the way these three phenomena were inseparable in popular thought, and to show how the period produced stock interpretations of abortion in terms of Callous Men and Foolish Women, characterizations that are very much a part of contemporary *mizuko kuyō*. This study seeks to explicate the relations of power that result in contemporary young women becoming unwillingly pregnant and seeking abortions, later seeking rituals to commemorate, explain, or lay to rest that experience. This book tries to understand men's and women's different attitudes toward intercourse, contraception, pregnancy, and abortion, as well as differences between older and younger women on these issues. Such an understanding is crucial to a comprehensive grasp of *mizuko kuyō*.

An anonymous reader earlier said of the present study that, in exploring gender tensions regarding abortion as these are revealed in *mizuko kuyō*, it was "trying to do too much." In the reader's view, there could be studies of abortion rituals and their commercialization, and there could be studies of gender, but the two do not belong in the same book, and the topic of tension or conflict is unwelcome in either case. A proper approach, the reader seemed to say, would describe women's and men's attitudes toward abortion and show how *mizuko kuyō* resolves any differences between them, leaving out the topic of commercialization altogether, or it would describe how *mizuko kuyō* is performed and commercialized, excluding gender altogether.

A book modeled after this reader's advice would closely mirror older ethnographic studies of Japan, in which the qualities of harmony and social consensus have been taken to distinguish Japan from other societies and to constitute important pillars of its "uniqueness." In such studies, social harmony and consensus become almost foreordained conclusions, and elements of conflict or divergence of interest are buried, on the assumption that they are destined to be ironed out, naturally.

Over the postwar decades, a view of Japanese society as being exceptionally harmonious became deeply entrenched. Since around 1980, however, that view has increasingly been called into question. Studies of Japan's modernization through the 1960s and 1970s, a major theme of postwar scholarship on Japan, sharply depicted Japan as having achieved the massive social transformations of modernization (urbanization, industrialization, and others) unusually rapidly and painlessly, compared with Western countries. This interpretation was made possible by focusing on the macro level and ignoring nonelite groups' experience of modernization.[12] Disregarding the experience of those who bore the brunt of modernization's inevitable social dislocations made it appear that harmony and consensus must inevitably prevail. When, nevertheless, a major conflict erupted, it was treated as an exception to the rule. The resulting view, that the West had much to learn from Japan about maintaining social order, undoubtedly assisted scholars' attempts to combat racism and other negative attitudes about Japan following World War II. Together, these trends produced an image of Japan as highly atypical.

In the 1980s, however, a number of significant works contesting the exceptionalist view of Japan began to appear.[13] An increasing interest in social history gave rise to studies of such nonelite groups in Japanese society as women, the poor, and minority groups such as the Ainu, Koreans, and the former outcaste group called *burakumin*.[14] Studies by Western Japanologists appeared along with works by Japanese historians of the "People's History" school (*minshūshi*), which sought to bring to light the experience of ordinary people during Japan's modern history. These studies gained credibility and prestige within the Japanese academy.[15] Significant studies concluded that conflict was a central element in Japanese history, no less than in other countries.[16] Sociologists demonstrated the ideological nature of valuing harmony; those in authority can use this ideal as a means of silencing dissent.[17] Harmony had previously been so deeply entrenched as a foregone conclusion in studies of Buddhism that an earlier Buddhologist, Edward Conze, could say that Nichiren (1222–1282), a particularly contentious medieval Buddhist figure, was not a Buddhist at all, though millions in Japan today belong to religious organizations founded to perpetuate Nichiren's understanding of Buddhism. Even in studies of Japanese religions, however, conflict is increasingly recognized as a continuous feature of Japanese religious history.[18]

While previous idealized, stereotyped images of Japan as a uniquely harmonious society have been significantly revised, it is probably fair to say that the full implications of newer understandings are still being worked out. This is particularly true in studies involving women or issues of gender, where, in order to maintain the image of Japan as uniquely lacking conflict, some serious scholars continue to deny the reality of significant discrimination against women in the workplace.[19] The majority of scholars now researching contemporary Japan would, nevertheless, probably find obfuscating and false an uncontested portrait of abortion rites as being entirely severed from sexual culture. Anyone acquainted with the abortion debate in the United States recognizes both the centrality of religion to it and the gendered character of the overall debate. They know that the entire question is a matter of great conflict in contemporary American society. Is it really to be believed that Japan's cultural priorities of harmony and consensus mean that gender, sexuality, and conflict are irrelevant to the rituals marketed to those who have experienced abortion?

Abortion and the rituals surrounding it are—emphatically and thoroughly—gendered phenomena. Thus, it is not possible to partition off something called gender from abortion in a study of *mizuko kuyō*. The subject requires us to see the intersections of gender and power in abortion and to interrogate the meanings of these conjunctions in the lives of women and men who perform *mizuko kuyō*. The commercialization of *mizuko kuyō* is gendered in its targeting young, unmarried women, in its assumption of an ideology of motherhood (the view that all women have a duty to become mothers), and in the way it averts the gaze from men's roles in women's becoming unwillingly pregnant. Abortion's meanings are different for each sex, and the topic of abortion inescapably engages the relations of power that structure sexuality. Furthermore, abortion is experienced in terms of power and conflict, as many studies of abortion in the United States have shown. Many of the same themes of power and conflict detailed by Rosalind Petchesky and Kristin Luker also exist in the eight personal narratives of abortion presented in chapter 3.

Given the many different issues inevitably involved in *mizuko kuyō*, no single approach could address them all. Thus, this study is necessarily interdisciplinary, and the remainder of this introduction describes how and why this book adopts the tools of different disciplines to treat particular aspects of *mizuko kuyō*. Historical research and textual analysis reveal enduring motifs in Japan's interpretations of abortion from the Edo period to the present. The book identifies a process of ritualization and deritualization over that span of time as central to cultural understandings of reproduction in Japan and to contemporary society's receptivity to *mizuko kuyō*. An analysis of print media materials since 1945 forms another important part of the study, in relation to the postwar history of abortion in Japan and Japanese women's experience of it. Translation and analysis of eight personal accounts of abortion reveal how historical themes are manifested in the experience of five contemporary women and three men, and how those themes have certain consequences for their relationships and full reproductive histories. Throughout, explication of religious ideas and ritual structures the analysis. These interpretations rest on both archival research and interviews with contemporary religionists involved with *mizuko kuyō,* either as practitioners or as critics of it. Ethnographic study of *mizuko kuyō* in four separate areas of Japan provides the basis for generalizing about its prevalence and future prospects.

The complexity of *mizuko kuyō* requires that multiple perspectives must be brought to bear on the problem, but this provides no guarantee of a final solution. Interpretations of so complex and contentious an issue as *mizuko kuyō* will inevitably be partial and contingent.

Writing *Mizuko Kuyō*'s History

In chapter 1, the study of contemporary *mizuko kuyō* is placed in an historical context of the ritualization of reproduction since the Edo period, beginning with a time in which midwives purveyed sex-specific knowledge and practice about pregnancy and childbirth, and in which a woman's first childbirth was a form of initiation into the status of adult woman, carrying great significance for her position within her affinal household. The practice of midwifery was highly ritualized, and midwives were regarded as conductors of the souls of the unborn into this world and of women into fully adult status. Physicians did not attend childbirth except in unusual circumstances. Pregnant women were subject to extensive food taboos and were symbolically joined to the midwife who would deliver them by a rite of tying on a special belly band. Men were excluded from the realm of female knowledge and practice presided over by the midwife, though it was frequently they, in consultation with their parents, who decided on infanticide when it was impossible to raise the newborn infant. The poor practiced abortion, infanticide, and child abandonment in this era.

Religious institutions of any kind were uninvolved in the ritualization of reproduction, and their sanctions upon abortion and infanticide were sporadic. Religion's involvement with the sexual culture of the Edo period can be seen, however, in the activities of Saint Yūten, a Jōdo-sect Buddhist priest who exorcised the spirits of aborted fetuses and the souls of abandoned children. His ritualization of aborted fetuses through rites of merit transfer was extremely eccentric, as his legend itself announces, because this was the liturgical formula for adult funerals, and at this time it was rare to accord such rites even to children, much less to fetuses, which were usually disposed of peremptorily to assure their speedy rebirth, rather than being gathered in among the Buddhas.

In 1868, after the Meiji Restoration, the state began to regulate reproductive practice. By 1945, this led to a deritualization of reproduction in favor of its supervision by state-licensed midwives who stigmatized the practice of former, unlicensed midwives as irrational and superstitious. At the same time, the regulations institutionalized birth in a prone position and made the practice of calculating and recording intrauterine events into the central account of pregnancy, thus supplanting folk religious ideas centering on the transit of the soul. Religious institutions remained uninvolved with reproductive practice, except in the case of new religions, which purveyed their own varieties of "magical midwifery"; at least two, Tenrikyō and Tenshōkōtai Jingūkyō, accumulated their original converts by this means.

Contemporary Frameworks

After 1945 physicians rapidly monopolized treatment of pregnancy and childbirth, which were progressively medicalized and completely deritualized. Chapter 2 examines the development of *mizuko kuyō* within this context of the deritualization of reproductive experience. Soon after the 1948 and 1949 amendments to the Eugenics Protection Law, which legalized the practice of abortion in a variety of circumstances, including economic hardship, the postwar rise in population decreased through the slow spread of contraceptive use and the rapidly introduced, widespread practice of legalized abortion. The major religious traditions remained little concerned with reproductive practice, though they occasionally joined with secular authority in stigmatizing abortion. Until the 1970s, they were almost entirely aloof from any ritualization of reproductive practice, with the exception of domestic-level ceremonies to welcome a newborn to the protection of the gods at Shintō shrines. An exception to this generalization was the attempt by the new religion, Seichō no Ie, to abolish the economic hardship clause of the Eugenics Protection Law.

The deritualization of reproductive practice that resulted from state intervention since the late nineteenth century left a gap, a cultural space available for reritualization, the renewed attachment of religious meaning and interpretation. The newspaper advice columns, *jinsei annai*, without obvious religious influence, propounded a "commonsense" attitude toward abortion that was highly sympathetic to it when it resulted from economic hardship, but condemnatory when it terminated pregnancies conceived in pursuit of sexual pleasure. This bifurcated view of the reasons for abortion was directly continuous with the motifs of the Edo period, motifs we first encounter in chapter 1's examination of Saint Yūten.

Mizuko kuyō has been the major form of ritualization to commemorate abortion. *Mizuko kuyō* fills the space created by the deritualization of reproductive life, allowing religionists of all kinds to offer a regimen of ritual, interpretation, and ideology that again ritualizes reproduction. This regimen coexists with the biologism of physicians' practice and with the social contract set out in the Eugenics Protection Law legalizing abortion, seeking neither to deny nor supplant those two things. In fact, *mizuko kuyō* depends upon both of them and upon the contemporary character of heterosexuality, which it attempts to construct along the lines laid down in the mirroring motifs of Callous Man and Foolish Woman, but giving far greater attention to the Foolish Woman.

Because *mizuko kuyō* has been promoted widely through print media, especially in those weekly tabloids marketed principally to women, chapter 2 also examines the development in tabloids of a symptomology and discourse of *mizuko kuyō*, which since the mid-1970s has stigmatized—even demonized—the nonreproductive sexuality of young women. The misfortunes and ills predicted for them come down to a list of physical symptoms associated with menopause, combined with problems women experience in disciplining their children and retaining their husbands' sexual interest and fidelity. National surveys of religious institutions and their patrons reveal that *mizuko kuyō* is rejected by the majority of institutions that have ever been surveyed. The variety of orientations that exist among the people—mainly, but not entirely women—who sponsor *mizuko kuyō* is introduced here.

Mizuko kuyō is intimately connected to contemporary sexual culture and abortion's many meanings. Chapter 3 examines this nexus, presenting eight personal accounts of abortion. These eight accounts show us also that by no means is the fetocentric ideology of *mizuko kuyō* universally accepted. To the extent that we can generalize from this small number of perspectives, we can conclude that abortion is a highly charged phenomenon for both sexes, but not necessarily one which is heavily influenced by *mizuko kuyō*. Previous studies have neither provided an historical framework in terms of the ritualization of reproduction, nor have they interrogated the medical, legal, and ideological supports upon which *mizuko kuyō*'s commercialization and proliferation depend. Far less have they looked to the character of relations between women and men in heterosexual life in Japan today as a basis for *mizuko kuyō*.

Chapter 4 examines the main ritualists who provide *mizuko kuyō:* spiritualists, new religions, and Buddhist priests. The rise to prominence of spiritualists, an occult-oriented group of religious entrepreneurs, reflects a changing religious ethos of uncertainty in Japan since the mid-1970s, roughly coincident with the "oil shocks" of those years. *Mizuko kuyō* is an important manifestation of this changing ethos, as is the rise of new religions mainly concerned with the occult. *Mizuko kuyō* also represents an economic strategy on the part of many ritualists to ensure revenues and to build an enduring relationship with clients on the model of temple parishes. This was the case in the new religion Bentenshū, which adopted the practice of *mizuko kuyō* only after its founder died and many members defected. In order to recoup a following, Bentenshū commenced *mizuko kuyō* and marketed it throughout western Japan. While some spiritualists, such as Miura Dōmyō of Enman'in, an Ōtsu City temple, may realize huge incomes as a result of *mizuko kuyō*, others, such as Morita Guyō of the Tendai temple Jionji in Tsuyama City, regard their practice of *mizuko kuyō* almost as a kind of social work that speaks to serious moral issues in Japan today. Their conduct of ritual is analyzed in this chapter, along with the ideology they promote.

Other practitioners, especially the Buddhist priesthood, are not active promoters of *mizuko kuyō*, but instead feel under pressure from their traditional adherents to provide rites for aborted fetuses. They are rather passive and reactive in their orientation, in comparison to spiritualists and those new religions that feature it prominently. Most Buddhist sects have avoided taking a position on *mizuko*, in part because there is no canonical warrant, and in part to avoid the appearance of political activity inappropriate to a religious body. Thus many parish priests, confronted with women parishioners such as Mrs. Niguma, are at a loss about what to do and can only improvise. When they do, they can only draw on the stereotypes of popular culture, apparently getting as much guidance from the tabloids as ordinary laypeople.

A major exception is the Jōdo Shinshū sect of Buddhism, which has prohibited its priests from performing *mizuko kuyō*. Since it is the largest Japanese Buddhist sect, its position is highly influential. There are also many priests of other sects who refuse to perform *mizuko kuyō,* for a variety of reasons. Not only is there no textual warrant, but some of these priests also do not wish to create any association between their temples and abortion, do not accept *mizuko kuyō*'s commoditization of ritual, or believe that it is profoundly exploitative of women. The latter view is shared by Japanese feminists, folklorists, Buddhologists, and many members of the general public.

This examination of *mizuko kuyō* rests in part on a field study of four sites: Tsuyama City (Okayama Prefecture), Yukuhashi City (Fukuoka Prefecture), Miura City (Kanagawa Prefecture), and Tōno Town (Fukushima Prefecture). The field study is the subject of chapter 5. The purposes of the field study were as follows: to survey the ways in which *mizuko kuyō* is carried out; to document how regional differences and the particular circumstances of a locale affect such questions as the timing of the ritual and the involvement of a variety of religious institutions; to look at generational differences in the religious orientation of participants; and to investigate the nature and degree of male participation. This study examines sectarian patterns within Buddhism, and the ways *mizuko kuyō* is practiced in Shintō shrines and in Shugendō.

In this chapter, we gain more insight into how older generations participate in *mizuko kuyō*. Many couples experienced abortion early in the postwar period, when no ritualization of it yet existed. Now, at the end of their reproductive lives, many feel the desire to register publicly their belief that they did not abort unfeelingly or callously. In fact, they use *mizuko kuyō* to deny symbolically that they acted as Callous Men or Foolish Women. They register this denial by holding the ceremonies in ordinary parish temples. In many cases, these rites have been established as part of the temple's ordinary liturgical calendar, with all parishioners called upon to contribute, regardless of whether they have experienced abortion. However, a paradox of *mizuko kuyō* in rural parish temples now is that, although many temples have invested heavily in stone statuary and large-scale installations for *mizuko kuyō,* the majority of them stand lonely and unattended. The wave has crested in rural Japan. Most parishioners, having satisfactorily ritualized abortions experienced long ago, are now no longer so preoccupied or troubled that they would continue ritualization. It seems likely that these installations will eventually be turned over to other purposes.

Sometimes, communities seek to promote tourism by advertising *mizuko kuyō,* by asking all resident households to contribute the equivalent of hundreds of dollars to religious statues and other ritual gear for tourists. This coercion on the part of a small-town mayor flies in the face of the constitutional separation of church and state, but this issue is not addressed in these rural locales. In at least one case documented in chapter 5, such a scheme failed conspicuously and completely turned the community against *mizuko kuyō*. Coercion effectively killed off any interest local people might otherwise have had in ritualizing abortion.

While this is perhaps an extreme case, it illustrates one significant aspect of *mizuko kuyō:* its ability to exist in communities without their support, to float above them, or to spark conflict. It is clearly quite naive to regard *mizuko kuyō* as a "natural" expression of collective sentiment—it is a ritual which is historically and culturally conflicted in every aspect. Recalling also that it is a minority phenomenon rejected by the majority of religious institutions in Japan, we would be very much mistaken to gloss it simply as "Japan's way of dealing with abortion."

Perhaps *mizuko kuyō* can serve to illustrate the character of religious life in Japan at the end of the twentieth century. The practice of *mizuko kuyō* reflects a loss of confidence and optimism, while the critique of it shows a desire to reject pessimism, determinism, and the stigmatization of sexuality. *Mizuko kuyō* also illustrates the way in which historical religious tradition is continually appropriated, transformed, and adapted to contemporary circumstances, and demonstrates the vital linkages between religion and popular culture.

CHAPTER I

Reproductive Ritualization Before *Mizuko Kuyō*

The social relations surrounding sexuality and reproduction are complex, constrained by law and social policy more in some eras than others. Within communities and families, sexuality and reproduction carry great significance at many levels simultaneously, from the cementing of communal ties, to the perpetuation of the group's existence, to the replication of familial patterns of authority based on sex and age, to the expression of intimacy and love. Between the principals, of course, reproduction originates in sexual relations, in which power is negotiated between women and men, and as such these relations are highly charged, becoming important sites where meaning is attributed to many aspects of sexual and reproductive practice. *Mizuko kuyō* is a ritualization of reproductive experience, and, as such, its history can be understood most comprehensively in terms of changing constructions of pregnancy and childbirth, the social relations in which sexuality and reproduction occur, and abortion's changing place within sexual culture. Religious institutions have not always been actively involved in ritualizing reproduction, remaining aloof until very recently because sexuality and reproduction were regarded as impure.

Because meaning is attached to abortion in and through sexual relations, the relevant historical context of its ritualization lies in the social relations surrounding sexuality, pregnancy, and childbirth, and in their changing cultural constructions. This chapter examines historical change in the way reproduction has been ritualized from the Edo period to about 1945. Over this time, we can see that aspects of premodern reproductive experience were ritualized extensively, that the involvement of the state in population policy after the Meiji Restoration of 1868 resulted in the deritualization of reproductive life, and that alternative forms of ritualization arose within new religious movements to fill this cultural vacuum. *Mizuko kuyō* follows in the tradition of alternative forms of ritualization, with a focus upon abortion, an experience which came to be shared by large numbers of women after 1945.

A given social practice may be the focus of much ritual in one era, but not necessarily in a previous era. Nor should we assume that this practice will always be ritualized. When the state takes an interest in the practice in question, the ritual practitioners may be displaced and replaced with state ritualists, or the state's involvement may cause a deritualization of the practice. It—or some aspect of it—may later be ritualized again, depending upon its continued cultural significance, depending upon whether entrepreneurial ritualists can create a need for ritual, and depending upon their ability to commoditize and spread rites in response to the "need" they created.

This book's approach differs from that of previous studies in taking the position that the history of *mizuko kuyō* is *not* equivalent to the sum of fragmentary data on abortifacients, numbers of abortions, or the type and number of Jizō statues ever erected for worship. Broadly speaking, aspects of *mizuko kuyō*'s material history can be identified in premodern practices of abortion, or in premodern traditions regarding the Bodhisattva Jizō; this is the approach adopted in virtually all existing works. That approach, however, fails to produce a comprehensive understanding of abortion's place in sexual and reproductive practice, the human relations that lead to abortion, and the range of cultural constructions of abortion.

Pregnancy and childbirth have been the object of ritual since ancient times in Japanese history, but we know most about their ritualization in the Edo period (1600–1868). In the first part of this chapter, on Edo-period ritualization, we will see how first childbirth constituted a rite of passage for women into fully adult status, into the company of other adult women who shared sex-specific knowledge. The midwife's role carried religious connotations, because she conducted both the woman's and the child's passages in childbirth. Midwives were not, however, connected with religious institutions.

Infanticide, abortion, and child abandonment were widely tolerated, and it was tacitly acknowledged that these practices were unavoidable, especially for peasants. Of course, no class had access to reliable contraception. Alongside this general toleration of abortion and infanticide for reasons of economic hardship, an acceptance punctuated by sporadic condemnation, there arose a second line of thought, holding that abortion should not be tolerated for pregnancies conceived in the pursuit of sexual pleasure. In the second section of this chapter, on religion and sexual culture during the Edo period, this tradition evolves in legends of a wonder-working saint named Yūten and in stereotypes about the Callous Man and the Foolish Woman.

The Edo period's dominant style of ritualizing pregnancy and childbirth, and that period's constructions of abortion, tended to characterize anything to do with sexuality or reproduction as impure and polluted. At the same time, a perception prevailed of midwives as semireligious figures, and of pregnant women as powerful in their ability to give birth. But near the end of the era, a new religion arose that originally made its mark with an alternative ritualization of pregnancy and childbirth. Nakayama Miki, founder of Tenrikyō, collected her first followers from among women to whom she taught a means of ensuring safe childbirth. She rejected the food taboos, belt tyings, separate cooking fires, and parturition huts that constituted the "women's knowledge" generally associated with pregnancy and childbirth, especially with the initiatory character of first childbirth. Nakayama created an alternative ritualization of pregnancy and childbirth. Taken up by a minority clientele on the basis of distinctive religious beliefs, this alternative stands as one premodern precedent for *mizuko kuyō*.

The development of the Meiji state's policies on population and public health greatly transformed Edo-period traditions of ritualizing pregnancy and childbirth. After the Meiji Restoration of 1868, abortion was criminalized, and the state became much more directly and systematically involved in regulating reproduction. A deritualization of pregnancy and childbirth was one result of state attempts to control reproductive practice, leaving a kind of cultural vacuum. In 1944, Tenshōkōtai Jingūkyō, another new religion offering another alternative ritualization and midwifery, arose and found a small number of adherents. The progressive medicalization of pregnancy and childbirth, driven by physicians' entry into obstetrics and gynecology, meant for most people that pregnancy and childbirth continued in their deritualized state. Given the great importance of reproduction and its multivalent significance, it is probably inevitable that it would come to be ritualized again. By the postwar decades, however, Japan underwent major demographic changes, including a massive lowering of the birth rate in a few short years, principally through induced abortion, which was legalized in

1948. When abortion became a reproductive experience shared by many Japanese women, they—and many of their male partners—supplied a kind of "market" for *mizuko kuyō*. This chapter treats these developments down to about 1945, leaving the task of describing the postwar demographic transition and the reritualization of reproductive experience through *mizuko kuyō* to chapter 2.

The Edo-Period Ritualization of Pregnancy and Childbirth

During the Edo period, midwifery was practiced outside any state or religious-institutional framework. Pregnancy and childbirth were extensively ritualized, and the midwife's role was highly ritualistic in character. Numerous local terms expressed the midwife's function as a mediator in different ways. For example, the widespread terms *toriagebāsan* and *torihikibāsan* refer to the "old woman who pulls" the child into a new existence.[1] The birth of a woman's first child constituted a rite of passage into the community of fully adult women, raising her status within her affinal family and cementing her membership in it.[2] This traditional mode of birth required women to accumulate specialized, sex-segregated knowledge based on their own experience and to transmit it over generations to younger women.[3]

Midwives were typically women who themselves had borne several children and who practiced and resided in the same village as the women they served, not generally traveling widely to deliver women outside their own areas. Because of beliefs that birth represented a soul's transit from another world into human form in this world, the midwife was seen as a conductor of souls and the master of their transition from the liminal state within the womb to a full-fledged member of the human community.[4] The phrase *futari de umu*, "to give birth as a pair," in reference to the midwife's central role, was an apt, much-used expression.

A woman's first pregnancy was initially recognized by a rite "binding" her to the midwife expected to deliver the child, in which the midwife tied a wide belt or belly band (*iwata obi*) around the pregnant woman's abdomen during the fourth or fifth month of pregnancy, a practice accompanied by feasting, where the midwife was treated as the guest of honor.[5] Typically, the band contained a charm for safe childbirth; the charms showed much regional variation, but a piece of the husband's loincloth was widely used. From that time on, the woman was subject to food taboos specific to pregnancy (again with much regional variation), and was instructed to keep the band tight, to prevent the fetus from growing too large. The pregnant woman would then refrain from visiting shrines and temples, lest she pollute their deities.[6] The midwife and the woman's female relatives would inform the pregnant woman about the foods locally prescribed or tabooed during pregnancy, and how to prepare for the birth itself by accumulating and specially cleaning old cloth and bedding for use at the delivery.[7]

It is important to note which moments of pregnancy were singled out for ritualization. The idea of a "moment of conception" attracted no ritual or ideological attention. The binding of the *iwata obi* marked the pregnancy's public visibility, the moment from which a woman attained the status of the *ninpu,* a "pregnant woman." The existence of the fetus was recognized from this stage, called by a number of regionally specific names, not all of which incorporated the characters *ko* or *ji,* which would mark it as distinctively human.[8]

In many areas it was considered important to induct the midwife into the pollution of the household in which the birth would occur by sharing a communal meal or by receiving a piece of the pregnant woman's clothing. This communal meal with the midwife provided a means for the pregnant woman's household to make an offering to the birth god(s) (*ubugami*), whose identity was variously construed in different areas.[9] The midwife herself was a representative of these gods, or acted on their behalf, a perception expressed in the custom of placing small stones on the midwife's tray. These stones represented a place for the birth god to rest and be present in the household.[10] In some places these stones were kept in the household Buddhist altar (*butsudan*), and if children had a serious illness, they were rubbed with these stones (round for girls, elongated for boys) to impart the healing power of the birth gods.[11] The midwife in this sense was not a mere technician, but someone who maintained an ongoing relationship, a fictive kinship, with the child. She attended the major life cycle rites of the children she delivered; in return, they gave her presents at the major annual gift-giving seasons and attended her funeral.

There are legends in which midwives were worshipped as gods of childbirth and were asked to offer formal prayer (*kigan*) for safe childbirth.[12] In Yamagata Prefecture, a group of midwives acted as a *kagura* (sacred dance) troupe and was invited to perform on auspicious occasions. In some areas (Ibaragi, Fukushima, Kōchi, Tokushima), the midwife sewed the child's first clothing, without which the child could not grow properly, it was believed. Elsewhere, the midwife was called upon to name the child.

The power perceived in childbirth is expressed in the belief that the gods attend and *ubugami* preside over the birth, and in the related belief that birth cannot take place unless the gods are present. Thus, childbirth and midwifery were not seen as being too polluted to involve divinity. For example, legends from Seto present the Suwa deities as forthrightly entering a house where childbirth is in progress.[13]

There was considerable regional variation among childbirth practices, but whether the woman grasped a rope thrown over a beam for support or leaned against a rice bale, squatting was the preferred position for the delivery itself.[14] A woman might return to her natal family to give birth, or remain with her affines, and the midwife might be accompanied by one or two assistants or mobilize the pregnant woman's mother, mother-in-law, or other female relatives. Women not directly involved in the birth itself would boil water and make rice when labor began.[15] If the midwife had assistants, one would support the woman in labor by holding her from behind, under the arms, while the midwife or other assistants pushed upward around the anus and perineum, so that the child dropped vertically onto the previously prepared cloth and bedding. Men were strictly excluded from the birth itself.

In general, mountain and fishing communities established the most stringent pollution taboos on childbirth, and it was here that parturition huts (*sanya* and other terms), built at a distance from human settlements and used exclusively for childbirth, remained the longest. The last one, in Fukui Prefecture, was in use until the 1950s.[16] A parallel custom was that of having the pregnant or postpartum woman's food prepared on a separate fire (*bekka*). The source of the pollution was the blood and afterbirth produced, and nationwide the disposal of afterbirth and cloth bloodied in birth was strictly ritually circumscribed.

The power ascribed to birth was seen as being most concentrated in the woman giving birth. Exclusive possession of that power at first childbirth was a woman's warrant for excluding men from the event, for joining other women in the new status and role of motherhood, and in stigmatizing childless women as "stone women" (*umazume*).[17]

The places designated for birth itself and for the disposal of afterbirth provide further indications that birth's power was construed positively. In rice-growing areas where birth did not take place in a parturition hut, it could occur in the domicile itself or in the grain store room, because the birth god was identified as the grain god, or before the Buddhist altar, because it was believed that the ancestors are the birth gods. Also, in rice-growing areas, afterbirth could be buried under the main house pillar (*daikokubashira*), hardly the place to put something with only negative influence.[18]

There is much evidence to suggest that the fetus was not regarded as fully human. Explication of this point requires a short discussion of premodern practices of contraception, abortion, and infanticide. All three of these practices were widespread, and although it is debatable how much any of them affected the population level during the era, no one seriously argues that they did not exist.[19] In the absence of reliable contraceptive devices, contraception and abortion relied heavily on locally variant pharmacopeia and magical means, prolonged breast-feeding, and men's seasonal migration to different areas for work, making them absent for long periods. Contraceptive pharmacopeia and botanical abortifacients were in the province of the midwife, and in many cases it was she who carried out infanticide if the former two measures failed.[20]

Contraception, abortion, and infanticide were not alternatives to each other in the sense of clearly bounded choices an individual might make (in any case it would not necessarily have been the pregnant or newly postpartum woman making any such "choice"). Instead, contraception, abortion, and infanticide existed along a continuum, corresponding to the level of development of the fetus or newborn.[21]

Both the shogunate and the domains (*han*) repeatedly inveighed against both abortion and infanticide (*mabiki* and other terms), but the frequency of famine and widespread poverty among the peasantry meant that numerous births constituted too great an economic hardship for many communities to bear, leading them to resort to both practices throughout the period. Neither practice was frequently punished, and neither was heavily stigmatized by religious institutions.[22]

Infanticide, generally by strangling or asphyxiation, was apparently carried out immediately after birth. Midwives asked whether the newborn was to be kept or "sent back" (*oku ka, kaesu ka*) to the world of the gods from which it had come. This question was not necessarily addressed to the birth mother, who might not be the senior woman of the household, but more likely to her mother-in-law or husband. Given the communal nature of the "choice" and "decision," little importance attached to assigning responsibility for the event, which might be carried out by the mother-in-law or husband if a midwife was absent, or if it took place after she had left the scene. There is no evidence to suggest that infanticide was regarded in the same light as homicide; "returning" (*kaesu*) is distinctly different from killing (*korosu*).[23]

Buddhism, Shintō, and Shugendō had virtually nothing to say about contraception, abortion, and infanticide.[24] In an age in which ethical thought was preoccupied with questions of public duty, and in which none of these three practices was seen to have a public character, they were simply not on the map of ethical thinking. Instead, religious institutions saw birth and related practices in a framework of purity and pollution, according to which childbirth was generally polluting because of the blood spilled. The mother and child, first and foremost, were polluted for a time after the birth, but the father and coresidents also were expected to refrain from visiting shrines and temples. Men in some occupational groups such as fishing and forestry (ruled over by female deities) even refrained from work for a period after their wives gave birth, because some of the pollution from the birth adhered to them.[25]

Ritualization of birth and rites for newborn children were absent from Buddhism and Shugendō, but Buddhism evinced a peculiar concern for the fate of women who died in childbirth, a horrible karma sending women to a "Pool of Blood Hell," mirroring the circumstances in which they were presumed to have died. During the Edo period, Buddhism developed a specialization in rites of death and ancestor worship. These rituals reflected this belief about women killed by childbirth, which further reflected the misogyny of the tradition and the way in which it absorbed folk notions about the pollution of women.[26] A particular funeral rite for women who died in childbirth developed, called *nagare kanjō*, "flowing funeral," picking up the liquid associations of the Pool of Blood image.[27]

At the end of the medieval period, and throughout the Edo period, the Sōtō Zen school performed special rites for women who died in childbirth. These rituals, which were also known in the Rinzai Zen school, had three aims: to prevent the woman from "giving birth" in the grave, to forestall any calamity arising from the woman's resentment about her early death, and to ensure the woman's salvation. Should the lurid prospect of "birth" in the grave occur, the woman might, it was believed, return as a ghost to haunt the living, wearing a bloody shroud and carrying her infant. This type of ghost was called an *ubume*. Instructions actually called for the officiating priest to kick the corpse, as it (the corpse) was given the tonsure and as the names of ten Buddhas were spoken into its left ear. Together, these actions effected a symbolic separation of the fetus from the womb (*beppuku*). Amulets warding off misfortune were laid in the coffin to ensure further that the woman would not return as a ghost. In all this, the mother was the obvious object of attention, and the ritual intended ultimately to ensure her salvation and to help her attain Buddhahood. Apparently, the hope for the fetus was merely that it be reborn, not, like the mother, that it attain Buddhahood. There is no indication that people believed that the fetus could take independent agency, become a ghost, or launch a spirit attack upon anyone. The word *mizuko* was not used.[28]

The term *mizuko*, literally "water child," bears fluid associations linking it to ideas about women dying in childbirth. The origins of the word are unclear, and inasmuch as it can refer to a baby or young child who has died, it is like other terms that place neonates and young children in a single category, such as *akago*, "red child" (referring to the red color of neonates), and *chigo*, "divine child." *Mizuko*, however, differs from these by also including the fetus before birth. Beyond this, *mizuko* is a term subject to significant regional variation. In Ehime, *mizuko* was used for children who died before being named, while in the Oki Islands children who died during the first year of life were called *mizuko*. Although neither of these two regional usages makes a clear link to abortion or has strong aquatic associations, it was the custom in northeastern Japan to float abortion remains away in straw sacks for disposal, and this may be one point of origin for the term.[29] The term is not found in the Buddhist canons in this form, or the variant reading of the same characters, *suishi*. The inclusion of fetuses, newborns, and young children in a single category reflects a perception of vulnerable lives not yet fully established in human existence, no doubt also reflecting high rates of infant and child mortality. The term has been susceptible to shifting interpretations, and, as we will see in chapters 2, 4, and 5, that is still the case.

A newborn generally made its "public debut" with a visit to a Shintō shrine (the *hatsu miya mairi*). The occasion marked the emergence of mother, child, and the domestic group from a state of pollution, shown by the lifting of taboos upon approaching the altars of the *kami*. The child was presented to the local tutelary deity, in hopes that the deity would bless and protect the infant. It was customary for the husband's mother (rather than the birth mother) to present the child before the altar, marking the incorporation of the newborn into the husband's family line, and also for her to present the child later to neighbors and relatives.[30]

Presentation before the tutelary deity rests on the rationale that the

newborn is a member of the human community under that deity's protection. In this sense, the newborn's "humanity" is unquestionable, but
other customs suggest a different tradition of thought in which an element of liminality remains much longer after birth. There are widespread proverbs, sayings to the effect that a child could not be fully
counted as a member of the human world until it reached the age of
seven. Until that time, it remained "among the gods" (*kami no uchi*
and other phrases). These proverbs undoubtedly reflect a recognition
of high rates of infant mortality from disease and famine, a fate that
could be construed as returning to the other world from which the
child had come.[31]

The Role of Buddhist Guardians
in the Ritualization of Childbirth

While religious institutions were not centrally involved in
ritualizing pregnancy and childbirth during the Edo period, the cults
of two guardian deities, the Bodhisattvas Jizō (Sanskrit: Ksitigarbha)
and Kannon (Sanskrit: Avalokiteśvara), established significant religious
ideas about children that were later incorporated into *mizuko kuyō*.
While we can identify continuities with premodern tradition in the general idea that both these deities act as protectors of children (living and
dead), we do not find any notion of vengeful fetal spirits in the Edo-
period cults of Buddhist guardian deities. In fact, we sometimes find traditions associated with these deities that explicitly deny that the aborted
have any basis for anger at their would-be parents.

Jizō and Kannon each have been the focus of independent cults aiming to secure a wide variety of religious benefits, such as health, safety,
and good fortune, throughout Japanese religious history, independent
of reproductive practice. Iconographic and cultic forms also depict both
deities as subordinates of the Buddha Amida, who presides over the
western paradise. In contemporary *mizuko kuyō* as it is conducted in
Buddhist temples, it is typical to find that the temple's ritual installation
has at least one statue of either Jizō or Kannon. More rarely, the two
may both be found in slightly separated *mizuko kuyō* sites within the
same temple. A common devotional practice today is to purchase and
leave at the temple's *mizuko kuyō* installation a small statue of Kannon
and Jizō for each abortion or stillbirth, depending which saint the

temple has adopted for *mizuko kuyō*. This practice is not found before the 1970s, but both figures have long associations with granting children and safe delivery to women, and with protecting children so they may mature safely. These associations are stronger in the case of Jizō, who is believed to protect children after they die, to guard them in the other world.

Buddhist scholars of Jizō's history and the texts associated with his cult in India, China, and Japan often express puzzlement about the figure's recent appropriation in *mizuko kuyō*. This is both because the term *mizuko* lacks any canonical basis, and because in traditional iconographical canons there is no such thing as a "Mizuko Jizō" or a "Mizuko Kannon." This means that the 1970s development of these iconographical representations of Jizō and Kannon is not continuous with the past. One scholar has written, "The current abnormal boom in *mizuko kuyō* inevitably produces misgivings. It is not a natural development of the desire for *kuyō*, but a promotion of a kind of belief in spirit attacks, in which someone fans the boom by saying that all misfortune comes from *mizuko*."[32]

There are numerous sutras associated with Jizō, of which three have been the most influential.[33] Probably originating as one of a group of earth deities in India, Jizō is represented in Indian cave paintings and at Buddhist sites in Orissa, India. The forms in which Jizō is best known in Japan took shape in China, where a cult of the Bodhisattva dates from the beginning of the fifth century. In China, Jizō developed under the influence of a cult of the Ten Kings of Hell, as a savior of people in hell. The idea developed that Jizō can intercede with the Kings of Hell on behalf of the damned, and forms of the deity emerged representing him as a god of wealth. These two types take different iconographic forms.[34]

Japan's first statue of Jizō arrived as a gift from the Korean kingdom of Paekche in 577. Illustrated scrolls and miracle tales from the Muromachi era (1338–1573) provided new motifs of Jizō as a guarantor of long life, safe childbirth, and the safety of children.[35] Jizō Bon, a children's festival still widely observed in the Kyoto-Osaka area, began during Muromachi. Statues of Jizō are used as road markers.[36] The association of Jizō with children really began to flourish in the Edo period, not because of a scriptural warrant (where this link is not an especially prominent theme), but more through miracle tales. These were popular devotional tales such as the *Konjaku monogatari* that were compiled earlier but circulated widely in the Edo period.

A striking motif called *Sainokawara* arose, one that is significant in contemporary *mizuko kuyō*. *Sainokawara,* "the riverbed of judgment," is where dead children were believed to congregate in the other world. In a lonely, stony riverbed, they spend their days grieving for their parents and piling up stones to make miniature pagodas or towers as a devotional act on their parents' behalf. Every day, however, they are chased away by devils (*oni*), who knock over the stones to torment the children further.[37] Numerous hymns about Jizō (*Jizō wasan*) address the *Sainokawara* theme, and Manabe Kōsai has published these.[38] The hymns express a variety of ideas about dead children, the most frequent being that children grieve for their parents, expressing filial piety by making the stone pillars, and that Jizō provides their only comfort. Beyond these, the hymns sometimes call for parents to have Buddhist rites performed, but others deny that *kuyō* has any ameliorating effect.[39] I could find only one mention of aborted fetuses, and in it the fetuses stand before the Buddha, bloodied and wearing their afterbirth as a kind of headgear, clinging to Jizō for help.[40]

These texts reveal no trace of fetal resentment. The hymns addressed to children occasionally tell the children that their fate originates in their own karma. They are exhorted not to imagine that they are innocent victims.[41] Thus the premodern history of the connection between Buddhist guardian figures and children does not establish a precedent for the idea of revengeful fetal spirits, which is central to *mizuko kuyō*. This means that the development of that idea in the postwar period represents a significant change from traditional understandings, rather than a continuity with the past.

Religion, Abortion, and Sexual Culture in the Edo Period

Through examining powerful representations of abortion, we can see the era's stereotyped scenarios explaining how abortion occurs, in what kind of relationships, and with what significance. In a highly exceptional case of premodern rites for aborted fetuses, a Jōdo priest named Yūten Shōnin, "Saint Yūten" (1637–1718), who was famed for many exorcisms, learns of the resentment of aborted fetuses by interrogating spirits of the dead who speak through a living medium. The exorcisms Yūten performed were made famous through works published in his lifetime and preserved thereafter in popular sermons, novels, and plays into the late nineteenth century. No less a part of the era's sexual culture, however, was the resistance and reaction that such representations provoked, establishing their exceptional character. This also forms a part of abortion's meaning in the sexual and religious culture of Japan during the Edo period.

This section centers on an account of abortion and its aftermath. It is supposedly a true record of events that occurred from 1682 to 1685. The narrative requires an introduction to the people involved and to the part of Edo in which the events unfolded.

Saint Yūten's legend is a mixture of biography and mythology, and he became the subject of long-enduring devotion in Edo's popular culture. Yūten's life was known principally through popular publications that began to appear even in his lifetime. The first, in 1690, was "A Tale of Salvation for Spirits of the Dead" (*Shiryō gedatsu monogatari kikigaki*), which recounts Yūten's successful exorcisms at Haniyū Village on the Kinu River in what is now Saitama Prefecture. From the mid–eighteenth century, several biographies of Yūten appeared, such as *The Legend of Abbot Yūten* (*Yūten daisōjō godenki*).[42] These legends uniformly portray Yūten as an incarnation of Jizō and as a powerful shaman and healer.

Yūten was born in northern Japan, in a locale now part of Aomori Prefecture, to poor parents who entrusted him at the age of eleven to an uncle serving as a priest at the temple of the shogunal house in Edo (modern-day Tokyo), Zōjōji. As an ordinand, Yūten began studying Buddhist scriptures immediately, but he was unable to learn. After several months of fruitless tutoring, Yūten's uncle demoted the boy to a general worker, taking away his priestly robes, placing him under an interdiction, and calling Yūten the dumbest novice he had ever encountered. Stung beyond measure at his failure, Yūten secluded himself to fast and pray with all his might to be relieved of his stupidity. On the seventeenth day of his fasting, Yūten had a dream in which an elderly priest appeared to him, exhorting Yūten to go to Shinshōji, a temple popularly known as Narita Fudō because of its cult of the deity Fudō, who was the patron of ascetics and was closely associated with shamanic powers. If Yūten continued his fasting, seclusion, and prayer before Fudō, the deity would surely give him wisdom.[43]

The image of the future saint facing an intellectual handicap in childhood can be seen as a rhetorical device backgrounding his later empathy for women and children. It also serves to explain why a new member of the orthodox Jōdo priesthood would seek out the patron saint of shamans and acquire magical powers otherwise forbidden to the Buddhist priesthood.

Yūten took up his vigil again at Narita, and on the twenty-seventh day, Fudō appeared to him in all his terrifying majesty, surrounded by a full-body halo of flames, fangs gleaming, a lariat and swords in his hands. Proclaiming that Yūten's dimwittedness was due to the accumulated karma of past lives, he thundered that many more lifetimes of virtue would be necessary to transcend this destiny if Yūten left matters to their natural course. The only way for the boy to cut off that karmic destiny immediately was for Fudō to cut it off in a more literal way, plunging his sword into Yūten's mouth, down his throat, and through the entrails. Yūten eagerly assented to this solution, whereupon Fudō thrust his sword down Yūten's gullet.[44] See Figure 1.

This scene is a shamanic initiation, in which the boy Yūten died to his former state of ignorance and was reborn to knowledge and mastery. He vomited out all of his blood, symbolizing his lifetimes of accumulated karma, and Fudō replaced the old blood with new blood, giving Yūten the intelligence he desired. Thereafter, Yūten bested his old masters at Zōjōji in doctrinal debate, significantly, on the topic of women's salvation. The interdiction remained in effect for many years, however, no longer because of any intellectual handicap, but instead because of suspicions that Yūten was more shaman than priest. He was frequently depicted preaching to large crowds, as in Figure 2.

Yūten remained at Zōjōji, holding various offices in its monastic administration until 1687. During that time, he performed celebrated exorcisms (see Figure 3), such as those at Haniyū Village (1672), and the one from 1682 to 1685, which we will examine in detail. The 1690 publication of a "A Tale of Salvation for Spirits of the Dead" brought him to the attention of women in the shōgun's castle harem, the ō-oku, especially Katsura Shōin, mother of shōgun Tokugawa Tsunayoshi.[45] Katsura Shōin thereafter backed Yūten in becoming abbot of several great Jōdo temples, finally becoming abbot of Zōjōji, with the highest rank, great bishop (Daisōjō) in 1711.

The tale of abortion we will shortly examine, which is drawn from the legends of Yūten, concerns Takano Shinuemon (1639–1727), who was neighborhood chief (*nanushi*) of the Nakabashi area of Edo. Shinuemon came from a family that had held considerable power even before Tokugawa Ieyasu set up his capital and erected his castle in Edo. Shinuemon's great-grandfather had been chosen from among fellow

Figure 1. Saint Yūten's initiation by Fudō

SOURCE: *Yūten shōnin go ichi daiki*, courtesy of Rev. Iwaya Shojyo of Yūtenji.

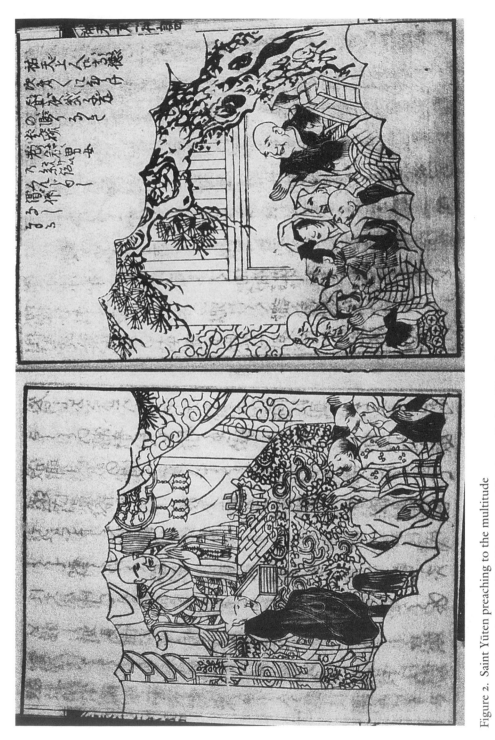

Figure 2. Saint Yūten preaching to the multitude

SOURCE: *Yūten shōnin go ichi daiki*, courtesy of Rev. Iwaya Shojyo of Yūtenji.

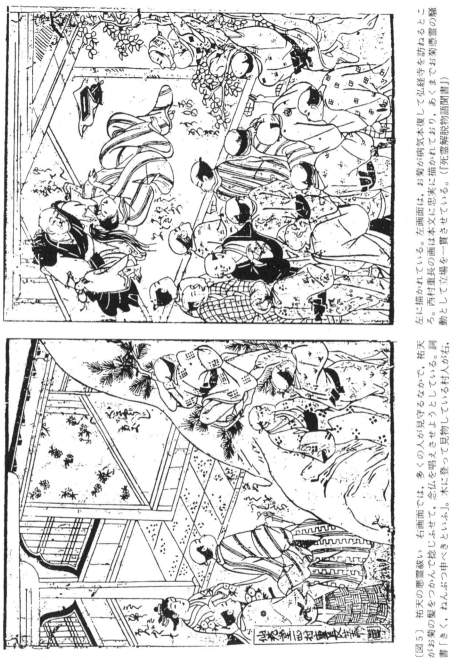

［図5］祐天の悪霊祓い。右画面では、多くの人が見守るなかで、祐天がお菊の髪をつかんで捻じふせて、念仏を唱えさせようとしている。詞書「さく、ねんぶつ申べきといふ」。本に登って見物している村人が右、左に描かれている。左画面は、お菊が病気本復して弘経寺を訪ねるところ。西村重長の画は本文に忠実に描かれており、あくまでお菊悪霊の騒動として立場を一貫させている。（『死霊解脱物語聞書』）

Figure 3. Saint Yūten performing an exorcism
SOURCE: Courtesy of Chikuma Shobō.

local notables to greet Ieyasu and pledge fealty. In return, his family was given the official job of running a courier station, supplying horses and labor for the transmission of official documents (*denmayaku*).[46]

By the 1660s, when the fourth Takano Shinuemon was neighborhood chief of Nakabashi, the office was an important part of shogunal administration, and Nakabashi was a flourishing area in Edo, the territory now called Gofukubashi, roughly between the contemporary Kyōbashi and Ginza areas. The shogunate appointed about 260 neighborhood chiefs, one for every five to seven residential quarters (*chō, machi*), of which there were more than 1,500 in Edo. The *nanushi* "stood at the point of articulation between state and neighborhood, communicating upward the wishes and demands of the commoners while at the same time assisting the superior city elders and magistrates and working with the five-family groups to make certain that they fulfilled their responsibilities."[47]

According to one recent study, Nakabashi in the 1630s had been the "haunt of a sizeable and varied demimonde," home to many theaters, public baths, teahouses, and a variety of places of amusement "that range from target shooting and *nenbutsu odori,* a salvationist dance performed by mendicants . . . , to such damnable pastimes as dallying with *wakashū* [young male prostitutes]."[48] By the 1650s, however, Nakabashi had become a mercantile district, where a great variety of goods were purchased, including fans, mirrors, and medicines. The theaters and denizens of the demimonde moved over to Negi-chō.

The main character of the story that follows, Takano Shinuemon, was the scion of a powerful family, incumbent of an important public office in a flourishing part of Edo. The following is a translation of "The Attainment of Liberation by the Maidservant of Takano Shinuemon" (*Takano Shinuemon ga gejo tokudatsu no koto*).[49]

Takano Shinuemon was the Neighborhood Chief of Nakabashi in Edo. He had an affair with a maidservant named Yoshi, and she became pregnant. Shinuemon's wife was jealous when it became known publicly, so, using an excuse of illness, Shinuemon sent Yoshi back to her family and had her drink an abortifacient. Instead of its intended effect, however, the drug poisoned Yoshi, and she died in agony. Her parents were grief-stricken, but there was nothing they could do, so they held her funeral at the Jishō-in Temple in Asakusa.

Later on, Shinuemon's daughter Miyo married, but she was soon divorced and returned home. She became ill and gradually began to waste away. She looked as if she were terminally ill. One night, she collapsed in agony. Rising after a while, she confronted her father asking, "Who do you think I am? I am Yoshi, who used to work in this house, the one you callously took to your bed, in whom, without love, you planted your seed. Then you made me drink an evil medicine, and both mother and child lost their lives. Even without this, women's sins are deep [*nyonin wa tsumi-fukashi*], but you had no pity for me in my condition. You did not even have Buddhist rites performed for me, so I was forced to wander from darkness to darkness, confused and grieving."

She screamed and cried in resentment. Shinuemon was terrified and consulted many spiritualists of *kitō*, but all were ineffective. Miyo became weaker and weaker. At one time she said to one of her nurses, "No matter how fine his doctrine, no spiritualist of *kitō* can enable me to escape this suffering. I want you somehow to persuade Saint Yūten to pray for me and perform merit transfer [*ekō*]."

Shinuemon's temple was Zōjōji, so he prevailed upon its priest, and Saint Yūten accepted the case. He came and prayed for Miyo. Addressing the spirit within her, he said, "There is ample reason for you to hate Shinuemon, but why attack Miyo?"

The spirit answered, "I do not hate her, but, without attacking Miyo, I had no way to make my pain known, so I had to use her as a medium."

Yūten replied, "Whatever pain you now endure is the bitter fruit of your own actions."

Hearing this interchange, the people listening felt every hair on their bodies bristle up in terror.

But the saint spoke with infinite pity, tears rolling down his cheeks: "You must not be resentful. Even though Shinuemon seduced you, had you refused, you would not have become pregnant. Even though he gave you medicine, if you had not drunk it, you would not have lost your life. All this is your own doing."

The spirit was unconvinced, "Even seeing my fate in this light, with my unbearable pain, I cannot help hating Shinuemon."

Yūten said, "No matter how much you hate him, even if you kill his whole family, you will only succeed in accumulating more sinful karma, and your own suffering will find no relief. Instead of that, open your heart and repent of your sin. Rely on Amida's original vow and seek rebirth in the Pure Land. Repent and recite the *nenbutsu*. Lean on the power of the Great Vow to be reborn in the Pure Land," he warmly exhorted her.

The spirit relented. "I will follow your instructions, but there are many other spirits who hate Shinuemon. Please save those resentful spirits [*onryō*] also." Yūten inquired, "Who are these other spirits of the dead [*shiryō*] who hate Shinuemon?"

The spirit replied, "There are fifteen others besides myself. All of them are children whom Shinuemon caused to be aborted." She then provided the names and present whereabouts of all the women whom Shinuemon had made pregnant with these children, all precisely and without error, as if looking into a bright mirror.

Hearing all this, Shinuemon was terrified. In his complete and utter loss of face, his chagrin knew no bounds. He just sat there, silently repentant.

Yūten instructed Shinuemon as follows: "Repent for your sins, and recite the *nenbutsu* for the sixteen who have died. Grant each one a posthumous name."

Returning to the temple, Yūten recited the *nenbutsu* for seventeen days, repeatedly giving sermons and religious instruction [for these spirits of the dead].

Nevertheless, Miyo continued to worsen. After a three-day fever, she turned at last to Shinuemon and said, "It was my karma to become the medium for those children. Relying on Saint Yūten's instructions and his merit transfer for me, the cloud of illusion has dissipated, and I will now go to the Pure Land." Thanking him again and again, she appeared to lie down to sleep, but her sickness only worsened, and she died.

Yoshi died in 1682. Miyo was possessed in 1685.

[A commentary adds:] The life of all beings is uncertain. . . . In spite of that, it regularly happens that when pregnancy occurs in a secret affair, the result is abortion. In this there is no difference between city and countryside. It is truly regrettable, as is the case of poor peasants who commit infanticide when they have too many children. This is commonly called *mabiki*. And even among people who are *not* poor, local customs can prevent them from raising many children.

In examining this text as a representation of abortion and its relation to religion and sexual culture, it is important to remember that it was made known to people not primarily in its written forms, but as *performed*—as a popular sermon. In the Edo period, sermons were performed as a kind of verbal art form, didactic storytelling. Popular preaching was known in all varieties of Edo Buddhism, but it was especially developed in the Jōdo (Pure Land) and Jōdo Shinshū (True Pure Land) schools. The preacher sat on his heels on a cushion, and except for his stationary position, he used all the skills of an actor, inclining the torso in all directions, using a fan as a multivalent prop, gesturing expressively, and adopting a variety of voices, accents, and styles of speech to convey the words of the characters in a narrative. The popular storytelling of the day, as well as the later form, *rakugo*, owes much to Edo-period preachers for their repertory, acting styles, and verbal proficiencies.[50]

Good preachers enjoyed the same popularity as famous actors, and, similar to secular theater and literature, sermons sometimes took up current events to didactic effect. In this they had a kind of tabloid function, embellishing on well-known incidents in a sensational way, much like the puppet theater (*bunraku*) and novels, which they directly influenced. The biographies of great religious figures such as Yūten provided excellent material, and, in fact, the several versions of his life story were originally composed in the form of sermon chapbooks.[51] In the hands of a skillful preacher, the story of Takano Shinuemon could easily become a multifaceted tearjerker, allowing the preachers from the Jōdo school, in particular, to use Yūten's awe-inspiring ability to communicate with spirits of the dead as an advertisement of the school, its doctrines, and its magical powers of exorcism.

The influence of popular preaching on society was decried in many quarters, however, and this critique was an important element in preaching's overall significance. First, sectarian scholars within Buddhism denigrated the sentimental and emotional approach of preaching, finding the sensational subject matter vulgar and the resulting piety cheap and shallow.[52] Contemporary intellectuals, especially Confucians, attacked shamanic figures such as Yūten for deceiving the people, beguiling them, and undermining their rationality. Confucian scholar Ogyū Sorai (1666–1728) called Yūten unlearned and bemoaned the populace's allegiance to him,[53] while fellow Confucian Arai Hakuseki (1657–1725) wrote the following words in *Kishinron:*[54] "There are people even now, who, sunk deep in jealousy from some amorous obsession, or pining after someone, or holding a grudge, pray to the gods and Buddhas, or work curses. Then the object of their obsession appears to them in a dream or like a shadow. This makes them feel confirmed in their suspicions, so they hasten—*away* from the gods—to shamans, mediums, magicians, women wizards, *yamabushi,* and other male and female quacks of all stripes."[55]

Ogyū Sorai also criticized Buddhist, Taoist, and shamanic attempts to pacify spirits, advising that one "steer clear of this issue." "It is not," he said, "for mortals to look deeply into the depths of what is unknowable to speculate on the nature of ancestral and heavenly spirits."[56]

Unmoved by the cranky gripes of the intelligentsia, however, the masses clamored for tales of exorcism and the occult. As a closer look at the narrative of Yūten's pacification of Yoshi's spirit shows, however, advertising Yūten's shamanic power was not the sole point of the sermon. Instead, the account can be seen as a promotion of merit transfer (*ekō*) over *kitō*, and the story upholds rebirth in the Pure Land as the proper end of exorcised spirits, surpassing simple pacification of them. These doctrinal points—rather than a special message about abortion or the aborted fetuses' desire for revenge—are the aim of the narrative in a sermonic context.

Many Buddhist scriptures expound the idea of merit transfer, according to which a priest's meritorious prayers or recitation of sutras confers a positive benefit upon the dead when the priest "transfers" that merit to them through ritual. The sutras concerned with Jizō, such as *Jizō hongan kyō* (Taishō 13.777, no. 412), explain merit transfer as a purification of ancestral spirits and an abolition of their negative karma. Only an ordained Buddhist priest can transfer the merit of devotional acts by the living to the dead.[57] *Kitō* is very different. In the first place, *kitō* refers to a large category of rites, only some of which are connected with the dead, and not necessarily performed by an ordained Buddhist priest. *Kitō* originally means invoking the assistance of Buddhas and Bodhisattvas through prayer, in order to be rid of misfortune or to increase good fortune. It was not originally performed in Buddhism, and the word itself is scarcely found in Chinese translations of Indian scriptures. Because of the belief in the magical powers of the sutras themselves and the idea of merit transfer, however, people began to seek the Buddhas' protective power and to believe that prayer is sufficient to secure that protection.[58]

The Takano Shinuemon narrative above tells how Shinuemon approached several *kitōshi,* spiritualists of *kitō,* to heal his daughter before consulting Yūten. Yūten appears in the story only after all the *kitōshi* have failed. Yūten's shamanic powers of exorcism only work on the rationale of merit transfer, in which he recites the *nenbutsu* and scriptures and gives sermons for the religious instruction of the unsettled spirits, allowing them to be reborn in Amida's Pure Land. When *kitō* is successful, it results in pacification or exorcism of a spirit, but not necessarily its salvation, as is claimed for merit transfer in this narrative. The text has a special point to make here, because, as we will see below, as infrequently as Buddhist clergy sought out any public connection to sexuality and reproduction, it was even more rare for rites of merit transfer to be performed for *mizuko*.

Aside from its didactic, doctrinal content, this story takes the form of an exposé. A neighborhood chief of one of the city's prominent mercantile districts, charged with ensuring that all in his bailiwick know and obey shogunal edicts and social convention, is unmasked as a lecherous hypocrite. Not content with affluence, influence, pedigree, and public office, he ruins a poor maidservant, giving her a poisonous abortifacient and packing her off to her parents, sick and pregnant, unlikely to be able to marry even if she had lived. Shinuemon had also been the source of another fifteen pregnancies, which he also caused to be aborted. The libertine gets his comeuppance at last, however, when

Yoshi's spirit, bent on vengeance, suddenly manifests itself in Shinue-mon's own daughter Miyo.

When Yoshi appears in Miyo, we understand why life has turned out as it has up to this point for Miyo: her fate mirrors that of her father's pitiful victim. Miyo's divorce and disgraceful return to Shinuemon follow the pattern of Yoshi's dismissal and return to her parents. Both die in agony. Yoshi attacks Miyo, not out of ill will toward her personally, but because Shinuemon long ago had hardened his heart so much against women that Yoshi had no hope of getting through to him.

Shinuemon is represented as responsible for seventeen deaths (the sixteen fetuses plus Yoshi and her fetus, not counting Miyo's), and they are treated as a unitary category called "spirits of the dead" (*shiryō*) or "resentful spirits" (*onryō*) interchangeably.[59] The fetuses are not distinguished as a subcategory, and while they may be resentful, it is only the spirit of an adult woman (Yoshi) who actually works a spirit attack and assails a living person. Fetal spirits in the Edo period are not represented as causing spirit attacks, and this point is worth special emphasis. Even in Saikaku's famous story in which fetal spirits appear, they do not cause *tatari*.[60] Thus there is a significant gap between Edo-period representations of the fetus and those in Japan today. Nothing establishes this difference more clearly than Edo-period sermons portraying the spectacle of spirits of aborted fetuses and dead children at the dry riverbed in the other world, Sainokawara, where the spirits spend their days piling up stones to make little stupas. In sermons, the spirits sing a song as they pile up the stones: "One for father, two for mother," and so on. They are represented as *honoring*, not hating, their parents.[61]

Instead of condemning abortion by the device of fetal spirit attacks, this text is much more preoccupied with the paired problems of women's attachment and men's callousness. Yoshi embodies the former problem, nursing her grudge even after death, determined to ruin her seducer. Following the general lines of Buddhist misogyny, Yūten takes a kind of "libertarian" view of Yoshi's situation, arguing that she had a choice whether to accept seduction by her employer and whether to drink the abortifacient he gave her, ignoring the cold-blooded way in which Shinuemon abused his position of power and authority over Yoshi. She could have said no, Yūten argues, and Yoshi is represented as accepting this verdict in the end. Yūten's interpretation here overlooks the inequality between Shinuemon and his servant, and all the circumstances preventing her from taking more agency—the prospect of immediate dismissal and disgrace—all of which, and more, she eventually suffers anyway. Yūten warns her against nursing her grudge, pointing out that her continuing attachment to her sense of injury and victimization will only bring continued suffering for herself, even if she wipes out Shinuemon's whole family in the process. Yūten exhorts her to relinquish this obsession and to concentrate on her own salvation.

The tale's dramatic power lies in its depicting callousness so great that it causes intense resentment that lives on, even in death. Men's exploitation of women on this scale (fifteen *other* abortions!) is a revelation of uncommon proportions, no doubt rendered by preachers to maximize audience disgust and to magnify the audience's satisfaction when the once-mighty Shinuemon is laid low. The tragic death of his daughter Miyo—a karmic victim if there ever was one—is not sufficient to atone for Shinuemon's wrong. How satisfying to imagine him scurrying from spiritualist to spiritualist, frantic to be rid of Yoshi's spirit, only to learn through Yūten that he can't be let off so easily. He must atone by repenting, by further sponsoring Yūten's rites of merit transfer through the provision of posthumous names (at considerable expense, no doubt), and by underwriting seventeen more days of Yūten's devotions, one for each of the deaths Shinuemon caused. An independent record informs us that Shinuemon was eventually cowed to the point of taking the tonsure in 1687.[62]

The story of Yūten and Takano Shinuemon contains several elements that continue to appear in representations of the sexual culture surrounding abortion in later eras. In both the story and the later culture, abortion is seen as arising in illicit, extramarital relationships characterized by significant inequality of power in sexual negotiations between women and men. Representations are not, of course, uncomplicated mirrors of reality, such that we may conclude that more abortions occurred between master and servant than between husband and wife, but we find little critique of the latter case by religious figures on religious grounds. Instead, we find stigmatization of foolish, obsessive women in sexual relations with callous men, who are also criticized. This stereotyping extends to an assertion that women deserve what they get (disgrace, physical injury, and death), because they could have refused. Women and men are really on a level playing field, Yūten seems to say, and he stops short of explicit critique of Shinuemon. The implication that Shinuemon deserved much more than he got is clear, but while he is humiliated by the spirit's revelation of his cold-blooded exploits, he is spared the tongue-lashing that Yūten gave to Yoshi's spirit.

The spirits of the dead who do not receive merit transfer, including aborted fetuses, are said in this text to wander pitifully "from darkness to darkness," a characterization frequently heard in *mizuko kuyō* today. But this is supposed to be true of all spirits without someone to ritualize them, not just fetuses. In this sense, abortion is not the issue, illustrating a relativism uninterested in blanket characterizations of abortion in the abstract as always being evil.

Ritualization of abortion was extremely rare in the Edo period, partly because abortion, infanticide, and child abandonment were at once disparaged and widely tolerated, much as prostitution is today. Physicians in Japan had practiced abortion since the mid–fifteenth century. In 1667, a directive was promulgated in Edo telling abortion clinics to take down signs advertising their businesses. This means that abortion was openly practiced until that time, and even thereafter the clinics were not required to close—simply to refrain from advertising. In Edo, fetuses arising from abortion, stillbirth, or other causes were typically disposed of as trash, and visitors to the city regularly commented that the Edo River stank of death as a result. In 1680, an abortionist whose patient died was required to give up his practice, a relatively light punishment, indicating continued tolerance for abortion itself.[63]

While there are scarcely any records of ritualizing abortion or infanticide during the Edo period, there are a few exceptions, such as two temples in rice-growing areas of what is now Gifu Prefecture, Ōkanji and Senshōji, which are said to have provided rites for infanticides, and the Edo temple Jizōin Konzōji, which catered to the female prostitute population of the former licensed quarter, Yoshiwara.[64] Fetuses and infants were not usually given ordinary funerals, because the end desired for them was a speedy rebirth in the human world. This desideratum conflicted with the declared goal of adult funerals, which was the attainment of Buddhahood, not rebirth. In fact, in some areas babies were buried with a dead fish, precisely so that the Buddhas would be offended by the smell and leave them alone, allowing the child to be reborn quickly. When Buddhist rites of any kind were performed for fetuses and infants, it was usually a rite of "feeding the hungry ghosts" (*segaki-e*), thus symbolically combining dead fetuses and babies with spirits who had no relatives to tend them and lived a miserable life in limbo as a result.[65] Graves were not built, nor were periodic memorial rites held.[66] The idea of performing rites of merit transfer for them, as in the legend of Saint Yūten, is exceptional, even anomalous.

The mild portrayals of fetal spirits' resentment pale beside those of spirits of abandoned children. In the Edo period, child abandonment was prohibited outright in a 1687 law.[67] The phenomenon still occurred with sufficient frequency to elicit commentary, as shown by remarks the peripatetic poet Bashō made about the pitiful spectacle of children abandoned by the roadside. Abandoned children were a major problem through the nineteenth century in Europe, as well. This phenomenon has been amply demonstrated by historian-anthropologist David Kertzer.[68] Child abandonment is thus hardly an aberration found only in Japan, but instead a widespread technique of population and reproductive control. Distinctive to Japan, however, is an image of the wrathful spirits of abandoned children. In "A Tale of Salvation for Spirits of the Dead," the work that originally made Yūten famous, he is said to have encountered a truly frightful spirit of an abandoned child in the course of yet another exorcism, the one at Haniyū Village in 1672. After he made several attempts to exorcise one spirit from the daughter of a man, Youemon, a second spirit possessed the daughter. The first spirit had shown an amazing tenacity, but the second, the spirit of the abandoned child Suke, surpassed all others in sheer grotesqueness. Suke, the son by a previous marriage of Youemon's father's wife, was severely handicapped: he was crippled, blind in one eye, and ugly to look at. First abandoned and then drowned in a river by Youemon's father, who did not care to raise Suke, his spirit became a water spirit called a Kappa, and in that form he had nursed a grudge for the sixty-one years since he was killed. He came forth to possess Youemon's daughter as a way to torture and kill the descendants of his murderer. The spirit's eyeballs lolled on his cheeks as if attached with elastic, his body was swollen, and all his limbs were bloated and red, as if with fever. Truly a loathsome sight, he was eventually saved by Yūten, who granted him a posthumous name that allowed him to be reborn in the Pure Land.[69]

In premodern Japan, as in Europe, abortion, infanticide, and child abandonment were all well-known responses to economic inability to raise more children. For the most part, Edo-period Japanese did not believe that spirits of aborted fetuses were vengeful or that those spirits were inclined to attack the living. Yūten's example shows a rare case of imagining the possibility that spirits of the aborted could be resentful. The saint assuaged them by praying for them and giving them posthumous names. Thus the problem these spirits presented for the living was solved by fairly simple ritual. But the vengeance of the spirit of an abandoned child was a much weightier matter, calling for a full-scale exorcism of the spirit by Yūten. The greater fear aroused by the spirit of

Suke than that caused by spirits of the aborted is mirrored in the scale of ritual. It seems clear that the spirit wrath of abandoned children was dreaded far more than that of the aborted.

Miki the Midwife

In this section we examine an alternative ritualization of pregnancy and childbirth that arose late in the Edo period, developed by Nakayama Miki (1798–1887). Miki was born in a family of village headmen (*shōya*) and married into another headman's family at age thirteen. Relations with her husband were poor, and when she was about twenty, one of his concubines tried to poison her, hoping to displace Miki and marry her husband, Zenbei. Miki interpreted the event as a supernatural purging.

She had been an ardent practitioner of the *nenbutsu* (recitation of the name of Amida, Buddha of the Western Paradise, the central religious practice of the Pure Land Schools) before marriage and married only on the condition that she would be allowed to continue *nenbutsu* recitation daily.

In addition to Miki's family affiliation with the Pure Land School, the Tanba area in which she lived was much influenced by the Shugendō tradition and by major temples and shrines. In Tanba, there was a Shingon temple called Uchiyama Eikyūji, which particularly promoted the cult of the Ten Kings. Eikyūji had a Shugendō temple-shrine complex called Isonokami Jingū attached to it, a complex with which Miki had considerable dealings in her later life.[70]

Motherhood was a major motif of Miki's life. Miki had six children in all; five were daughters. When she lactated, her breast milk was always sufficiently plentiful to feed infants whose mothers could not nurse. Around 1828, she took in a neighbor's child to nurse, but it contracted smallpox and nearly died. Miki prayed that two of her daughters be taken in exchange for the life of this child. The foster child lived, and in 1830 and 1835, two of her own daughters died.

In 1838, when Miki was forty-one, her only son developed a painful ailment of the foot. She prayed to Kōbō Daishi, founder of the Shingon school, and made barefoot visits to the local tutelary shrine for 100 days. This connection with the Shingon school led her to the Isonokami cult center of Shugendō, the subsidiary temple of the Shingon temple

Uchiyama Eikyūji. There, she consulted a high-ranking *shugenja* named Ichibei, who was also a village headman (Nagataki mura). Miki began a ten-year period of religious practice under Ichibei, which included a forty-nine-day retreat for esoteric instruction. She received instruction concerning the cult of the Ten Kings, as well as lessons in shamanistic ritual (*kaji kitō*).[71]

Miki had many rites of shamanistic exorcism performed by Ichibei and his *miko* partner, Soyo, in order to cure her son. On one occasion when the *shugenja*'s usual *miko* was unavailable, Miki took her place. Instead of an oracle regarding her son's complaint, she announced to Zenbei in the voice of a male deity possessing her, "I want to take Miki as a shrine within which to dwell" (*Miki o kami no yashiro ni morai uke-tai*).[72] The exorcist was unable to rid Miki of this spirit, and Miki remained in a state of spirit possession for three days, sometimes sitting quietly, holding *gohei* (wands topped with paper streamers, representing the perch onto which deity descends to the human world) in each hand, and at other times delivering oracles in an awesome voice, with her hands and body shaking violently. The possession was so violent that at times she seemed to be dragged about the floor by the god, leaving her skin raw and bleeding.[73]

The god had announced himself as Tenriō no Mikoto (one of the Ten Kings), the True God (*Jitsu no kami*), the Original God (*Moto no kami*), and the Heavenly Shōgun (*Ten no shōgun*) come down from the heavens to save all humanity. The full meaning of the god's request was not initially clear, but in demanding that Miki become his shrine, he was calling for her to be released from all the demands of her current position as wife and mother in the Nakayama household. She would take up a new position as a full-time servant of this deity. All further sexual relations between Miki and Zenbei would be precluded by accepting the deity's demand. When nothing could be done to exorcise her of this spirit, Zenbei reluctantly acceded to the demand, and Miki's initial possession ended. Tenrikyō dates its founding from the day Zenbei gave in.[74]

Little is known of Miki's life for the sixteen years between the time of her first possession in 1838 and 1854, the year she became known locally as a living god of safe childbirth. She and her children were very poor, and far from trying to reestablish the family fortunes, they continued to sell off their lands and other possessions. Apparently, Miki had no followers outside of her children. Her own regimen seems to have focused upon reciting the name of her deity, "Namu Tenriō no mikoto," clearly an adaptation of the *nenbutsu* recitation that was the center of her prerevelation religious life.

Things changed, however, when her daughter Oharu became pregnant in 1854. Miki rubbed Oharu's abdomen and stroked it three times, and as a result, Oharu had a very easy birth. When a neighbor woman requested the same treatment, however, she suffered from fever for thirty days following the birth. When she confronted Miki, Miki told the woman that she had been wrong to follow the local dietary taboos on pregnant women, and that this meant that she doubted Miki's method. This doubt caused the fever. When this same woman became pregnant the following year, she followed Miki's advice and observed no taboos. She had a remarkably easy birth and recovery, which she attributed to Miki's treatment. The word spread rapidly that Miki was a living god who could grant safe childbirth. Thereafter, the number of her clients increased rapidly, and she received significant economic assistance from them.

Miki traveled to many villages to practice her method on pregnant or postpartum women, creating a community of women linked by common beliefs, rather than practicing midwifery as a resident of a neighborhood. Miki's prescription called for pregnant women to wear an ordinary *obi,* the sash holding the kimono in place, thus making it unnecessary to wear any special *obi* during pregnancy. Miki's approach to pregnancy and postpartum recovery was called *obiyayurushi,* meaning "forgoing the parturition hut" (*obiya* was the local term for parturition hut). She promised safe childbirth as a result of faith in her and a simple application of hand and breath. She treated childbirth as a natural event that did not require the pregnant woman to be placed in a special category of pollution. She said, for instance, that postpartum women need not abstain from normal social life for seventy-five days after birth. In this, she built upon the religious associations of the midwife as mediating two realms of existence.

In order to deny the strong and widespread idea of the pollution of childbirth, Miki had to address the idea that women are polluted by menstruation. Miki told people: "Look at the pumpkins and eggplants. They bear large fruit because their flowers have bloomed. Without the blooming of flowers, there can be no fruit. Remember that. People say that women are polluted [*fujō*], but they are not at all. Insofar as women and men are both children of god, there is no difference between them. Women must bear children, and it is a real hardship. Women's menstruation is a flower, and without that flower, there can be no fruit."[75] Thus,

Miki described menstruation and childbirth with an agrarian metaphor, likening it to the ordinary blooming of flowers as the inevitable prelude to the production of fruit. This naturalistic approach took menstruation and childbirth out of the category of the sacred and put them on the level of the ordinary.

Miki's alternative ritualization of pregnancy and childbirth probably did not affect vast numbers of women, though this consideration does not affect the religious significance of her innovation. We can see that the changes Miki enacted for the treatment of pregnancy and childbirth required corresponding changes in contemporary notions about female pollution, ideas directly linked to women's status and position in relation to men. Miki arrived at her alternative ritualization following a thorough renegotiation of the power relations between herself and her husband. We can hypothesize on this basis that future alternative ritualizations of reproductive experience (including *mizuko kuyō*) will likewise carry implications about the negotiation of power between women and men. But it is by no means a given that those implications would necessarily work to women's advantage.

State Deritualization of Pregnancy and Childbirth

The Meiji state reiterated previous prohibitions on abortion and infanticide. Significantly, infanticide was made punishable on the same terms as the law against homicide in 1873 (Articles 114 and 164). With these exceptions, however, the state did not directly become involved in the practices surrounding contraception, pregnancy, abortion, and childbirth until the early twentieth century. Beginning in the 1920s, as a part of a more general campaign to improve Japan's public health (*eisei*), measures were established to license midwives, calling them by a different term than earlier (*sanba*, for the licensed midwives, rather than *toriagebāsan* and regional variants for earlier, unlicensed practitioners). Following a period of instruction and certification, licensed midwives then operated within the state bureaucracy for public health, delivering the majority of births, as physicians before 1945 did not routinely attend births unless there were complications requiring surgical intervention. The licensed midwives served to promulgate authorized sanitation practices as well as government policy regarding pregnancy and childbirth. During the years 1939 to 1945, this included an aggressive policy of pronatalism. During a transitional period that lasted until 1945, licensed and unlicensed midwives practiced side by side, but the state-authorized status of the licensed midwives helped them gradually undermine their predecessors and gain a preeminent position.[76]

Oral histories of licensed midwives from before 1945 show that they perceived a great difference between themselves and traditional midwives. For one thing, licensed midwives tended to be younger, receiving certification after completing a course of education before they had had children themselves. They practiced in a "scientific," which is to say medicalized, bureaucratized, and professionalized, context. They had uniforms and were able to practice midwifery over a much wider territory than their own place of residence, typically being summoned by telephone and traveling by bicycle or rickshaw. Uniforms, bicycles, telephones, and rickshaws also were conspicuous markers of bourgeois class status. Licensed midwives instructed women to give birth in a prone position, a departure from the former, universal practice of a squatting posture. They taught women how to calculate the day of birth, and they conducted prenatal physical examinations, as well as using rolls of waxed paper, white cotton cloth, and disinfectant at the birth itself. Whereas the *toriagebāsan* were expected to handle the effluvia of afterbirth, wash blood-stained bed linens, and generally clean up after a birth, the licensed midwives seem to have regarded these menial tasks as beneath them. Unlike the ritualization of pregnancy overseen by *toriagebāsan,* the licensed midwife was not a ritualist, and she formed no ongoing relation with either mother or child. As these midwives themselves frequently lacked roots in the communities they served, their services could not conduct women in a rite of passage into the company of the fully adult women. Because they were concerned with transmitting *public* knowledge exoterically, they did not initiate women any longer into sex-segregated gnosis. Thus, the meaning of childbirth for women conducted by licensed midwives differed radically from before. The licensed midwives effectively deritualized pregnancy and childbirth, even before the institutionalization of hospital birth.[77]

While some licensed midwives instructed women on contraception, and while some also practiced abortion, neither practice was considered a proper part of midwifery. Plus, from about 1930 until 1945, contraception and abortion were greatly stigmatized through repeated state prohibition and regulatory vigilance. The Criminal Code of 1907 reaffirmed

Table 1. *Criminal convictions of abortion providers, 1904–1955*

1904	293	1921	340	1937	127
1905	307	1922	266	1938	103
1906	367	1923	258	1939	188
1907	294	1924	215	1940	119
1908	377	1925	171	1941	144
1909	508	1926	418	1942	83
1910	672	1927	308	(1943–	
1911	580	1928	193	1947)	—
1912	639	1929	170	1948	68
1913	630	1930	178	1949	69
1914	605	1931	223	1950	44
1915	545	1932	121	1951	33
1916	—	1933	143	1952	15
1917	497	1934	280	1953	7
1918	563	1935	249	1954	7
1919	387	1936	254	1955	5
1920	306				

NOTES: These convictions include self-induced abortions, abortions performed on others, and the provision of abortifacients. Numbers of convictions after 1955 remain in single digits. A dash denotes that data are unavailable.

SOURCE: Takayasu Itsuko, "Kanri sareta sei, sono kaihō e," *Sabetsu to tatakau bunka,* Special issue of *Kaihō kyōiku* 12 (1984): 31.

that abortion was a criminal offense, and Table 1 shows the changing number of criminal convictions of abortionists. Related laws governing sterilizations for eugenic reasons were established; these were later revised to create the 1948 Eugenics Protection Law.[78] The popular press treated incidents of abortion as scandals and greatly magnified the sense of guilt and shame surrounding it. The treatment of abortion in such a public forum, combined with state prohibitions upon it, contributed to its attaining a public character, whereas previously it had been relegated to the realm of the private and domestic.[79]

In spite of the growing public stigmatization of abortion, many progressive midwives became staunch advocates of both legalized birth control and abortion after having to promote the state's pronatalist policy, especially following 1939. This experience seems to have radicalized many who entered the profession with the intention of instructing women in the state's requirements of them.[80]

A birth control movement arose early in the twentieth century, stimulated by European and American advocacy for the promulgation and spread of contraception. The Japanese government's celebrated 1922 prohibition on Margaret Sanger's public lecturing greatly stimulated birth control advocates such as Hiratsuka Raichō, Katō (Ishimoto) Shidzue, Shibahara Urako, and Majima Kan. Besides contemporary intellectuals' considerable involvement, a wide range of social groups advocated birth control in the face of state prohibition, including feminists, tenants' unions, and labor unions. These activists opened birth control clinics and surreptitiously provided birth control supplies and instructions to thousands of women. Physician Ōta Tenrei developed a contraceptive intrauterine device, while Ogino Kyūsaku correctly identified the periodicity of ovulation, making possible the rhythm method that still bears his name in Japan. Katō Shidzue traveled to the United States to receive instruction at Sanger's clinic on the manufacture of pessaries (diaphragms) and spermicides. After returning to Japan, she duplicated these materials, personally boiling up creams and jellies, squeezing them into tubes, and writing hundreds of letters responding to women whose families refused to allow them to visit Katō's clinic in person. Though leaders of the movement were repeatedly interrogated and jailed, they persisted until around 1940, when the clinics were shut down by government orders. The movement had a number of factions and included various philosophical positions; some advocated contraception and abortion for eugenic reasons, while others, like Katō, emphasized contraception over abortion and based their advocacy on the feminist position that women should be free to control their reproductive potential by any available means.[81]

During these decades, there were no conspicuous changes in religious institutions' attitudes toward contraception and abortion, nor was there any marked change in their ritualization practices, which remained low-key and customary (Shugendō was officially disbanded early in the Meiji era). The sole exception to this generalization lies in those new religions that began to assume a mass character during these years. Numerous new religions founded outside the Buddhist line denied older ideas about the pollution of women and childbirth. Some, such as Kurozumikyō and Konkōkyō, male-founded religions, upheld the equality of the sexes and their equal worth in the eyes of a deity, denying in the process notions such as that women should not engage in religious observances during menstruation. Others, like Tenrikyō and Tenshōkōtai Jingūkyō, female-founded religions, began their own ritualization of pregnancy and childbirth, attaching a variety of positive meanings to both, and, in the latter case, seeking to involve husbands in childbirth, as well as denying more general ideas of female pollution.[82]

Tenshōkōtai Jingūkyō was founded by Kitamura Sayo (1900–1971). Sayo was deprived by her stingy mother-in-law of all assistance in pregnancy and childbirth, and for unexplained reasons, her natal family did not step in to aid her. Thus Sayo's sole experience of childbirth in 1922 was characterized by a complete absence of ritualization, and she had no opportunity to receive a transmission of women's knowledge or for her child to form any ongoing relationship with a midwife. Typically, her husband was no help, either.

Sayo's prescription for a wife and husband to deliver their own child made pregnancy and childbirth essentially an affair of a nuclear household, in which men received knowledge traditionally monopolized by women (e.g., how to cut and tie the umbilical cord) and were called on to assist in their wives' births as a fulfillment of obligation stemming from the conjugal bond, their sexual relationship with the wife, and as a duty of paternity. While a role in midwifery was created for men, there was, however, no suggestion that the man become the main actor in childbirth. Instead, the idea of a husband's duty and obligation to his wife was more central, and the community of women (who had failed to come to Sayo's aid) was excluded from any meaningful role, as were the state and medical institutions. At the same time, however, in acting as midwife for the births of followers' children and her own grandchildren, Sayo preserved aspects of the traditional religious significance of midwifery and was widely perceived by her followers as a deity of safe childbirth, representing a living deity presiding over a child's passage into a new existence. Acting as midwife at that time without a license also constituted a violation of law, albeit one that was not likely to be prosecuted.

The Postwar Completion of Deritualizing Pregnancy and Childbirth

The state's attitude toward contraception and abortion changed radically after 1945. Immediately after the defeat, Japan faced severe food shortages and the prospect of a staggering population increase from the repatriation of military personnel and colonial settlers to the home islands. With the neutral oversight of the Allied Occupation, the newly reorganized Ministry of Health and Welfare (Kōseishō) embarked upon a policy of limiting population growth.[83] A hallmark of this policy was the Eugenics Protection Law of 1948, which legalized abortion (by licensed physicians only) in a number of circumstances, including (by an amendment of 1949) economic hardship. The licensed midwives were reorganized, given a new title, *josanpu,* and placed explicitly within a medical framework (the *jo-* part of the new title, meaning "to assist," implied that they were to help and function under the direction of physicians). While midwives were authorized and charged to spread knowledge of contraception, they were forbidden to prescribe drugs or perform abortions. These prerogatives were held exclusively by physicians, who came in a few short years to monopolize treatment of pregnancy and childbirth. The practice of hospital birth attended by physicians was speedily universalized, thus obviating midwives, who have all but disappeared as independent professionals.[84]

With these measures, the medicalization of pregnancy and childbirth was complete, as was their deritualization. Women came to depend entirely upon physicians for obstetrical and gynecological services, a commoditized relationship in which no ongoing bond was formed between physician and mother or child. Technological innovations made it possible to regulate the timing of childbirth minutely to suit hospital schedules (in the morning rather than late at night), and the later introduction of national health insurance made it profitable for hospitals to keep postpartum women in the hospital for several weeks following birth.[85]

First childbirth retained the character of a rite of passage for women, but with a much changed meaning. In this medicalized context, and in a social context constructing motherhood in a desexualized way, pregnancy came to constitute passage from a state of "unmarried or childless woman," a state characterized as maximally sexually desirable and autonomous, to maternity, a state of circumscription within the domestic realm under a physician's direction and a husband's control. The transition was marked by the assumption of a desexualized appearance (with maternity clothing much like children's clothes—sturdy, loosely cut fabrics—no makeup, flat shoes and socks, simple, unadorned hair style, usually short and pinned back from the face). While motherhood undoubtedly constitutes its own type of authority (and can still be lorded over childless women), its desexualized and subordinated representation injects a note of considerable ambivalence into it, as it represents a "death" of desire and desirability. The phrase women now use is *umasete kureru,* or "causing to be allowed to give birth," *caused,* that is, by the physician. This expression casts the pregnant woman in a passive position in relation to the physician. This is a far cry from the active expression *futari de umu,* "giving birth as a pair," which was characteristic of premodern midwifery's attribution of religious power to both a midwife and a pregnant woman, and is an accurate index of the degree of change that has occurred since that time.

Conclusion

In this chapter, we have seen how extensively ritualized reproductive experience was during the Edo period. Ritualization focused mainly upon pregnancy and childbirth. By contrast, ritualization of abortion and infanticide was exceptional and rare, though not unknown. Where Buddhist rites were performed, they usually took the form of "feeding the hungry ghosts," or rites of prayer and intercession (*kitō*), rather than rites of merit transfer on which adult funerals and memorial rites are based. We saw one exception in the tales of Saint Yūten, which includes an unusual proposal to ritualize aborted fetuses through merit transfer. The new religion Tenrikyō provided an alternative mode of ritualization based on denial of the pollution notions that kept other religious organizations aloof from reproduction.

With the state's involvement in systematic population policy after the Meiji Restoration, and especially in the early decades of the twentieth century, bureaucratization of childbirth practices resulted in a deritualization of reproduction, producing a cultural vacuum filled on a small scale by Tenrikyō and Tenshōkōtai Jingūkyō. For the most part, other religious institutions continued to be uninvolved with reproduction. After 1945, the character of state population policy reversed the former pronatalism completely, lowering the birth rate in a few short years, mainly through abortion, a process that will be examined in detail in the next chapter.

CHAPTER 2

The Practice of *Mizuko Kuyō* and the Changing Nature of Abortion

This chapter examines *mizuko kuyō* in the context of the changing practice of abortion over the postwar decades. Following a discussion of the implementation of the Eugenics Protection Act, we distinguish three periods within the postwar years. In discussing each one, we use statistics on contraception and abortion, and attitudes toward both, as well as national surveys of opinion, historical studies, and letters that ordinary people wrote to the advice column (*jinsei annai*) of the national newspaper *Yomiuri Shinbun*. We next examine a political attempt by the new religion Seichō no Ie to repeal the Eugenics Protection Law's provision for performing abortion because of economic hardship. Seichō no Ie repeated its challenge several times between 1960 and 1983, but was defeated each time. Contrary to its intent, Seichō no Ie's actions renewed support for legalized abortion from a wide spectrum of the population, especially feminists and family planners. We then examine the role of the tabloid press in shaping and promoting *mizuko kuyō* as a media event, beginning in the mid-1970s. The media provided a nationwide forum for spiritualists, and the competition among publishers greatly magnified national awareness of *mizuko kuyō* at its beginning. Media coverage accelerated *mizuko kuyō*'s commercialization, while giving coherence to an associated symptomology, correlating abortion with a stereotyped list of menopausal symptoms. The next section of the chapter analyzes survey results to pinpoint the time of *mizuko kuyō*'s inception in various settings, and participants' sociological characteristics and beliefs. The concluding section identifies key areas of change since the Edo period.

The Implementation of the Eugenics Protection Law

Early in the Occupation, several prewar advocates of birth control, such as Ōta Tenrei and Katō Shidzue, were elected to the Diet as members of the Socialist Party. These Socialist MPs began to press for abortion rights, anticipating a population explosion as soldiers and colonists repatriated. In addition, they sought to protect women from the dangers of illegal abortion, the genetic legacy of the atomic bombings, and state pronatalism.

Diet members closely connected with physicians joined the Socialists in advocating "simplification" of the existing eugenics law to permit physicians to perform abortions. These negotiations began as soon as the war ended, but they could not proceed entirely autonomously. Instead, it was necessary to secure the support of the Occupation, specifically, General Crawford F. Sams, Chief of the Public Health and Welfare Section of the Supreme Commander of the Allied Powers (SCAP). SCAP's official position on abortion was one of neutrality. It preferred to remain uninvolved, but was pressured from all sides. On the one hand, the Catholic Church urged SCAP to block contraception (to say nothing of abortion), whereas Japanese family planners asked SCAP to assist in government programs to distribute contraceptives and legalize abortion.[1]

Family planners-turned-MPs found SCAP weak-willed and obstructionist, unpardonably ignorant of Japan's domestic situation and thoroughly intimidated by the Catholic Church's opposition to birth control. One MP accused SCAP of suppressing the birth control movement,[2] while Katō Shidzue attributed SCAP's reluctance to issue a visa to Margaret Sanger to fear of American Catholics' recriminations.[3] Japanese-American birth control advocate and physician Fumiko Amano held that fear of Catholic criticism made SCAP suppress the findings of its own consultants who advocated birth control.[4]

Both houses of the Diet passed legislation that became the Eugenics Protection Law of 1948, first implemented in 1949. The clause permitting abortion for reasons of economic hardship was added in 1949, and further revisions were made in 1952, allowing a single physician to decide whether abortion was merited, abolishing a previous requirement that local eugenics councils approve each abortion.

One reason for these amendments was the recognition that restrictions on abortion encouraged illegal abortions, which in 1950 were estimated at 120,000 to 150,000.[5] Since 1945, illegal abortion in Japan has not been a matter of back-alley jobs performed by nonprofessionals, but abortions that physicians performed without registering the procedure. All studies of Japan's postwar demography agree that abortion is underreported, but estimates of underreporting vary considerably, and there is no persuasive way to reconcile them. Physicians are expected to register all abortions, but since this results in a permanent record, patients frequently dissuade doctors from complying with this requirement. The 1957 implementation of the National Health Insurance system created an economic incentive for physicians to accept unreported cash payments for abortion, rather than utilizing this cost-regulating system. Knowledge of this widespread practice contributed to images of OB-GYNs as corrupt and moneygrubbing. Some estimate that the actual number of abortions performed in the early postwar years may have been as high as 70 percent more than reported figures.[6] Table 2 presents the changing ratio of abortions to live births from 1950 to 1989. However problematic the official statistics, they are nevertheless our only consistent guide.

Three Periods in the Postwar Culture of Abortion

The periodization adopted here represents an attempt to take account of a variety of factors influencing abortion and the practice of *mizuko kuyō*. These include the spread of contraceptive use, the incidence of abortion itself, and changes within the religious world. As it happens, the divisions identified here follow widely recognized demarcations in Japan's cultural, social, and economic history.[7] In that frame of reference, the period 1945 to 1955 was devoted to recovery and to rebuilding the economic infrastructure. From 1955 up to the oil shocks of the 1970s was an era of high economic growth. The period since then has been one of slower economic activity, adjustment, and stabilization. In advancing a parallel time frame for the changes in abortion and the economy, I do not mean to imply that abortion and *mizuko kuyō* are economically determined, nor to account for why changes in reproductive practice occurred when they did. The incidence of reported abortions peaked in 1955, and that is this study's

Table 2. *Ratio of abortions to live births, 1950–1989*

Year	Ratio	Year	Ratio	Year	Ratio
1950	20.9	1970	37.8	1980	37.9
1955	67.6	1971	37.0	1981	39.0
1960	66.2	1972	35.9	1982	39.0
1963	57.6	1973	33.5	1983	37.1
1964	51.2	1974	33.5	1984	38.2
1965	46.2	1975	35.3	1985	38.4
1966	59.4	1976	36.2	1986	38.2
1967	38.6	1977	36.5	1987	37.0
1968	40.5	1978	36.2	1988	37.0
1969	39.4	1979	37.4	1989	37.4

SOURCE: Mainichi Shinbunsha Jinkō Mondai Chōsakai, ed., *Kiroku: Nihon no jinkō, shōsan e no kiseki* (Tokyo: Mainichi Shinbunsha, 1992), p. 337, table 24.

rationale for declaring a break there. From 1956 to 1974, the rate of abortion declined; thus, this period marks a second distinctive unit. After 1975, the rate of abortion began to drift up again, especially for younger cohorts of women than previously represented prominently.

These changes paralleled transformation in the religious world. From 1945 to 1955, a great upsurge of religious activity occurred, and thousands of new religions, large and small, were founded. Some of these grew at unprecedented rates to become mass organizations. By 1955, many had failed or folded in with other organizations. Those that remained for the most part adopted a distinctive worldview stressing optimism and unlimited possibility.[8] By 1975, membership in the largest of these organizations began to peak, and some started to decline. The older, more optimistic new religions were joined by a new generation of "new-new religions." These differed from their predecessors in placing more emphasis on the role of fate, luck, and spirit influence over human affairs, and in adopting a more pessimistic attitude.[9] *Mizuko kuyō* emerged alongside such "new-new religions" with a shared emphasis on youth, a prominent role for spiritualism, and a belief that personal destiny is less influenced by one's own efforts at self-determination than by spirits' unknowable potential to protest, punish, or, in the case of *mizuko*, to menace, unless ritualized appropriately.

Japanese sociologists of religion hold that the country has, since the beginning of the 1980s, been experiencing a notable upsurge of religious activity, a phenomenon journalists have called a "religion boom," or an "occult boom."[10] The indicators include rising membership in religious groups of all kinds, and an increased number of persons who profess various religious beliefs or practice customary religious observances of a nonsectarian kind (grave visits, maintaining household altars, etc.).[11] Recent surveys show a conspicuous rise in the number of young people who believe in life after death, the existence of a spirit world, astrology, and the reality of such spiritual powers as the shamanic ability to communicate with spirits.[12]

New interest in religion has quickly been commercialized. Television programs featuring psychics and spiritualists now draw a huge viewership in prime time, no longer relegated to midmorning dead zones. Stores selling crystals, tarot cards, and amulets to attract love and banish acne, and offering fortune-telling, divination, geomancy, onomancy (divination of names), palmistry, and tarot readings are booming. Works on the occult, magic, and the prophesies of Nostradamus, as well as the works of Krishnamurti and other Indian spiritualists, have become best-sellers. The bookstores have established corners devoted to the spiritual life (*seishin no sekai*) in recognition of the increasing share of their sales derived from the new occultism. New magazines such as *Mū*, which started in 1979 and was renamed *Twilight Zone* in 1983, entered the market, followed shortly by others targeting specific subsections of the readership, such as *Harouīn* (Halloween), which started in 1986 and targeted teenage girls. These magazines advertise a variety of occult goods for purchase by mail through such appeals as these: "Is it enough for me alone to be happy? The Aztec bracelet that attracts happiness and miracles!" "The home-use Pyramid will give you supernatural powers without doing meditation!" "The mysterious Hiyanya lapis pendant [a six-pointed star] brings happiness to anyone—just by wearing it!" One could join "The Lapis Club," which sells lapis watches and pendants by mail. The stone brings many benefits, as frequent testimonies show; people claim that after buying the stone, they got a new job, found financial support, cured anorexia, and found a new boyfriend or girlfriend. Also available are correspondence courses on how to develop one's *ki* so that it is possible to perform miracles of physical strength. Occult comics (*manga*) have appeared, and two authors—Kuroda Minoru and Yamamoto Sumika—of those directed to teenage girls have even founded "new-new religions" drawing on the same clientele.[13]

In fact, the emergence of these "new-new religions" is the most revealing element of the "boom."[14] Compounding the absurdity of the certainly-destined-for-obsolescence term *new religion,* the new-new religions (*shin-shin shūkyō*) come in large and small varieties. The larger ones are Agon-shū, Glad Light Association, and Mahikari, plus offshoots of the latter two. The small ones are too numerous to mention in any detail, but they have important links with urban shamanism, and upon close inspection it often emerges that a founder was until recently operating either as an *ogamiya* or as a practitioner of one of the historical varieties of shamanism. The new-new religions are distinguished most significantly from the older new religions and from the so-called "established religions" (that is, temple Buddhism and shrine Shintō) by their high proportion of young members (some with as many as 60 percent under thirty), by a doctrinal concern with spirits, and in ritual by a concentration on techniques for manipulating spirits. They lack the tight-knit organizational structure of older groups and seem instead to be propagated as much by the founders' books and television appearances as by face-to-face evangelizing.[15]

Urban shamanism, whose practitioners are collectively called *ogamiya,* is another part of the occult boom. *Ogamiya* are religious professionals who worship (*ogamu*), often performing divination, geomancy, onomancy, and almanac readings in the course of advising clients. In order to ensure health, harmony, and prosperity for oneself and one's family, or to determine the spiritual causes of misfortune, anyone may consult an *ogamiya,* usually on a cash-for-services-rendered basis, not necessarily forming any ongoing relationship. Not all *ogamiya* are women and neither are their clients, but both seem to be disproportionately female.[16]

The Early Postwar Years, 1945–1955

From 1945 to 1955, contraceptive use remained very low, and abortion was the major determinant in lowering the birthrate. Table 3 shows the change in contraceptive practice from 1950 to 1992. Condom manufacture began in 1945 and accelerated dramatically after 1947.[17] No less than thirty private family planning institutes were opened, including the Japan Birth Control Institute, headed by Dr. Fumiko Amano, the Japan Family Planning Federation, sponsored by Katō, and many others. These institutes sponsored birth control clinics to provide contraceptives and education in their use.[18] The birthrate

Table 3. *Changes in contraceptive use, 1950–1992*

Year	Percentage of population practicing contraception	Year	Percentage of population practicing contraception
1950	19.5	1973	59.3
1952	26.3	1975	60.5
1955	33.6	1977	60.4
1957	39.2	1979	62.4
1959	42.5	1981	55.5
1961	42.3	1984	57.3
1963	44.6	1986	62.8
1965	55.8	1988	56.3
1967	53.0	1990	57.9
1969	52.1	1992	64.0
1971	52.6		

SOURCE: Mainichi Shinbunsha Jinkō Mondai Chōsakai, ed., *Kiroku: Nihon no jinkō, shōsan e no kiseki* (Tokyo: Mainichi Shinbunsha, 1992), p. 54, table 1.

peaked in 1947 at 34.3, while the population in 1948 rose to 80 million with predictions of 100 million by 1970. The earliest postwar surveys of popular opinion showed strong support for birth control and a desire for small families.[19] In 1951, the Japanese government declared its support for family planning, and after 1952, the Ministry of Health and Welfare began (re)training midwives and public health nurses as family planning workers.[20]

Letters to the popular advice column (*jinsei annai*) afford some insight into the dilemmas about contraception and abortion that couples faced at the time. Advice columns have been a standard feature of postwar Japanese newspapers. Because individuals explain their problems in their own words, the numerous letters on contraception and abortion provide a means to breathe life into statistics on these subjects, to illustrate the ways people have understood the meanings of these practices in their own lives. These understandings change over time, however, and they are shaped by the medium in which they appear—a commoditized publication for popular consumption, a newspaper. Because advice columns have never been extensively theorized, it is important to state clearly the purpose and assumptions informing their use in this study.[21]

Let us dispose at the outset of the notion that they can be taken as mirrors of social reality. Advice columns adopt a deceptively simple format: letter and response. But a look at the complex processes combining to bring a letter and its response to the newspaper page should disabuse us of any tendency to view them mimetically. First, because not all letters are published, an editorial decision invisible to us results in the printing of some and the exclusion of others, and in the assigning of selected letters to a staff writer. The Yomiuri newspaper, publisher of the collection of *jinsei annai* of 1945 to 1988 drawn on here, maintains a large staff of male and female staff writers.[22] The process of composing a response is similarly invisible to us and represents another mediation between reader and social reality.

Responses reveal the column's ideological function in constructing the "common sense" of the time, and treatments of abortion frequently bear extra, moralistic baggage beyond that seen in responses to other problems. A contrasting example may help to clarify this point. In *jinsei annai* up to 1970 or so, there were frequent letters from anguished young men who wished to preserve their virginity until marriage. Responses to letters of this kind are uniformly open-ended and encourage the writer not to be swayed by the derision of classmates and friends. They invite the reader's sympathetic understanding and do not necessarily prescribe a course of action or foreclose options. Readers of such *jinsei annai* take pleasure in forming an image of the letter writer and enumerating his alternatives.[23] Unlike responses to the problem of male virginity, replies to letters concerned with contraception and abortion are clear-cut, prescriptive, often judgmental, and frequently adopt a tone of great urgency. These characteristics tend to foreclose interpretations for readers, to shut down the speculative indeterminateness seen in treating other questions, channeling readers into a moralistic framework.

Although *jinsei annai* play a role in constructing the "common sense" of their times, and although the content of so-called "common sense" undoubtedly changes, *jinsei annai* cannot, by themselves, be taken as uncomplicated reflections of changing social values. Continuing with the example of queries about male virginity, we note that these cease to appear around 1970. Are we justified in concluding that before 1970 men valued male virginity at marriage, and that their values changed after 1970? That may be the case, but *jinsei annai* are only an indication—requiring separate, independent confirmation—not proof of this. The appearance of numerous letters on this theme—or on abortion—may be a more accurate reflection of the editorial staff's moral preoccupations and perceptions of social change. *Jinsei annai* cannot confirm that more or fewer men went as virgins to the altar, or that more couples who were not married to each other conceived pregnancies later terminated by abortion, but *jinsei annai* can alert us to a perception in Japan that such was the case. As letters about contraception and abortion accumulate in the newspaper, overdetermined images of abortion build up, alongside stereotyped scenarios about who has abortions and why. Both the images and the scenarios change over the postwar decades. My purpose in introducing these texts is to chart the changing images and scenarios about abortion as one representation of Japan's attitude toward abortion, without, however, assuming that these texts provide an immediate reflection of actual social change.[24]

Jinsei annai disclose two main trends in the "common sense" about abortion. The first recognizes that economic hardship necessitates abortion in many cases, and that such hardship can be construed in an absolute or a relative sense. The absolute sense, seen frequently until 1955 or so, is a situation in which a family will be economically devastated if another child is born. The relative sense of economic hardship emerges later on, and in it there is no immediate threat of poverty, but another child may mean denying a higher standard of living to the children a family already has, precluding such things as special schools and tutoring. Responses to women facing abortion in either sense of economic hardship are generally empathetic and invite the reader to see the letter writer's personal tragedy as illustrating problems facing society at large. There is a tendency for response writers to adopt an explicitly moral tone, and to define the dramatis personae not as rounded personalities, but as representatives of social types or moral positions.[25] The response writer determines moral values in terms of actions taken rather than intention. It is always assumed that the pregnancy was conceived within marriage.

Moralizing is raised to a great height in the second trend in "common sense" about abortion: a scenario in which abortion results from an illicit affair between a callous, older, married man and a foolish, unmarried, younger woman. This scenario is a staple of *jinsei annai* throughout the postwar decades, the major demarcation being teenagers' debut in the role of Foolish Women in our final period. There is a direct and striking continuity between this scenario as seen in the pages of *jinsei annai* and the popular and oral literature of the Edo period examined in chapter 1. Whereas men tend to be invisible or excused from direct scrutiny in scenarios about abortion and economic hardship, they are a central focus in the illicit scenario, resulting in a neat pairing

of Foolish Woman and Callous Man. Women are construed as originally innocent, if ignorant, but as infinitely corruptible by illicit sexual
liaisons. By contrast, men are not innocent, but neither does sexuality
so completely corrupt them. Women in this scenario lack self-respect
and are vulnerable to emotion that blinds them to the consequences of
their actions. Men, on the other hand, are egotistical and selfish, wanting the benefits and pleasures of both a wife and a lover.

The more indeterminate, sympathetic scenario invoking economic
hardship coexists with the overdetermined scenario about Callous Men
and Foolish Women. A sampling of *jinsei annai* letters for each period
should provide a guide to the evolution of stereotypical representations
of abortion.

In a letter published on June 22, 1952, a woman with two children
wrote that she wanted to use birth control, but that her husband opposed it. She thought of enlisting a physician's aid, but was worried
that using contraception without her husband's consent would constitute infidelity. The newspaper staff writer responding to this letter
replied that it is a woman's right to limit her fertility in order to give the
children she already has the best possible upbringing. The husband is
in the wrong. It is a woman's right (*onna no kenri*) to use birth control,
and this does not constitute infidelity.[26] A letter of March 4, 1953,
shows that economic hardship weighed heavily in motivating women to
limit their reproduction, as the following paraphrase illustrates:

Letter Writer: I am thirty-three and have four children. My husband is
a factory worker. We live with the in-laws, eight of us in all. I do piecework
and want to use that money for contraceptives, but it always seems to go
on food. I cannot refuse my husband indefinitely. What should I do?

Response: All the married women in Japan share your anxiety. In your
situation, pregnancy, childbirth, and childrearing are great sorrows, not
joys. Get contraceptive advice immediately and consider sterilization. The
procedure would be easier for your husband than for you.[27]

These letters to the advice column may be anecdotal, but because
their worth to the newspaper depended upon their credibility with the
public, as the voice of realism and pragmatism, they can reveal much
about the channeling of public opinion. We can see from sampling such
letters that contraception was promoted straightforwardly, and that
women were urged to take responsibility for it, not to wait for men to
change their minds. An unspoken corollary of this latter idea, which
emerged with greater clarity in later periods, is the idea that it is
utopian for women to try changing men, either in the sense of refusing

them sexually, or by pressuring them to share responsibility for contraception. Women should act as independently as they can, within the sphere of activity they can control.

While contraceptive use was just beginning to spread, abortion was mainly responsible for lowering the birthrate. Demographers Hodge and Ogawa summarize the situation this way: "The total fertility rate fell by over one-third, from 3.26 to just over 2. This period provides the major evidence that abortion was the primary means by which Japan negotiated her demographic transition."[28] The equivalent change in European societies took more than a century. In 1955, the number of registered abortions peaked at 1,170,143, or 67.6 percent of the number of live births that year. Half of these abortions were performed because of economic hardship.[29] A 1950 report stated that curettage was the method of abortion most frequently adopted, and that about 2.1 deaths per 1,000 abortions occurred.[30] Among the reasons demographers noted for this high reliance upon abortion were such factors as the lack of condoms, their high cost, and their low reliability.[31] One observer noted that an abortion could be procured in 1955 for the equivalent of U.S.$5, a sum less than the cost of a year's supply of contraceptives.[32] Another study noted the absence of religious impediments to abortion: "Since the Shinto and Buddhist religions are ethically blank on the subject of induced abortion, and since infanticide had in past centuries been an accepted means of family limitation, it has not been difficult for legalized abortion to be readily accepted."[33] As of 1950, about 60 percent of the population favored the practice of birth control, but different surveys on abortion showed contradictory results, with majority approval in one survey contradicted by the lower findings of another.[34]

The population was at the same time highly motivated to limit family size, exclusively dependent upon expensive and unreliable condoms, and left with no choice other than abortion when contraception failed or could not be implemented in the first place, leaving attitudes volatile. In 1955, women in their twenties and through the age of thirty-five had the majority of abortions. The proportion of women experiencing abortion increased after thirty, and women of thirty-five had more abortions than births. We can assess the significance of this change if we compare the average number of births for women born between 1911 and 1915, namely 4.8, with 2.65, the figure for women born between 1921 and 1925. This was a decrease of almost half. With a generation of women born in the 1920s setting the example, abortion became a widespread experience.[35]

A variety of attitudes accompanied the practice of abortion in this period. A Japan Medical Association report noted the prevalence of abortion among the middle class, calling it a "normal" development, while women's magazines of 1955 expressed some concern. Nevertheless, the women's magazine *Shufu no tomo* affirmed abortion in the event of contraceptive failure, reflecting the tendency we first identified in discussing the Edo period, to see contraception and abortion on a continuum. The Mainichi newspaper recommended that women who had more than two or three children, or who had repeated abortions, be sterilized, identifying sterilization as a new end point of the continuum beginning with contraception.

The women experiencing abortion early in the postwar period frequently voiced a sense of being forced into the procedure, mostly by economic circumstances, and they expressed both pity for the child who might have been born and grief at their own victimization. One woman wrote in response to a 1955 survey carried out by the women's magazine *Fujin Kōron*, "I considered questions of health and the economic hardship, but more than anything else I felt [that the fetus was] to be pitied, and a sense of sin [*tsumi no ishiki*]," while another wrote, "Abortion is a tragedy for women. [It is terrible] to feel so ashamed and to endure the horror of abortion." [36]

These brief statements make it clear that abortion's social and sexual contexts are essential to an understanding of its meaning. A letter to *jinsei annai* published with a response on April 30, 1956, reveals one kind of context for abortion and the judgment passed upon it.

Letter Writer: I am twenty-two, and for the last four years I have been involved with a thirty-eight-year-old, married Section Head in my company. At first we only saw each other socially, but gradually we became more deeply involved. I have had two abortions so far, and now I am three months pregnant again. The last operation went poorly, and I want to raise the child I am carrying now. It is truly a child conceived in love [*aijō yue no onaka no ko*], but my lover says to abort it. I understand his position, and that he is thinking of his family, but I cannot kill the child in my womb a third time. I would be so much happier choosing death. I don't feel like breaking up with my lover and marrying someone else after all this, but I have resigned myself to die many times before. And every time I have an abortion, I am so sad that I want to die.

Response: Every time I encounter suffering like yours, I want to scream in anger, both at men's selfishness [*mushi no yosa*] and at women's lack of self-respect. If you think that love is above all questioning, then there is nothing to do but imitate the unhappiness women suffered in the old times. The same sin is committed by selfish, willful men who want both a family and a lover, and by women who allow themselves to be stepped on and kicked around, thinking pathetically that this is love, and thereby let men get away with it.

The reason your lover doesn't want a woman other than his wife to bear a child is that he wants pleasure from love but has no intention of taking responsibility for a lifetime. You are very proud of your "child conceived in love," but while your child may come to hate you, it will never take pleasure in being made to bear the lonely consequences of illegitimacy. The child will be shamed by its parents' irresponsibility. Continuing your relationship even after the poor results of your last surgery, if you repeat this abortion again and again, it could cost your life if worse comes to worst. And you are likely to become sick and weakly in any case.

Have more respect for your young life of twenty-two, and do not waste it. Have the courage to put an end to your relationship with your lover and to make your third abortion your last. It's a great fool who lets a failure at the beginning of life be an excuse to sell off the rest of a long life at bargain basement rates. Nobody can demand true love on the basis of sloppy weakness, and happiness cannot be nurtured from an unstable position.[37]

This exchange counterposes a woman's sentimental attachment to her third "love child" and a response that must have come like a bucket of icy water. The response writer had no sympathy for her sentimentality, but instead expressed utter disgust with her "sloppy weakness." The response casts the scenario as a Foolish Woman in love with a Callous Man and calls on the woman to realize the social stigma of illegitimacy with which she would saddle any child born of this sorry union. The woman should summon the self-respect to rid her life of this man who only uses her. No sentimental illusions about a fetus should deflect her from the urgent task of putting her own life in order.[38]

The Era of High Economic Growth, 1956–1975

This middle period saw rising rates of contraceptive use, which gradually overshadowed abortion's role in bringing down the birthrate. These trends occurred alongside unprecedented economic growth, accompanied by rising rates of female labor force participation, rising levels of education for both sexes, and rising age for both sexes at marriage. A comparison of Tables 2 and 3 shows that the rate of abortion had fallen under 50 percent by the time contraceptive use rose just over that level, around 1965.[39] Thereafter, contraceptive use steadily increased, while abortion declined until 1975. The most conspicuous exception to abortion's retreat between 1955 and 1975 was 1966, the astrological year of the Fire Horse (*hi no e uma*). The belief that girls born in the year of the Fire Horse could not get married evidently played a role in the decision of many couples not to give birth that year, a potent indicator of the continuing salience of such quasi-religious beliefs.

As many commentators have noted, condoms have provided Japan's most widespread contraceptive device, usually used in combination with rhythm (calculating the day of ovulation), and periodic abstinence. Women's reluctance to handle their genitals rules out the diaphragm, while the intrauterine device (IUD) is not widely diffused, because of its reputation for side effects. The pill was not prescribed as a contraceptive during this time, because of a judgment by the Ministry of Health and Welfare that it endangers women's health. In addition, women's own hesitation to use the pill, based both on fear of its side effects and dislike of altering their bodies' cycles, has remained strong to the present.[40]

As the population came to rely more upon contraception for birth control than abortion, more people approved of abortion, as shown in Table 4. Abortion apparently gained acceptance as it lost its earlier character as a substitute for contraception and became instead a fallback in the event of a contraceptive failure. A 1964 survey by the Ministry of Health and Welfare showed that about half of all married women who were either thirty-five or who had two or more children had had an abortion.[41]

The inception of *mizuko kuyō* dates to the end of this period, as will be explained in greater detail below. It is paradoxical that the end of this period should show both a high rate of approval of abortion and the beginnings of religious anxiety about it, at a time when incidence of abortion hit a postwar low. Before the mid-1970s, however, the evidence from *jinsei annai* suggests that many of the pragmatic, unsentimental views of abortion we saw in the early postwar years were still in effect. We can see, for example, that abortion is always regarded as preferable to birth out of wedlock. Women who imagine that their married lovers will either recognize their paternity, or divorce their wives to marry women who do not require this commitment before having sexual relations, are regularly told to have more self-respect, abort their pregnancies, and get rid of the men.[42]

At the period's end, however, we find the first mention of supernatural punishment for abortion and the suggestion that a woman should

Table 4. *Attitudes toward abortion (percentages), 1969–1992*

Year	1969	1972	1973	1975	1977	1979	1981	1984	1986	1988	1990	1992
Approve	9.5	8.6	9.4	9.2	12.5	10.9	16.3	17.4	15.8	17.3	22.2	26.2
Approve with conditions	62.6	64.2	68.2	68.2	66.3	63.8	66.3	68.1	65.5	68.1	57.3	56.6
Do not approve	16.3	14.0	12.7	11.1	10.1	9.1	10.8	10.3	12.7	9.4	13.6	10.5
NA/DK	11.6	13.2	9.7	11.5	11.1	16.2	6.6	4.2	6.0	5.2	6.9	6.7

SOURCE: Mainichi Shinbunsha Jinkō Mondai Chōsakai, ed., *Kiroku: Nihon no jinkō, shōsan e no kiseki* (Tokyo: Mainichi Shinbunsha, 1992), p. 83, table 7.

repent to an aborted fetus, as appears in this letter published on January 24, 1975:

Letter: I am a thirty-four-year-old housewife, married (by an arranged marriage) twelve years ago to a thirty-nine-year-old merchant. We have a daughter and two sons and were living happily. But last spring I got pregnant. I was surprised, because my husband and I were agreed that we wanted no more children, and we practiced contraception. Nevertheless, as a mother, having become pregnant, abortion was unthinkable to me. My husband, however, was greatly opposed, and he said we didn't need four children, so I should get an abortion soon. I was a weak-willed, foolish woman. I hated it, but I had the abortion.

I have been suffering continually ever since. I wonder if I am not being punished for it; after all, I shouldn't have had an abortion. But the doctor said, "Four is too many, and abortion is simple." When I recall that, I get angry, and I think I will go on hating him and my husband for the rest of my life. Every day is bitter and sad. When I see a pregnant woman or hear that someone has become pregnant, I am as miserable as if stabbed in the chest, and I want to repent to the dead child.

Response: You complain that you are a foolish woman, lacking will, that you are being punished, but that is ridiculous. I was moved by your letter, even though I see much pain in many of the letters I read. I thought, this precisely is motherhood, the wellspring of human love. Having experienced the difficulties of raising many weakly children myself, and from the standpoint of the world's limited food resources, I am of an opinion close to your husband's, but in the face of your feelings, which came out to me from the lines of your letter like the great mercy and compassion of Kannon, I felt that my view was superficial and shallow, the sort of fool's wisdom that would blow away in an instant. The doctor was even more so— the sort who would probably start marching to a new tune the instant the government started to beat the drum of "Bear and Multiply!" [*umeyo, fuyaseyo*] again, the minute the policy changed.

You should cherish your sunlike feeling and have confidence. But isn't it going too far to say that you will hate the doctor and your husband for the rest of your life? The two of them (and I'm sorry to include your husband in this) are neither sun nor earth, but mere droplets or branches that have emerged off from them. In other words, they are on the level of a child. They aren't equals whom it would be worth hating and resenting. You should treat them with kindness, as you would a child.

I hope you will reapply your feeling of wanting to apologize to the dead child to your living daughter and sons.

In this letter, the writer voices a kind of proto-*mizuko* view: it was wrong to have had an abortion, her unspecified present sufferings are due to the abortion, and she seeks a means of repentance. The reverse face of these emotions is strong anger against her husband and physician, who together encouraged her to have an abortion. Not reconciled to the procedure, she burns with resentment after the fact. The response endorses the writer's sentimental portrait of the maternal, but demurs from the notion of spiritual punishment, seeking instead to redirect the woman's emotions toward renewed devotion to her three children.

1976 to the Present: Teenagers and Abortion

From 1976 to the present, the rate of abortion in Japan has risen slightly overall, and is consistent with much of the developed world.[43] In most age groups it has actually declined. Teenagers are the exception to this generalization; the number of abortions among women fifteen to nineteen years old doubled from 3.4 to 7.6 per 1,000 between 1974 and 1991. Hodge and Ogawa draw this conclusion: "As the gap between the completion of schooling and first marriage has widened, the incidence of premarital intercourse and unwanted teenage pregnancies has also increased, prompting a rise in abortions."[44] The intention of this book is not to advance a comprehensive explanation for a rise in teenage abortion, but later sections of this chapter will show how cultural factors such as media campaigns aiming to popularize *mizuko kuyō* have highlighted and stigmatized pregnancies among young, unmarried women.

Rates of approval for abortion have remained high, as shown in Table 4. In general, higher levels of education and higher ages of marriage for women tend to mean more approval of abortion. Even if a woman has a negative reaction toward her own abortion, she will not necessarily disapprove of abortion. According to Hodge and Ogawa: "A woman's feelings about her own first abortion are . . . unrelated to her attitude toward abortion. Women who feel guilty about their first abortion, women who feel sorry for the fetus, and those concerned about possible damage to reproductive organs equally favor abortion."[45]

Strong support for abortion seems likely to continue to increase as more generations are born into families that have practiced abortion, tending to normalize it and remove from it illicit associations. Because the previous generation has had so many abortions, however, young women seem likely to be more aware of the physical pain and emotional anxiety that their mothers, other female relatives, and friends have suffered. Any ambivalence they personally may experience makes them more vulnerable to media barrages about *mizuko kuyō*.

Perhaps, paradoxically, because of society's growing overall acceptance of abortion, a new preoccupation with pregnancy and abortion among teenagers has emerged. Abortion is still seen as absolutely preferable to birth out of wedlock, but there is a new focus upon inappropriate sexual activity among young women, paralleling widespread knowledge of growing rates of teenage pregnancy. The following letter printed in *jinsei annai* on November 13, 1976, illustrates this trend.[46]

Letter: I am a third-year high school student, eighteen years old. I have been involved for the past three years with a boy two years older than me, who is now a university student. We became sexually involved after dating for a year, and I have had two abortions. I continued to hemorrhage for a long time after the second abortion and went many times to the hospital. Now I am worried that I won't be able to have a child, and I can't get the thought out of my mind. I am planning to take the entrance exams for the same university as my boyfriend next year, but I can't seem to throw myself into my studies.

I suppose I should get a medical diagnosis, but I am afraid of hearing the verdict, and I can't work up the courage to go to the hospital. This summer my boyfriend coached me in my studies, but I can't tell him, either. Since the second abortion, we haven't slept together even once. Adding this worry to my study problem, I think I'm becoming neurotic. I am suffering, unable to talk to my friends who are caught up in studies, or to my parents.

Response: People can usually judge the actions of others very well, but when it comes to themselves, they become confused. It is the same with your problem. If a friend came to you with this problem, I wonder what advice you would give? I think you would probably tell her to go to a doctor if she is so worried, or that the hospital where she had the abortion didn't say she would be unable to conceive, so she's all right, or that she should forget all this and concentrate on her studies.

But you may say that you can't, being so overanxious. However, in order to be happy, people have to do the appropriate thing at the appropriate time. For example, you see a doctor if you can't sleep at night. There is nothing as stupid as failing your exams because of anxiety. Aren't you really doing nothing but inappropriate things at an inappropriate time?

The response writer seems to say to the anguished teenager that the girl knows perfectly well that she is making a mess of her life. The response writer stigmatizes neither the letter writer's sexual relationship nor her abortions but seems to say instead that both are inappropriate to her stage of life. The message between the lines seems to be that the girl's most pressing task is to concentrate on her studies and shake off unnecessary anxieties stemming from the abortions. The response writer's main concern is practical rather than moral; if the teenager doesn't throw off these morbid obsessions, she will fail her university examinations. The teenager receives a disciplining response, to be sure, but one underlining an absolute priority on educational achievement, rather than a moralistic response in terms of Foolish Woman and Callous Man.

Let us attempt to summarize changes over the three periods of the postwar era. During the period 1945 to 1955, abortion was advocated straightforwardly, and women were encouraged to shed sentiments and attachments hindering them from achieving emotional independence. Japan's economic circumstances at the time were understood to require population limitation, and in a situation in which contraception was not yet affordable or widely distributed, abortion was realistic and necessary. At the same time, however, male irresponsibility paired with a theme of female emotional weakness emerged.

Over the second period, 1956 to 1975, the earlier themes of economic hardship and contraceptive unavailability were eclipsed by the theme of a couple in which one (generally the man) coerces the other to consent to abortion. This change paralleled the increased practice of contraception and the beginning of abortion's decline. Women's anxieties about abortion sometimes assumed religious overtones, as the cult of *mizuko kuyō* came to be promoted, and as spiritualistic religions began to flourish.

In the third period, 1976 to the present, we see a further decline in the salience of economic hardship. People are less concerned with being unable to afford another child, but still concerned about how a new child would affect their existing family. Alongside this change, we find a new disciplining of the sexuality of young women, which we will see given a new form through *mizuko kuyō*.

Seichō no Ie's Challenges to Abortion

Serious legal challenges to the Eugenics Protection Law have come from only one source since its passage, the new religion Seichō no Ie. Founded in 1929 as a breakaway from Ōmotokyō (f. 1892) by

Taniguchi Masaharu (1893–1985), Seichō no Ie inherited much of the spiritualism of Ōmotokyō, especially an interest in the soul and questions about its existence before birth and after death. Seichō no Ie only began to oppose abortion around 1960. At that time, the group's membership was about 1,500,000, the same level it had had since about 1955. The group entered the political arena not uniquely because of its concern with abortion, but because of the founder's keen support for a number of conservative and nationalist causes, such as state support for the Yasukuni Shrine, the presurrender national shrine for the war dead, anticommunism, abolishing Article 9, which renounces the use of war, and reinstitution of the prewar educational system (with abolition of the industrial rights of teachers' unions).

To achieve these aims, and to abolish the economic hardship clause of the Eugenics Protection Law, in 1964 Seichō no Ie founded a political action and lobbying group called the Seichō no Ie Seiji Rengō, "The Political Association of Seichō no Ie." This group began to support conservative candidates for national and prefectural elections. Meanwhile, Seichō no Ie's Youth Group began urging right-leaning religions to support an official Cabinet tribute at the Yasukuni Shrine and a host of other rightist causes, in addition to opposing abortion. Vitalized by this political activity, membership grew significantly from 1970 to 1980, to about 3,500,000 in 1980. In the Diet, the group cultivated politicians from the right wing of the Liberal Democratic Party. In some cases, such as conservative Ishihara Shintarō, these were MPs who had ties to a range of religious organizations. Seichō no Ie hoped that sponsorship by multiple religious groups would deliver them large blocks of urban votes.

Seichō no Ie's abortion opposition rested on the fetocentric position that abortion prevents a soul from being born in human form and is thereby tantamount to homicide. As fetocentrism was expressed in publications of the religion's Women's Group, the White Dove Society (Shirohata kai, also known by the English title, Truth Movement for Women), it relied obliquely upon images supplied through fetal photography. The following excerpt from a testimony presented at the group's annual meeting in 1978 is representative:

I believe that you know that in this world there are fetuses [*taiji*] who are aborted and sent from darkness to darkness. I want to consider the Eugenics Protection Law. In a word, this law is a law to promote abortion. Because induced abortion is legally established, fetuses which should have been born as loveable babies are ripped out upon the surgical benches of hospitals with tools, cut up and bloodied, and thrown away just like trash. What a tragedy. This law was established in 1948, through the work of Diet members supported by the medical establishment, and every year it has gotten worse. In 1952, in order to legalize secret abortions [*yami chūzetsu*], these medical Dietmen completely removed all restrictions. From that time on, abortions have increased rapidly. In 1956, the reported number of abortions was 1,600,000, and if you include the secret abortions, the number of aborted fetuses is three million. This is seventy times the number of deaths in traffic accidents. A fetus is killed every twenty seconds. In the age of color television, refrigerators, and automobiles, in this affluent life, I think we must seriously consider this situation. Abortion is not a surgery on the order of that required for uterine cancer or appendicitis. This is life sheltering in the maternal body, which will be born in a few months as a loveable baby. No—even from the time it is sheltering in the womb, it is a fine baby. It has cute little ears and a nose. All five fingers are there. Abortion is murder. Abortion leads to the decay of sexual morality and is the cause of juvenile delinquency. We must bind our hearts together to revise the Eugenics Protection Law in order to be rid of this tragic situation and to protect the life of the fetus.[47]

Seichō no Ie's opposition to abortion rested not only on fetocentrism, but also on ideas about the harm done by spirit fetuses (*taiji* or *ryūsanji;* the religion avoids the word *mizuko*), usually to a couple's children.[48] The idea that spirit fetuses try to get their "parents'" attention by causing problematic behavior in their "siblings," from bedwetting to juvenile delinquency, is the main theme expounded in Seichō no Ie's publications. This theme was regularly addressed by the founder's wife, Taniguchi Teruko, in an advice column she wrote for the Women's Group's monthly magazine, *Shirohata*. One letter came from a thirty-six-year-old housewife and mother of four, who had aborted a pregnancy seven years earlier. Her letter sought advice about her six-year-old son's bed-wetting, and a strange experience he had of seeing furtive images of a small child dressed in white; what should she do? The response was as follows:

You must apologize from the bottom of your heart to the child you aborted seven years ago. It was wanting to be born into this world, and the gods were wanting to cause it to be born—this is a precious life that you have killed. You have done a terribly wrong thing. Repent deeply and enshrine the soul with proper respect, as soon as possible. The tears and sadness of your murdered child have appeared as bed-wetting in the child you bore next. The child is crying out to its parents. It appears to your six-year-old child dressed in white. Have mercy on this pitiful child and comfort it with a warm heart. There can be no doubt that what your son saw dressed like a spirit in white was the fetus you killed seven years ago. . . . You should read the book on ancestor worship [referring to a Seichō no Ie publication], and as it teaches, give your aborted child a name.[49]

Fetocentrism, the notion of fetal spirits causing harm to "siblings," the linkage of abortion with a breakdown of sexual morality and juvenile delinquency, and a religious prescription to ritualize fetal spirits like ancestral spirits (by bestowing a posthumous name) were the main religious elements emerging from Seichō no Ie's abortion opposition.

In the late 1970s, however, the electoral fortunes of candidates backed by Seichō no Ie began to suffer from the repeated corruption scandals exposed within the Liberal Democratic Party. Seichō no Ie's fifth and last initiative to restrict access to abortion failed in 1983, and the political action group was disbanded. The founder's death in 1985 ended the religion's political involvement, and by 1985, membership had dropped to about 600,000.[50] The abrupt end of political involvement coinciding with the founder's death suggests that his personal support was a key element. Once it disappeared, there were no pressing doctrinal reasons to continue in politics, and thus the group's opposition has effectively ended. Small groups of Seichō no Ie members have demonstrated and tried to collect petition signatures to oppose abortion in provincial cities such as Sendai as late as 1990, but they do not seem to attract widespread support. The membership's allegiance in political activity may have been more to the founder than to the issue itself.

Other religions did not join Seichō no Ie in opposing abortion; nor did politicians or the general public. Perhaps Seichō no Ie did not really expect that it could significantly undermine the broad support abortion has among people of all religions, but used this issue and other favorite issues to stake out a position on the far right of the political and religious spectrum. Even if five defeats were not enough to convince everybody that this was a losing issue, Seichō no Ie's history suggests that while political activity can temporarily swell the ranks, those gains can dissipate rapidly.

Japanese feminists rallied in opposition to Seichō no Ie. They pointed out the cynicism of right-wing politicians' accepting support from the religion in the hope of capturing votes, not from any committed stand on abortion. Feminists suspected that the real aim of the religion and its political allies was to turn back the clock on postwar social reform of all kinds, returning Japan to an emperor-centered regime of militarism and pronatalism.[51] Many of the personal experience narratives of abortion presented in chapter 3 were written specifically to oppose Seichō no Ie's attempt to abolish the economic hardship clause. They show vividly that Seichō no Ie's use of fetocentric rhetoric was not, by any means, accepted wholesale.

Both feminists and family planners take exception to Seichō no Ie's attribution of all social problems, including delinquency and crime, to abortion. They also call it a pretense when people oppose abortion out of "respect for human life." As Katō Shidzue writes, "The anti-abortionists base their stand on the principle of 'respect for life': abortion is murder. But the life to which they accord respect is that of the fetus only: the life of the mother is totally ignored." [52]

Doctors and the physicians' lobby in the Diet joined feminists and family planners in opposing the elimination of economic hardship as grounds for abortion. It is not possible to say with certainty how much income physicians derive from abortion, because of the problem of underreporting, but it is believed to be considerable. But it is not entirely fair to place too much emphasis on the profit motive for doctors' support of abortion, which is also based on serious considerations regarding public health.

Mizuko in the Media

Early postwar media portrayals of abortion focused on the pain and suffering women endure in abortion, as in the 1961 film *Pigs and Battleships,* in which the female lead drags herself off the abortionist's bloody table in agony. Another early portrayal, the movie *Kandagawa,* focuses on the pain of a man accompanying his lover to an abortion, when the doctor shows him the tissue removed. The film *The White Tower* has as one of its main characters a corrupt gynecologist whose abortion mill lines his wallet handsomely. Novelist Sono Ayako's *Watcher from the Shore* is a didactic Catholic critique of abortion.

By the mid-1970s, when *mizuko kuyō* was first commercialized, abortion was well accepted and contraception was widely diffused among the population. Abortion had survived political attack from a right-wing religion. *Mizuko kuyō* emerged as part of what the media labeled "the occult boom," at a time when the actual incidence of abortion was in decline for all age groups except teenagers, and when a variety of representations of abortion in film, fiction, and advice columns presented a rich diversity of viewpoints within an overall framework of acceptance.

This section describes the media campaign from the mid-1970s to the early 1990s that promoted and shaped the practice of *mizuko kuyō*. It should be noted that those promoting *mizuko kuyō* have not done so from opposition to abortion. Rather, they seem to assume that there will be a continuing need for abortion. If nothing else, their livelihood depends upon it. The weekly tabloids frequently print articles on temples and other religious facilities for *mizuko kuyō,* including travel directions and a schedule of fees for various grades of ritual. These same articles introduce the views and rites of particular spiritualists, while pages devoted to paid advertising allow spiritualists to promote themselves without editorial intervention. Because such publications rely on sensationalism to outsell competitors, the most frightening spiritualists' predictions of fetal wrath and the most anguished accounts of the sufferings of their young, female victims have provided a gravy train for the tabloids.

At the time of the media blitz, the women whose postwar abortions had brought down the national birthrate, those born from 1920–1935, were entering menopause. *Mizuko kuyō* had not been faddishly promoted at the time of their abortions. The deritualization of pregnancy and childbirth characterizing the postwar decades meant that their abortions had passed without religious interpretation or observance. At the end of their reproductive lives, many were drawn to the possibility of appropriate ritual, whether or not they feared spirit attacks or believed that they had experienced one, as a means to demonstrate that they had neither acted callously nor forgotten the abortions.

Religion traditionally receives media coverage only in limited circumstances—when some religion or religious leader is apprehended in a scandal, when there is a news vacuum on other fronts, and in the late summer coinciding with the ancestral festival *obon*. The last is also a time for ghost stories and the release of horror films. Like news on any other topic, coverage of religion is expected to sell. News on religion of the last ten years or so has been commoditized in a new way, focusing on "booms," such as the "occult boom" or the "divination [*uranai*] boom." The trigger for these can be the smallest upturn in statistical indicators of religious participation, the appearance of a striking founder, or an eccentric religion. To convey the sense of a boom, the media magnify the significance of these facts, calling them unprecedented and using other superlatives to attract readers. The coverage, especially in the tabloids, is typically formulaic, sensational, and excessive. In short, it is the epitome of "trash." [53] The hyperbole tends to inflate popular interest in that which is being covered, thus actually making that religion or practice bigger as it receives sustained exposure transmitted instantly to masses of people. This information would take exponentially longer to travel by word of mouth.

Tabloid magazines are linked to publishing houses and television networks producing other commoditized representations of the "occult boom," of which *mizuko kuyō* is understood to be one element. All share an obvious commercial interest in magnifying the extent of the boom in order to attract television viewership and to sell books and magazines. Publishers, especially, have created a subindustry of publications on the occult, and the bookstores are full of their output. Because it is to the economic advantage of many people to expand the pool of consumers as much as possible, representations of occult phenomena, *mizuko* included, are vague, allowing for open-ended readings that attract a wide variety of consumers.[54] The interlocking of these various media creates a phenomenon of intertextuality,[55] and students of the tabloid press elsewhere have found that tabloids are linked for readers with television and popular literature, including folkloric oral literature, so that representations appearing in a wide variety of forms "reflect and feed into each other."[56]

An article published in the young women's magazine *Josei 7* in 1973 presented a Tokyo temple called Shōju-in Mizukodera that was devoted exclusively to *mizuko kuyō*. Its priest claimed to have memorialized 300,000 spirits, including Hawaiian *mizuko*, whose "mothers" came to Japan for their abortions, because the procedure was still not legal in Hawaii. The priest said that in the summer of 1972 alone, he had performed 50,000 memorials. The article carried a title worthy of the *National Enquirer:* "I have heard the cries of 300,000 *mizuko* and seen their mothers' tears."[57] A 1976 article advertised a Chiba temple exclusively for *mizuko kuyō* founded in 1973 by a nun who had lost both arms. Accompanying the article was a description of nearby amusement parks and beaches, plus details on how to get there, suggesting that clients for ritual stay the night and enjoy local tourist attractions.[58]

Full-page or two-page advertisements of Enman'in, a national center for *mizuko kuyō* in Ōtsu City, and its priest, Miura Dōmyō, have been a staple of the *mizuko* media blitz. Miura's views and practice are discussed in detail in chapter 4. He has advertised in a variety of magazines besides those principally marketed to younger women, including *Asahi geinō,* a weekly devoted to the doings of media stars, *Shufu no tomo,* a magazine for housewives, and general interest magazines such

as *Sunday mainichi* and *Shūkan sankei.* Stating that spirit attacks can
be expected unless aborted fetuses are ritualized, these advertisements
set out Enman'in's fees and services, with ¥30,000 (U.S.$300) the ba-
sic cost to memorialize a single spirit in perpetuity.

The media blitz for *mizuko kuyō* consisted of a barrage of fetocentric
rhetoric in tabloids.[59] The fetocentrism in tabloid accounts of *mizuko
kuyō* erases the distinction between fetus and infant, and attributes full
humanity and agency to a fetus from the moment of conception. It
further separates the pregnant woman from the fetus as "mother" and
"child" and positions them in opposition to each other. Tabloid fetocentrism posits that abortion is an act of homicide by the pregnant
woman upon the fetus. It is misogynist in ignoring the man's role in
the pregnancy and in its assumption that only the "mother" bears moral
responsibility for abortion. It assumes an ideology of motherhood that
all women have a duty to bear children.

Fetishized images of wrathful fetuses are created from fetal photography and graphic art based upon it in order to heighten sensationalism
and fear. It should be stressed, however, that fetal photography in and
of itself carries no moral message about conception, pregnancy, or abortion. A separate, ideologically motivated interpretation must be supplied in order to fetishize and "deploy" this technology. In the media
blitz of *mizuko kuyō,* fetocentric rhetoric provided this interpretation.

Numerous articles on the fees for certain kinds of *mizuko* rites have
appeared. Jizō statues in plastic go for about ¥5,000 (U.S.$50), while
those in stone can be purchased for between ¥40,000 (U.S.$400) and
¥150,000 (U.S.$1,500). One company manufacturing stone statues for
mizuko kuyō reported that it had no such business before 1979.[60] In
1980, an Osaka temple charged as little as ¥3,000 (U.S.$30) for prayers
for one *mizuko,* with monthly prayers for ¥2,000 (U.S.$20), and dis-
counts for three *mizuko* or more.[61] The articles indicate that *mizuko
kuyō* can be had in nonsectarian religious facilities and shrines, as well
as temples.

Articles that provide travel information and fees convey an important message—the client for these rites should not or would not usually
approach the temple to which her family is affiliated, but should instead
try to have rites performed in a setting in which she can preserve her
anonymity. This clearly communicates that there is something secretive
about *mizuko kuyō.* Much of the paid advertising for *mizuko kuyō* states
prominently that all sectarian affiliations are welcomed, and that clients
need not provide identifying information.

Articles appearing in magazines directed mainly to men or to general readers, such as *Shūkan post, Heibon punch,* and *Shūkan gendai,* for example, have adopted a different tone. They take an unsentimental attitude toward religious anxieties about abortion, for the most part, and they focus instead on the way obstetricians and spiritualists parasitically profit from exploiting and inflaming those anxieties. One cracked cynically that OB-GYNs will start performing *mizuko kuyō* the day the birthrate takes a nose dive.[62] Such articles cite the recency of the *mizuko kuyō* craze to imply that the trappings surrounding the practice and giving the impression of antiquity are vulgar and fake. It is pointed out that one of the best-known *mizuko* sites near Tokyo—Shiunzan (in Chichibu, Saitama Prefecture)—was not established until 1971 after a fundraising drive by its self-styled priest Hashimoto Tetsuma,[63] and that Miura Dōmyō of Enman'in started operations in 1975. The magazine calculates Enman'in's annual budget at ten million yen, noting with horror the huge numbers of fetal memorials he and his ilk claim to have performed. The side businesses generated by *mizuko kuyō,* such as the sale of ritual goods at obscenely inflated prices, the twenty-four-hour hot lines established to advise the perplexed about their *mizuko* problems, the titillation value for readers of ritual clients who have supposedly had twenty or more abortions—all these lead the men's magazines to the unanimous conclusion that *mizuko kuyō* is a "fear industry" (*kyōfu sangyō*). One article says, "This is an industry [prospering by] fastening on to human weakness."[64] Calling *mizuko kuyō* an "industry" denies any claim to religious significance, and rejects the fetocentrism of the media blitz. Even among the tabloids, *mizuko kuyō* is rooted in conflict, not a bland social harmony or consensus.

Tabloid articles aimed at young women uniformly have as their centerpiece reports of spirit attacks suffered by women who have had abortions. Lurid graphic art or fetal photographs show the vengeful *mizuko* hovering near its erstwhile "mother." The pictures show girls crying, covering their faces in shame, and hiding under bedclothes to escape the malevolent fetus. The victims report a complex of symptoms combining elements of folkloric ghost stories and menopause. One symptom drawing on ghost stories is *kanashibari,* the sensation that something damp, heavy, and clammy is sitting on one's chest. Women see images of infants and hear babies crying, though no one is there. They report strange blotches on the skin, and, looking closely, they are horrified to see the outlines of a fetus in the blotch. They experience "spotting," small emissions of blood from the vagina between their periods, menstrual irregularity, cramps, headaches, and pains in the shoulders and lower back. Some report sexual problems, such as frigidity or nymphomania, infertility, or strange growths on the genitals. There are no reports of men suffering physical and sexual problems following a partner's abortion; this complex of symptoms applies exclusively to women.[65] See Figures 4 through 9.

Spiritualists are interviewed as "experts" for these articles, and they often offer advice on stubborn cases (in the manner of *jinsei annai*), as well as their opinions and interpretations of the current rise in fetal wrath. They regularly cite rising rates of teenage abortions and sexual promiscuity. Nakaoka Tetsuya, a spiritualist featured in a three-part series on *mizuko kuyō* that appeared in July and August 1985, has written books on *mizuko* spirit attacks.[66]

Here is a sampling of some of the problems that Nakaoka addresses in that series. One woman complained that after an abortion she was turned down four times by partners for arranged marriage (*miai*). Another said that she began performing *mizuko kuyō* after reading Nakaoka's statements to the effect that wishes can be granted through these rites.[67] Nakaoka offers a typology of *mizuko*-related problems: courtship and marriage difficulties (including a husband's infidelity), illness (including uterine tumors and cancer), sexual problems, trouble with children (delinquency, refusal to study or attend school, violence against parents, etc.), and work problems. In response to a woman who wrote that she was injured in a traffic accident, one year to the day after she had an abortion, Nakaoka responded that she should not have told her current lover about having aborted a pregnancy conceived with a previous partner. To a woman who complained that she has become unable to conceive after having four abortions, Nakaoka explained that because she failed to perform *kuyō* for these spirits, they have all turned into hungry ghosts (*gaki*) who seek to obstruct her happiness. Another woman wrote that she feared that her engagement had ended because of interference from a *mizuko* created by an abortion her mother once had (the writer herself had also had one). To this, Nakaoka recommended that mother and daughter perform *mizuko kuyō* together, repenting to the *mizuko* for murdering them, and practice contraception thereafter.[68]

How do readers react to coverage of *mizuko kuyō*? We have seen that it generates a critique within men's and general interest magazines. Some female readers may also react negatively to these articles, viewing them as vulgar trash or camp, the way some people view soap operas to laugh at how preposterous they are.[69]

Lacking an ethnographic study of the readership of tabloid articles on *mizuko kuyō*, we can hypothesize that readers retain all the major

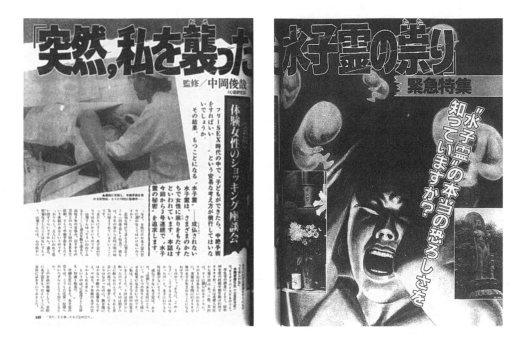

Figure 4. "The *Mizuko* Spirit Attack Which Suddenly Assaulted Me!"

SOURCE: *Young Lady* (23 July 1985): 144–45.

Heading: Do You Know the True Horror of *Mizuko* Spirits? A Shocking Roundtable Discussion from Women with Experience!

Smaller type text, left: Aren't we overrun in this age of free sex with the easy notion, "If I get pregnant, I'll just get an abortion"? And as a result, lots of women are attacked by the spirits of *mizuko* who can't achieve Buddhahood. This magazine presents a three-part series searching for the secret of *mizuko* spirits.

Photo caption, upper left: The number of women who get abortions after a contraceptive failure is increasing dramatically, especially teenagers.

Text, lower left: "Why is it that only women have to suffer *mizuko* spirit attacks?" asked twenty-one-year-old office worker Yamanashi Kyōko plaintively. Since spring this year, she has been experiencing numerous illnesses of unknown cause. "My friends wonder whether my problems could be caused by *mizuko* spirits," said Ms. Yamanashi, looking back on her past. "Now that I think about it. . . ." She recalled the time during summer vacation during her third year in high school when she had sex just one time with a boy she picked up. She ended up having an abortion.

Nakaoka Tetsuya, a researcher of spiritual phenomena, gave this advice: "If it was plain enough for her friends to bring it up, I expect she never had proper rites performed in the past. Now she'll have to apologize to her *mizuko* from the bottom of her heart." According to the Ministry of Health and Welfare, the number of abortions in 1984 was 569,000. That's how many were reported by gynecologists. Actually, however, the number of abortions performed illegally is probably three times that amount. That means that every year 2,500,000 *mizuko* come into being. But of these, the number of women who sincerely apologize, saying, "I'm so sorry. There was no other way out," is very small. Then one day, these spirits who cannot achieve Buddhahood latch onto their erstwhile "mothers" with a spirit attack and give them trouble.

"I have had meetings for arranged marriages five times. On one of them, I was the one to turn the other party down, but in four cases out of five, I was rejected. They didn't turn me down on the spot, but within a few days they all rejected me. It must be a spirit attack from that *mizuko* from three years ago," says Hiroike Hiroko, a twenty-one-year-old office worker.

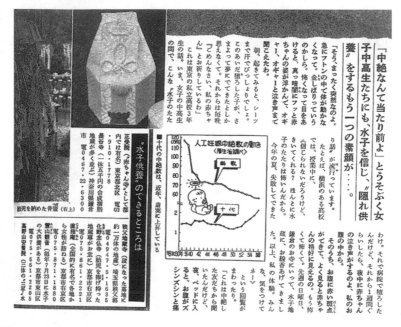

Figure 5. Textual concatenations: image, statistics, horrific testimony, and list of ritual service providers combined

SOURCE: *Josei Jishin* (4 November 1982): 194.

Caption: Even among teenage girls who say, "Abortion's no big deal," there are those who believe in *mizuko* and secretly have ceremonies performed. That's how it is. . . .

Chart: Changes in Abortion, 1955–1980. Upper line shows overall decline; lower line shows increase among teenagers.

Box, upper left: Cremation remains of aborted fetus, in silk-wrapped box.

Inset, lower left: List of temples performing *mizuko kuyō*, with prices, addresses, and telephone numbers.

Text at right: "That's right—it was a bolt from the blue. All of a sudden, lying under the covers, I couldn't move, like I was being sat on by a ghost. I was so scared, and when I opened my eyes, a baby had floated up out of the darkness. I could hear it crying, 'Ogyaa, ogyaa. . . .'

"When I got up the next morning, my sheets were soaked with sweat. All I could think was that the child I had aborted a little while ago had somehow wandered into my dreams. So after that, every night I've been praying, 'My baby, I'm so sorry.'"

This is the story of a girl in her third year at a private high school. These stories of *mizuko* spirit attacks are tremendously popular now among middle school and high school girls. For example, take the following story of a girl in a Yokohama high school:

"You probably won't believe it, but *mizuko* spirit attacks are really frightful. Last summer, I got knocked up. I went to the hospital for an abortion, but about a week later, I started hearing the crying voice of a baby in the middle of the night, coming from inside me.

"Soon after that, a red blob came out of me, and when I looked at it closely, it looked like a baby. I was so scared! So last Sunday I went to a temple in Kamakura and offered incense before a statue of Mizuko Jizō. That's what happened to me. Be careful, everybody!"

decoding possibilities outlined by Hall: dominant, negotiated, and op-positional.[70] Men's magazines adopt this last approach, with a blanket rejection. Undoubtedly, there are women readers who also adopt this stance. Research on United States tabloids, soap operas, and popular romances has shown that women tend to be somewhat more accepting, even when they disbelieve much that they read or see. Both sexes use the tabloids as conversation topics, and committed fans tend to believe in such things as Bigfoot, ESP, UFOs, and astrology. Skeptics among them believe in some but not others, such as one woman describing herself as a "gifted medium" who pooh-poohs UFOs. "Negotiating" readers may be slightly titillated, sometimes amused, and sometimes skeptical. The reader may derive pleasure from assuming several contra-dictory attitudes in sequence, enjoying brief emotional roller coaster rides in the time it takes to read a two- or three-page article.[71]

Some readers may derive a sense of imaginative possibility from thinking that excessive stories about *mizuko* might be true. This stance characterized some of Bird's readers of the *National Enquirer,* such as one who said of bizarre birth stories, "It's difficult, but yeah, I believe it could happen, I sure do, stranger things are going on all over the world right now. . . . It's kind of intriguing you know, it's like a lot of people let their imagination run wild."[72] Some may also take imagina-tive pleasure in these texts by concluding that however messy their own situations are, plenty of people have worse problems.[73] Bird writes, "Like sensational 'tabloid television' shows, the papers dramatize threats to the ideal world of family harmony, allowing readers to explore these threats vicariously and compare other people's problems with their own good lives."[74]

It is hard to understand why readers would endure the heavy-handed, blatant, ideological policing of young women's sexuality that is so obvi-ous in the media blitz on *mizuko kuyō* if they did not derive some plea-sure from reading those texts. Much like *jinsei annai* portrayals of sex-ually active, young, unmarried women, in tabloids we find a constant theme of women's degradation as a result of sex, a consequence from which men are immune, and of which women can never be free. Im-ages of *mizuko* symbolize their pollution and degradation.

One manifestation of this degradation is that abortion is portrayed as causing the physical symptoms associated with menopause in Japan, as well as distinctive problems in the Japanese family. As a recent study by Margaret Lock shows, the symptoms most associated with meno-pause in Japan are pain in the hips and shoulders and ringing in the ears.[75] Family problems currently highlighted in Japan are husbands'

Figure 6. "The Secret of *Mizuko:* Fetuses Unable to Receive Ritual Cry Out in Sorrow!"

SOURCE: *Young Lady* (13 August 1985): 159.

Photo, upper left: Young woman prays before a Mizuko Jizō statue.
Graphic, lower right: Mizuko float above a temple.

Text boxes: (upper right) It's unbelievable, but there are sicknesses that medicine can't explain. *(lower left)* It isn't only the mothers who are the objects of *mizuko* spirit attacks.

Smaller text: Says that a variety of misfortunes and illnesses can be caused by *mizuko*'s wrath, such as the breakup of marriages and romantic relationships, as well as chronic pain in the shoulders or hips, boils, inability to have sexual intercourse, breast cancer, chronic nasal congestion, uterine cancer, headache, all gynecological problems, heart disease, neurosis, weak vision, bed-wetting, sterility, and more.

Figure 7. "Do You Know the Horror of *Mizuko* Spirits?"

SOURCE: *Young Lady* (13 August 1985): 155.

Caption: Urgent Special Issue 2: Do You Know the Horror of *Mizuko* Spirits?
Is there a sure method of pacifying them?
Forgive me, my baby, and then sleep peacefully.
Below, right: An application form for having an abortion.

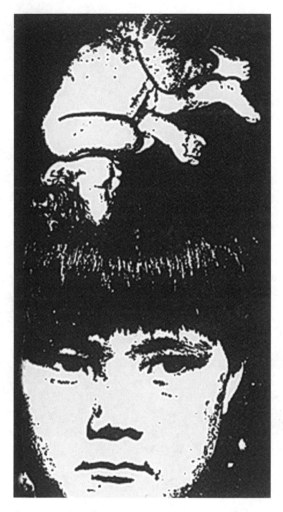

Figure 8. *Mizuko* spirit in the thoughts of a
young woman

SOURCE: *Young Lady* (13 August 1985): 158.

Figure 9. "The Horror of Those Wildly Popular Tales Among Teenage Girls—*Mizuko* Spirit Attacks!"

SOURCE: *Josei Jishin* (4 November 1982): 193.

Caption: Report from the Coldface: Dramatic Increases in Teenage Abortions!

The Horror of Those Wildly Popular Tales Among Teenage Girls—*Mizuko* Spirit Attacks!

Upper left: Out of complete darkness floated the shape of a baby . . .

Lower left: "*Mizuko*"—you wouldn't think that an arcane word like that would have anything to do with these girls. But they are more affected by stories of spirit attacks than anyone else, in their sorrowful motherhood.

infidelity, children's school phobias and violence against their parents, and difficulties in caring for the elderly at home, usually with a daughter-in-law as the primary caregiver.

Tabloid representations of women suffering the spirit attacks of *mizuko* regularly report this list of symptoms and in so doing create a logic of retribution applicable to most age groups of the female population. For teenagers and unmarried women, the message would seem to be that illicit sex and abortion damage the body and spirit. If you refuse to carry pregnancy (especially first pregnancy) to term, you may not only lose all future opportunity to bear children (the threat of infertility), but also your youth and beauty, the qualities that originally made you desirable as a sexual partner. To married women in middle age, the logic of *mizuko kuyō* says, in effect, "All the problems you now experience with your husband and children are due to abortions you have had. Your husband's infidelity and your children's failures are simply the reflection and consequences of your earlier undisciplined sexuality." To women in menopause and older, the logic says, "There is a reason for the physical ailments you suffer now. Earlier abortions demand an accounting at the end of your reproductive life. You must recompense through ritual."

Fetal photography has made a distinctive contribution, strengthening and giving a visual form to *mizuko kuyō*'s logic of retribution. The first popular-media fetal photography appeared in two magazines with Japanese editions, the June 1962 issue of *Look* and the April 30, 1965, issue of *Life*.[76] By now the image of the fetus has become very familiar, and we are accustomed to the erasure of the female body from it, giving the impression that fetus and female are separable. "The curled-up profile, with its enlarged head and fin-like arms, suspended in its balloon of amniotic fluid . . . has become a metaphor for 'man' in space, floating free, attached only by the umbilical cord to the spaceship."[77] In a Japanese context (and elsewhere), the idea of fetal existence apart from the mother that fetal photography made conceptually possible is radically new and a distinct departure from religious and folkloric conceptions examined in chapter 1, in which the unity and oneness of the pregnant woman and fetus was the dominant theme.

The novelty of seeing a fetus in utero presents a new field of conceptual possibility, a tabula rasa on which to project emotion, social preoccupations, or a kind of moral drama pitting women against fetuses; in abortion, women become "murderers" of the hero-astronaut fetus. It is no accident that this appropriation of the fetus diverts attention away from men's roles in abortion. The fetus cannot oppose any projection applied to it, so it can be variously labeled: scarcely differentiated human tissue, a homunculus, or a "baby." Any projection making sense of the visual information in a fetal photograph can stick, so long as the speaker and surrounding rhetoric carry sufficient authority.

Fetus as fetish is a creation of *mizuko kuyō*. Several artistic techniques are used to make fetal images seem human and menacing. One is to combine sketches of a fetus with a photograph, thus enhancing the sense, given in the text of an article, that fetuses are everywhere and innumerable. Another is to show them in as late a stage of development as possible. This technique blurs the distinctions among embryo, fetus, and baby, further underlining the sense of an existence independent of the mother and somehow capable of autonomous action. To achieve this effect, however, it is necessary to turn the fetus upside down, because a real one at full term is moving into a head-down position for birth. By contrast, the vengeful fetus image of *mizuko kuyō* appears head-up. Finally, enlarging the size of the fetal image relative to adults pictured elsewhere in the article increases the sense of the fetus's power.[78]

Popular culture shows no small concern with the menacing fetus, a preoccupation that Hollywood probably first introduced to the international scene. Consider the fantastically successful three-movie series *Alien,* shown widely in Japan, which revolves around beings of hyperhostility and the purest aggression. Their only activity is mindless reproduction of their kind, implanting parasitic fetuses into human beings who serve as incubators, completing the monsters' gestation in the human body. The human host dies in screaming agony when the neonate aliens burst forth from the chest in a bloody, fatal birth scene. The greatest ogre of all is the "queen," mother of the colony, whose entire existence is devoted to the perpetuation of her demonic species. The antipathy to femininity, reproduction, and motherhood inherent in these films feeds into the same sentiments conveyed less obviously in media coverage of *mizuko kuyō*.

Mizuko Kuyō in Practice

Studies of large numbers of religious organizations, temples, and spiritualists illuminate the institutional context of *mizuko kuyō*. Surveys of *mizuko kuyō* worshippers at Kyoto temples in the mid-1980s provide significant data on the sociological characteristics of the clients at urban temples at that time, the attitudes they hold toward abortion, and their goals in performing these rites. This section examines the practice of *mizuko kuyō* in its institutional context.

A 1986 survey of 209 religious institutions registered as Religious Juridical Corporations found that 55 percent of them did not recognize *mizuko kuyō* as a legitimate religious practice, while 43 percent responded that they practiced it. Forty-six percent reported that they took a negative view of the fad *mizuko kuyō*, and 45 percent denied the reality of spirit attacks.[79] This finding accords with results reported in chapter 5 of a field survey of about 200 temples and shrines in four provincial locations. There, too, a majority of religious institutions reject *mizuko kuyō*, for reasons discussed in that chapter. From these combined results, we can conclude that *mizuko kuyō* is practiced at roughly 40 to 45 percent of the religious institutions—mostly temples—that have ever been surveyed.[80]

In the introduction and in chapter 1, it was explained how premodern ritualization of pregnancy and childbirth occurred within a community of adult women, not within religious institutions. With that history, it is not surprising that a majority of the institutions surveyed should reject the idea of ritualizing abortion. Added to that historical hurdle is the fact of *mizuko kuyō*'s original popularization in a "trash" format, the weekly tabloids. Religious institutions concerned with their own respectability have frequently found it difficult to reconcile the illicit associations of abortion with religion in any case. Their stance of authority within a community disinclines them to be in any way associated with such a dirty business, or with sexuality and reproduction. Indeed, the more remarkable finding is that 40-odd percent *do* practice *mizuko kuyō*, that so many should have been drawn into a novel ritual form that others reject for historical and traditional reasons.

The 1986 survey revealed significant variation in definitions of *mizuko*. Fifty-three percent of surveyed institutions defined *mizuko* as spirits of aborted and stillborn fetuses, while 25 percent added infant deaths to the category.[81] This variation is possible, of course, because of the absence of any textual anchoring of the idea of *mizuko*.

The largest number of religious institutions listed 1980 to 1983 as the period when their clients for *mizuko kuyō* were most numerous. On an annual basis, most clients apply for rites to be performed around *obon* or the equinoxes. Roughly equal proportions perceived a decrease, no change, or increase in the number of requests for *mizuko* rites in recent years.[82] External observers report a decline since around 1985.

A 1991 survey of 284 temples advertising *mizuko kuyō* found that of the people requesting *mizuko kuyō* at any particular temple, most were not parishioners of that temple. Most ritual clients (61 percent) came in male-female couples, while women alone made up 37 percent of the clientele. It seems likely that these figures conceal a bifurcation by generation. We saw above how media shaping of *mizuko kuyō* creates and reinforces a desire for secrecy and anonymity. Probably no one sponsoring *mizuko kuyō* is proud of a past abortion or inclined to advertise the fact of having had one or more. Because whole families normally establish temple affiliations, an individual's approach to a temple could become known to the rest. Not only that, younger women tend to have grown up without any direct acquaintance with the temple and the priest's family. Their choice is between a stranger who might "blab," and one who guarantees anonymity. The matter is different for older women, who may be somewhat more likely, especially in rural areas, to have close, ongoing personal ties with a temple. For them, the parish temple may well be the place they would prefer to go, not only because their abortions took place a long time ago when many of their friends also had them, but because they are *not* ashamed to have the rites performed. Not only that, but as we will see in chapter 5, they frequently use the temple's mediation in a way that calls on men to assume equal moral and financial responsibility by making *mizuko kuyō* a standard rite that *all* parishioners are expected to support. Unlike younger women, older women may be ashamed to go to a place where they are *not* known.

These temples reported that about 23 percent of *mizuko kuyō* clients came from each of two sects, Jōdo and Shingon, with Nichiren and Sōtō sects each comprising another 13 percent.[83] This list of the four Buddhist sects most frequently providing clients for *mizuko kuyō* is slightly at odds with the conventional wisdom associating the rites most prominently with the esoteric sects, Tendai and Shingon, but not with Jōdo or Sōtō sects. The list accords precisely with the finding of my 1994 survey reported in chapter 5, which found that Shingon, Nichiren, Sōtō, and Jōdo temples most frequently perform *mizuko kuyō*.

Table 5 allows us to compare the timing of *mizuko kuyō*'s inception in various religious settings. We can see that most purveyors of *mizuko kuyō* became involved in the practice between 1975 and 1984, and that there was some tendency for spiritualists to begin before other religious institutions. This finding parallels the popular view that most clients first get the idea of doing *mizuko kuyō* from contact with a spiritualist (whether in person or through the media) and only later approach temples and other institutions to have it performed.

Table 6 shows the average fees charged for *mizuko kuyō*. We can discern a wide variation, with a notable concentration of ritualists charg-

Table 5. *Timing of* mizuko kuyō's *inception by various religious organizations and practitioners*

	Organizations actually performing *mizuko kuyō*[1]	Temples advertising *mizuko kuyō*[2]	Independent religious entrepreneurs, spiritualists[3]
Before 1965	15.2%	25.3%	20.4%
1965–1974	13.8	16.9	22.0
1975–1984	42.1	47.5	33.9
After 1985	11.8	8.5	8.5
NA/DK	17.1	1.8	15.2

[1] Data collected in 1986; 152 organizations surveyed; includes new religions and spiritualists.
[2] Data collected in 1991; 284 temples surveyed.
[3] Data collected in 1991; 59 spiritualists surveyed.

SOURCE: Takahashi Saburō, "Mizuko kuyō ni kansuru tōkei chōsa shiryō" (Unpublished survey, Kyoto Daigaku Kyōyōbu Shakaigaku Kyōshitsu, 1992), pp. 14, 18, 22.

Table 6. *Average fees for* mizuko kuyō

	Organizations actually performing *mizuko kuyō*[1]	Temples advertising *mizuko kuyō*[2]	Independent religious entrepreneurs, spiritualists[3]
Less than ¥1,000 (U.S. $10)	8.5%	5.3%	16.9%
¥1,000–4,999 (U.S. $10–$49.99)	19.1	28.9	18.6
¥5,000–9,999 (U.S. $50–$99.99)	18.4	24.3	10.2
¥10,000–29,000 (U.S. $100–$290)	15.9	23.6	25.4
Over ¥30,000 (U.S. $300)	4.6	7.0	15.3
NA/DK	33.5	10.9	13.6

[1] Data collected in 1986; 152 organizations surveyed.
[2] Data collected in 1991; 284 temples surveyed.
[3] Data collected in 1991; 59 spiritualists surveyed.

SOURCE: Takahashi Saburō, "Mizuko kuyō ni kansuru tōkei chōsa shiryō" (Unpublished survey, Kyoto Daigaku Kyōyōbu Shakaigaku Kyōshitsu, 1992), pp. 17, 19, 24.

ing from ¥10,000 to ¥30,000 for basic services. Meanwhile, Table 7 shows that most purveyors of these rites have ten or fewer requests per month. This means that most spiritualists, temples, and other religious institutions performing *mizuko kuyō* are not, in fact, doing a bustling trade in these rites, and that those which realize significant income

Table 7. *Average number of clients per month for* mizuko kuyō

	Organizations actually performing *mizuko kuyō*[1]	Temples advertising *mizuko kuyō*[2]	Independent religious entrepreneurs, spiritualists[3]
Less than 10	43.4%	59.5%	44.1%
10–100	19.7	22.2	27.0
Over 100	7.3	4.6	3.4
NA/DK	29.6	13.7	25.5

[1] Data collected in 1986; 152 organizations surveyed.
[2] Data collected in 1991; 284 temples surveyed.
[3] Data collected in 1991; 59 spiritualists surveyed.

SOURCE: Takahashi Saburō, "Mizuko kuyō ni kansuru tōkei chōsa shiryō" (Unpublished survey, Kyoto Daigaku Kyōyōbu Shakaigaku Kyōshitsu, 1992), pp. 16, 18, 23.

Table 8. *Age distribution of survey respondents, 1983*

Age	Female	Male
11–20	19.2%	17.6%
21–30	44.3	46.4
31–40	15.4	15.2
41–50	10.7	10.4
51–60	4.6	5.0
61–65	0.6	0.5
NA/DK	5.2	4.9

SOURCE: Kamihara Kazuko et al., "Nihonjin no shūkyō ishiki ni kansuru kyōdō kenkyū no hōkoku, oyobi ronbun," *Tōkyō Kōgei Daigaku Kōgakubu Kiyō* 8 (1985): 8.

from them are in the minority. These are indications that the "boom" in *mizuko kuyō* has peaked.

When surveys of 1983 and 1984 were conducted to assess the strength and character of *mizuko kuyō*, researchers at that time concluded that approximately 100,000 persons performed these rites annually, and that the fad was already beginning to decline.[84] Researchers distributed questionnaires to Kyoto-area temples, which in turn prevailed upon their clients for *mizuko kuyō* to complete them. The number of respondents was 558 in 1983 and 1,127 in 1984. On both occasions, women made up over 85 percent of the respondents, and 60 percent resided in urban areas. Table 8 presents the age distribution of respondents in 1983. Over

Table 9. *Personal meaning of* mizuko kuyō

Meaning of *mizuko kuyō*	Percentage (multiple answers)
Atoning for a sin (*tsumi no tsugunai*)	73.9
Easing my feelings	44.6
A natural thing to do, arising from natural feeling	39.9
A comfort to support me in my life	31.6
Relief from the sense of a weight upon my heart	26.1
Becoming happy	20.3

SOURCE: Takahashi Saburō, "Mizuko kuyō ni kansuru tōkei chōsa shiryō" (Unpublished survey, Kyoto Daigaku Kyōyōbu Shakaigaku Kyōshitsu, 1992), p. 10.

one-fourth of both sexes had graduated from university. The fact that the survey was carried out in Kyoto, which is also a major tourist site, may partly explain the high representation of those under thirty. This accords with general observations in which urban temples, especially in tourist areas, tend to attract a younger clientele than those in rural areas.

In both years the survey was conducted, about 77 percent of respondents reported that their *mizuko* were created by abortion, 20 percent by miscarriage, and 3 percent by stillbirth. Some 85 percent of respondents reported that they feel a sense of sin (*tsumi*) toward their *mizuko,* and over 70 percent fear that they will suffer a spirit attack if they do not perform rites for *mizuko.* Table 9 sets out respondents' beliefs about the personal meaning of *kuyō* for them.

Other questions revealed that those who sponsored *mizuko kuyō* anticipated that it would enhance their lives. The leading benefits expected, in order of frequency, were the health of oneself and one's family, the absence of spirit attacks, and a happy marital life. These results generally agree with other ritual performances in Japan, in which, aside from the benefits expected for ancestral or other spirits, benefits for the living are anticipated, partly because ritual establishes and reinforces a reciprocity.[85]

Survey results that indicate a mixture of regret, guilt, and anticipation of benefits for oneself for the performance of ritual are directly continuous with the mix of sentiments we identified for the Edo period in chapter 1. To contemporary mentalities, it is perhaps paradoxical that a feared spirit could be looked to for dispensing benefice, but ritual is assumed to mediate the gap. The assumption is that a fearsome or vengeful spirit can be transformed by ritual into a benevolent protector. In the present day, however, these ideas are being eclipsed by an image of the *mizuko* as perpetually malevolent, as the next group of data show.

Table 10. *Beliefs regarding the present state of* mizuko

Beliefs about where *mizuko* is, after ritual	Percentage (multiple answers)
It/they is/are always in my heart	45.2
Existing in the other world as a soul	33.9
Returned to that place where the ancestors dwell	25.8
Gone to heaven	20.8
Has been reborn	19.9

SOURCE: Takahashi Saburō, "Mizuko kuyō ni kansuru tōkei chōsa shiryō" (Unpublished survey, Kyoto Daigaku Kyōyōbu Shakaigaku Kyōshitsu, 1992), p. 9.

Table 10 reflects surprising beliefs about what happens to *mizuko* after the rites. The multiple responses from the same respondents may indicate that people are uncertain about where the *mizuko* are now; feeling unsure, they selected several answers. Those believing that *mizuko* are with the ancestors, in heaven, or reborn presumably believe that the spirits have attained contentment and comfort in a new existence. However, large numbers of people affirm the idea that the spirit is still in proximity to the believer or in an indeterminate state as a soul, a perpetually uncertain state of being. The principal researcher of this study, Kamihara Kazuko, notes that the belief in *mizuko*'s rebirth is unexpectedly low, given that through the Edo period and probably up until the early postwar decades, the hope for the aborted, stillborn, miscarried, and dead children was precisely that they would immediately be reborn, not go to the ancestors, the Buddhas, or any other destination. From the fact that so few respondents now affirm the idea of *mizuko*'s rebirth, Kamihara concludes that these people believe that "the *mizuko* will always be with them, always near, very familiar, and an inseparable part of personal identity." She interprets the current weakness of belief in rebirth to the prestige of science and the diffusion of Christian ideas of a single existence.[86]

Concluding Remarks

Mizuko kuyō emerged in the mid-1970s at a time when the rate of abortion for all groups but teenagers was in decline. It emerged as part of the media-promoted "occult boom," which included the rise of religious entrepreneurs, some of whom founded "new-new religions," operated as independent spiritual counselors, or specialized in ritualizing abortion. Together, these elements of the occult boom rejected the open-ended optimism of a previous generation of new religions and looked instead to a variety of spirits, whose attitudes toward humanity could not be assumed to be benevolent, but who could be manipulated and placated through ritual of various kinds.

The idea of *mizuko* seen in *mizuko kuyō* is continuous to a certain extent with a minor category of spirits known in the Edo period's folk and oral literature, as examined in chapter 1. The continuity is fragmentary, however, because Edo-period tales and other texts envisage them as almost entirely benevolent, and as being speedily reborn in human form. By contrast, present-day conceptions tend to stress the malevolent character of *mizuko,* though surveys reveal a minor theme of tutelary benevolence. The media appropriation of fetal photography has created a radical change in conceptions of *mizuko,* first by separating mother and fetus, and second, by fetishizing the fetus as an omnipresent menace. The decline of the idea of rebirth strengthens the idea that one can never be freed of spirit wrath. When these representations are attached to a text demonizing the sexuality of young women, the misogyny increases. An intense, competitive commercialization of tabloids, a central medium of the cult's promotion, creates an excessive, vulgar, "trashy" patina that causes a majority of religious institutions to reject *mizuko kuyō.*

Just as in the Edo period, there is a tolerance today for abortions necessitated by economic hardship alongside stigmatization of abortion resulting from sex deemed illicit. "Illicit sex" is itself a representation created through a stereotyped scenario of the Callous Man and Foolish Woman. By contrast, ritual has not been so continuous. This bifurcation of cultural judgment seems to allow the exercise of both compassion and condemnation. In the condemnation mode, a vicious misogyny is exercised through the retributive logic of menopausal symptoms as punishment for any problem likely to afflict a woman at virtually any age. Where the scenario of Callous Man/Foolish Woman is invoked, men's roles in abortion are identified and interrogated. In scenarios about economic hardship, on the other hand, this sort of scrutiny is rare.

Because *mizuko kuyō* has only recently been commercialized on a wide scale, we cannot know what proportion of abortion recipients would have utilized it if it had been available earlier. Many of the women in late middle age and old age who now participate in *mizuko kuyō* for much earlier abortions might have done so at the time if they had had the opportunity. Their participation is very different from that of younger women, but this is a point which must await a fuller elaboration in chapter 5, where it will be shown that these older women have succeeded in incorporating *mizuko kuyō* into the standard rites of parish temples with parishioner sponsorship.

The biennial population surveys by the Mainichi newspapers, which provided so much valuable data for this chapter, present data on questions that were standardized, for the most part, in the 1950s. In 1963, in a departure from the standard list, respondents who had experienced abortion were asked a question which, most unfortunately, was dropped after that year: Do you memorialize or want to memorialize the fetus? Nineteen percent answered affirmatively. Twenty years later, in both 1983 and 1984, researchers estimated that about 100,000 people performed *mizuko kuyō,* or, about 18 percent of the reported number of women undergoing abortions in those years. Undoubtedly, the abortion figures in any year are underreported, and it is certain that in the early 1980s many participants in *mizuko kuyō* were older women and men, memorializing abortions that occurred many years earlier. But even in the face of these slippages, might we not speculate on the basis of these figures? An interesting possibility, impossible to confirm with the data of this chapter alone, is that there may be a "market" of 15 to 20 percent of people who have contact with abortion (not only the client herself, but female relatives, male partners, and children) who are inclined to ritualize the event in some way. These people's actions can be seen variously as the legacy of a long history (only interrupted in this century) of ritualizing pregnancy and childbirth, and as resisting the progressive deritualization of these phenomena in the present. This is the "pool" for *mizuko kuyō,* originally produced through Japan's religious heritage and sustained now, in part, through newspaper advice columns, political-legislative challenges to abortion, the portrayal of abortion in films and novels, and through the tabloids.

However we construe the market for *mizuko kuyō,* it remains the case that much about the culture and sexuality of abortion remains obscure when viewed only through the lens of ritual. We can see through this chapter's investigation of the mighty industries that have produced the *mizuko kuyō* "boom" that it would be extremely naive to understand the phenomenon primarily as a "natural" outgrowth of collective religious sentiment. Nor should we understand the continuities from the Edo period as evidence that *mizuko kuyō* can be glossed over uncomplicatedly as "Japan's way of dealing with abortion." This is a minority practice, rejected by most abortion recipients and most religious institutions.

It is the task of chapter 3 to examine abortion and contemporary sexual culture. There we can look further into representations of economic hardship, and the making of Callous Men and Foolish Women.

CHAPTER 3

Abortion in Contemporary
Sexual Culture

This chapter turns to the perspective of individual women and men involved in abortion. It presents eight personal accounts of abortion in order to discern the influences of "common sense" about abortion and the fetocentrism of *mizuko kuyō,* and to see how individual representations of abortion are related to the representations in popular culture. Most of these accounts were originally written to resist Seichō no Ie's attempt to overturn the economic hardship clause of the Eugenics Protection Law, so they clearly illuminate the meanings "economic hardship" has for individuals of both sexes. In the texts, individuals alternately accept, resist, and reject stereotypes of themselves as Callous Men and Foolish Women. In addition, these texts offer rich insights into the range of thought and sentiment surrounding abortion, which cannot be captured by quantitative investigation.

This chapter discusses heterosexual intercourse, contraception, and abortion as part of sexual culture, that is, "the systems of meaning, of knowledge, beliefs, and practices that structure sexuality in different social contexts."[1] The term *sexual culture* calls attention to the fact that the sexual is "one of many domains of culture,"[2] and in so doing denies that biology is all-determining. After each textual representation of abortion experiences comes an analysis of what meanings people attribute to intercourse, contraception, pregnancy, and abortion. This analysis inevitably raises questions about the relationship between individual and collective patterns, as the meanings that individuals attribute to these practices and phenomena both shape their own experience of sexuality and contribute to meanings shared by Japan's collective sexual culture. Both individual and collective levels of sexual culture exist in a matrix of mutual influence with meanings deriving from religion and popular culture.

As recently as the 1960s, the suggestion that such physical phenomena as menstruation, lactation, and menopause are subject to cultural conditioning might have met with derision. In the intervening years, however, medical and cultural anthropology,[3] as well as interdisciplinary gender studies,[4] have chipped away at presuppositions of biological determinism, replacing that perspective with an emphasis on cultural construction and showing how these phenomena are culturally constructed, experienced differently within specific cultures, and subject to historical change. Meanwhile, historical and cross-cultural studies of sexuality illustrate its nearly infinite malleability, as well as its constructed, culture-specific, and historical character.[5] Studies of the histories of femininity and masculinity similarly underline change and cultural specificity, further undermining older assumptions about an immutable physical substratum.[6]

Contraception and abortion are viewed in this book as *sexual* practices arising from a man and woman's sexual negotiation and erotic exchange. The partners practice and interpret contraception and abortion within a context of expectations about their future relationship. The partners' families and employers (or schools) partly determine these expectations, but the man and woman's own vision of their future has the largest effect on the meanings they give to intercourse, contraception, pregnancy, and abortion. Constructions of gender form an important part of sexual culture, and partners continually measure themselves and each other against these constructions, testing their boundaries and occasionally subverting and resisting them. Accounts of sexual experience reflect all these elements of sexual culture.[7]

The meanings a couple assigns to contraception, intercourse, pregnancy, and abortion depend upon their feelings about their relationship: Will it continue? Will it culminate in marriage if they are not already married? Do either or both desire to commence or continue childbearing? Each of the associated practices becomes a polysemous and ambivalent signifier in the relationship: besides being undertaken consensually, intercourse can be withheld or coerced, practiced in a drunken state or sober. Such modulations of any of these practices send complex messages between the partners. It is not clear that either partner is fully aware of what he or she wants to communicate, nor that the partner will "get" the message and interpret it in the terms intended.

This is particularly true of contraception, and ambiguity surrounding the question of who is responsible for contraception is a major theme in the accounts of abortion presented below. Not only is there vagueness about who should take charge, but the texts also reveal that, like intercourse itself, contraception is subject to withholding, coercion, and, in many cases, inconsistency because of fatalistic attitudes, carelessness, and drunkenness.

Pregnancy is saturated with meanings for couples, and these vary with their age, marital status, and with the balance of power between them. Each party may use pregnancy to shift that balance and to clarify the other's feelings and intentions. The ready availability of legal abortion and the relative weakness of fetocentric rhetoric in Japan mean that pregnancy is seldom seen as a sufficient reason, in and of itself, to compel a reluctant partner to marry. On the other hand, if the couple is already married but has not yet commenced childbearing because one party is reluctant, an actual confrontation with pregnancy may help him or her overcome that reluctance. Similarly, if one or both spouses have declared their intention to limit the number of their children to the status quo, a (further) pregnancy can test that resolve.

Abortion, like pregnancy, has no set meaning, but shifts widely depending on the context of the relationship within which it is undertaken. It may result from a joint decision, but the texts presented below suggest that this is by no means the norm. Like intercourse, contraception, and pregnancy, abortion can be withheld and coerced; it can also be undertaken with positive purpose, or with great reluctance and fear. The families of either partner may play major roles, seldom obstructing a decision for abortion, but more likely urging the woman, especially if unmarried, to decide in favor of abortion. A man may command a woman to have an abortion as a prerequisite to continuing the relationship. Similarly, a woman can present the man with her own decision as a *fait accompli,* either before she carries it out, or, as in several texts, after everything is over. When a story such as the latter is told from the man's perspective, we can vividly see abortion's power (if only momentary) to demonstrate that the woman retains autonomy whatever the man's attitude to her and can make an emotional impact upon him far greater than he can through intercourse. Either partner can "deploy" abortion as a way to gain a better position within the relationship, though the texts below suggest that this is usually self-defeating. In relationships between unmarried partners, abortion not infrequently signals the end of the liaison.

Distinguishing Representations
from Representativeness

It is important to underline that these texts are all representations of abortion by an individual who experienced the narrated
events. Except for narratives 5 and 6, all of them were written to help
maintain the economic hardship clause of the Eugenics Protection Law
and to oppose Seichō no Ie's attempts to overturn this provision (described in chapter 2). These texts originally appeared in a book published by the Japan Family Planning Federation in 1983, titled *Can Sadness Be Judged? Against the Prohibition of Abortion,* a volume which
also contained criticism of Seichō no Ie.[8] Produced in this highly politicized context of the early 1980s, these representations are ideological documents, as much as (although not in the same way as) *jinsei annai* or tabloid coverage of *mizuko kuyō.* Because of abortion's highly
charged meanings in sexual negotiations, all representations of it are inherently political, and there is no possibility of there being a nonpoliti-
cized representation of it. That being the case, these texts are not invalidated nor is their content compromised by their political character.

There is value in presenting personal accounts of abortion in order
to study the meanings attributed to contraception, intercourse, pregnancy, and abortion. Such accounts are virtually impossible to collect in
large numbers, because of the emotional sensitivity of the subject matter and a general desire for privacy. In order to establish any ethnographic base at all for the study of abortion and *mizuko kuyō,* it is therefore necessary to use the few available texts, for lack of opportunity to
collect better ones, and to be very clear about both their strengths and
limitations.

Studies based on a small number of personal narratives cannot supplant large-scale surveys that establish representativeness, but neither
can the largest survey produce the depth of insight into the type of
interaction, negotiation, and emotion that a single personal representation of abortion experience affords. What we have is individual reflection on experience, giving it coherence after the fact, making connections not necessarily visible at the time, relating it to the theme of a
perceived threat to the law that made their abortion possible. Reading
these texts will not yield a representative picture of "what abortion is
like in Japan today," nor are these texts necessarily representative of
particular constituencies. Eight texts are too few to sustain sweeping

generalization, but their thematic similarities and shared elements may provide material for the formation of hypotheses in other kinds of studies, including surveys. It is also true that although some of the most suggestive studies of abortion from other countries are also based on small samples, this has not disqualified their findings.[9]

It is a given that every abortion terminates a pregnancy conceived between one man and one woman, and that every personal narrative of abortion presents the interpretation of one party only. We can take it for granted in every case that the other partner has a distinctive point of view, not identical to the one voiced, and that we will not have access to it, though our appreciation of events would undoubtedly be enriched if we could. The absence of the partner's perspective does not limit our access to the meanings these writers attribute to the sexual practices under investigation here. We need not assume that the absent partner would validate these meanings, the portrait obliquely conveyed of himself or herself, or that the writer's perspective is thereby invalidated by any reaction the absent partner might have.

The texts in this chapter are presented in two parts. In part 1, four women talk about themselves, their abortions, and their reproductive histories. Part 2 consists of four narratives, each of which focuses on one abortion in the speaker's experience. All concern the abortion of a woman's first pregnancy. Three of these are related by men, and one by a woman. Table 11 presents an outline of part 1 narratives to facilitate comparison of them. Table 12 shows the chronology of all the pregnancies mentioned in part 1, occurring from 1955 to 1980, in relation to the changing national rate of abortion.

Part 1

All of the narratives presented in this section were volunteered by individuals in response to the legal challenges to the Eugenics Protection Law. Since the narratives were assembled in this highly politicized context, the women represented here are necessarily more activist, more politicized about abortion, than the general population probably is. This politicization is further registered by the fact that each woman uses her real name, as opposed to having submitted an account anonymously. Only one of the women is not employed outside the home. The other three are professionals: a nurse, a dentist, and a designer.

Table 11. *Summary of reproductive histories in part 1*

	Name			
	Tamada Makiko	*Koyama Chizuko*	*Miyaguchi Takae*	*Ōbata Kyōko*
Approximate date of birth	1935	1948	1948	1943
Age at the time of the account	48	35	35	40
Occupation	Designer	Dentist	Nurse	Housewife
Number of pregnancies	3	5	6	2
Number of abortions (and other terminations)	1	3	4	1
Number of children	2	2	2	1
Which pregnancies were terminated?	No. 3	Nos. 1, 3, 5	Nos. 1, 4, 5, 6 (?)	No. 2
General attitudes toward sex, childbirth, abortion	Differentiates self from mother's "very severe code of sexual morality"; "Never once have I given birth to a child in happiness"; "Abortion still weighs on my heart"; "It is no good to think that it is possible to raise . . . children purely because of the emotional desire to do so. . . . You	Thinks about sex seriously, as "the highest expression of love," and "a pleasurable kind of communication"; About abortion: "a great burden that you must always carry with you"; "As if grinding rocks with my teeth, I decided to bear a second child. . . . [The decision] is impossible to accom-	"All my pregnancies have been unplanned"; "If the mother's health is in danger, one has to give priority to the mother's health over that of the fetus"; "I started to hate pregnancy"; [After an abortion]: "I felt as if a nemesis had been expelled from me, thor-	". . . Sometimes sex seems really stupid to me [now]"; [In her youth] "Rather than thinking of sex as physical pleasure, I thought of it as that greatest closeness . . . in which you can become vulnerable to the point of throwing away all shame"; [After the birth of a handicapped child and the deterioration of her emotional

Table 11 (continued)

	can't do it unless you are in appropriate circumstances."	plish in happiness"; "I hope I will never be pregnant again."	oughly refreshed"; "Pregnancy is hardly different from disease."	relation to her husband]; Sex began to seem "worthless"; [About abortion] "I hated all men."
Pregnancy 1				
Age	20	20–25 (?)	27	22
Marital status	Unmarried	Unmarried	Married	Married
Employment	Had to quit work—no maternity leave in non-unionized company	Student	Nurse	Housewife
Was the pregnancy planned or unplanned?	Unplanned	Unplanned/failed coitus interruptus	Unplanned	Planned (?)
Own reaction	Fear, ambivalence	"Unthinkable" to carry pregnancy to term	Feels that pregnancy is pathological	Pregnancy welcomed
Others' reactions	Partner optimistic; both sets of parents opposed originally; own mother relents and supports her	Partner remorseful	Unspecified	Unspecified
Outcome	Carried to term	Abortion	Abortion	Carried to term; child is handicapped
Pregnancy 2				
Age	21–22	22–27 (?)	28	30+
Marital status	Married	Married	Married	Married
Employment	Self and husband unemployed; heavily in debt; husband seriously ill	Dentist	Nurse	Housewife

Table 11 (*continued*)

	Name			
	Yamada Makiko	*Koyama Chizuko*	*Miyaguchi Takae*	*Ōbata Kyōko*
Was the pregnancy planned or un-planned?	Unplanned (?)	Unplanned/condom failure	Unplanned	Unplanned
Own reaction	Ambivalent; but sees this pregnancy as her last chance	Unwanted, but economically feasible	Resolved; wanted a child	"I hated all men"
Others' reactions	All others favor aborting this pregnancy	Unspecified	Unspecified	Unspecified; relation with husband had broken down
Outcome	Carried to term	Carried to term	Carried to term	Abortion
Pregnancy 3				
Age	32–33 (?)	24–29	30	
Marital status	Widowed; pregnant by a married man	Married	Married	
Employment	Marginal piecework/part-time work, followed by full-time employment at unionized company	Dentist	Nurse	
Was the pregnancy planned or un-planned?	Unplanned	Unplanned; IUD failure suspected	Unplanned	
Own reaction	Desperation; fearful of economic consequences and mother's reaction	Extreme ambivalence; retching; hatred of pregnancy	Unspecified	
Others' reactions	Partner advises abortion; own mother and all others assumed to favor abortion	Unspecified	Unspecified	

Table 11 (*continued*)

	Abortion	Abortion: false pregnancy revealed	Carried to term
Outcome			
Pregnancy 4			4, 5, 6
Age		24–29	No other information
Marital status		Married	provided, except that
Employment		Dentist	all were unplanned,
Was the pregnancy planned or un-planned?		Unplanned; after removal of IUD	and all were terminated
Own reaction		"Grim resolution"; "I hate this—never again!"	
Others' reactions		Unspecified	
Outcome		Carried to term	
Pregnancy 5			
Age		29–34	
Marital status		Married	
Employment		Dentist	
Was the pregnancy planned or un-planned?		Unplanned; contraceptive carelessness	
Own reaction		Gives priority for need for continued income, since she must care for husband's mother	
Others' reactions		Husband ambivalent or opposed to this abortion	
Outcome		Abortion	

Table 12. *Part 1 pregnancies, national rates of contraceptive use and abortion (high and low estimates), 1955–1980*

Year	National rate of contraceptive use (percentage)[1]	National rate of abortion Low[2]	High	Yamada b. 1935 Pregnancy[3]	Age	Koyama b. 1948 Pregnancy	Age	Miyaguchi b. 1948 Pregnancy	Age	Ōbata b. 1943 Pregnancy	Age
1955	33.6	50.2	131.9	P1	20						
1956				P2	21–22						
1957	39.2										
1958											
1959	42.5										
1960		42.0	138.0								
1961	42.3										
1962											
1963											
1964											
1965	55.5	30.2								P1	22
1966											
1967	53.0			P3 abortion	32–33						
1968						P1 abortion	20(?)				
1969	52.1										
1970		29.8				P2	22(?)				
1971	52.6										

Table 12 *(continued)*

Year								
1972				P3 abortion / P4	24(?)			
1973	59.3				25(?)			P2 abortion / 30+
1974						P1 abortion	27	
1975	60.5	25.0	84.0			P2	28	
1976		21.8						
1977	60.4	21.1		P5 abortion / P5	29(?)	P3	30	
1978		20.3				P4–P6 Timing unclear—all terminated		
1979	62.2	20.1						
1980		19.5						

[1] SOURCE: *Basic Readings in Population and Family Planning in Japan*, ed. Minoru Muramatsu and Tameyoshi Katagiri (Tokyo: JOICFP, 1981), p. 102, table 4.

[2] Expressed as number of abortions per 1,000 women.

[3] P1, P2: Pregnancy number 1, pregnancy number 2, etc. Pregnancies not specified as terminated by abortion were carried to term.

Thus they have higher than average education. The nurse and the dentist mention both that their husbands provide limited assistance with child care and that their own incomes are crucial to the family's support. The designer was widowed in her twenties and was the sole support for herself, her children, and her mother until she remarried more than a decade later. Each of the employed women makes a connection between the need to continue working and the decision to abort a pregnancy.

Each of the narratives is necessarily brief, and they frequently touch upon matters that cannot be fully clarified by the information contained in the text. In the analysis that follows the translations, therefore, the focus must necessarily be the *representation* of abortion as it appears there. It is not possible to ascertain the truth of the events reported, nor to go far beyond the text itself to clarify its relation to other events in the women's lives.

Narrative 1: Yamada Makiko, age forty-eight, a designer

The first time I became pregnant, my partner's parents as well as my own refused to recognize the match, and our plans of marriage broke down. Caught between my parents and my lover, I was terribly upset and thought I would have to give him up. I knew how angry my parents would be when they found out that in the middle of all this I had become pregnant, and I felt weighed down. At twenty this first experience was a great weight upon me.

My lover said optimistically that things would work out, and my mother, concerned for my physical condition because I had been weakly since birth, said that I could probably manage one child. Their outlooks were different, but between them they were agreed that I should carry the child to term, so I gave birth to a son. That was when we got married. I was working at a small company with no union, so of course I had to give up my job.

My son was a year and four months old when I learned that I was pregnant for a second time, and around the same time it was discovered that my husband had progressively deteriorating tuberculosis. My husband thought that the only way was to abort the child, as we couldn't afford it. He had just quit his job and started a project with some of his friends. We had large debts. But I had a premonition that if I did not bear this child, I would not have another chance, and I wanted to have it even though we were not in circumstances that would allow it. Besides that, I was an only child and had always envied people with lots of brothers and sisters, and I didn't want my son to grow up an only child. Eventually I gave birth to a daughter, though everyone around me was very critical of my decision and looked at me as if to say, "Why are you bearing this child?," even long after the fact.

My husband's condition was mistakenly diagnosed, and a year after my daughter was born, my husband died after being four months in a critical condition. As a woman with two small children, I could not find work, nor anyone to take care of the children. In spite of that, I prevailed on my mother and took a job as a waitress in a coffee shop two months after the birth. Then I worked as a clerk, a decorator, and went through many part-time jobs. All this time I was suffering from lack of sleep and poor nutrition from having to nurse my husband. I had no breast milk for the second child, though I had been overflowing for the first. Probably because of pushing myself so hard, I had tuberculosis, ulcers, and a kidney infection. My body was worn out.

I couldn't go to the hospital, so I did piecework at home, and somehow made enough to eat by sewing. Poverty and illness go together in a vicious circle, as I found out through bitter experience. I just barely got by from day to day, thinking that even if I committed suicide, I didn't want to kill my children as well. My mother had separated in bitterness from her own husband, my father, so she came to live with me and the children in a six-mat room. A struggle began in that one room where we all lived.

Nine years later I had my third pregnancy, when I was in love with a certain man. He was married and unable to break up his family, and he had neither the economic means nor the physical strength to raise his own child, my two children, plus a new child, he said. Compared to my first two pregnancies, I was a little better off economically, and because the company where I was working then was unionized, I could get maternity leave. But maternity leave had never yet been granted for a pregnancy outside of marriage. Thinking of my mother, who subscribed to a very severe code of sexual morality, not to mention the neighbors, the company, and society in general, I didn't have the courage to go through with it. I could not quit work. I was the family breadwinner, and I liked my work as well, and wanted to continue it. So, to make a long story short, nursed through it by my lover, I ended up having an abortion. I couldn't even stay in bed afterward, because I kept it a secret from my family. I took two days menstruation leave but then had to do stiff overtime, no matter how I felt.

I don't know if this was the reason or not, but thereafter, since I married my present husband, I have never since become pregnant. Previously I had got pregnant even though I was careful about contraception, but now by a cruel joke I had to go to the doctor [because I wasn't pregnant]. However, having had that abortion still weighs on my heart as I watch the growth of my two children and pains me.

Looking back on it, I see that never once have I given birth to a child in happiness, but always as the inevitable result of mental distress. Not everyone can give birth without doubt and with pride. A great resolve, with much self-questioning, is required whether one does or does not decide to give birth. And if the Eugenics Protection Law were revised as proposed, and abortion were prohibited, there would be no way out. If both the woman and the physician were made to bear the crime of abortion, it would be women who have to pay. Physicians can just refuse to perform abortions, but the woman can't run away. Even now my heart and body are wounded. If on top of all this I had to go forward and face the danger of committing a crime, could I bear it?

It is no good to think that it is possible to raise one or two children purely because of the emotional desire to do so, or in the belief that spiritual fortitude [*kiryoku*] will get you through. You can't do it unless you are in appropriate circumstances.[10]

Yamada Makiko is the eldest of the four women in part 1 and the only one born before World War II. She grew up during the war and the immediate postwar years, becoming an adult just as Japan began a period of high economic growth and the abortion rate was at an all-time high. It was in 1955, at the age of twenty, that Yamada experienced the first of her three pregnancies. That pregnancy came at a time when she and the man she was later to marry found their prospective match strongly opposed by both sets of parents. She faced defeat by this opposition, and, as a young woman, was probably not yet clearly "adult" in the eyes of the parental generation.

Pregnancy seems to have provided the means for Yamada to shift the united parental disapproval toward approval of her planned marriage. Because Yamada had been sickly in youth, her pregnancy called forth her mother's sympathies and attention. Pregnancy also carries the meaning of adult status, whether or not the parents realize this, and confronting her daughter's first pregnancy likely assisted the mother's change of heart. Yamada presents her decision to carry the pregnancy to term as resting on a new alliance with her mother and lover, a sign that pregnancy succeeded in shifting the balance among those perceived as exerting authority in her life.

Even after the economic takeoff in 1955, life was severe, as is apparent in the husband's illness from overwork, and in Yamada's later health problems. The lack of any provision for maternity leave in small, non-unionized enterprises forced Yamada to quit her job and to rely entirely upon her husband's income. She represents society as rigid, leaving her little scope to negotiate any exception to the rules.

Yamada's second pregnancy came at a time of even greater crisis than the first, coinciding with her husband's worsening tuberculosis, a period of unemployment, and significant indebtedness. Although he had supported Yamada's desire to bear the first child, the husband favored aborting the second, and Yamada agreed that they "were not in circumstances that would allow" the birth of a second child. Everyone else concurred, and in bearing the child anyway, Yamada had little support and faced universal criticism of her decision. Legal abortion was probably more readily available than reliable contraception in 1955, when only about 34 percent of married couples consistently used it, and Yamada's critics undoubtedly envisioned abortion as her best alternative to an inadvisable pregnancy. Yamada's story shows us the other side of *jinsei annai* advice in these years—she would surely have been advised by the advice column to abort this second pregnancy. When she failed to do so, she had to brave social opprobrium.

The second child's arrival precipitated great physical and emotional strain for Yamada, coinciding with the need to nurse her husband through his last illness and continued financial problems. She became quite ill due to overwork. In the midst of all this, her husband died, her parents separated, her mother came to live in a one-room apartment with Yamada and her children, and Yamada became the sole breadwinner for four people. Although Yamada should have been hospitalized in order to recover from her serious illnesses, she could not afford to stop working, leading her to realize that, "Poverty and illness go together in a vicious circle." Society's negative judgment on her decision to bear a second child can only have seemed justified to her.

Nine years later, around 1966 or 1967, Yamada became pregnant again. Although her employment conditions had somewhat improved, she was a widow who was pregnant by a married man. The factors bearing on Yamada's decision to abort this child were the man's opposition to the pregnancy, the impossibility of receiving maternity leave, her mother's anticipated disapproval, and the expectation of universal opprobrium. She was still her family's only source of support, but she would have been forced to quit her job if she decided to bear the child, and she could not afford that consequence.

Though pained by her decision years later, and suspecting that abortion might have caused her to become unable to conceive, Yamada stood by her decision, pointing out that sentiment is not a sufficient condition to bear and raise a child. She does not express feelings of guilt, demonstrate any acceptance of fetocentrism, or construe her situation as an abortion between a Callous Man and a Foolish Woman, though this is one cultural reading that was doubtless available to her. She represents this abortion as a clear case of economic hardship. The situation she sees as "appropriate" for childbirth would include sufficient economic and social support. Nevertheless, reflecting on her own reproductive history, each birth came as "the inevitable result of mental distress."

Narrative 2: Koyama Chizuko, age thirty-five, a dentist

No woman talks offhandedly of having an abortion. It can't be spoken of at all—it's a secret experience. The depressing feeling up on the surgical bench as you start to go under the anesthetic, the sensation of shame when you are informed that you are pregnant.

And when you cut off the possibility of nurturing a new life, no matter how firm the decision, there comes the feeling of having brought upon yourself a great burden that you must always carry with you. In the sense that you must continually answer a sharp accusation against yourself as a woman, as a person living in society, as the real you, a human being with some possibility of accomplishment.

I was a student when I first became pregnant. My first goal was graduation, after which I had to pass a national examination in order to practice my profession. The appearance of a child was completely unthinkable. There was a classmate of mine who did continue her studies even after having a child, but I had no prospect of being able to raise a child. You could say that the social pressure on me was not as heavy as it might have been, because although I was not married, my partner and I were discussing marriage. Nevertheless, I could not bear a child and accomplish my goal of becoming a financially independent woman. Having made up my mind firmly not to bear the child, I said to my partner, "Don't blame me if I should become unable in future to bear children [as a result of the abortion]." I had heard that it is common to miscarry if a first pregnancy is aborted, and I was both regretful and uneasy. Pregnancy is a dual responsibility, so there was no reason for me to be the only one to suffer. My partner must have felt remorseful as he sat in the waiting room on the day of the surgery. We resolved that once married we would build a life that could support a child in exchange [for the one lost in abortion].

I thought of sex seriously, as the highest expression of love. So it was important to me, and a pleasurable kind of communication. I think it would be most natural if one could have sex without thinking about contraception, but able-bodied men and women are made so that sex leads to pregnancy. It is really a big problem to choose a method of contraception that is neither unnatural nor a physical burden. My first pregnancy resulted from a failure at coitus interruptus.

When I tried to chart my menstrual cycle by taking my temperature each morning, I found that I was highly irregular, so I couldn't keep that up as a contraceptive measure. That left condoms, and even though I didn't like the interruption necessitated by their use, it was the next best thing.

Within two years I had another unwanted pregnancy. This time I would have to interrupt my practice, but giving birth was possible in the situation. More than anything else, however, was my feeling of the threat that if I missed this chance to have a child, I would become incapable of carrying a pregnancy to term, so I ended up having my first child.

About six months after the birth, my doctor told me that I shouldn't use birth control pills, because over time they would alter the original rhythm of my cycle, so I decided to use an IUD. But I continued to hemorrhage for a month after its insertion, and I was afraid of inflaming the uterus or its leading to cancer. I was very uneasy. Nevertheless, as far as sex was concerned, I was released from the emotional pressure of [other contraceptive measures], and it seemed to be effective. However, after about two and one-half years, just when I was thinking of getting the IUD replaced, I became pregnant. I had been told that they weren't 100 percent effective, but I was faced again with a bitter decision.

For a while I thought of carrying it to term, but having raised the first child enough to return to work fully engaged in [my practice], I decided to have an abortion after all. After the surgery, the doctor said to me, "You weren't really pregnant after all." At one and the same time I was both glad to hear it and much conflicted in my feelings. On the way home, possibly as an aftereffect of the anesthetic, I began to retch violently, and said to myself, "I hate this—never again!" But I had had the IUD removed, so three months later I was pregnant again. With a grim resolution, as if grinding rocks with my teeth, I decided to bear a second child. Whether bearing a child or deciding not to, the decision for a woman is immense and impossible to accomplish in happiness. I was only able to get over it because I had day care and because my husband helped in my work.

Four years later, my husband's mother had a stroke and we had to provide for her nursing care. Just as we were wondering whether to move house or how to manage, I became pregnant again. I could be accused of being careless [about contraception], but the fact is that there was a greater demand on me as an economic breadwinner than as a mother, so I was unmoved by my husband's remark to the effect that, "Children are lovable." As I was being dragged into the issue of caring for the elderly, I couldn't give birth to a third child.

It is impossible to give birth purely in proportion to fertility, and in deciding whether to give birth, one is always pressured by severe restrictions of one's own physical and life circumstances. I hope I will never be pregnant again, and that I will never be forced to give birth.[11]

Born around 1948, Koyama is a dentist, and it appears that at the time of this account she may have been in practice with her husband. Koyama's first pregnancy occurred when she was making the transition from student to professional status. Though she does not specify her age, we can estimate (since dentistry is an undergraduate degree in

Japan) that she would have been twenty or slightly older at the time.

Since Koyama's first pregnancy resulted from failed coitus interruptus with the man she was later to marry, her partner may have hoped that a confrontation with pregnancy would cause her to relinquish her "goal of becoming a financially independent woman," but if that was the case, he was disappointed. *She* retained full authority to decide whether to carry the pregnancy to term. The suspicion that Koyama's partner may have hoped that pregnancy would alter the balance of power between them in his favor is strengthened by what Koyama says to him. She tells him plainly that she will accept no more than half the responsibility for the pregnancy and that she will not be made the only one to suffer. She describes *him* as remorseful, and speaks little of her own emotions, except as they contribute to the couple's resolution to build a life together that eventually could support a child properly. In other words, Koyama was not prepared to accept fetocentric rhetoric or any sort of spiritual defeat in abortion.

Koyama seems to have had a pregnancy for each method of contraception she tried. Her irregular periods made the rhythm method unreliable, coitus interruptus led to her first pregnancy (around 1969), and condom failure or inconsistency of condom use to her second, around 1970. Her doctor warned her against the pill, so she next tried the IUD, which failed (she thought) after two and a half years, around 1972 or 1973. Deciding in favor of abortion, she was informed after the procedure that it had been a false pregnancy. No doubt bitter and resigned after all this, she lapsed into inertia and for a time used no contraception, resulting in her fourth pregnancy, which she bore to term, around 1973 or 1974. Around 1976 or 1977, carelessness resulted in a fifth pregnancy, which she aborted. Koyama seems to think that choosing and implementing a contraceptive method involves a trade-off between her health and the need to preserve an erotic flow without interruption. Apparently, she could find no reliable form of contraception that would preserve one without compromising the other.

Koyama seems to have assumed a preponderance of the responsibility for contraception after the first pregnancy. She regarded this responsibility as "a big problem," and was relieved that for a time the IUD facilitated sexual exchange uninterrupted by the necessity to stop midway to attend to contraception, even though the IUD produced serious side effects. The experience of a false pregnancy left her disgusted with contraception and pregnancy, retching violently. This may have made her too weary to face another decision about adopting some form of contraception.

It is evident that Koyama's husband did not step in to compensate for her temporary inertia by providing contraception himself. It is also possible that Koyama's momentary weakness gave him an opportunity to pressure her to have a second child, a decision she eventually took with no enthusiasm, "with a grim resolution, as if grinding rocks with my teeth."

Her fifth pregnancy, resulting from "carelessness" about contraception, coincided with other pressure from her husband: the demand that Koyama care for his mother after a stroke. He tried to dissuade her from the decision to have an abortion. This time, however, she says, "I was unmoved by my husband's remarks to the effect that, 'Children are lovable.'" Although Koyama only presents his role obliquely, she pictures him throughout her reproductive history as having taken progressively less responsibility for contraception, and to have presented her with more restrictive circumstances. Koyama's strongest defense against him has been her professional income as a dentist, which has evidently supported her at each point of decision about whether to carry a pregnancy to term, vindicating her original struggle to become financially independent.

Narrative 3: Miyaguchi Takae, age thirty-five, a nurse

I have had two births and four miscarriages and abortions. I am a nurse working at a hospital with three shifts, which is far from the ideal working conditions for motherhood. I have night shifts ten to twelve times per month, and on those days the burden falls on my husband. He must pick up the children from kindergarten, feed them dinner, tend to them if they are wakeful at night, fix their breakfast, and take them to kindergarten for one-third of every month. Often, he and the children are alone on Sundays. . . . Continuing to work as a nurse is really difficult. Nurses are always tired. It is quite normal for the menstrual cycle to be thrown off, causing us to end up with unplanned pregnancies.

I'm not an exception. All my pregnancies have been unplanned, but I haven't been able to carry them all to term. The reason is that my life is under great strain. The rent and utilities cost ¥100,000 per month, and if we had a child we couldn't get by on a single salary. My living depends on my physical health and strength. The life of a fetus depends on its mother's body, and if the mother's health is in danger, one has to give priority to the mother's health over that of the fetus. This is what I have learned from my three-shift job.

Two nurses work the night shift, and if you are scheduled for a particular rotation, you can't suddenly shift the schedule just because you feel rotten with morning sickness and can't keep food down, so you go to work even if your head is dizzy and your face pale. I nearly became neurotic, and I started to hate pregnancy itself. I couldn't continue the pregnancy, so I decided to have an abortion. After the surgery, I felt as if a nemesis had been expelled from me [*tsukimono ga ochita yō ni*]; I felt thoroughly refreshed. As if a spell had been broken, my appetite returned, and food tasted good again. Feeling my health return, I felt that pregnancy is hardly different from disease. Having this dramatic experience, I came to think of a fetus as all-controlling of a woman's life and health.

It was a year after that when I gave birth to my elder daughter. It was forbidden to have children in our apartment. The place was only a four-and-a-half mat room plus a three-mat room, so I was worried about space, for one thing. Morning sickness wasn't so bad as before. I was twenty-eight, so I resolved to have the child. I thought that every nurse believes that working conditions for nurses will be improved if nurses continue to work while they are pregnant, but above all else I wanted a child.

However, I couldn't find an apartment we could afford which allowed children. While I was still searching, my daughter was born, and the landlord asked me to vacate before the child started to walk. My days were consumed with the search for apartments and nursery schools. My maternity leave had nearly ended. I tried to get the union to encourage the hospital to open a nursery for the workers' children, but it never materialized, and I realized how long it would be before the hospital would do so. But fortunately one of my coworkers told me about an unlicensed nursery. The licensed ones take children from the age of four months, but maternity leave is only seven weeks, and when I took my daughter to this unlicensed nursery on my first day back at work, there was no bed for her! I threw myself on the mercy of the superintendent, saying that I would have to quit my job if the nursery couldn't take care of my daughter.

My parents had already passed away, and I couldn't afford a private baby-sitter. Even at that, the fees then were ¥30,000 per month not counting extra fees for milk and diapers, so that there was almost nothing left of my salary by the end of the month.

I was so sad that I could take no simple pleasure from seeing my daughter's growth day by day. We had to vacate our apartment but still couldn't find a new place we could afford that would allow children. So on impulse we took a huge loan and bought a place—even so, it was only two four-mat rooms. It was near my work, which solved one problem, but when my daughter became active, the nursery school superintendent said, "Sumi-chan is walking around so much on her bed that we can't take our eyes off her, but we can't provide this kind of care, so please enroll her in a public nursery."

So then I started going back and forth to the city welfare offices. No place would admit a new child in the middle of the year unless another child left, so it was six months before we could enroll her in a public nursery. She was a year and six months old by that time. I was pregnant with my second child, frequently having to carry the first one when she didn't want to walk, back and forth from the hospital to the nursery to home. It was a tightrope act every day. When I think what it would be like to have to raise a child alone, my spine goes cold. I think I might rather choose death.

Am I exaggerating to imagine an age in which, because of this "reform" movement [of the Eugenics Protection Law], it will become even less possible to dream of a better life? [12]

Miyaguchi's life is dominated by her stressful schedule as a nurse, family finances, housing problems, and the double burden of managing work and child care. While she appreciates her husband's help on days that she works the night shift, there is little indication that his assistance is available on a daily basis. Even with her contribution to the budget, the couple can barely get by, which suggests that neither Miyaguchi's nor her husband's employment is lucrative. That he can pick children up from kindergarten suggests that he has unionized employment, perhaps as a civil servant of some kind, allowing him to maintain fixed working hours.

Miyaguchi and her husband could only afford to have children if she continued to work, but pregnancy was so physically stressful for her that she could not continue pregnancy *and* work. In the background of this account is a system of hospital management that made no allowances for Miyaguchi's pregnancy. As she perceived her situation, Miyaguchi was forced to delay first childbirth in order to continue working and earning an income necessary for the couple's living. Pushed into this corner, Miyaguchi wanted desperately to terminate this pregnancy, saying that she hated it, feeling fresh and revitalized when the abortion was over, as if exorcised of a malicious, parasitic spirit.

Miyaguchi's second pregnancy (at twenty-eight) and her third (at twenty-nine or thirty) were pressured by the search for affordable housing and day care. Since her parents had already died, she had no one upon whom she could rely for occasional relief, and there is no indication that her husband shared these burdens. Her double burden was increased, no doubt, by the skyrocketing price of real estate in the 1980s, as well as by the tight market of day care provisions. All the while, she continued her hellish schedule at work. It is little wonder, indeed, that her menstrual cycle was irregular, and that she terminated three more unplanned pregnancies.

Narrative 4: Ōbata Kyōko, age forty, a housewife

I have been sexually active since I was twenty, which means that for twenty years I have known what physical relations between men and women are all about. At times I think I've done pretty well to be as little involved as I have, and sometimes sex seems really stupid to me, but that makes it sound like I've transcended the human condition somehow, though I haven't at all.

When I was young, I thought that human existence was on a higher plane. I thought I could live with a man as I pleased, as if I were building a fortress against the prospect of being just one of the herd. I imagined that we would read books together, whisper sweet nothings together, that this would be wonderful, and then to feel so close to each other that we would embrace. Rather than thinking of sex as physical pleasure, I thought of it as that greatest closeness, to just one person, in which you can become vulnerable to the point of throwing away all shame. So I thought it would be wonderful to be pregnant, to feel a fetus moving within me, to wait for a cute little baby to be born.

I burned with anticipation, waiting for the baby, determined to build a home in which we could openly discuss anything. I wanted nothing to do with my violent and depressing parents. My mother had died at forty-four, leaving a note asking that she be buried with my father. There was no one to protect [my husband and myself], young as we were, but my support and my confidence came from my strong sense of being tightly bonded to my partner.

However, I was mortified from the day I returned home from the maternity ward with a baby that cried like it was on fire. Wailing, "Gyaa, gyaa," it wouldn't wait for me to drink a single cup of tea, and it didn't care if I was deep in sleep at night. I'd think, "Damn, I should have waited." In spite of that, my body responded with overflowing milk to the child's cries, no matter what I was feeling. Frequently my clothing would be soaked. I would hurry to give the child my breast, but I was miserable, feeling all the while, "Give me a break." I felt piteous, that I was turning into an animal, as my days were completely taken up with caring for the baby. At twenty-two, I was certainly immature, but I would have been able to get perspective on things if only somebody else had been able to wash some of those diapers instead of me every once in a while.

It was around that time that I started to worry that my child was developing late. We had only just moved into our home, and we were a nuclear family with only shallow roots in the area. I was devastated when these worries arose and didn't know what to do. Unlike today, there was little information and few public services devoted to the early discovery of disability, so all I could do was rush from one place to another, carrying this child who knew nothing at all about himself. Until

I found a training facility, every day was black, and I was constantly bursting into tears.

After that, I was determined to throw myself into motherhood, even though it was hateful. I trained my child vigorously, to raise him so that he could be accepted in society. The child hated it, but I would grab him and teach him for four to six hours at a stretch, and when he made a mistake in vocabulary or pronunciation, I would correct him. Later I heard that all the other kids in the neighborhood used to say they were glad they didn't have such a scary mother. Although I was completely involved with raising my child, I couldn't stand it that he was not as good as other children. I would raise my hand every time he failed to meet my expectation. No matter how loudly I tried to teach him, he couldn't master sounds beginning in *s* or *r*. I couldn't suppress my feeling that he should be able to do something so simple, that I wanted him to try until he got it right, so I'd hit him as he tried to get away. At times like that, I'd think to myself, "My life wasn't supposed to turn out like this." What had happened to the person who was so unspoiled, who used to talk so passionately? After I would strike the child, I would suddenly return to my senses and think that it was myself I should be hitting. But while I always seemed to have the strength to strike the child, I never seemed to have the strength to strike myself. I could always be easy on myself. I'd throw myself on the floor, thinking, "I'm not a mother; I'm a devil who tortures the weak." I wanted someone to punish me, because I felt so apologetic to the child. But the child just looked at this mother of his with eyes trembling in fear.

That's why it took a long time for me to come to the feeling of kindness that a mother should have. I appeared from the outside to be a very principled and engaged mother. I went to the Mothers' Group, the primary school PTA, and groups for the parents of children with disabilities. I spoke out against discrimination against the handicapped. But no matter how much I spoke out, the criticism always fell on myself. I knew that it was I, the mother, who was unable in kindness to accept my child as a handicapped person. Around that time a group was formed by the handicapped themselves, called the Green Lawn Club, speaking out about how oppressive their parents were to them, and I as a mother could not remain unconcerned.

It was around that time that I became unexpectedly pregnant and had an abortion. My relationship with my partner at the time had broken down. The more critical I became of myself and society, the more worthless sex seemed to me. But even so, I would embrace my partner in the hope of retrieving our former closeness. Nevertheless, I found myself turning my face away from him. I was a little over thirty at the time. Even though my period stopped, I couldn't possibly believe that a life had come into being within me. So much for a small, new life—I could hardly believe in my own existence. In misery, I had an abortion. I hated all men.

But somewhere deep within myself, I was relieved. With this, my principles and righteousness would be destroyed. I could see myself as one member of mistaken humanity, the herd. I would be released from the hard and bitter sense of duty that I must raise my child to be "normal." I could be free of my self-criticism, my belief that I must be strict and severe with others, and free from being a frightening mother.

It was a long time after that until I was able to take any pleasure from motherhood. I was a mother physically, but I had to wait a long time before I was able to raise someone else. First I had to raise myself. Now my own son, who is taller than I, speaks of his bitterness in jest. He says, "Mom used to knock me around, bang me against a post." Shrinking at this, I am still ashamed. I'm not the kind of mother who can be respected, but I wish I could think that my son had affection for me.[13]

Ōbata relates her story as a *bildungsroman* of tragic loss: a loss of ideals, loss of hope for her congenitally handicapped son, and the disintegration of her bond with her husband. Whereas her early experience of sex was suffused with the ideal of a pure bond, sex dwindled alongside her hopes and ideals, until it seemed hopeless, idiotic, and she conceived a great hatred for all men.

Ōbata's first pregnancy is the only one in these texts that was welcomed and eagerly anticipated. The pregnancy is given the meaning of cementing Ōbata's bond with her husband, providing the foundation that will prove decisively that she has broken from her parents. Although they are dead, they are described as "violent and depressing," and Ōbata wanted only to be free of them, protected by an ideal love from becoming "one of the herd." While she does not spell out very clearly what she means by her desire not to become "one of the herd," the specialness she desired would evidently distinguish her from her parents. More than anything, she feared recapitulating the patterns in their relationship.

Ōbata focuses mainly on the meaning that pregnancy had in establishing her independence and as the fruition of her bond to her husband, which is to say that, by comparison with these considerations, she was much less attuned to the reality of demands on her attention and physical strength posed by a newborn child. She was shocked by that reality when her son arrived, crying as if "on fire." Smashing her ideal of perfect union with her husband, the child's endless demands and her body's mindless, automatic response of overflowing breasts made Ōbata feel that she was turning into an animal. She was horrified at her own transformation.

Whereas a woman whose mother was still living might have called upon her for advice and assistance, Ōbata was entirely on her own. Ap-

parently she could not get her husband "to wash some of those diapers
. . . every once in a while," either. Thus, the child's arrival broke the
spell of naiveté and idealism and confronted Ōbata with the prospect
she feared most: a breach in her bond with her husband, exposing his
unwillingness to share her burden, and the specter of her own transformation into one of the bestial herd, like her despised parents.

Awakening to the reality of her son's handicap, Ōbata threw herself
into motherhood with a vengeance, determined that, at the very least,
she could make her son "as good as other children." In effect, she tried
to beat his speech impediment out of him, completely unable to accept
his limitations. Again, she was horrified by her own transformation,
this time into "a devil who tortures the weak." To the outside world,
she presented a convincing disguise of engagement and activism on the
part of the handicapped, but, knowing that this was a sham, she was
tortured by her own hypocrisy and disappointment that life failed to
meet her expectations.

Sunk so low in self-criticism, Ōbata tried to revive her former closeness to her husband through sex, but she could no longer make it work
to cement their bond—it seemed worthless. She was unable to engage
fully. At this nadir, involving a genuine crisis of self-loathing, broken-
down relations with her husband, and the ongoing disappointment of
her son's handicap, she became pregnant and had an abortion.

The meaning Ōbata attached to the abortion spoke to all elements
of her distress, albeit with deep ambiguity and ambivalence. It became
for her simultaneously a sign of failure, destroying "my principles and
righteousness," and a symbol of accommodation, enabling her to accept
both her own limitations and her son's. Apparently, the abortion also
allowed Ōbata to express an emotion that seems to come out of nowhere, yet must have had its genesis in her relations with her father and
her husband: "I hated all men."

§

These four texts enable us to see abortion in the context of a longer
reproductive history and in relation to contraception and family planning. See Table 11. All four women married their first sexual partner,
though two were not yet married at the time of their first pregnancy.
Only one had more than one partner; Yamada did after the death of her
husband. None of them divorced. Koyama and Miyaguchi aborted
their first pregnancies, postponing first childbirth to lengthen a period
of study or work. While only Ōbata aborted a second pregnancy, all

those experiencing pregnancies after the birth of a second child aborted them, following a pattern in industrial societies.[14] All but Ōbata found pregnancy a great physical burden, virtually never planned and hardly ever welcomed.

The four women seem to have had generally positive attitudes toward sex, at least at the beginning of their sexually active lives. Yamada distances herself from her mother's "very severe code of sexual morality." Miyaguchi reveals little about her attitudes toward sex, but neither does she mention anything negative about it, though she says she hated pregnancy and regarded it as virtually pathological. Koyama and initially Ōbata idealized sex, Koyama calling it "the highest expression of love," while Ōbata thought of it as the greatest human closeness, in which all defensiveness and shame could be abandoned. Ōbata's attitude later changed, however, following the birth of her handicapped son. None of them subscribe to fetocentrism.

In total, these four women experienced sixteen pregnancies, of which only one was planned. Of these sixteen pregnancies, nine (or 56 percent) were terminated or ended in miscarriage, and seven (or 44 percent) were carried to term, yielding a ratio of terminations to births of 1.29. All of the contraceptive methods used are reported as failing to prevent conception: rhythm, condoms, withdrawal, and the IUD. Factors mentioned in connection with contraceptive failures included severe bleeding as a side effect of the IUD, the unreliability of withdrawal, carelessness, and the failure of condoms, whether from material defect or inconsistent use.

It is important to grasp the experience of pregnancy and abortion in the context of relations with sexual partners and family. The timing of first pregnancy for Yamada, Koyama, and Miyaguchi coincided with periods of transition and stress. For Yamada, the issue was parental opposition to a proposed marriage. For Koyama, first pregnancy coincided with the transition from student to professional status. Miyaguchi's first pregnancy coincided with great physical strain brought on by overwork and frequent night shifts, compounded by ongoing anxiety about finances. But whereas first pregnancy provided a means for Yamada to gain support, approval, and a more adult status, for Koyama and Miyaguchi, it was the last straw, a further burden they could not accept along with the other responsibilities already facing them.

Significantly, in none of these sixteen pregnancies does anyone voice strong opposition to a woman's decision to abort a pregnancy. No one seeks to prevent women from carrying out a decision for abortion, and no one assumes the right to enforce a different decision upon a woman.

If anything, lovers, husbands, and family more often argue in *favor* of abortion than against it. Most importantly, no one reports a religious objection to abortion, much less fetocentric rhetoric about *mizuko*.

Women voice regret about abortion, but consistently construct that emotion as unrealistic and impractical. Far greater importance is accorded to the desirability of raising a child in material circumstances and with sufficient social approval to ensure a viable life in society. Besides being impractical and frequently impossible, raising a child without requisite economic and social security would be constructed as an egotistical act on the part of the mother. Religious anxieties hardly come into view at all and seem to be regarded as sentimental and inappropriate concerns for so important a decision.

Part 2

Part 2 examines four narratives of first abortion, three told by men, and one by a woman. Table 13 summarizes these narratives. Narratives 5 and 6 differ from the texts examined in part 1 in that they represent a combination of direct testimony and a compiler's interpolations. They are drawn from a collection of interviews and articles about pregnancy and abortion.[15] Narratives 7 and 8 are drawn from the same source as narratives 1 through 4. The awkwardness of juxtaposing these two sources is compensated to a certain extent by the rare opportunity that narratives 5 and 6 afford to see a first abortion from a man's perspective. Collectively, the texts in part 2 complement the reproductive histories presented in part 1 in two ways: by directing sustained attention to a particular experience of abortion, and by focusing on the abortions of a generation of women younger than those in part 1. As in part 1, each translation is followed by separate analysis, and collective analysis appears after that.

Narrative 5: A, the man, is now employed at a trading company specializing in machinery; B, the woman, has married someone else

Man A was twenty-seven in 1984. The abortion he describes occurred five years ago. He and the woman, B, have since separated.

   A: "It was her first pregnancy and her first abortion. The day before the surgery she had to have a device inserted [to dilate the cervix], so she had to spend a night at the hospital. I went along and stayed by her bedside, but she was in such pain that she couldn't sleep, so I asked the

Table 13. *Summary of part 2 narratives*

Narrative	5		6		7		8	
Sex	*Male*	*Female*	*Male*	*Female*	*Male*	*Female*	*Male*	*Female*
Name	A	B	C	D	Kadota Nobuo	Reiko	Unnamed boyfriend	Kawashima Haruyo
Approximate year of birth	1957	1957	1954	1958	1948(?)	1951(?)	1951	1952
Age at time of abortion	22	22	27	23	22	19	29	28
Year in which abortion occurred	1979		1981		1970		1980	
State of relationship at time of abortion	College graduation; job search		C out of town for work assignment		Job search		Anticipated separation	
Relationship duration at time of abortion	3 years		2 years		About 4 months		1.5 years	
Contraception methods adopted	Rhythm and condoms		Withdrawal		Rhythm		Condoms(?)	
Partner mainly responsible for contraception	Responsibility shared(?)		X		X		X	
Reason for contraceptive failure	A was careless; inconsistent condom usage		C failed at coitus interruptus		Nobuo lost control and did not withdraw as planned		Boyfriend was careless; inconsistent condom usage(?)	
Relationship outcome	Separation after 1.5 years following abortion		C married, continues sexual relation with D in secrecy		Unclear; continuation(?)		Unclear	

nurse to give her a painkiller. She took two pills. She had eaten nothing, but she felt nauseous and vomited. Nothing came up but stomach acid.

"I felt so sorry for her. I felt that I had done something terribly wrong, and that feeling pained me deeply. She said nothing, and neither did I. She was just in pain. She took the medicine and was asleep in thirty minutes.

"I was a university student at the time, so I had to go to class the next day. Everything was over by the time I got back to the hospital. She was terribly pale. I felt so bad to see her that way. I can picture it vividly even now."

A met B ten years ago, when they were both students at a private university in Tokyo, majoring in British and American literature. They got to know each other originally as classmates, borrowing each other's notes and so forth. A was from Niigata Prefecture. During the summer vacation, he used some money he had earned at a part-time job to take a short trip that included a stop at B's hometown, Sendai. B's family owned a dry goods firm there. They arranged to meet at the Tanabata festival. In the excitement of the huge crowd, they held hands, and when they tired of walking they stopped at the edge of a park where they had their first, clumsy kiss.

Their first sexual encounter took place right after the end of summer vacation. A went to meet B's train back to Tokyo, and it was the next day that it happened. B invited A to dinner at her apartment. It was the first sexual experience for both of them. Their relationship continued for three years. During that time, they even managed to meet in London, where they had traveled separately. It was very dramatic.

A: "It was then that it came to me for the first time that I wanted to make my life with B. It is very lonely to be all by yourself in a foreign country, and when we were able to meet there, it really affected me. Besides that, she had agreed to my plan for the trip and had come all that way to be with me. So I thought that I wanted to be with her always. I told her how I felt, I asked her to marry me, and she said yes."

It was a year after that, in the autumn of their senior year, when A was intensely preoccupied with finding a job (to begin after his graduation), that B became pregnant.

B had an aunt living in Tokyo, someone whom B could confide in. One day the aunt called A out to meet her and told him that B was pregnant and had decided to have an abortion. B had felt lethargic for a long time and had been running a low fever. When she told her aunt about these symptoms, the aunt suspected that B might be pregnant and so took her to a gynecologist for a pregnancy test. B was three months pregnant.

This was the couple's first contraceptive failure in their three years together. A had used a condom on the "danger days" of B's menstrual cycle, and he believed that he had been careful, but there had been one day when he didn't bother, and B must have conceived at that time. This was the beginning of a bad dream for A. The couple had talked together of their hope to marry one day, but they had no concrete plans, except as expressed through sex and love. To their surprise, that which should have followed the marriage had unexpectedly come first.

The pregnancy was confirmed just at the time that both of them were maximally caught up in the search for work. Neither of them was in a state of mind to make way for a new life. Besides that, B's father was an influential man of very conservative views, for whom the opinion of society mattered above all else. There was no question of his permitting the birth of a child before marriage. To make a long story short, this new life would be welcomed by no one, and it was absolutely clear how to dispose of the matter. This was the reason B did not discuss with A the question of whether or not to give birth to the child. She was under pressure to make a decision, and she was not about to entrust the decision to her partner. She decided to take care of matters herself.

A: "B's aunt told me that B had made up her mind. But I couldn't see why a decision had to be made so suddenly. I guess I wasn't very practical. I figured that things would work out one way or another after we graduated. But there was no room for me to say, 'Wait a minute, please,' or to try to put off a decision.

"I know that I was being devious [*zurui*], but I wanted to put it off as long as possible. However, she had made up her mind firmly." When A went to see B after the abortion, he recalled a scene in the movie *Kandagawa,* on the theme of couples living together out of wedlock. In this scene a doctor shows a woman's lover the bloody fetus he has just taken from her body. Although A wasn't shown the fetus, in recalling this scene from the movie, he felt thoroughly disgusted with himself. Although he bore half the responsibility for the creation of this life, he had silently assented to its destruction. His feelings were confused and upset.

A: "I think she was not in a position to make any other decision. She was under terrible pressure. But the truth of it is that she was able to endure the abortion because of her aunt's support. I think that my support wasn't enough for her. And I feel deeply ashamed to say so."

Interviewer: "But did A want B to have borne the child?"

A: "I thought things would work out somehow."

Interviewer: "Does that mean that you wouldn't have minded if she had decided to bear the child?"

A: "No, not exactly. I just thought that if I could get a job, then we could be together and raise the child somehow. I know I wasn't being very realistic, but I did feel this hope. Looking back on it, I can see that I was really running away from the problem. To be blunt about it, women are the ones who feel the pain—not men. Men can afford to be vague about it. But as long as a decision is delayed, the fetus grows steadily bigger, and women are forced to make a decision."

Interviewer: "Did B want to have the child?"

A: "It was before she became pregnant, but at one point she did say that she wanted a child."

Interviewer: "Would B have had the child if you had agreed to it?"

A: "I don't think so. I may have been careless, but her father was very severe. He would never have permitted her to have a child before marriage. I think she was well aware of that."

The two went back to their everyday lives, the new life having been sent away. They both found jobs and graduated. A took a job with a trading company dealing in machinery, and B went to work as a clerk in a bank. But an undiscussable, unpleasant feeling grew up between them.

A: "It may have been the transition from student life to working. I felt she had changed from the girl I used to know, and that feeling grew stronger. Eventually I grew cold toward her. I think she sensed keenly that my feelings had changed, and in the end we grew unpleasant to each other. I know that she wanted to forget the wounding feeling of the abortion. She spent a lot of time with her workmates, and even though I didn't want to grill her about it, we'd end up quarreling. That's how our relationship changed."

They stayed together for another year and a half, and then finally broke up. A year before the interview, B married another man.

A: "I wanted to marry her. But something about the abortion kept me from it. I couldn't make myself say to her, 'I'll take responsibility. Please marry me.'"

A still keeps B's letters in his apartment in a desk drawer, along with a box of chocolates she gave him on Valentine's Day. The lace curtains she put up for him are as she left them.[16]

The relationship between A and B began as a student romance. After they had known each other as classmates for a year or so, A visited B at her hometown, where they first became romantically involved, on the occasion of the Tanabata festival. This festival, held on the seventh day of the seventh month, commemorates the astrological convergence of Altair and Vega, mythologized as the meeting of a celestial Cowherd and Maiden. Charged by this romantic meeting in the provinces, when A and B met again in Tokyo after the vacation, they initiated a sexual relationship immediately.

They apparently shared responsibility for contraception, which for them consisted of a combination of rhythm and condoms. A was aware of the timing of B's menstrual cycle, and the couple seems to have regularly used condoms for a time each month around B's ovulation. This method prevented conception successfully for three years. A attributed the pregnancy that occurred in 1979 to his failure to use a condom on one of B's "danger days."

The pregnancy occurred at a time of major transition for the two individuals. Both were finishing their final university requirements and seeking jobs. The occurrence of pregnancy at such a time of transition can be recognized as a theme of narratives 1, 2, and 3 in part 1, and it will appear again in narratives 7 and 8.

Since this account is presented by A, we can only view the couple's relationship through his representation of it, but by the time of the pregnancy, he had begun to think that he would eventually like to marry B. He began to feel this way after another emotionally charged rendezvous, this time in London, where he and B had traveled secretly and alone to be with each other. The meeting must have had certain associations for them because of their study of British and American literature, and these were probably heightened by associations with famous travel accounts by such Japanese modern writers as Natsume Sōseki, whose experience of loneliness among strangers in London is legendary. A, the romantic student of foreign literature, must have felt his attachment to B deepened by the exotic setting and the possibility of projecting his own odyssey upon the path to London so well worn by Japanese literary luminaries. Whereas he invoked the motif of Japanese abroad confirming their sense of life purpose and ethnic identity through the difficulties and cultural differences encountered in foreign lands, however, A only vaguely arrived at a sense that he and B should marry.

For all the drama of the way in which A came to want to marry B, however, it is not clear that A ever actually communicated this desire to B, or that the couple had any contingency plan for what to do in case B became pregnant. It seems likely that A remained vague about his intentions, further motivating B to fend for herself when the pregnancy was confirmed.

B seems to have been of a more practical mind than A. She turned to a female relative, an aunt, when her pregnancy was first suspected, and she decided in consultation with the aunt to abort the pregnancy. It would appear that the anticipated wrath of B's father weighed heavily in the decision. B turned to her family for support, realizing that A would be useless and impractical. He proved them right.

What he seems to seek is some recognition of the very real pain he suffered in the abortion. There was a paucity of cultural scripts for him to turn to, no defined role for him in the situation. The lack of roles for men in abortion is also noted in U.S. studies of men and abortion.[17] This lack may be one reason A could not bring himself to remain at the hospital, one reason he deserted B while she had the abortion. All he can think of is the film *Kandagawa*, a scene which he apparently takes to be an accusation against him.

A's youth and inexperience undoubtedly contributed to his inability to act in the situation. He felt that events had overtaken him before he could grasp what was unfolding before him. B and her aunt united in the decision to abort before he even learned of the pregnancy. The only honorable courses of action left to him were either to interrupt his job search, oppose the abortion, confront B's ogre of a father, marry B, and raise the child; or agree to B's decision to abort the pregnancy, support her through the procedure, and reestablish their relationship (hopefully with an improved contraceptive regimen). In the end he was unable to clarify his position, and as a result he could only appear irresponsible, cowardly, weak, and unreliable to B, who was, as he points out, the one who was really under pressure in the situation. For all this, he feels ashamed. In fact, he can only represent the situation in this light to the interviewer (that is, he can only say that just women really suffer in abortion—men do not) by removing himself ("running away," as he puts it), acting as if the pregnancy—and hence the decision regarding abortion—belongs more to women than men. This approach conveniently excuses him when the decision is made, just as he absents himself from the procedure itself with the excuse that he must attend class. His approach also allows him to smolder resentfully after the fact, making the separation pretty much inevitable.

Narrative 6: C, a thirty-year-old male employee of a stock brokerage house who is married, with one child; his partner, D, is several years younger

C became acquainted with D five years ago, through a literary circle at a city university of which C was an alumnus and D was a currently enrolled student. C was already busy with his job as a stockbroker, but he had not lost his interest in literature. One day he was engaged in literary debate at his old school with some of the current students. He spoke romantically, passionately, and the students looked up to him in a spirit of reliance and admiration. D, who came from Kagoshima, was one of several who fell for him. Eventually, D started visiting C at his apartment. For all that, the two had never even held hands. It was a one-sided campaign on D's part. She cleaned up his room, washed his dishes, and did his laundry. Sometimes she cooked for him. She might as well have been his wife.

C had a fiancée in Osaka, where he came from, but he saw her only once or twice a month. Even though D knew all this, she kept visiting C as his "commuting maid." At first, C had no particular feelings for D. Since she came from his school and was junior to him, he didn't feel moved to refuse her advances outright, so he thought he would let her do as she liked. The result was that he sometimes felt she was a bother, and he did not let her into his heart. To be blunt about it, he ignored her.

But even though this was his attitude towards her, as she kept coming around to do things for him, he began to be attracted to her. Then one night, about two months after she started visiting him, C got quite drunk at a party held by the literary circle, and D ended up seeing him home. That was the first time they had sexual relations. Right after that, the two took a short overnight trip, and from then on their relationship was a sexual one.

Two years later D got pregnant and had an abortion. C was on a three-month out-of-town assignment at the time, so he had no contact with D until it was all over. C called D when he returned to Tokyo, but D's mother answered the phone. It was clear that she was not pleased to hear from him. C could not understand why she was being unpleasant. He thought there must be some reason, so he called D out to meet him to learn what was up. When he heard that she had been pregnant and had an abortion a month earlier, it was like pouring water in the ear of someone sleeping.

Up to that time, C had had a number of lovers and a variety of sexual experience, but he had never had a contraceptive failure. C's method of contraception was withdrawal; he did not use condoms. This is the most dangerous contraceptive practice, but C was very confident of his ability, based on his success up to that time. But looking back on it, he could recall one sexual encounter with D of which he could not be certain. He had been slightly uneasy about it at the time, but since he had heard nothing from D, he had forgotten all about it.

Not only had that uncertainty borne fruit, but without involving C at all, D had disposed of the matter entirely. D had not even told her parents about her relationship with C, let alone informed them of the pregnancy, but in the middle of it all D's mother had come up to Tokyo for a visit and found out about it. The mother forcibly took D to the gynecological clinic and had her receive an abortion.

C described his shock at the time as follows: "When I learned of the abortion, my reaction was one of extreme pain. I realized keenly that a human life had been destroyed. Honestly speaking, I wanted to go with her to a Mizuko Jizō, I felt for the first time in my life that I had committed a genuine sin. Not on the level of stealing or quarreling—something completely different—the feeling of a weighty sin."

Interviewer: "What had D herself planned to do about the child?"

C: "She had planned to have it. She said, 'I want to quit school, get a job, and raise your child.'"

Interviewer: "Then why didn't she tell you she was pregnant?"

C: ."She said that if she had told me, I surely would have told her to abort it."

D knew that C was engaged to marry another woman; she was planning to be his "second wife." She had no thought either of marrying C or of having him legally acknowledge his paternity of the child. She seemed to accept that she would be "the woman in the shadows." And knowing how D felt, C did not seek any different kind of relationship with her.

Interviewer: "What would you have done if you had known about the pregnancy earlier?"

C: "I would have told her to have an abortion. I think that would have been the only way. I had absolutely no intention of marrying her, you see. This may sound cold, but even if I had wanted to have a child with a lover, I wouldn't have wanted it with her. The meaning of sex with her and with my fiancée is entirely different. Sex with my fiancée was for the purpose of communication, to fill the gap made by the time when we couldn't be together. But sex with D was just for our mutual pleasure. Both she and I were agreed on this point. And we still are."

Two years ago C married his fiancée, and his first son has been born. Unknown to his wife, he continues to see D.[18]

The relationship between C and D originated in D's "one-sided campaign" to be noticed by C. Several years older than D (three or four years?), C presents himself to the literary circle of his Tokyo alma mater as a passionate and worldly "older man." Along with several other women in the student literary group, D, who came from the provinces, was smitten with this handsome *senpai.**

Although C made no secret of his engagement to a woman in Osaka, with whom he was apparently already sexually involved, D gave little consideration to C's engagement. Her "campaign" was very direct and involved no negotiation on her part of the terms of the relationship. She asked for no mutuality, reciprocity, or public acknowledgment, nor did she make consistent application of any contraceptive method a condition of her continued sexual availability.

C presents himself as sexually experienced with a variety of partners. Because D relinquished all power in the relationship from its inception,

---

**Senpai:* a "senior," one to be consulted, his or her advice heeded, as one more advanced than oneself in some common organization or group.

C held virtually all the cards. His greater age and sexual experience and his engagement enhanced his position over D. In fact, she only occupied any place in his life at all on sufferance, on condition of her making no requirements of him whatsoever.

C was, it turns out, overly confident of his ability to provide effective contraception through withdrawal. He was stunned to learn that D had discovered a pregnancy and aborted, all in his absence. He regarded the abortion as a sin to which he was party (neither he nor A criticizes the women's decision to abort on moral grounds). His receptivity to feto-centric rhetoric and his reference to *mizuko* are unique in these texts. Momentarily, he experienced a desire to ritualize the aborted fetus through *mizuko kuyō*, though it does not appear that he actually did so. Along with the shock he received, however, came the recognition that he would—if consulted—have told D to abort.

C seems content to personify the stereotype of the Callous Man. He has no intentions toward D beyond continuing a convenient sexual relationship, and it is clear that he does not regard marriage or the birth of his wife's child as an impediment to this plan. He maintains that he and D have agreed that the sole purpose of their relationship is mutual sexual pleasure, and he will probably continue to see her as long as she remains sexually available to him. He recognizes that his view of the matter is "cold," but he evidently regards himself as entitled to avail himself of the windfall D provides, as long as she is receptive to him on a nonreciprocal, illicit, no-strings-attached basis. He has no feeling of responsibility toward her or any child she might conceive if he fails again at coitus interruptus. The gratification that makes it worth his while to continue granting D his sexual favors seems to lie precisely in the absence of any requirement for responsiveness, which he seems to experience as an enhancement of his masculinity.

The real mystery in this story is D. Why does a university-educated woman who participates in literary salons make herself available to a man so callous and cold to her as C? Seeing her only through his eyes, we cannot hope to reach any final conclusion, but it may be useful to examine her devotion to him and society's attitudes toward women who spend their lives attached to men clearly unworthy of their loyalties.

D originally offered C all the advantages of a wife: free cleaning, cooking, laundry, and sexual services, but with none of the social and financial responsibilities of marriage. Instead, she devotes herself to him single-mindedly, renouncing any possibilities of marriage that might otherwise have awaited her. She is represented as wanting nothing more than to go on in the same vein with C and to bear his child. He need not even acknowledge his paternity, so far as she is concerned.

C presents this picture of D to the interviewer, evidently in the expectation that his representation will be taken at face value, which is to say that he evidently believes that such a representation of women is at the very least within the bounds of actual possibility. One of its implications is the proposition that C is a terribly attractive man, and everything about his self-representation suggests an ego proportionate to the proposition. Leaving C aside, however, the representation itself has several points of significant interest.

One is the image of a woman so devoted to a man that she ignores all his faults and disregard for her, though she may not be unaware of them. Instead, she wraps herself in a cloud of devotion so intense that the man, his faults, and the vulnerability of her position become irrelevant. The spectator's gaze instead is directed to the beauty and purity of the woman's selflessness. That selflessness then becomes the focus of eulogy as "women's beauty" (*onna no bifū*). Countless masculinist ideologues propound such devotion as the essential ingredient in "women's happiness."

In any event, the focus on the beauty of a woman's pure devotion to a man, *especially* if he is as cold, callous, and egotistical as C, produces a kind of relativism, to the effect that such a life is not only acceptable, but beautiful. It hardly matters, in this view, who the *object* of the devotion is, as long as the woman bases her entire life on it and is satisfied with it.[19]

This representation conveniently diverts attention away from men, their actions toward women, and the real-world consequences for women (and their children) who choose this kind of life. Men can be invisible within this representation, while attention is directed to the sanctification of female self-sacrifice. C's momentary capitulation to fetocentric rhetoric seems not to have altered the relationship in any way.

Narrative 7: Kadota Nobuo, thirty-five, a male high school teacher, and his lover, Reiko

I first met Reiko in a neighborhood coffee shop eight years ago at the end of September. We began a sexual relationship in October. By November, Reiko was hardly going back to her own apartment at all. I lived in Nakano, and Reiko lived in Itabashi,[20] and it was too far to commute between the two. She probably couldn't stand living alone. Reiko was a student at a cram school [*yobi kō*], but she went to class less and less often, and instead she seemed to be enjoying cooking and doing the laundry. I was a fourth-year university student. I had financial help from home, but it wasn't enough to live on, so I was teaching part-time at a different cram school than Reiko's, but nearby. Sometimes we would arrange to meet and go home together.

Reiko really had a great figure, not too skinny, but nicely rounded. At night, her body bathed in light coming in from the window, her nakedness shown blazingly white, and when she lay on her side, and her lustrous black hair was spread out in a tangle down to her hips, the voluptuousness of her flesh was emphasized even more. I burned to the core of my skull. My desire for her was unquenchable, boiling up all day every day, and every night I embraced her. I used a contraceptive method I had learned from an older woman, a variation on the Ogino [rhythm] method, in which the six days of menstruation and a week before and after were considered safe. Reiko's period was regular, and even such a simple method ought to have worked. However, Reiko was completely ignorant about sex and had very little awareness of safe days and dangerous days, so I was the one to remember when her last period was, and it was up to me to take control.

From our first night together, I had never used a condom. Since childhood I had thought of condoms as disgusting. I had once used one with a prostitute, and that memory was another reason why I didn't want to use one with Reiko. It isn't that I despise prostitutes but rather that I felt guilty myself. Reiko was still just nineteen, and she had been a high school student up to six months ago, and I didn't want her to see me fumbling around trying to put on a condom.

I had taken several employment tests since autumn, and my greatest hope was to become a high school teacher. I was traveling all over Tokyo and the encircling prefectures for these tests. My determination to become a teacher produced a tendency for me to treat Reiko like a student. I was maintaining my own code of behavior toward her, and Reiko's complete lack of distrust in me for failing to use a condom actually made her lovable to me.

We went home to our separate families for winter vacation. I had planned to talk to my parents, but wondering how to do it and how much to tell them, I couldn't reach a decision. It wasn't that Reiko had asked me to marry her, and I had never heard Reiko say what her hopes for the future were. So the evening before I was to return to Tokyo, I said to my mother only, "There's a woman I'm fond of named Reiko. Would you please remember that name?" When my mother asked me what sort of person Reiko was, I said only that she was a good person, and returned to Tokyo the following day.

Reiko came right over. After two weeks of abstinence, I went for her, regardless of its being a danger day. I thought that I could handle the situation with coitus interruptus, and I held her tight. At the height of my desire, Reiko suddenly looked to me like an adult woman, and I suddenly exploded and lost control. The shock of it nearly made me faint. I tried to think of a contraceptive method that would work after the fact. All the methods I had read about in the tabloids ran round and round in my head. I knew that all of them were too vulgar and unlikely to be effective, so I gave up in disappointment and did nothing. I finally calmed down, thinking to myself, "You've only just ejaculated. It isn't that she's already pregnant," relieved that the verdict could at least be postponed.

My interviews and tests for becoming a high school teacher weren't going very well. I thought it was strange, but the reason was a lack of ability and humility. The interviewer for a certain prefecture asked me, "Are you planning to stand up before your students like that?" At first I didn't understand the meaning of his question, but then he said, "Will you be teaching in that red sweater?," pointing painedly to what I was wearing. I said with confidence, "Yes." That prefecture didn't hire me. It was a little late, but I finally grasped the character of the education profession. Then I decided to postpone graduation and remain a student for another year to take the tests again in the following year.

I found a job in a cram school for primary and middle school students through a friend, to begin in March and last for a year. When my mother called, I told her not to send money and that Reiko was pregnant. This was the first time her period failed to come, and she felt certain that she was pregnant. I felt glad that a child had been conceived the first time I lost control. In my joy, however, I was also confused. I decided to marry Reiko, though she was still a minor. That decision was one reassurance that I could be confident of being able to take responsibility. But when I thought of the child, I was continually confused, and I wondered if in the first instance we would be able to raise it. How we would raise it would depend on how I was making a living and was directly connected to my problems of employment. The cram school manager might be sympathetic, but I wondered whether anyone else in authority would be. That interviewer had refused to allow my red sweater. Would Reiko's parents permit her to marry and bear a child? If they wouldn't, that would mean that they wouldn't recognize our child. If unable to find social recognition, would it be possible for the child to live at all? The cram school would probably not permit me to keep working until retirement. No high school would permit a student marriage. It wasn't that I actually went around to confirm these suspicions, but I was sure I was right.

There was no way we could have the child. I wanted to hear Reiko say that she wanted to bear the child, but that would just be the voice of motherhood, so what good would it do? I had to announce the conclusion before Reiko started talking that way. I told her to go along to the gynecologist, and she obeyed. She came home having had an examination and bringing the consent form. I set my seal to it. The next day Reiko went alone to the hospital. I realized that it wasn't only our child that was trying to cling to life inside Reiko's womb—it was myself as well. When I realized that, I was overcome with shame. That was two hours after she had left, but I leapt up and went after her.[21]

Nobuo and Reiko were separated in age by only three years, but this difference was magnified by Nobuo's tendency to treat Reiko as his student and by the fact that he was considerably more sexually knowledgeable than she. They began a sexual relationship within a month of their first meeting. Both were students at the time, though Nobuo was already working part-time at a preparatory school where students ready themselves for college entrance examinations. Having just graduated from high school, Reiko was extending her study for a year at a cram school similar to the one where Nobuo was teaching. Both came from the countryside and were living alone in Tokyo before Reiko moved in with Nobuo.

Nobuo took virtually complete responsibility for contraception, while Reiko apparently gave over all authority to him, depending on his calculation of her ovulation and on his willingness to abstain from sex on "danger days." Nobuo evidently understood that rhythm can be supplemented by condoms, but he disliked them for two reasons. First, he associated them with an earlier experience with a prostitute, and, second, he objected on aesthetic grounds, not wanting Reiko to see him "fumbling," handling his genitals in an attempt to put one on. His attachment to Reiko was enhanced by the fact that she made no demand of him that he use one. His masculinity gratified by this abdication of authority, he felt responsible for her, "maintaining my own code of behavior toward her," manifesting a teacherly attitude, simultaneously experiencing burning desire for her.[22]

While the two were separated for the two weeks of winter vacation, Nobuo began to think about marriage, but he returned to Tokyo without having spoken clearly to his parents. In any case, he had never even consulted Reiko on her future plans. His pent-up desire from the separation completely overwhelmed him when for the first time, during intercourse, Reiko looked adult to him. He lost control and failed to withdraw as he had evidently planned, knowing that unprotected sex at this time in her cycle might well make her pregnant.

Something about this sexual encounter introduced an idea that was new to Nobuo: Reiko was an adult, not a child, and not his student. Since his earlier regimen of monitoring his own behavior toward her was based on his image of Reiko as still a child, a sudden contradiction of that image triggered a loss of control. This incident became the occasion for Nobuo to reexamine his own childishness, naiveté, and immaturity, so embarrassingly pointed out to him by the prefectural examiner who found fault with his red sweater.

The color red has many cultural associations in Japan, but the examiner's objection to Nobuo's wearing it probably stemmed from a sense of incongruity: red is appropriate for young children and girls—not for mature males, and certainly not for men at work. Young men seeking employment in Japan are instantly recognizable by their unaccustomed appearance in grey or navy suits, the resume folders they carry, and their fresh haircuts. Nobuo's first mistake in the interview was deviating from this norm. It wasn't, apparently, that he was flouting convention, but that he was too absorbed in himself and his girlfriend even to know at first what the interviewer meant by asking sarcastically if Nobuo planned to teach in such inappropriate attire.

This incident and the pregnancy pushed Nobuo to "wise up," and to get it through his head that the educational system was unlikely to accommodate itself to his idiosyncrasies. He realized also that he was not prepared to begin professional life, but must postpone his goal and study for another year. The relation of these belated realizations to the insight that Reiko was not a child remains obscure, but one possibility is that he conflated her adulthood and his own, and that the intimation of the enhanced power this new status would bring him was expressed in the only manifestation of potency available to him: impregnating Reiko.

He was momentarily gratified that this first loss of control should have borne fruit, and a part of him wanted to hear Reiko say that she wanted to have his child. Nevertheless, a realistic assessment of their situation quickly yielded the conclusion that his job chances would be effectively destroyed if he married Reiko and raised the child. In any case, she was a minor, and Nobuo was not confident that her parents would permit the marriage. That being the case, he sent Reiko out alone to abort the pregnancy.

The ending of the narrative is elliptical. We are not certain whether Nobuo finally went after Reiko to prevent the abortion, or whether, having started two hours after she left, such an attempt would have succeeded. It may be that he merely intended to accompany her and provide moral support. The narrative alone would support either interpretation, but based on the logic of the text up to that point and on the fact that he later volunteered his story for a compilation aiming to maintain legal abortion's economic hardship clause, I believe the latter is the more persuasive reading of Nobuo's story.

We gain almost no sense from this text of Reiko, beyond her physical beauty and erotic attraction. To Nobuo she is the personification of eros, but what else? Was it something she actually did or said that led Nobuo to see her—if only briefly—as an adult? The story is Nobuo's to the end, and Reiko remains a beautiful cipher who helped him to grow up, whose humanity was ultimately irrelevant to the meaning she held for Nobuo.

Narrative 8: Kawashima Haruyo, thirty-one, employed

My period, which was almost always regular at thirty-day intervals, was a week late. I was full of dread, thinking, "It couldn't be." That was three years ago, in the spring. I was twenty-eight and living in San Francisco.

I had quit the nursery school where I had worked for three years and had been in this foreign country with my lover for a year and a half where he wanted to start a new life. He was used to speaking English and to living conditions there. At school he was involved with the Japanese-American community, striving to accomplish something, and working out for himself the meaning of American life. We had practiced contraception, and things had been all right up until then, but it was no good making excuses. The first thing was to be sure, so I picked up the telephone receiver heavily and dialed a health center in the city. With my heart beating like thunder, I said that I wanted to have a pregnancy test, and asked about the cost, when I could have an appointment, and so on. They told me that the test was free for foreigners [as well as citizens], that I didn't need an appointment, and that I should come the next day between eight and nine a.m. So I decided to go the next day.

The health center was downtown, next to Chinatown, in a small building. As I went up to the third floor, there were signs marking the offices for counseling on diet, prevention of illness, health, contraception, pregnancy, childbirth, and family planning. There was also an office for men's counseling on sex, at which my eyes opened wide. There were handouts and pamphlets in English and Chinese. The place was already full, I guess, because densely populated Chinatown was so near. There were lots of people speaking Chinese, but I seemed to be the only Japanese. Most of the workers were women. I filled out my name and address in the pregnancy testing office, as well as the dates of my last period, and then had the urine test. After I waited a while, they told me that it was too early to tell, and that I should come back in a week. That meant I would have to wait a whole week for the verdict.

I made up my mind to decide during that time what I would do if it turned out that I was pregnant. I went home and talked it over with my lover.

As I expected, he had a clear sense of what he wanted to do. He said that he did not want a child then. He had been a year ahead of me at the university, and when he graduated he had traveled alone to an America that nobody knows.* He had built a life for himself from nothing, going to school as he worked. For five years he had thrown himself into the Japanese-American minority movement. But at that time he was planning to end his stay in America and travel to Europe and Africa in the autumn, returning to Japan from there. He was about to set out on this last, solitary, decisive† journey. Having known him for so long, I knew very well how important this long trip was to him.

My position wasn't as clear-cut as his, but for myself, if I were to have a child, I wanted to do so at a time when I could do so with a firm sense that I had accomplished something in my life. I didn't want to give birth passively, just because I fell pregnant or because I thought I was getting old. I didn't want to absorb myself totally in bearing and raising a child, but instead to follow my own instincts and concerns, widening my connections with other people continuously. My associations with people here [in the United States] had been very enjoyable; I wanted to continue my studies and to become more involved in the women's movement and the Japanese-American movement. And although I didn't say so, if I *were* going to give birth to a child, I wanted to share its care with my lover, and I was concerned about such a long separation. We agreed that we did not want a child now.

I went back to the health center. Even though I knew that there was a high probability that I was pregnant, I still had a glimmer of hope. They told me to go to the counseling room for the results of the urine test. I knew that the reason was because I was pregnant. Now feeling under great threat, I waited for my turn. Looking around me, I saw many others with the same hunted look as myself. There were Caucasian women about my age. One was bent over, and another was filling in a form. One was saying that she couldn't stay there waiting, because she had to go to work, and that she couldn't take off from work just because she was having an abortion, complaining to the staff people with a pained expression. I could see that they suffered irresolutely in the same way as I, and that life was hard, even though they were the majority in that society and could pay for an abortion through insurance.

---

*Not an unknown geographical location, but to live among Japanese-Americans, "unknown" or not known very well to Japanese living in Japan.

†"Decisive" (*sōkessan*), apparently in the sense of helping him resign himself to returning to Japan and making up his mind what sort of life he would take up there.

A slim, professional-looking Caucasian woman called my name and showed me into an office. She told me that I was pregnant. Although I had expected it, for a moment everything before me went black. She asked me softly whether I did or did not want to give birth to the child, and whether I was confused. When, trembling, I said as I had planned, that I did not want to bear the child. I asked her to tell me where I could find a doctor. She wrote down several names for me, and put a check by Planned Parenthood. It was close to my home, very reliable, and inexpensive, she said. She asked me what method of contraception I used, and encouraged me to get instruction. She told me that the health center offered contraceptive instruction and distributed contraceptives free of charge, and that there was a group meeting held there to show people how to chart the menstrual cycle and determine the day of ovulation.

Leaving the health center with the heavy reality, "I'm pregnant," I couldn't imagine going to school, so I wandered around the harbor and the local tourist sites. This was my first pregnancy, and I found it amazing and tender that a bud of life could be being nurtured inside my womb. I had said just before that I didn't want to give birth, but was that really true? I asked myself whether I really had no feeling of wanting to bear this child. It wasn't a choice of yes or no, but I couldn't say that it was 100 percent no. I asked myself if I were in a position to give birth, and I reflected back on my life. Working as a waitress in a Japanese restaurant, or as a baby-sitter, I barely made enough to keep myself going. I was only able to manage because my lover and I split the rent and living expenses, but even if I had no child, I couldn't afford my own apartment. I was a foreigner who could not work openly, so there were only a limited number of jobs for me, and none of them paid well. If the Immigration Office found out, I might get caught, so I was always afraid. In those circumstances, I had no confidence that I could raise a child on my own.

If I had to have an abortion, then the sooner the better. I went straight home and called Planned Parenthood. In my clumsy English I told them as best I could that I was pregnant and that I wanted an abortion. When the appointment was finally made, the voice at the other end told me to bring a translator with me. Having brooded so much over the problem, I was really wounded by those words. I was still an immigrant, a foreigner who could not use the language fluently. Not only was I incapable of bearing a child, I couldn't even manage a trip to the doctor easily. I couldn't do anything without depending on someone else. Tears came to my eyes to think that my situation should be so wretched.

I told my lover that the pregnancy was certain. He seemed to have no doubt that abortion was the way to go. He had his own life to live, so he thought it was fine to live as he pleased, but there was within me a thing that could be blown away like a dandelion ball. I wished that just once he would experience sufficient doubt about it to say that maybe he should give up his trip and try to raise the child with me, that he would reconsider.

It was ten days until the abortion, and I went to school and to work as usual, trying to spread my feelings over the busy daily routine, but it was a time of terrible suffering for me. I was dried up with wanting to scream out in anger at myself, or I was sunk in depression, or my feelings all welled, and I couldn't stop crying. I helped out at a food stand for a festival, went on a day trip to see historical sites of Japanese immigrants, and was active as usual, but even that was hateful and isolating to me. The feeling I had toward my lover of wanting him to comfort me, to understand how I felt, was betrayed and turned into a snowballing anger and distrust. Although the thought of the abortion never left me for even a moment, though I was suffering so badly, how could that jerk go on so pleased, as if he'd forgotten all about it? Would he not even be tender toward me? Could he even consider having sex with me? The reason I'd ended up like this was that time when the jerk just bulldozed ahead to have his way with me and messed up the birth control.* Each day I couldn't help criticizing him, making him responsible, turning away from my own responsibility.

The weather on the day was clear. I took off from work, and my lover took a half day off. We got up earlier than usual and went to Planned Parenthood. The morning train was crowded with people going to work. When we changed trains, I was overcome with nausea, probably morning sickness. If I had decided to raise it, would it have become a baby, like my friend's child? "Let's not think about it," I said to myself. "You've made up your mind, haven't you?" My heart started to pound with fear and uncertainty as we approached the clinic.

Planned Parenthood was near Japan Town, where we went frequently. The murals at the entrance, in blue, white, and pink, reminded me of a nursery school, but I felt relieved to a certain extent. We went into the waiting room, and I wrote down my history of illnesses, answered questions about allergies, with the help of my lover and a dictionary. I was told that before the abortion there would be a counseling session, that my blood type and blood pressure would be checked, and that I would have a pelvic examination to check for cervical cancer. In the counseling session they inquired whether I truly wished to have the abortion and then explained the surgical procedure to me, had me choose the degree of anesthesia, and had me sign a consent form in case anything should go wrong. I felt fear in spite of the counselor telling me that everything would be all right. The blood type and blood pressure tests were finished quickly. After a moment, I

Konna fū ni natta no wa, ano toki, aitsu ga gorioshi shite hinin o chanto shinakatta no ga gen'in da.

was told to go to the next room. And now for the surgery at last. I was afraid. The fear of my body being cut open spread out before my eyes along with the terror of killing something that might become a human being, and a cold, dark, inexplicable, stunned fear. What could I do if I should break down? I felt somewhat relieved in that my lover would stay by me during the surgery, but I was stiff with fear as I opened the door.

It was a small sunny room, with houseplants hanging down. There were no intimidating medical machines or sharp, shiny instruments in sight, no odor of disinfectant. I sat down on the examination bench, and the only thing in sight was a little box the size of an orange crate. A young woman came in and spoke to me in a friendly voice. As we chatted, my fear began to be calmed. She told me that the doctor who would see me was a very experienced woman doctor, and I began to feel better.

After a little while, a nice woman a bit older than me came in and began to speak to me in a friendly way. She asked me about my work, was I a student? As we talked, she said that before doing anything she would explain each step to me. The speculum had been warmed. She said there was no danger of uterine cancer. She said she would apply a local anesthetic to open the cervix. Because I was entirely conscious, I knew from beginning to end exactly what was happening and could be sure, so I felt relieved. A small tube connected to the box like an orange crate was inserted into my uterus. When the switch was turned on, the machine began to make a noise. As the doctor had said, I felt a sharp pain of contraction in my pelvis. That meant that the thing inside me had been removed. My feeling was, "I'm sorry. I'll never do this again."

It was over. The surgery was incredibly simple. It was over in a few moments. I wanted to review exactly what I had done. I requested to be shown what had been removed from my body. It was a little red, slimy thing. You couldn't tell anything about it with the naked eye. The fact that nothing could be told about it reassured and relieved me. Then I was told what precautions to take; I received some medicine to take in case of hemorrhaging, and was told to be in touch if there was anything I needed. I would have a checkup in two weeks, and they would show me how to use a diaphragm at that time.

I was shown to the recovery room, and there too were houseplants like in a living room, a bright and cheerful room, with two other women already resting there. I was glad that my lover stayed with me. Then right away they brought me hot tea and cookies. I was glad. Each small kindness echoed in my heart. The abortion itself was an awful experience, but at least I had it in a good environment. These women supported me wordlessly, and it was clear that I would have broken down with a single word. I felt keenly that I had been kindly encouraged through the whole process. I think that I experienced the fruits of the women's movement as expressed in *Our Bodies, Ourselves*.[23]

Haruyo is a university graduate who has interrupted the expected path for women, which includes a period of employment, followed by marriage. Instead of remaining in Japan to follow that well-worn trajectory, she followed a man (never named) who had dropped out of Japanese society to live in the United States and join forces with the political movement of Japanese-Americans seeking compensation for internment during World War II. He had been there for a year and a half when Haruyo went to join him. He has evidently adopted the pattern seen earlier in an incomplete form in narrative 5 of attempting to confirm an "off-track" life course or sense of ethnic identity by a period of residence abroad.

Haruyo's boyfriend planned a journey back to Japan by way of Europe and Africa, and Haruyo was not a part of that plan. The couple seems to have had no intention of marrying. The boyfriend meant to travel alone, and Haruyo was anxious about the meaning of that long separation for their relationship. It was in the midst of confronting that question that she became pregnant.

The boyfriend evidently had some plan for rejoining Japanese society, though his future there was probably not straightforward, since he had departed from the usual trajectory for male university graduates, in which employment immediately follows graduation. His involvement in the Japanese-American movement suggests a degree of politicization not common among Japanese university students of the late 1970s or early 1980s. He is clearly a man of high purpose, and Haruyo admires this quality.

Haruyo's life course up to the abortion had not been so purposefully planned as her boyfriend's. She had graduated from university, worked for a nursery school, and then traveled to the United States. She was attending a school when she became pregnant, and may have entered the country on a student visa, supporting herself meagerly by baby-sitting and waitressing, looking over her shoulder for Immigration officers all the while. She had no clear plan other than remaining in the United States and continuing her involvement in the women's movement and the Japanese-American movement. It is not clear that at the time of her pregnancy she was involved in more than a peripheral way with either one; instead, it appears that she followed the boyfriend's lead without developing a clear direction herself.

The couple practiced contraception, and since Haruyo attributes her pregnancy to the boyfriend's bungling, they were probably relying on condoms. The man seems to have been mainly responsible for contraception in their interaction. The incident of intercourse in which Haruyo was impregnated was characterized by some degree of coercion and haste on the man's part, not exactly rape, but sex under pressure from the urgency of the man's desire, leaving Haruyo feeling taken advantage of and resentful.

The pregnancy provided an occasion for Haruyo to test her boyfriend's commitment to their relationship, and she was disappointed that he did not relinquish his plans for the trip, show remorse, or attend to her emotional distress. She felt betrayed and abandoned by his pragmatic attitude toward the abortion. Although her own emotions ran high and left her feeling bewildered and chaotic, however, she did not confront the boyfriend or require him to commit to any long-range plan that included her. Showing no receptivity to fetocentrism, he didn't want a child, and that was that, though he was prepared to provide some emotional support on the day of the abortion itself. For her part, Haruyo was not prepared to challenge him.

Haruyo felt regretful about the abortion, but was reassured by the appearance of the embryo, which bore no resemblance to a baby. From this point in her account, her focus shifts away from the boyfriend and settles on the sense of female solidarity in the clinic. The supportive community of women she encountered as doctors, nurses, and fellow clients for abortion contrasted with the boyfriend's self-centeredness and made a lasting impression on her.

§

In the background of all four of these abortions is Japanese society's zero tolerance for childbirth out of wedlock. Two of the four women, B and D, reached a decision to have an abortion in consultation with their female relatives. B was probably going to abort the child in any case, whereas D was originally determined to have the child. B feared her father's reaction to an unwed pregnancy, and she was unwilling to defy him. Her aunt confirmed her in this approach. D was unable to overcome her mother's opposition to an unwed pregnancy and allowed herself to be virtually dragged to the abortion. Both women were university students at the time of the pregnancy and abortion, and at that stage of life, they were both probably financially dependent on their parents, as well as reluctant to damage their parents' social position by having a child out of wedlock.

The female relatives in these narratives seem to endorse the view that women before marriage "belong" to their natal family. The natal family has a right to make decisions about their daughter's pregnancies, a right that outweighs the daughter's opinion, especially since she can be considered immature and uninformed about the problems precipitated by an unwed birth. The damage to the family's prestige is a consideration that looms large. Another consideration is the weak position of children from female-headed households and the economic problem of supporting a family on the earnings of a single woman. Not least in a family's decision to have an unmarried daughter abort an unwed pregnancy is the stigma of illegitimacy. How egotistical, vain, and pointless it would be, parents may well say to their pregnant daughters, to bring a child into the world before marriage.

When both B and D faced unplanned pregnancies, neither of them initially turned to her male partner for assistance or support, or in order to learn his views on whether the pregnancy should be carried to term. Neither the women nor the men approached the matter as one in which men's views should be considered or even necessarily aired before a decision is made. In the pregnancy of A and B, A recognized that he was "devious," "vague," and incapable of supporting B emotionally. In the case of C and D, D knew that C would tell her to abort the child; she did not seek his emotional support. In neither case is the financial cost of abortion presented as a major issue, nor is there discussion about who should pay. Given the women's independence of action, it seems reasonable to suppose that the women (and perhaps their female relatives) paid the bill without asking the man to contribute.

By contrast, Reiko and Haruyo turned to their male partners and were told to terminate the pregnancy. Nobuo made up their mind in a hurry, anxious to gain the initiative before Reiko could start talking motherhood. By contrast, Haruyo and her boyfriend discussed the decision, though Haruyo's flimsy sense of her own direction meant that her part in it was as much informed by a vague desire to hang on to the relationship as by any clear sense of goals for her life. She concurred with his decision mainly from reluctance to differ with him. Had he unexpectedly said that he wanted to marry her and raise the child, she probably would have gone along.

The difference in age between C and D (narrative 6) and between Nobuo and Reiko (narrative 7) clearly enhances the man's power in both cases. The age difference is also linked to the man's near complete control of contraception in both cases. It is further linked to a style of masculinity that sees itself enlarged by the passive attitude that the woman assumes in response to the man's much greater power. The corresponding style of femininity emphasizes self-sacrifice, abdication of authority, and relinquishing of power and negotiation in favor of complete reliance on the man.

The beautification of this style of femininity may be further linked (though it is not explicit in these narratives) with a corresponding style of religiosity.

Conclusion

Let us return to the problem of understanding the phenomena surrounding abortion as a part of sexual culture, beginning with a review of the meanings assigned to intercourse, contraception, pregnancy, and abortion in the eight narratives presented in this chapter. First, intercourse and contraception are major sites for the negotiation and exercise of power in all eight narratives. Women are almost never (narrative 2 being a partial exception) represented as negotiating or exercising power; more frequently, they are represented as abdicating power and negotiating position, as the women in narratives 6 and 7 do with particular clarity. Women seem to fear that they will lose power in the relationship if they set conditions, negotiate, criticize, or are otherwise uncompliant to male-initiated intercourse. Men significantly older or more sexually experienced than their partners consistently take the initiative in sex, and this construction of male initiative is paired with female passivity.

Men's pleasure in intercourse is enhanced by a woman's entrusting all responsibility for contraception to them and by the following circumstances in which intercourse can be constructed as a transgression: (1) when it includes an element of coercion; (2) when the woman is a minor; (3) when he is married to someone else; (4) when he knows that the timing of intercourse could result in impregnation. In general, transgression, aggression, and risk are eroticized for men. In intercourse, women regularly report valuing a sense of emotional closeness with a man; they do not cite eroticization of risk, transgression, or aggression as giving them pleasure. The experience of abortion is linked for women, but not for men, to diminution of pleasure in intercourse.

Even if a couple eventually adopts a woman-borne device, the first contraceptive measure adopted is man-borne: condoms or withdrawal. Both sexes represent themselves as being occasionally or habitually "vague" about contraception, knowing logically that unprotected sex leads to pregnancy, but unable, for a variety of reasons, to implement an effective contraceptive regimen. Sometimes, as in narrative 2, women become dispirited about previous contraceptive failures, and this state of lassitude leads them to do nothing about contraception. They also lack the energy either to insist that the man take the initiative to supply and use condoms, or to abstain from sex and insist that men do likewise. Sometimes habituation leads to carelessness, as in narratives 2 and 5, while drunkenness becomes an excuse for carelessness in narrative 6, and the intensity of male desire is represented as the cause of contraceptive carelessness in narratives 7 and 8.

The reproductive histories suggest that in married couples, contraception over time increasingly becomes the woman's responsibility, but this tendency contradicts norms of femininity in which the man takes the initiative in intercourse. The relative unavailability of woman-borne forms of contraception also makes it difficult for women to take this responsibility. Assuming coital frequency declines after thirty to thirty-five, the woman has less incentive to believe that intercourse is a regular probability. Even if she keeps condoms on hand, the idealization of male initiative acts as a disincentive for her to make it a condition of intercourse that he use one. The more rare intercourse becomes, the more incentive the woman has to accept it on his terms, in the hope of creating, enhancing, or reestablishing emotional intimacy, even if his terms include coercion, drunkenness, and carelessness about contraception.

Women not married to a male sexual partner are most likely to entrust full responsibility for contraception to him in these circumstances: when she is significantly younger or less sexually experienced than he; when she is living at a distance from her natal family; or when she has no profession or full-time employment. Women are likely to take an active role in contraception in these circumstances: when they are close in age to the man; when they are in close communication with their natal families; or when they have a profession or full-time employment.

Pregnancy is virtually never planned and frequently occurs at a time of stress or transition in the relationship. This timing of pregnancy is a sign of a struggle for one partner's ascendency in the relationship, or one partner's desire to divine or confirm the other's feelings and commitment. Alternatively, the women in narratives 1, 2, and 3 represent their pregnancies as occurring when their endurance was stretched to the limit by financial hardship, the stress of work, the difficulties of balancing the physical and emotional burdens of work and domestic life in which their partners' assistance was minimal, or the emotional deterioration of relations with the man. All of these factors are part of what the Eugenics Protection Law's "economic hardship" clause means to these women.

Although pregnancy is interpreted as conferring female adult status and confirming femininity, it is virtually never greeted with enthusiasm. Pregnancy is experienced as a great physical burden, sometimes hateful, especially when the woman continues to work until the delivery, suggesting that its meaning is continually conflicted. Because of pregnancy's potential use by either party to test a relationship, to elicit support and sympathy, and to shift a balance of power, it retains a changing, ambivalent meaning.

Abortion appears most frequently at two points in a marriage: at the beginning (to prolong the woman's work income and in the context of relationship strife or transition) and after the desired family size has been reached (normatively, two children). The main consideration in abortion is the couple's socioeconomic circumstances, as measured by parental recognition and income. This is described as realistic, by comparison with which birth is construed as vague, impractical, and unrealistic. No one disputes a woman's authority to decide in favor of abortion, but her inclination to carry a pregnancy to term is sometimes contested in favor of abortion if she is a minor, unmarried, or if she is seen to lack appropriate economic and social support. Religious considerations are acknowledged as relevant or appropriate only if socioeconomic realism is weighed more heavily in the end. Mention of religious anxiety about abortion is rare. Ideas of fetal personhood are absent, or arise with such infrequency that they bear little weight in decisions about abortion.

Narratives 5, 6, and 7 give us some insight into men's reaction to abortion. Narrative 5 represents a man as both saddened by abortion and perplexed by the lack of a defined role for men in the situation of a lover's abortion. By contrast, man C in narrative 6 realizes after the fact that he would have wanted his lover to get an abortion, and is relieved that his lover does not attempt to impose responsibility upon him for anything about the incident. The men in both narratives 6 and 7 represent themselves as somewhat discomfited or humiliated by having lost control of their orgasms, but these feelings were salved by the enhancement of their masculinity as experienced through the woman's renunciation of all initiative in contraception and by pregnancy's confirmation of their virility. The narrator of the seventh text particularly derives great joy from the pregnancy's confirmation of his potency. None of these men seem to have any confidants with whom they can discuss the abortion and their feelings about it. Fetocentric rhetoric may be mentioned, but it is impossible to discern that it makes any difference in men's decisions or in the conduct of their relationships.

Like men, women are also saddened by abortion, though in neither sex is this sadness represented as a factor that can overrule the financial and other concerns that led them to decide on abortion. Narrative 8 is eloquent in its description of the difficulty in reaching a decision, and of holding to it, but this emotion is not portrayed at all by the women whose families depend upon their earnings. For them, a hatred of pregnancy and a concomitant perception of the fetus in negative terms, as in narrative 3, is much more central. All the women's narratives express a hatred of being unwillingly pregnant. No one makes decisions on the basis of fetocentric rhetoric.

Can we perceive in these texts the influence of postwar Japan's "common sense" about abortion or the influence of *mizuko kuyō*? Since fifteen of the twenty pregnancies represented here occurred during the time of *mizuko kuyō*'s currency, it is not unreasonable to think that some evidence of the phenomenon should be discernible if it is to be treated as an influential movement. Only narrative 6 mentions *mizuko,* and only narrative 3 mentions the fetus as nemesis. All but narrative 6 avoid the stereotyped scenario of abortion as occurring between Callous Men and Foolish Women, though the women represented in narratives 7 and 8 come close, and the man in narrative 5 represents himself as "devious." By contrast, narratives 1, 2, 3, and 4 show a rejection of the stereotype. These women assert that, for them, sex has a "higher" meaning than the stale terms of dominance and submission upon which the Callous Man and Foolish Woman stereotype revolves. Overall, almost no evidence of *mizuko kuyō*'s influence, whether in the sense of accepting or rejecting it, can be perceived here; much stronger is the "common sense" that abortion is necessitated by a wide range of difficult circumstances that the umbrella "economic hardship" usefully covers. The misogyny of *mizuko kuyō* is nowhere to be seen, though the misogyny of the Callous Man is palpable in narrative 6. *Mizuko kuyō* can apparently coexist with experiences of abortion that implicitly deny its rationale, as a minor phenomenon without ubiquitous influence. It will be the task of chapter 4 to examine the practice of ritualists and religious organizations purveying *mizuko kuyō* as their stock in trade.

The Practitioners of *Mizuko Kuyō*

The oil shocks of the 1970s spelled an end to the era of high economic growth that had begun around 1955.* Although the 1980s provided a considerable financial "boom" of affluence for some, based largely upon speculation in the stock market and a bloated real estate market, significant inequalities of wealth became conspicuous. The beginnings of pessimism were visible in religious life by the mid- or late 1970s, and that mood persists to the present. For one thing, the huge rates of growth of those new religions (Sōka Gakkai, Reiyūkai, Risshōkōseikai, and others) that had paralleled the growing Japanese economy had peaked and begun to level off. New religious groups of a more spiritualist character came to the fore; these included Mahikari, Agon-shū, and many other smaller organizations, as well as a host of independent religious entrepreneurs. The tight-knit organization and communalism seen in previous generations of new religions gave way to atomistic or individualized organizational forms. It was also in the mid-1970s that the cult of *mizuko kuyō* came to public attention and was promoted on a mass scale.

By the 1970s, a more pessimistic mood overshadowed the optimistic perspective of unlimited human possibility that characterized the new

---

*The term *oil shock* refers to the massive economic impact on Japan and other developed nations of a sudden quadrupling of the price of Middle East oil due to a change in the pricing policy adopted by the Organization of Petroleum Exporting Countries (OPEC) in 1973. The oil shock caused an economic recession in Japan, and its impact was felt for several more years.

religions of the early postwar years. In place of the view that no spiritual accomplishment is out of reach for the dedicated and cultivated individual came a preoccupation with unpredictable spirits and a concern with divination techniques premised on the notion that many things are controlled by forces entirely beyond human influence. The flourishing of diviners, fortune-tellers, and prognosticators of all kinds, collectively known as *uranaishi,* paralleled the appearance of other religious entrepreneurs promising healing, spiritual counsel, and a host of rituals to deal with spirit influence of all kinds. Many of these spiritualists gave a prominent place to *mizuko kuyō.* The rise of spiritualism in these several forms signals a significant change in Japan's contemporary religious ethos.

This chapter examines the practice of spiritualists who promote *mizuko kuyō* among their clients and the parish priests of Buddhist temples who practice it, on the whole, less enthusiastically. In part 1 we look at a range of religious entrepreneurs, some of whose practice is quite localized and independent of the Buddhist priesthood, such as Shōzaki Ryōsei, who operates mostly in Kyūshū. Later sections discuss Jionji and its priest Morita Guyō who works at a Tendai-affiliated temple in Tsuyama that functions as a regional center of *mizuko kuyō.* These examples include female religious entrepreneurs inside and outside the Buddhist priesthood who expound a rationale for *mizuko kuyō.* Their rationale contains an analysis of the general phenomenon of abortion in Japan, a distinctive construction of gender, and pointed commentary on contemporary history. In particular, we can see from part 1 how the concept of *mizuko* can be extended, due to the lack of any canonical "anchor," until it becomes virtually indistinguishable from wandering spirits. In the process, the association with abortion is muted, and the rite takes on a routinized character by linking *mizuko* to the stem family, the *ie.* This linkage facilitates male participation and legitimates *mizuko kuyō.*

Part 2 examines the variety of attitudes toward *mizuko kuyō* among the Buddhist priesthood. In general, the Buddhist priesthood has been slower to clarify a position toward *mizuko kuyō* than spiritualists, and has tended to be passive and reactive. With the exception of Jōdo Shinshū, which rejects *mizuko kuyō* outright, Buddhist sects have not issued a clear policy on these rites, partly from the desire to avoid political involvement, and partly to avoid offending parishioners, who themselves have a wide spectrum of views. This means that Buddhist institutions had been overtaken by religious entrepreneurs and an outpouring of popular religious sentiment before they could reach a clear policy within each sect. Because there are few opportunities for ecumenical dialogue on such issues, most sects have not had occasion to air a range of views, nor to inform themselves systematically on the practice of other religionists.

Part 1: *Mizuko Kuyō* Performed by Spiritualists

The following exchange is a good example of the ease with which spiritualists introduce the subject of *mizuko*, even if the client shows no inclination to do so. This account of a shamanic consultation comes from a recently published transcription of a researcher's interview. The shaman is Funakoshi Tokiko, who heads the Japan Institute of Spirit Communication (Nihon Reikōgaku Kenkyūkai) in the Ueno district of Tokyo. On this occasion, she was consulted for the first time by an unnamed woman in her late fifties. They begin the interview facing each other across a low table.[1]

Client: Our family [*ie*] is all messed up and coming apart. I have had collagen disease for eight years, and I also have gallstones. My abdomen is cold, and I feel like wind is blowing through it. What kind of misfortune or retribution could it be?
Funakoshi: You have aborted a child. When you suddenly pull out a child into whom the soul has already entered, it is like creating a wind tunnel. The reason you feel cold is that the abortion cuts off the hormones, so the balance of the uterus breaks down, and you lose energy.
[The client repeatedly denied any experience of abortion, but Funakoshi insisted that this was untrue. Finally the client admitted it after Funakoshi said to her:]
Funakoshi: I'm talking about an abortion you had in middle age.
Client: Well, yes, I was in my forties.

Although this spiritualist had never laid eyes on this client before, she could say immediately in response to the woman's vague complaints, "You have had an abortion" and have at least a 50 percent chance of being right. She was so sure of this that she persisted even in the face of the client's denials until she extracted a confession. This interchange shows vividly how vulnerable older women are when unresolved feelings about abortion are suddenly exposed. The sentimentalized portrayal of spirits wandering "from darkness to darkness" mirrors their own conflicting emotions. The suggestion that ritual will provide a resolution thus finds a ready audience.

Shōzaki Ryōsei is a female spiritualist headquartered in Saga Prefecture whose practice is known throughout Kyūshū (and thus to people in Yukuhashi, one of the field sites discussed in detail in chapter 5), and to a lesser extent throughout Japan, due to media coverage in the early 1990s. Shōzaki is illustrative of a loose category of religionist called *oga-miya*, "one who worships," or prays, on behalf of a client who is seeking healing, improved material fortune, or better relations with other people. *Ogamiya* such as Shōzaki are independent religious entrepreneurs who attract a clientele on the basis of their personal charisma.[2] The more successful sometimes construct a "temple" or "shrine," erecting for worship statues or other representations of the deities who are supposed to inspire them with their ability to heal and counsel. The *ogamiya* may organize a membership system for their followers, allowing them to regularize revenues and to establish an annual calendar of communal rites. Even in the most developed form, these temples only rarely provide funerals and ongoing memorial rites for the dead in the manner of a Buddhist temple, so in most cases their followers remain affiliated with a temple of one of the established Buddhist sects.

Spiritualists frequently form an affiliation with one of the established Buddhist sects, especially Shingon and Tendai, which have provisions for laypeople to undergo training and become certified to proselytize. A spiritualist just beginning, say, to receive revelations and the ability to heal may seek such training and certification as a means to interpret these experiences. Emerging from such instruction, the spiritualist can claim affiliation with the sect. In some cases, the person may even be ordained, and thereafter function in a way combining spiritualism and the priesthood. Unless spiritualists were born into a temple and thus could succeed to its headship upon the death or retirement of, say, their father, however, they are unlikely to be put in charge of a regular parish temple of the sect. Parish temples generally manage a traditional group of adherents based on the performance of funerals and ancestor worship rites for the parish's separate stem families (*ie*), funneling a part of the revenue back to the sect headquarters.

Spiritualists operating outside parish temples, by contrast, generally do not have a stable group of parishioners, but instead receive revenue chiefly from performing rites that clients request. In the past, people approached spiritualists mainly for rites of healing, improvement of material fortune, and the improvement of relations with other people.

As Japan has grown in health and affluence, however, illness and poverty have declined in salience as sources of spiritual malaise. Lacking the routinized revenue of a parish priest, spiritualists have necessarily adapted to the changing spiritual anxieties that clients express. Unresolved feelings about abortion are widely reported, especially by women in their fifties and older; the majority of women born between 1920 and 1940 have had abortions. Spiritualists have taken a major role in highlighting ambivalent emotions about abortion and in *creating* the sense of spiritual anxiety motivating these women to patronize *mizuko kuyō*.

The following testimony from Shōzaki's client shows a spiritualist responding to a client's preexisting desire to have *mizuko kuyō* performed. The following exchange between a spiritualist and client at their first meeting illustrates how spiritualists promote the idea of *mizuko kuyō*'s necessity.[3]

> Having miscarried three times, I had wanted to provide *kuyō* for these children for a long time. I hesitated, however, thinking that I would have to become a parishioner of a temple before I could request its services, and I didn't know what to do. Then one day a neighbor took me to Shōzaki Sensei, saying that she would consult with me regardless of sectarian membership. That was ten years ago, in 1982.
>
> When I asked Shōzaki Sensei to perform the *kuyō* for the miscarried children, *mizuko* appeared to her in a spirit message,* complaining that they were in a cold well and were very cold. Her voice was exactly the voice of *mizuko*. I was filled with the feeling, "I'm so sorry I didn't perform *kuyō* for you." Shōzaki Sensei told me that I should bring candy and milk to offer to the *mizuko* the next time I came, so I went to visit her again, bringing these things. The sutras used in *mizuko kuyō* and Jizō *wasan* sank into my heart, and I could not stop crying. When Shōzaki Sensei said in a spirit message (in the voice of *mizuko*), "Thank you for the *kuyō*. Thank you for drawing us up [to a higher level of existence]," my feelings were finally settled.
>
> However, I could not help feeling that this wasn't the end, and I realized that I could have Shōzaki Sensei perform *kuyō* if I went to her again. In later spirit messages the *mizuko* made me understand the vital importance of *senzo kuyō* [memorial services for ancestral spirits].
>
> On one occasion, Shōzaki Sensei said to me, "I think you have something like a hanging scroll. Please search for it." I recalled a scroll that I had put away and forgotten about. It was a scroll of the Bodhisattva Manjusri. At work I had been instructed to throw it out along with

---

Omikuji, the word this spiritualist uses for all messages received from deities and spirits.

other things, but I held it back. When Shōzaki Sensei prayed over it, the following revelation came to her: "I wanted to appear in this world. Pray for me, and I will protect your family for future generations." I had the scroll repaired and hung in my house as a family treasure. Since then I have been protected by this scroll. We are self-employed, and this event happened when at the end of the month I went to the bank to deposit payments we had received. I realized that I had left a necessary memo at home, and I ran back to get it, leaving my bank book, seal, and important papers behind at the bank. I went pale and started to tremble when I realized what I had done. Racing back to the bank, everything was just as I had left it. I didn't lose any money. Returning home, I prayed before the scroll in tears. I went straight from there to Shōzaki Sensei and shouted out, "I've been saved [*tasukeraremashita*]."

Manjusri appeared in a revelation, sending Kappa and the Dragon God to the bank . . . , and the Dragon God revealed that. . . .

Then the Dragon God told her that she must clean out a well. She went back to her natal family where there was such a well, cleaned it out, and the Dragon God then sent her a beautiful dream. She receives revelations in dreams regularly and consults Shōzaki about each one. These consultations reassure her in each case that she is taking the correct action. She feels certain that she is being protected by the *kami*, Buddhas, and ancestors.

This testimony illustrates the position of *mizuko* in the spiritualism of *ogamiya* and their clients. In this case, the client's own interest in *mizuko* was the occasion for her original consultation with Shōzaki, but after that her interest shifted to other spirits: the ancestors, Manjusri, the Dragon God, and Kappa. After the first incident, the client does not return to the theme of *mizuko*. For her, the *mizuko* seem to have provided the gateway to a kind of pantheistic spirituality in which deities of all kinds appear in an unexpected manner, which itself is part of the client's attraction.

The client need no longer be concerned with *mizuko* after the original *kuyō* and the message (transmitted through the *ogamiya*) that the *mizuko* are now at rest. The lesson she takes from the consultation about *mizuko* concerns the importance of ancestor worship, so it may be that from the time the *mizuko* are put at ease by Shōzaki's *kuyō*, the client can regard them as receiving appropriate rites through ancestor worship. If this is the case, it would mean that one function of the *mizuko kuyō* rite is to elevate the *mizuko* into the category of ancestors. This aligns with the expression "drawing up," which was used in the spirit message. The change means that they are no longer part of the unsettled dead, spirits that can provoke misfortune to punish or awaken those who should provide them with appropriate rites. Instead, they have become benign, protective spirits who watch over the client.

JIONJI: INDEPENDENT BUDDHIST SPIRITUALISTS AND *MIZUKO KUYŌ*

Some religionists in Buddhist orders closely mirror spiritualists in their practice. This is especially true of temples lacking parishioners (as is the case at Enman'in, discussed below) and when the priest is particularly entrepreneurial in offering rituals for fees, has a background as a spiritualist, or is female, as at Jionji.

Morita Guyō of the Tendai-affiliated temple Jionji in Tsuyama, one of the four field sites discussed in chapter 5, is a good example of a Buddhist priest who has many of the characteristics of a spiritualist. Taking the tonsure after a successful career in social work, Morita opened a temple in loose affiliation with the Tendai sect, but not under its direct authority. Jionji has no parish, nor does it maintain graves, conduct funerals, or perform periodic ancestral rites. Instead, Morita receives clients daily and counsels them on whatever problems they present to her. She established *mizuko kuyō* at Jionji in a very unusual form, and the temple now functions as a regional center for these rites.

An important and frequently voiced idea in the folk knowledge concerning *mizuko kuyō* is that while Buddhist temples may be the major providers of these rites, people who request them get the idea not from Buddhist priests, but from independent spiritualists and diviners. In some cases, prayer healers and diviners refer their own clients to temples to have *mizuko kuyō* performed, while others, such as Morita Guyō of Jionji, are equipped to provide *mizuko kuyō* themselves.

The performance of *mizuko kuyō* in Tsuyama as a whole confirms the suggestion that the Buddhist temples providing *mizuko kuyō* mostly do so in a passive manner, which is to say that while they may erect the necessary statuary, hang out a sign, or even make ancestral rites available along with *mizuko kuyō,* they do not promulgate a doctrinal rationale for the rites. They cannot offer a doctrinal rationale, of course, because there is no canonical basis for the idea of *mizuko.* They do not go out of their way to explain in a promotional way that *mizuko kuyō* should definitely, necessarily, be performed; in other words, they do not take a proselytizing stance about these rites. In this respect, the attitude of the Buddhist priesthood in Tsuyama differs fundamentally

Figure 10. Group-dedicated Jizō statues at Jionji (Tsuyama)

from that of spiritualists. While Jionji's *mizuko kuyō* clientele come from all over western Japan, this temple is locally known for the practice and provides consultation to many local people who sponsor the rites on the basis of what they are told by the temple's priest, Morita Guyō.

Three separate observations of this temple were carried out, including a four-hour interview with Morita. One observation period at Jionji was devoted to its seventy-two Jizō statues for *mizuko kuyō*. These are placed along a winding path ascending a steep hill in the rear of the temple buildings. These statues are about thirty inches high and bear inscriptions of donors' names on the base. See Figure 10. The temple would not reveal the fee for dedicating one, but the cost must be considerable, because only fifteen have been donated by individuals. Most have been erected by groups of people. Married couples have dedicated twenty-seven, and the rest were dedicated by groups of people who are unrelated.[4] The temple has composed these groups on the basis of which followers have expressed the wish to do so and how much they are able to invest. See Table 14 for a breakdown of who donated statues.

Among the groups of three or more donors, groups of seven are a

Table 14. *Categories of people who dedicated statues*

Identifiably donated statues	72	
Statues for which no donor was designated or which were unidentifiable [1]	7	
Identifiable donors	194	
Male	68	(35%)
Female	126	(65%)
Groups of donors for a single statue		
Single individual	15	
Unrelated, two-person pair	5	
Married couple	27	
Groups of three or more	18	
Unidentifiable	7	

[1] There were seven statues either for which no donor was designated or which were unidentifiable, because only a group name was followed by the expression *ichidō,* "all members" [of the group]. This category also includes people of indeterminate sex using religious names, probably bestowed by Morita.

favored pattern; there were seven of these. Other identifiable combinations among these larger groups were mother-daughter pairs, a group of two men and one woman with the same surname, and uneven groups of individuals listed singly, in such groups as five men and three women, or seven women and one man.

The erratic character of the groupings suggests that while all the donors have a concern for *mizuko* and probably believe that they have been affected by one, it is not necessarily the case that they have been sexually involved with any of the other people with whom they combine to dedicate a statue.

Undoubtedly, *mizuko kuyō* provides a means to create a firmer tie between follower and temple than would be possible on the basis of sporadic consultations with the priest. It seems unlikely that people would dedicate a statue unless they intend to establish and maintain a long-term relation with the temple. It also seems likely that the fees involved are out of reach for most people before middle age and the attainment of considerable wealth. Significantly, no *ie*-groups are represented among these statue donors. Jionji has no parish, per se, but instead a nationwide group of followers.

Morita was born in 1932 in Kume County, an agricultural area in Northern Okayama Prefecture just west of Tsuyama. She graduated from *jogakkō* (women's high school) and at twenty-one married a sculptor of Buddhist statuary, to whom she is still married. They have two sons, both of whom have been ordained in the Tendai sect, as has the husband.[5] One son is the resident priest (*jūshoku*) of a Tendai temple in Hyōgo Prefecture.

During her twenties and thirties, Morita was involved in a kind of social work (*kōsei hogo*) in the Tsuyama area. At that time, local communities identified individuals known for strong character and principles and put them in charge of rehabilitating those recently released from prison. To perform such work, resting as it did upon the community's high estimation, was a mark of honor. Morita worked with Okayama's Big Brother and Big Sister organizations to rehabilitate all types of former criminals, from petty thieves and con artists to prostitutes.

When she was forty, Morita received the first stage of ordination (*tokudo*) in the Tendai sect, on Mt. Hiei under Yamada Eizan, then chief abbot (*zasu*) of the sect. Following this ordination, she performed austerities at Yokawa, a site on Mt. Hiei historically noted for the severity of its ascetic regimen. In this same year, 1972, she registered her temple, Jionji, with Okayama Prefecture as a religious corporation (*shūkyō hōjin*).[6] Three years later, Morita received full ordination (*teihatsu*), and since that time has resided at Jionji, where temple practice is based on Tendai rites and doctrine, but which operates independently from the Tendai sect. The first of Jionji's *mizuko* Jizō statues was dedicated in 1980.

Morita's beliefs concerning *mizuko kuyō* are akin to her earlier involvement in social work. She sees on average fifty clients per day, of whom seven or eight, she says, seek consultation regarding *mizuko*. She regards *mizuko* and abortion as serious social and religious problems, which she seeks to address on the basis of a correct understanding of the history of the cult of Jizō, and the history and changing meaning of abortion and infanticide in Japan. When I applied to the temple for an opportunity to meet with Morita, she took particular care to ensure that I, too, would approach the question of *mizuko kuyō* with this basis of historical understanding. She wrote to the son of her deceased teacher at Mt. Hiei, requesting that he send her the most thorough, scholarly, Buddhological studies of Jizō. When she had received these, she made copies and sent them to me, asking me to read them before talking with her, and saying that she, too, planned to study them carefully. In a letter, she made it clear that she regards many current appropriations of Jizō as perversions of the cult in its classical form. She wanted me to be under no illusions, she said.

When we met, she explained her understanding of the original connection between Jizō and the *mizuko,* which she identifies with Osorezan, a mountain in Aomori Prefecture which is taken to represent Sainokawara. In order to investigate Osorezan, Morita traveled there in 1988 with her husband. She was deeply impressed by her perception that myriad spirits were congregated there, full of bitter attachment (*shūnen*) to this world and unable to be at peace. These were the spirits of all those involved in any capacity with premodern practices of abortion, infanticide (*mabiki*), and abandoning the elderly to die.

Morita's understanding of these practices is as follows: the northeastern region of Japan has always been poor, and large families spelled great economic hardship and sometimes even starvation for all. A woman expecting her twelfth or thirteenth child would approach the midwife before the birth and say to her, "Now Granny [*obāsan*], I think you can see how things are. My husband and I are poor. We have more children than we can properly raise even now. I don't know what will become of us if we have to raise another. It's a pitiful thing, but I want you to call this one a stillbirth." Recognizing that another birth could only increase the misery of the whole family, the midwife would sorrowfully comply with this request. As soon as the infant was delivered, she would place a small piece of damp paper over its nose and mouth, preventing it from drawing breath, and it would die before uttering its first cry of birth.

Then the mother would bury the child in a shallow grave in the gravel of Osorezan and pile stones over it, praying for forgiveness, for Jizō to protect the child, for the child to forgive her, and for the child's immediate rebirth. This could not be the end of it, however, because in fulfillment of "women's karma" (*onna no gō*), the mother's breasts would fill with milk. She would visit Osorezan again and again, each time carrying with her a small, red cloth bib drenched in her breast milk, to tie at the neck of statues of Jizō, praying again for the child's forgiveness and rebirth. Thus, in Morita's view, premodern infanticide (and abortion, as well) were carried out because of genuine economic hardship—even desperation—and were extensively ritualized and surrounded by a climate of prayer and repentance. The proper role of the Buddhist priest in this situation is for Morita exemplified by Ennin (794–864, third chief abbot of the Tendai sect, also known by the posthumous title Jikaku Daishi), who, in the course of founding many Tendai temples in the northeast, gathered huge amounts of human remains at Osorezan, ritualized them properly, and set up the main temple, Bodaiji, there.

Morita illustrated her understanding of the current situation of abortion, infanticide, and the proper role of the Buddhist priest through two linked narratives:

Narrative 1

Several years ago a young woman of about twenty contacted Jionji by telephone and requested a consultation, saying, "I have had a baby, and I'm in trouble. This is a temple, isn't it? Help me." Her story as she related it to Morita was that she had come up to Tsuyama from Kyūshū to attend college, and her mother had set her up in an apartment. Living alone, away from home for the first time, she fell in love with a boy and soon found herself pregnant. Her pregnancy went unnoticed by others, and she gave birth alone in her apartment, either killing the child immediately afterward or simply allowing it to die from neglect. In any case, she put it in the freezer compartment of her refrigerator, but it was beginning to smell, and she was at a loss about what to do. She wanted Jionji to dispose of the body.

Morita called the girl's mother and had her come to Tsuyama immediately. The mother was horrified to learn what had happened. Morita explained to them that it is illegal to dispose of a body without a proper death certificate, and that if she were to procure the certificate on the girl's behalf, the whole story would come out and irrevocably disgrace the girl and her family. She told them to bury it in the graveyard at their family temple in their hometown, where, with luck, it could be kept out of the papers. The mother yanked the girl out of college, took her home, and apparently persuaded the home temple to help cover things up.

Morita drew two conclusions from this story. First, unlike premodern times when abortion and infanticide were carried out as described in her earlier account of Osorezan, young, unmarried women today think of sex as a form of amusement or play (*asobi*) and commit abortion or infanticide merely for their convenience (*tsugō*). In their eyes, children are a bother, so they just want to get rid of them. Evaluating the girl in this way, Morita felt no sympathy for her. Second, Morita greatly resented the girl's evident assumption that a temple could be called upon to dispose of her dirty little problem. Morita's interpretation of the girl's assumption was that because some unscrupulous, self-styled religionists do, in fact, make themselves and their so-called temples available for precisely this sort of thing, calling it *mizuko kuyō*, the girl thought that Jionji would accept her business as, essentially, a financial transaction. Commercialization of the original ritualization of the spirits of the aborted, stillborn, and the victims of infanticide is no more than a crass and cynical perversion, however, of what should be a sincere and pure expression of repentance. This Morita finds unforgivable, and she makes it clear that the *mizuko kuyō* practiced at Jionji is entirely different from this, and that hers is not a temple that sells ritual pap as a cheap sop to the momentary "trouble" that abortion precipitates for people who think of sex merely as a form of recreation. The most lasting comfort to *mizuko* would be sincere repentance and a change of heart. Without this, the rites themselves are empty.

Morita elaborated her views further through the following narrative:

Narrative 2

There was a family of five, in which the husband was an MP, the wife a physician, and their three children were at the nation's finest universities, the boys at the University of Tokyo and Waseda, and the girl at Aoyama Gakuin. There was every reason to expect that the three children would match their parents' achievement of prestige and contribution to society. The only fly in the ointment was a weakness of character in the second son (the one at Waseda).

Unlike the other two children, the second son lacked the judgment and resolution necessary to discern that unscrupulous individuals might use him as a means to get at his parents. He was vulnerable to sob stories and constitutionally unable to say no, even to the most unreasonable and patently exploitative requests. Thus, when he was approached by someone who later proved to be a con artist, he naively signed a document guaranteeing that person's loan. Needless to say, the crook absconded with the money, leaving the son holding the bag. The loan sharks went straight to the boy's parents and demanded the cash to repay the loan. More upset about the boy's weakness of character than the money, the parents went to Morita in search of an answer.

Morita explained to the parents that there could be only one explanation for a single flaw among the three children: *mizuko*. The *mizuko* created by an entirely unrelated person, like the girl from Kyūshū of the previous story, can suddenly appear out of nowhere and blight the hopes of someone with an otherwise bright future.

WHO ARE THE *MIZUKO*, AND WHAT DO THEY WANT?

The conclusions Morita reached by linking these two narratives produce a general interpretation of the changed meanings of *mizuko* and abortion in contemporary Japan. In her view, it is entirely reprehensible that women should treat sex as a form of play. They end up ruining not only their own lives, but others' as well. The *mizuko* represent the consequences of their misguided behavior. Together, the *mizuko* wreak havoc in the lives of people who are guiltless and otherwise on a good, positive trajectory. According to Morita, abortion carried out irresponsibly therefore has horrible consequences for all society. The women who are responsible for this show a heinous lack of respect for life and lack of concern for the quality of life in society.

Abortion and infanticide as they were practiced in premodern society were inescapable in situations of desperate economic hardship. It is very wrong, however, to extend tolerance for abortion to pregnancies that originate from carelessness and a cheapened view of human sexuality. In Morita's perspective, sex is not a plaything, and it is not meant as a simple means to gratification. Abortion or infanticide as practiced by the young woman from Kyūshū epitomizes this mistaken, vulgarized understanding of sexuality. The plight of the parents in both narratives epitomizes the problems caused for the wider society. *Mizuko kuyō* is the only means to deal with the situation.

This understanding of *mizuko* focuses on their bitter attachment (*shūnen*) and their malevolent power to attach themselves even to people entirely uninvolved in the mistaken sexual relations that produce *mizuko*. In this view, *mizuko* are essentially indistinguishable in terms of their social consequences from the *muenbotoke*, the spirits with no living relations to ritualize them properly. They roam about the human world aiming spirit attacks (*tatari*) at all and sundry, until they can somehow be properly ritualized and thus laid to rest.

With abortions (and, as a result, *mizuko*) so numerous in Japan today, *mizuko*'s bitter attachment can lead them to make a spirit attack on anyone, any time. This is the simplest explanation for any otherwise inexplicable misfortune. Jionji's role in alleviating the distress of the *mizuko* and their victims is to provide a form of ritualization that victims can perform to assuage the *mizuko*, who then cease the spirit attacks. Conceptualizing *mizuko* in this way makes it possible for Morita to counsel her clients without ever asking whether they, personally, have ever been involved in abortion. If Jionji's practice of *mizuko kuyō* can alleviate the distress of any of those involved, then surely that contributes to the good of society and is a legitimate form of ritual of the same character as Ennin's at Osorezan.

Morita has a complex view of the legal and moral issues surrounding abortion and infanticide. The fact that it is legal to commit abortion now does not mean that it is morally permissible; similarly, the fact that infanticide may have been stigmatized in premodern times did not make it less inevitable. Knowing the law, Morita was unwilling to involve her temple in an illegal activity such as burying a corpse without a death certificate. She was not interested, however, in alerting the law to the infanticide or murder that the girl in narrative 1 committed; no one was likely to be helped by this course of action. Instead, Morita recommended repentance and a change of heart.

While Morita believes that abortion is equivalent to destroying what would have been a human life, she does not object to it on the basis of a fetocentric discourse on the rights of the unborn, nor would she favor total abolition of legal conditions for the practice. Morita is not principally interested in judging abortion as right or wrong in the abstract. There are circumstances when it is unavoidable, but it is always regrettable, and it must always be addressed with a combination of the proper rites to show respect to the soul and sincere repentance. Ritual alone, without repentance, is empty and meaningless; a woman who approaches a temple thinking that she can avoid self-examination and repentance is in the wrong, and temples that provide such rites for fees, without educating the client about the need for repentance, are also in the wrong.

Readers of this account will probably be struck, as I was, by the complete silence about men at every stage. As an adult, married woman with two children of her own, Morita is hardly ignorant of the facts of reproductive biology. What, then, accounts for the invisibility of men in her understanding? How is it that this way of looking at abortion and *mizuko kuyō* can seem to her a coherent religious response, when it is patently so counterfactual, even counterintuitive? First, let us review the examples separately, observing first that her separate stories are framed in an overarching contrast between a pure and genuine (if materially impoverished) past and a degraded and spiritually polluting present. This rhetorical device accords with the pan-Buddhist notion of time as devolution from a pure age in which a Buddha is preaching in the human world through ages that become progressively worse. Worse, that is, in the sense of offering ever poorer conditions for spiritual progress, ending in the Latter Days of the Law (*mappō*), the age in which we currently live.

In Morita's description of abortion and infanticide in premodern Japan, we saw only the interaction of a pregnant woman and a female midwife, who between them plan and carry out infanticide. No men are present, though in past time as well as the present it was frequently they who made the decision for abortion or infanticide and perhaps carried out infanticide themselves. In the course of another discussion with me, Morita brought up the idea that Edo-period women did not cut their hair in case they died in childbirth. Such a death condemned a woman to the Pool of Blood Hell, according to folk Buddhist notions. Their only hope for salvation from it was that Jizō would extend his staff into the blood, entwine their hair, and then lift them out to a higher plane. The husbands of such women suffered no such fate. Men are entirely absent from Morita's reconstruction of the past. She lays all guilt and retribution associated with sexuality and reproduction at women's door, even as she admits that abortion, infanticide, and death in childbirth have occurred unavoidably. This is "women's karma," a greater burden and obstacle to salvation than that borne by men, as fruitless, sorrowful, physically painful, and inevitable as lactation following infanticide.

Men are also curiously invisible in her accounts of present events. The partner of the girl from Kyūshū is mentioned only in his capacity as inseminator, after which he disappears from the story with no assignment to him of guilt, responsibility, or retribution for the pregnancy or infanticide. The boy whose lack of judgment in narrative 2 caused his parents such grief is, similarly, never held responsible for his actions. Instead, it is as if the girl from Kyūshū were to blame for his troubles as well as her own. In short, even when it requires resolute suspension of disbelief to make men invisible, and thus unassailable, that is the approach Morita recommends. In a significant departure from the "common sense" on abortion inherited from the sexual culture of the Edo period, and from representations in contemporary newspaper advice columns, where the Callous Man receives his share of scrutiny, the Foolish Woman is alone in the limelight in spiritualists' accounts.

From one perspective, Morita evidently uses this device as a strategy to encourage female clients to take charge. That is, in saying that women are responsible for mistaken ideas of sexuality that produce *mizuko,* she is saying, among other things, that women have it in their power to reject involvement in sexual relations that are no more than a form of play. They can and should reject male desire in that form. This position offers women some scope for protecting themselves. It also casts men in a position of irrelevance to the woman's spiritual state, determined by seriousness, self-respect, and purpose. Morita would probably recommend, in terms common to all varieties of religion in Japan, that women avoid criticizing others and focus instead on self-examination and repentance.

While Morita's strategy offers this limited empowerment to women, it is not clear that they could ever escape her bleak portrayal of "women's karma." The frequently identified misogyny of the Buddhist ideas at its basis would seem to limit women severely. No hope is extended here, as it frequently is in Japan's new religions, that "women's karma" (however called) can be transcended. The feature of male invisibility and the device of focusing all moral qualifications regarding sexuality on women are standard characteristics of a wider discourse about sexuality that surrounds *mizuko kuyō*. We will return to this issue in a later section.

Finally, let us consider the significance of Morita's practice within Tsuyama as a whole. In chapter 5 we will see a passive attitude taken in other local temples' practice of *mizuko kuyō*. By contrast, Morita is an active advocate of *mizuko kuyō*, based on an understanding of *mizuko* that casts them as wandering spirits who can attack anyone, regardless of their experience of abortion or lack of it. On this basis, anyone might need to perform the rites. Morita diagnoses clients' problems in terms of *mizuko* spirit attacks, encourages them to perform rites, and provides the means to do so. She views the social roles of priests and temples in terms similar to her former social work. Priests have a responsibility to contribute to the public good, and temples should be places for reflection, self-examination, repentance, and character building. Priests are not just the custodians of buildings, altars, and graves. They have a responsibility to educate and "rehabilitate" the people who come as clients—to tell them in no uncertain terms where they are mistaken in their thinking, resigned that if the clients do not like what they hear, they are free to take their business elsewhere.

Morita's spiritualism and practice of *mizuko kuyō* at Jionji has made the temple a regional center not only in the sense of erecting a large group of statues and attracting significant numbers of people, but also in the more active sense of providing a rationale for the rites. Morita has developed a very broad interpretation of *mizuko* that widens its application and potentially implicates anyone. Morita's style of combining spiritualism and the priesthood can be seen on a wider scale at Enman'in, a national center of *mizuko kuyō*.

MIZUKO KUYŌ ON A GRAND SCALE: ENMAN'IN

Enman'in was established in 987 and a son of Emperor Murakami (r. 946–967) was installed as its abbot (*monzeki*). Since that time it has been headed almost continuously by relations of the imperial family, and is now affiliated with the Tendai sect. It is a large temple complex of over twenty separate buildings and extensive gardens and grounds. Some of the buildings themselves are designated as important cultural properties (*jūyō bunkazai*), as are a number of works of art displayed there. Enman'in is especially noted for its collection of *Ōtsu-e*, a kind of folkloric, frequently humorous, painting.[7]

An interview with the vice abbot of Enman'in in August 1994 disclosed circumstances directly relevant to the temple's decision to practice *mizuko kuyō*. Until 1945, Enman'in received significant government support, in recognition of its imperial connections and its conservation of important works of architecture and art. Now, however, except for a token amount, that support has almost entirely disappeared, and as a *monzeki* temple, Enman'in has no parishioners. This has meant that new sources of revenue had to be found, or Enman'in would have to close its doors.[8]

The present abbot, Miura Dōmyō, fifty-sixth-generation head of the temple, assumed the job of creating new sources of support for Enman'in. Miura instituted *mizuko kuyō* at Enman'in in 1975, after a female client requested that Miura perform rites for the spirit of an aborted fetus, though there was no previous practice of it in Tendai Buddhism or in this temple. The temple had not, prior to that time, offered ritual to large numbers of the general public, as this would have sullied the temple's imperial connections. Nevertheless, Miura Dōmyō tirelessly promoted *mizuko kuyō* and attracted much media attention. He has written several books on *mizuko kuyō,* one of which has been translated into English as *The Forgotten Child.*[9]

It is uncertain how many people who come to Enman'in would purchase and read an entire book. Much more likely to be read in its entirety is a forty-two-page pamphlet titled "How to Perform *Kuyō.*" In it Miura presents his rationale for *mizuko kuyō,* and includes testimonials about its beneficial results, along with a detachable application form to be sent in with the fees: $300 for the first *mizuko,* plus $100 for each additional one.

Miura defines *mizuko* as the souls of the miscarried, stillborn, and aborted fetuses, linking this explanation to a ten-part analysis of the human life span to be found in the Buddhist canons, divided into five stages in the womb and five after birth. The death of a fetus for any reason goes against the Buddhist precept prohibiting the taking of life (pp. 5–6). He demolishes the notion that there could be such a thing as a Mizuko Jizō or Mizuko Kannon, because traditional Buddhist iconography has never recognized such a thing. People who erect such statuary in the mistaken idea that it might be effective will be sorely disappointed.

Mizuko cannot receive any benefit, Miura writes, until they are given a material form. A spirit tablet (*ihai*) bearing a posthumous name must be prepared for each one, just like the practice for ancestors. The name is necessary to give the *mizuko* a genuine existence, and Miura has initiated the practice of choosing a name from scripture, so that when that scripture is recited, the *mizuko*'s name will also be called (pp. 7–8).

Miura denies that *mizuko* can cause spirit attacks (*tatari*) and pooh-poohs the spectacle of unscrupulous religionists who attribute their clients' problems to *mizuko,* warning darkly that further misfortune will befall them if they do not pay for extensive rituals (pp. 9–11). In a later passage, however, he identifies twenty maladies that frequently appear when a couple fails to perform *mizuko kuyō* after a miscarriage, stillbirth, or abortion. These include continual illness of family members, loss of good fortune in spite of strenuous effort, pain in the hips and shoulders (especially in women), repeated illness and accidents in children, strange behavior in children and grandchildren, traffic accidents, seeing a child's face in a dream, seeing in a dream a number of lit candles equivalent to the number of *mizuko* one has produced, seeing furtive shapes, hearing voices or a crying child though no one is there, and so on (pp. 23–24). If these results of failing to perform *mizuko kuyō* are not spirit attacks, they just as well might be, insofar as the message to perform the rites is the same.

The pièce de résistance of this work is its fetocentrism, combined with a perspective on Japan's postwar history characteristic of *mizuko kuyō* ideologues, in a section of the pamphlet titled, "The Frightful Notion of Cutting Off a Small Life."

In the newspapers of May 3, 1981, there was extensive coverage of an event in which, just before her planned marriage to one man, a woman gave birth to a baby boy by another man and strangled it. She threw the corpse into a trash can and was arrested. She was a university graduate. More surprising was the fact that on January 1, 1980, she had had a baby girl by this same man and had killed her as well. On that occasion, at her wits' end, she asked the man to dispose of the body. One can only find this greatly surprising.

The television reporter relating these events was obviously disgusted by the insensitivity of these two. At first he couldn't believe it. No one could imagine something so completely surpassing common sense. Even a dog that gives birth does its best to raise its young, and if the young are taken away from it, it will search for two or three days, so distressed its blood might change color. However, the idea that human beings, supposedly the most intelligent of animals, could not even reach the level of a dog but would throw away a baby as if it were a thing is truly disgusting.

But I had a different perspective on this story. This incident was a sensation, because the child had already been born, and it attracted a great deal of attention as something highly unusual. But what if the baby were disposed of by abortion, before birth? In that case it would not have been out of the ordinary and would never have been reported.

Certainly, to kill a living child with one's own hands is murder, and that should never be, but in abortion, even if not executed by one's own hand, the same willful intention is there—to cut off the life of a child.

On the one hand we have a scandalous incident and on the other an ordinary, everyday occurrence. Although the substance is slightly different, the thought behind both conceals the same horror. And contemporary people are not aware of this horror. A child can be called the result of love between men and women. But contemporary people do not think of the fetus in the mother's womb as a child until it has emerged from the womb and been born. Is this the correct understanding? I think that everyone knows that this is mistaken. A baby is a life from the moment of conception, when egg and sperm are united. That life develops through pregnancy and is born with a cry of life. Whether inside or outside the mother's womb, whether its size increases, or whether there's a difference [in the stage of pregnancy] is irrelevant.

Since the war, people have become more liberal and knowledgeable about sex. Previously, sex was hidden, and there was a tendency to think of it as shameful, but recently, sex has been discussed more lightheartedly, as a basic human instinct, as natural, and sometimes as a type of human pleasure. I am not criticizing this, but it is frightful that a baby, the result of love between men and women, should be discussed as a "by-product" of human pleasure, as if it were a mere object. Even if you step back from that point of view and see sex merely as a form of pleasure, then it is irresponsible to conceive a child. Contraception should be used.

Now that we have become affluent and people's needs for food, housing, and clothing are satisfied, the Japanese have achieved material wealth beyond belief before and during the war. As in the expression "To know courtesy and moderation," the Japanese should be more temperate and moderate, going forward on the way of humanity and not departing from that way. But as we become more materially wealthy, we seem to have become spiritually impoverished, and this tendency is rapidly progressing.

Because children are the result of love between men and women, as parents and as children, they should be given birth, and I pray that they may be born.

This passage is characteristic of the combination of misogyny, fetocentrism, and nationalism just beneath the surface of *mizuko kuyō* rhetoric. Because the strategy is so frequently recapitulated, it is worth analyzing in some detail. First is the equation of infanticide, murder, and abortion, placing all on the same, subhuman, even subcanine, plane. Second, the narration of the newspaper and television coverage spotlights the woman's actions and leaves the man uninterrogated; she is apparently more reprehensible than he because she was engaged to a second man while pregnant by the first, and more unforgivable yet, because she had been given the rare privilege—for a woman—of higher education. This way of viewing abortion casts it as murderous with women as its principal perpetrators. Unlike the dominant "common sense" on abortion examined in chapter 2, the Callous Man is nowhere to be seen; the Foolish Woman must assume all the blame. The third step is to evoke an intuitive affirmation that human life is fully present from the moment of conception. As if to answer why people fail to recognize something so obvious, it is asserted that things have changed since 1945, and that "sexual liberation" and the affirmation of sexual pleasure are to blame. The qualification "since the war" means since Japanese came under foreign—that is, American—influence and lost their traditional virtues of "knowing courtesy and moderation." Materially rich, but spiritually impoverished, people, especially women, treat sex as a form of amusement and fetuses as bothersome "by-products" to be got rid of like a wart or a bad tooth.

MIZUKO FESTIVALS

With the foregoing presumptions about the contemporary practice of abortion and the plight of *mizuko,* Enman'in conducts its rites of *mizuko kuyō.* As above, individual installations of *ihai* (spirit tablets) are the first step. Upon payment of the fee, the abbot composes a posthumous name, which is inscribed on a gold-lacquered tablet about three centimeters wide and twelve centimeters high. That tablet joins thousands of others after its consecration in a parlor where the tablets line four walls. On one wall, there is an altar, before which the Heart Sutra is recited for the *mizuko.* Ritual sponsors are encouraged to attend an annual "Mizuko Festival" (*Mizuko daihōyō*) on August 23. Smaller-scale rites of the same type are held on the twenty-third day of each month.

I attended the Mizuko Festival in August 1994, the eighth year of the ceremony. It is held over four days, on which identical rites are performed, twice each day, a total of eight separate rites. About 200 attended, of whom about 150 paid to have *kuyō* performed for their

Table 15. *Attendance at the 1994 Mizuko Festival*

Age	Male	Female	Total	Percent
20–29	3	15	18	9
30–50	10	50	60	30
51+	37	85	122	61
Total	50 (25%)	150 (75%)	200	100

mizuko, meaning that their names would be read aloud as sponsors in the course of the ceremony. For a breakdown of who attended the ceremony, see Table 15. The attendants registering people for the ceremony provided the information that the average offering for *kuyō* (there is no set fee on this occasion) was $50, ranging as high as $400. Given the minimum offering and the average number of sponsors per rite at 150 for eight ceremonies, Enman'in's minimum gross income from the four-day rite would be $60,000.

The grounds of the temple were decorated as for a fair, with numerous vendors of clothing, food, and children's snack items suitable as offerings to *mizuko.* While the general mood at the Mizuko Festival was more festive than funereal, a number of people were visibly engaged deeply in devotions for the *mizuko,* even before the ceremony began. One woman in her thirties was performing *mudras* and moving her lips in silent prayer, while another woman in her sixties prayed aloud, saying to the *mizuko* how sorry she was to have prevented its or their birth into this world. Many women arrived in groups or in pairs. All of the men in attendance were accompanied by a woman; none seemed to have come alone. Conversation with those nearby revealed that some recite the Heart Sutra for *mizuko* at their homes; other than that, no special domestic devotions are prescribed for Enman'in's adherents. Probably the majority were in attendance because they had previously paid the basic cost of $300 for an *ihai* to be installed at Enman'in and therefore were on its mailing list, which informed them of the times of this year's ceremony. Thus the initial memorialization can establish the original connection for an ongoing link to Enman'in in a way loosely similar to a temple-parishioner connection.

The rite itself was conducted by the abbot and fourteen people in priests' robes, including the abbot's wife, for a total of four women. Five of the men had shaven heads, but the rest did not, suggesting that the unshaven are not full-time priests. In fact, Enman'in maintains its own independent, nonsectarian training program for the priesthood. This course accepts women (seventy female matriculants so far) and does not require enrollees to give up their lay occupations or marriage. A pamphlet on this program, "Priesthood in Lay Life" (*Zaitaku no mama no sō nyūmon*), describes the course as consisting of monthly training sessions on the conduct of Buddhist rites and study of Buddhist teachings. Those who continue for three years are admitted to the En-man'in Mahayana Society (Enman'in Daijōkai), the highest level of ordination available there. As the ceremony unfolded, it was announced that liturgists other than the abbot were members of the Mahayana Society.

The ceremony for *mizuko* is carried out in a way that presents a dense concentration of traditional Buddhist symbolism, simultaneously elevating the roles of the abbot and accompanying liturgists, and creating participatory roles for the laity, much as if they were parishioners of the temple. The overall effect owes much to the creation of a remarkable ritual space (see Plan 1). A long, rectangular room about 25 feet by 50 feet is divided lengthwise into a 15-foot section in which the priests perform and a second section about 35 feet long where the audience sits. The two sections are divided by two long, low tables for audience offerings and boxes of incense later passed among the audience. As the audience assembles, they first register their names and places of residence along with paying the offering, so that this information can be read out and thus direct the rite to their *mizuko*. Passing into the ritual hall, most placed bags of children's snacks and candy on the offering tables as they seated themselves.

Large paintings of the Diamond World (left) and Womb World (right) mandalas flank the central object of the workshop, a large *ihai* for "All *Mizuko* Spirits" (*mizuko sōrei*). The *ihai* is set in a bank of chrysanthemums in a lacquered cabinet (reminiscent of a domestic Buddhist altar [*butsudan*] in its dark wood construction), surmounted by a statue of Jizō. Arranged in front of the mandalas and the *mizuko ihai* are eight Buddhist figures. From left to right, they are the Buddha Amida, Fudō Myōō, the Buddha Dainichi, Sei'chi Bodhisattva, Fugen Bodhisattva, Monju Bodhisattva, Kokuzō Bodhisattva, and a thousand-armed Kannon Bodhisattva. Their placement makes clear that these figures are to guide and protect the *mizuko*. The pamphlet received by those in attendance advertises that replicas of these statues, carved from wood and covered with gold leaf, can be purchased for $1,980 each. Offerings of fruits and vegetables are placed before each one, along with large votive candles on stone stands.

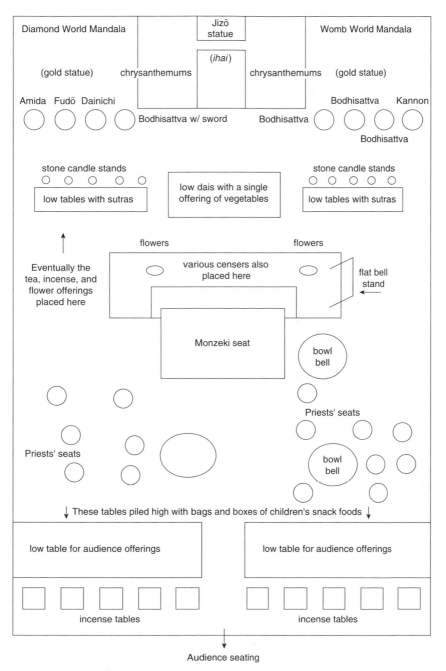

Plan 1. Enman'in Mizuko Festival ritual space

Two low tables with sutra books atop them demarcate the area where the Buddhist figures, *mizuko ihai,* and mandalas are set out from the zone where the priests perform. Between the tables is a low dais where offerings of tea, incense, and flowers are placed as part of the ritual.

The zone where priests perform is also divided into two areas: one for the abbot, and, behind it, a space where the other liturgists sit and chant sutras when not performing offerings. The abbot's seat is a raised, square dais on which he kneels, setting him apart vertically from the other liturgists, who use small pillows, and from the audience (lower still), who kneel directly on the room's straw mats. The elevation of seating, of course, communicates different hierarchical positions in the rite. The abbot's seat faces a lacquered desk wrapping around three sides of the seat. It is decorated with flowers, set with a cup of tea for the abbot, and arranged with censers and other ritual gear. To his right, set into the desk, is a raised, red lacquered frame in which a flat bell is hung, which the abbot strikes with a hammer at various points in the rite. Also to his right is a large metal bell bowl, which he strikes with a padded lacquered wand. The zone for the other liturgists is marked only by the placement of six cushions on the left, eight on the right, small plates of colored paper cut in the shape of lotus leaves, with a wooden drum (*mokugyo*) on the left and another metal bell bowl on the right.

The construction of the ritual borrows elements from two traditional ritual forms: the Jizō Bon, practiced in a variety of Kansai locales annually on August 23 and 24, and the *segaki-e,* or "Feeding the Hungry Ghosts," a rite usually combined with ancestral rites at *obon,* the August "All Souls Festival." The Jizō Bon originally was intended to change negative karmic influence to positive, and to cut off accumulated sin. From the medieval period, Kyoto wards of various areas have observed the festival by setting up tents with an image of Jizō, before which many offerings are placed. The assembled spend a night drinking and feasting. In both Osaka and Kyoto, children participate by making offerings, recognizing the role of Jizō as (among other things) protector of children.[10] The rite of Feeding the Hungry Ghosts has also become combined with *obon,* and its efficacy is understood to extend not only to the hungry ghosts themselves, but to the spirits of the dead as a whole, especially those who have died in the last year. In recognition of this connection, *ihai* of the newly dead are set up near offerings for the hungry ghosts, partly in the hope that the ghosts will not interfere with the progress of the newly dead toward rebirth and the eventual attainment of Buddhahood.[11] Both of these ceremonies are performed in several Buddhist sects and thus have a kind of ecumenical character. Their combination establishes a conjunction of Jizō and *ihai* not seen in traditional Buddhist rites.

After a solemn entry by all the liturgists, which is announced over a loudspeaker, the rite consists of four parts:

1. Offerings of lights (*kentō*), flowers (*kenka*), incense (*kenkō*), and tea (*kencha*).

2. The abbot's reading of a prayer of his own composition for *mizuko*.

3. The *kuyō* proper, in which the abbot reads off the names and places of origin of each ritual sponsor, while the other liturgists continue to recite sutras. During this time, the incense boxes are passed through the audience, and each person takes a pinch of the granulated incense, lifts it level with the forehead, and then sprinkles it on a small piece of burning charcoal in a separate compartment of the lacquered box, igniting the incense and releasing its odor.

4. Two readings of the Heart Sutra by all in attendance, from sheets distributed at the time of recitation.

The abbot's prayer (the second step above) invokes all the Buddhist figures represented in statuary at this rite, plus Enma-ō, the guardian of hell, to watch over the *mizuko*. In a semiclassical verbal style typical of formal prayer, he evokes their pitiable fate, plucked from the womb before they could complete the ten stages of human development. The power of ritual can, however, be the first step in the opening of their destiny, and the awakening of the "aspiration to Buddhahood" (*hosshin*). Through the prayer and devotion of their parents here at this ritual, they will be set at rest and receive the protection of all the Buddhas. Prayers will be granted and sickness and misfortune avoided through the great mercy and protection of the Buddhas.

The abbot's reading of the individual names of ritual sponsors integrates the *mizuko* into the stem family, the *ie*. He announces each as "the *suishi* [another reading of the characters informally read as *mizuko*] of the such-and-such *ie*." This attaches these spirits to the *ie* in question and asserts that the *ie* has an ongoing responsibility for them. In the context of this rite, ritual sponsorship, offerings of food, and recitation of the Heart Sutra constitute fulfillment of responsibility.

The ritual as a whole constitutes a kind of merit transfer, *tsuizen kuyō,* as the abbot later explained in an informal talk to the audience following the conclusion of formal rites (*hōwa*). Creating a *mizuko,* he said, creates bad karma (*gō*), and the only redress is prayer. He encouraged the group to attend as many monthly *mizuko* services as possible, and to participate in other Enman'in activities.

In fact, the abbot's *hōwa* did not mention *mizuko,* other than the remarks immediately above. Instead, he mainly discussed his own recent activities, such as trips to China and New Zealand, and other temple activities unrelated to *mizuko.* In other words, his remarks presupposed that the audience were already in an ongoing relation to Enman'in analogous to a parishioner tie, that they had an interest in its affairs, and that they looked to him for continual and diverse ritual services.

The abbot's talk also seemed to assume that members of the audience had rather weak ties to any other temple, including the temples where they actually were parishioners. The services the abbot advertised on the occasion of the Mizuko Festival included the sale of a special altar built to accommodate cremation remains and membership in Enman'in's "Living Posthumous Name Club." No one with a firm status as a parishioner in a temple would either need or be able to use either of these services. Parishioners of temples in most cases have access to a family grave where cremation urns are interred, and a domestic altar (*butsudan*) where ancestral *ihai* are enshrined. Though graves and ancestral altars are separate in ordinary Buddhist practice, Enman'in combines the two, recommending that people purchase such an altar and have it placed at Enman'in in a hall connected by a sliding door to the parlor where *ihai* for *mizuko* are enshrined. Printed advertising for the altar emphasizes that one can always make a "grave visit," regardless of the weather (since it is inside), that perpetual ritual is assured, and that it is ideal for single people or those without descendants (who might otherwise become wandering spirits for lack of someone to ritualize them in perpetuity).

Similarly, the "Living Posthumous Name Club" offers to create a posthumous name for people before they die, thus saving their survivors a significant expense ($100 per character is a standard rule of thumb for even the simplest posthumous names), and assuring that one receives a long and dignified name (rather than depending on survivors' generosity). It is the abbot who composes the names. Entry to the club costs $300, plus an annual membership fee of $30, entitling members to attend lectures on Buddhism, and including a special prayer for health and happiness on each member's birthday. In a Buddhist parish, the temple priest composes the posthumous name, but not until the parishioner dies. Each Buddhist sect follows its own conventions regarding the choice of characters and phraseology for posthumous names, and these services are central to the economic support of temples.

The combination of these two customs allows Enman'in to offer funeral rites and to sell altars and rites for the dead (including emplacement of cremation urns and the composition of posthumous names), even in the absence of a parish organization and grave sites. Further, it is the temple's reputation for *mizuko* rites that has afforded it access to a clientele or market for all these ritual services. *Mizuko kuyō* is thus the key to the creation of a parishlike network of ritual sponsors connected to it in an ongoing way. Creating a stable group of adherents from people cut off from traditional temple affiliations and lacking strong ties to Buddhism is clearly the heart of the sales pitch, and a crucial requirement for Enman'in in the face of its postwar loss of official economic support. In this, *mizuko kuyō* has played the central role.

Enman'in's commercialization of rituals stemming from *mizuko kuyō* is largely driven by economic necessity. Since it is not presently affiliated with Tendai or any other Buddhist sect, and since it has no formal parish, it is under no obligation to answer to any authority above or below it. It is free to attract sponsorship by any and all possible means, including the promotion of fetocentrism in a spiritualist framework, turning the abbot toward a practice of the priesthood which is much like that of a spiritualist. Miura Dōmyō, like Jionji's Morita Guyō, is an *ogamiya* in a priest's vestments. His clientele are those without a firm Buddhist parish membership, who nevertheless wish to provide rites for *mizuko* and for themselves after death. They are women (and a significant number of men) predominantly over fifty years of age. They evidently seek to solemnize and dignify an experience of abortion long in the past, integrating these spirits into the *ie* framework and transforming them into a benign and protective character.

TESTIMONIALS BY ENMAN'IN ADHERENTS

Those who have *mizuko kuyō* performed by Enman'in report receiving a wide variety of benefits as a result. The following three testimonials are representative.[12]

A woman from Hokkaidō: Since I had *mizuko kuyō* performed, my business has flourished miraculously, and my health has returned. I want very much to come to Enman'in again to give thanks, but I am too far away. Can you consider building a branch of the temple here [in Hokkaidō]?

A woman from Kyoto: Thank you very much for performing my *mizuko kuyō.* For many years I had kept this secret heavy in my heart, deeply disturbed, with no one to talk to about it.

Since the *kuyō,* I am filled with a pure feeling, purged of my former distress. Countless times I had previously felt that a large, black thing was sitting on me, so heavy that I could not breathe, strangled. Then on the day of the *kuyō,* I dreamed of Jizō, with a dark, thin smoke curling about the hips. I thought this was strange, and I had a feeling of dread and unease. I experienced nerve pain and had to stay home from work for five or six days, and pain in my arms and rheumatism. Hateful misfortune seemed to go on and on. But two or three days ago the pain in my hips disappeared miraculously, and I have been able to return to work. I know that this is due to *mizuko kuyō.* . . .

A (second) woman from Hokkaidō: It has been three months since I had *mizuko kuyō* performed. I was granted a superb posthumous name [for my *mizuko*], much finer than I deserve. The pains in my neck, shoulders, and hips have disappeared. I have since had many miraculous experiences, all due to *kuyō,* and I am deeply grateful.

During twenty years of marriage, life was full of family troubles, my son was severely ill and introverted, and my husband was undependable. I had halfway given up on life. But in the twentieth year of marriage I am now experiencing the greatest happiness, and my days are filled with deep repentance and gratitude.

I have realized how deep is the karma of my body. In the past, I was selfish, willful, and full of myself. I wonder why I didn't realize earlier, and even now I regret it. Now, however, my son's introversion is improving daily, and I am sure that he will be completely cured.

As a wife and mother I am far from ideal, but as I face the *butsudan* in prayer daily to perform *kuyō,* I feel that I am gradually coming to understand, and I am filled with tears of gratitude.

I am grateful for the preciousness of life, and I want to visit the temple again to receive religious training. Not only has my son's condition improved, but my husband recently has a new will to work and is working hard from early in the morning. This would have been unthinkable before now. I thought this might not last long, but now I see that his heart has really changed, and I can only think that something is pushing him from behind. Now that I feel this gratitude, my home is bright and cheerful and peaceful. I thank you with all my heart.

A notable characteristic of these testimonies is the origin of two of them in Hokkaidō, showing that Enman'in's adherents sometimes come to the temple from great distances. The first of these three testimonies is a straightforward assertion that *mizuko kuyō* has brought "miraculous" success in business. The second testimony comes from a woman whose abortion or miscarriage evidently occurred many years ago. The experience produced sensations typically reported in ghost stories, the feeling of *kanashibari,* a heavy being sitting on one's chest, which we saw promoted in the tabloids as a symptom typically linked to *mizuko* spirit attacks. After *kuyō* was performed, she had ominous dreams of Jizō and strange pains of the type that Japanese women frequently report during menopause: rheumatic and nerve pains in the arms and hips, the same *mizuko* symptomology we saw expounded in the tabloids. There seems also to be a relation between the smoke seen around Jizo's hips and this woman's pains in the same area, with the suggestion of a further connection between hips and the reproductive organs. When after five or six days these pains vanished, however, the woman experienced a feeling of purity, which she attributes to *mizuko kuyō.* In this testimony and in the third one, the writers are relieved of miscellaneous pains typical of menopause and experience lasting results from *mizuko kuyō* (apart from whatever effects it has on the spirits) as a kind of purification of body and spirit.

The third testimony is the most comprehensive, reporting not just material success, relief from physical discomfort, or a lifting of spirit, but a more general reorientation of life as a whole. This adherent's abortion or miscarriage happened sometime within her first twenty years of marriage (meaning that she is probably between forty and fifty years old) and those twenty years were lackluster and unhappy, owing to her own selfishness and lack of purpose, her son's strange, introverted nature, and her husband's undependability. *Mizuko kuyō* evidently afforded this woman an opportunity to realize "the karma of [her] body," an enigmatic phrase here, but connected to her previous selfishness and willfulness, which she now regrets and which she presumably links to an abortion.[13] This is "women's karma," probably in the sense expounded by Morita Guyō. Repenting for her earlier attitudes and the resulting negative karma, the third writer now disciplines her life through daily *kuyō* before the domestic Buddhist altar (Enman'in adherents perform *kuyō* by reciting the Heart Sutra). The first result of this new discipline is the transformation of pain and dissatisfaction to gratitude. Her new attitude is mirrored in her husband's new will to work and an improvement in her son's condition, leading to a cheerful home life. The writer now hopes to deepen her discipline by going again to Enman'in. Thus this woman has experienced a comprehensive reorientation of life in a more positive direction, and she attributes the change to *mizuko kuyō,* promising an ongoing relation to Enman'in.

These three testimonies attribute a range of benefits to *mizuko kuyō,* and a corresponding range of experience in terms of how much change in life the writers sense as a result. The testimonial form adopted here is much like that seen in the Japanese new religions, and their variation from simple success story to comprehensive life reorientation is also similar. The attention to vague physical discomforts associated with menopause is particularly characteristic of testimonials about *mizuko kuyō*. All three texts make clear that *mizuko kuyō* is promoted not only for any benefits the spirits may receive, but equally for concrete results for the sponsors of these rites, a theme we first identified in the surveys on *mizuko kuyō* introduced in chapter 2.

MIZUKO KUYŌ IN THE NEW RELIGION BENTENSHŪ

The initiation of *mizuko kuyō* in Bentenshū in 1981 represented an attempt to recoup membership lost after the founder's death.[14] Bentenshū was founded in 1952 by Ōmori Kiyoko (later called Ōmori Chiben, 1909–1967), wife of the priest of a Shingon temple in the Ikoma area to the east of Osaka. Stricken with a persistent pain of unknown cause in the shoulder, Ōmori consulted a spiritualist who told her to worship the Buddhist goddess Benzaiten (Sanskrit: Sarasvati). Searching in her husband's temple, she discovered a statue of Benzaiten from which one arm was missing. She began to worship this statue, and not only was her own malady healed, but she began to receive revelations from the goddess, enabling her to cure others and to provide general spiritual guidance, beginning in 1933.[15] People flocked to her in such numbers that they soon outgrew the capacity of a Benzaiten confraternity established within her husband's temple in 1948. In 1952 the religion was officially established on a basis of independence from Shingon, and its own temple was built two years later beside the original temple of Ōmori's husband.

In 1955 the new religion set up a second headquarters in Takatsuki City, Osaka Prefecture, moving its entire administrative operations there, while the original site continued to be used for some rituals. When the founder died in 1967, Bentenshū was a small but flourishing new religion based largely on the cult of Benzaiten, healing, and the founder's personal charisma.

It is frequently the case, following a founder's death, that Japanese new religions show erratic membership statistics, generally with a net decline. Bentenshū was no exception; from 1975 to 1980 the group suffered a sharp decline, from nearly 600,000 to about 150,000, or a loss of three-fourths of the membership. No conspicuous schisms or scandals rocked the group in these years. Instead, it appears that adherents principally attracted to the charisma of Bentenshū's founder simply dropped out when she died.

Mizuko kuyō provided the means to stem the tide. The founder's thought did not mention *mizuko,* and they did not figure at all in the revelations she received from Benzaiten or in the counsel she provided her followers.[16] In effect, her desperate successors appropriated the *mizuko* rites at the height of the cult's popularization by prayer healers, the media, and assorted religionists without any basis in Bentenshū's doctrine and practice up to that time.

Bentenshū has published a monthly magazine called *Mysterious Sound* (*Myōon*) since 1951, which includes the founder's sermons and revelations, testimonials, news of organizational activities, and reports on the activities of one of Bentenshū's most prominent supporters, Sasagawa Ryōichi (1899–1995). Sasagawa is associated with Japan's right wing and spent three years in jail for Class-A war crimes. The first mention of *mizuko kuyō* in *Mysterious Sound* occurred in 1979, when a campaign to raise funds for a great tower and associated ritual facilities for *mizuko kuyō* began.[17]

In 1981, the Takatsuki City headquarters built a seventy-three-meter high modernistic tower for *mizuko kuyō* at a cost of about $12,000,000. The tower houses an eight-armed statue of Benzaiten as a protector of *mizuko,* with smaller statues of infants on the palms of seven of the hands. See Figure 11. In addition, the group purchased land to accommodate five hundred graves, and these grave sites include not only the customary stone grave marker, but also statues of Mizuko Jizō and other *mizuko kuyō*–related statuary. This placement indicates that *mizuko* are integrated into the category of ancestors following their ritualization by Bentenshū.

The years 1982 to 1986 were a period of major expansion for Bentenshū, in which it more than doubled its membership, as Table 16 shows. The doubling seems to have occurred mainly between 1985 and 1986. It is no accident that a huge number of articles in *Mysterious Sound* concerning *mizuko kuyō* appeared around this time, beginning in 1984. These articles set out a rationale for the practice, integrating it with Bentenshū's original teachings. This rationale held that along with the *mizuko,* living humanity will be saved through *mizuko kuyō,* and that by experiencing the blessing and importance of this salvation, humanity

Figure 11. Statue of Benzaiten at Bentenshū Takatsuki City headquarters

will be enabled to walk the path of happiness. In addition to linking
mizuko kuyō to an understanding of salvation, testimonials of the concrete results received from *mizuko kuyō* aligned the practice with the
pursuit of such this-worldly benefits as healing, a pursuit already well
entrenched in Bentenshū. Testimonials proclaimed, for example, that
people had been cured of illness, became able to conceive, had avoided
traffic accidents, and that their children's behavior had improved, all as
a result of *mizuko kuyō*.[18]

Table 16. *Bentenshū membership, 1982–1992*

1982	148,555	1986	322,980	1990	304,669
1983	149,502	1987	318,155	1991	302,407
1984	150,114	1988	307,819	1992	301,793
1985	149,312	1989	307,027		

SOURCE: Bunkachō, *Shūkyōnenkan* 1981–1992 editions (Tokyo: Gyōsei shuppan, 1981–1992).

It is evident that *mizuko kuyō* made it possible for Bentenshū to bring in the families and friends of the group's original membership, and that these people swelled the group's ranks. Since membership has shrunk since that time, however, it would appear that *mizuko kuyō* may no longer be such a powerful attraction.[19]

Bentenshū recognizes the souls of aborted, stillborn, and miscarried fetuses as *mizuko*, and it ritualizes them in several forms: the *mizuko* created by each married couple, the *mizuko* created by one's own children or friends, and the *mizuko* of one's ancestors. Insofar as possible, each *mizuko* should be ritualized individually. *Mizuko* are symbolized in separate, golden-colored *ihai*, and in about 25,000 ceramic tiles that are stamped with the faces of praying children. Some 50,000 *ihai* are enshrined in a subterranean chamber beneath the Benzaiten statue in the tower at the Takatsuki City headquarters. See Figure 12. It is not necessary to be a member of Bentenshū to have its rites of *mizuko kuyō* performed. It costs $300 to have rites performed for a single *mizuko*, a price that includes the *ihai* and three-times-daily sutra recitation for them, as well as an annual festival on August 8 that features an impressive fireworks display. Unlike temples and shrines, which for the most part refrain from active proselytization regarding *mizuko*, Bentenshū promotes the idea that a variety of problems stem from *mizuko*, as in a pamphlet explaining why the rites should be performed:

Children always fighting with their parents, making them worry, always weakly and frequently sick, can't seem to find a good marriage partner, nothing they do ever seems to turn out right.

Children are treasures, a child loved above all else. Do your children have problems like this? In such cases, spiritual damage from *mizuko* (*mizuko no reishō*) is frequently the cause.

Miscarriage, stillbirth, abortion—any of these can produce *mizuko*—a pitiful, small, unlucky life that is banished from darkness to darkness. They are small lives preserving the lamp of life in the mother's womb. Their only

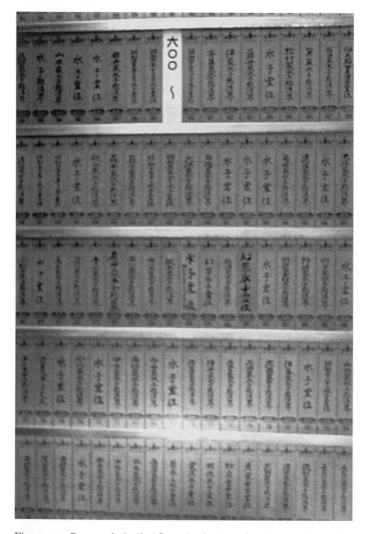

Figure 12. Bentenshū's *ihai* for *mizuko,* in a chamber underneath the Benzaiten statue

prayer is to be born into this world, trusting in their parents' love. Then suddenly one day the lamp of life goes out, and they are plunged into darkness. They have no way to make anyone ever think of them again.

The parents undoubtedly had their reasons for what they did, but *mizuko* can't understand. They especially hate selfish parents who commit abortion, and they continually complain bitterly of their sadness to the parents and the rest of the family in a variety of ways. These ways are manifested especially strongly among the siblings of the *mizuko.*

This is only to be expected. The siblings have the same parents and have been raised lovingly, but though they share the same parents, the *mizuko* cannot make their parents think of them or do anything for them. It is only natural that they would be sad and resentful.

So what is to be done? There is no other way than to repent sincerely and offer sincere *kuyō*. Apologizing from the heart, expressing repentance, and showing them the same love as a living child by offering up *kuyō*. This is what must be done. There is no other way to ease the resentment of these pitiful little souls. Unless we think of them and offer them *kuyō*, the souls of the *mizuko* will never be able to rise up, and they will always be among us in this world, forever seeking *kuyō* and consolation from those of us in this world.[20]

Bentenshū also has a song for *mizuko:*

"Souls of the Mizuko *Set At Ease"*

Sent away in tears, abandoned without a tear,
The crying voices of small souls blow about in the wind
The Founder, Chiben Son'nyo, savior of the world, also cried,
Praying only for the peace of the souls of her children.

Carrying out our founder's will, we built a *kuyō* tower with a clear
    spring and blooming flowers
Morning and night, we will send the sound of ease that opens the way
    for these children
Sending them ample, pure food
Offering them flowers
Giving them the warmth of our founder's heart.

Sleep, soul, upon a cloud
The day of salvation draws nigh
Held in gentle hands, sleep in peace, *mizuko.*

The decline of Bentenshū membership was arrested by the adoption of *mizuko kuyō*. This can be seen in Table 16. Thus, the generation of Bentenshū's leaders succeeding its founder effectively saved the group from falling into obscurity. Even though the core membership is aging (mid- to late fifties and older) and predominantly female, the particular interpretation seen here of efficacious rites for *mizuko* allows the group to cast its net more broadly than it might at first appear. The core membership may be beyond reproductive age itself, but even after a couple has memorialized their own *mizuko,* the sentimental appeal to save other people's *mizuko* remains a challenge for the stalwart. The *mizuko* of one's children, friends, and ancestors are not, by Bentenshū's interpretation, a matter that can be left to the actual progenitors of those spirits (and the progenitors may be dead in any case). If one's own children or friends should be insensitive to the fate of "their" *mizuko,* then it is up to the Bentenshū believer either to awaken these people to their responsibility or to undertake the proper rituals on their behalf. The absence of any blood relation between the *mizuko* in question and the sponsor of ritual is no obstacle to the efficacy of *mizuko kuyō* as performed and interpreted in Bentenshū. Furthermore, because Bentenshū does not make group membership a prerequisite for performing *mizuko kuyō,* it can accept as ritual sponsors people who do not intend to form a lasting relationship with the religion. In these various ways, *mizuko kuyō* provides a major source of revenue and vitality to Bentenshū, restoring in some measure that lost after the founder's death.

Part 2: The Buddhist Priesthood and *Mizuko Kuyō*

Given the central role of Western religious institutions seeking to influence social policy on issues in medical ethics, such as euthanasia, abortion, organ transplant, in vitro fertilization, and a host of other questions, the fact that Japanese religions have preferred not to involve themselves in such discussions may well meet with disbelief, but that is the case. In the first instance, abortion does not have a status in Japan today as an "ethical issue," because support for its legally regulated practice is so strong. By contrast, if Japan could be said to have entertained stirring ethical debate on medical issues in the last twenty years, the issue is organ transplant and the question of whether to recognize the idea of brain death. Japanese religions have only just begun to address this issue, and they show remarkable timidity in doing so. The exceptions to this generalization are the Buddhist-derived new religions Sōka Gakkai and Agon-shū.[21]

Buddhist institutions are reluctant to involve themselves in any activity that is political in nature or that might encourage divisiveness or lead to controversy. While this may be a camouflage for cowardice upon occasion, it is also the case that fomenting schism and division is seen as a great sin in the Buddhist tradition as a whole. Priests would not lightly sound off with their personal views on abortion or other medical issues if there were any prospect of contradiction. Also, Seichō no Ie's movement to abolish the economic hardship clause of the Eugenics Protection Law opened that group to charges of political activity inappropriate to a religious body, in violation of the constitutional separation of church and state, and Buddhist sects are understandably reluctant to make themselves targets for such accusations. Separate sects do not frequently have occasion to interact and consider a range of views, and in the case of medical issues, they may find themselves ill prepared to deal with complex scientific data. Not only that, in view of the twentieth-century history of reversals on Japan's population policies, Buddhist sects do not want to assume a strong position that might later have to be reversed and then justified to the membership. These are some of the reasons Buddhist sects have been cautious about setting out too clear a position on *mizuko kuyō*.

Of the major sects of Japanese Buddhism, only Jōdo Shinshū has developed a clear policy on *mizuko kuyō*—a policy of absolute prohibition. Other sects seem not (yet) to have taken a stand one way or the other, and the result is that provincial temples reach their decision in terms of the local situation rather than enacting policy worked out in their sect's central administration. The practice of *mizuko kuyō* is thus not centrally orchestrated except in the case of Jōdo Shinshū's opposition to it.

There is a sense in which temples offering *mizuko kuyō* must represent their decision to do so as a response to local demand. There is no canonical basis for these rites, nor any canonical basis to the concept of *mizuko*. This absence precludes any possibility of representing the rites as the enactment of something mandated in scripture. The usual way I have heard priests and others put the matter is to say that their parishioners get the idea that the "spirit attacks" (*tatari*) of *mizuko* are something to be afraid of from *ogamiya* or women's magazines, and then come running to the temples for *kuyō*. In this representation, the temples are merely responding to parishioners' demands by providing the rites requested. In other words, they respond to their parishioners' expression of a spiritual need without concerning themselves directly with the question of the existence of *mizuko,* their *tatari,* or the effectiveness of the rites (or the fabricated nature of the ritual).

The sole exception to the lack of a united ecumenical front on *mizuko kuyō* is the nonsectarian Buddhist Telephone Advice Service (*Bukkyō terefon sōdan*), run from a Tokyo office and staffed by priests of all sects. Most calls to the service concern graves and ancestral memorials, but questions on *mizuko kuyō* run a close third. Since the service is nonsectarian, it had to develop an ecumenical way to answer these questions, which must have been hard, given that the only sect with a clear position completely opposes these rites. The approach adopted denies the idea of fetal spirit attacks, stressing instead a respect for human life and deepening awareness of sin (*zaigō no ninshiki*). The service tells callers that they should go to their temple priest and accept guidance on precisely how to perform rites, underlining the implication that one's parish temple is preferable to a "*mizuko* specialist." This bland ecumenism seems to be a result of a search for the lowest common denominator, rather than of true engagement with abortion as an ethical issue.[22]

Jōdo Shinshū's opposition to *mizuko kuyō* is set out in a text titled *Nyonin ōjō* (Women's salvation), published for the continuing doctrinal education of priests and laypeople by the Doctrinal Bureau (Kyōgaku Honbu).[23] The discussion that follows is based on that work and an interview with Professor Kakehashi Jitsuen, vice-director of the Jōdo Shinshū Doctrinal Research Institute (Jōdo Shinshū Kyōgaku Kenkyūjo).[24] The sect's opposition is complex, but has two main parts, the first being an opposition to any form of merit transfer ritual, *tsuizen kuyō*, based on the teaching of the sect's founder, Shinran. *Mizuko kuyō* represents one kind of merit transfer and is thus opposed on the same grounds as other forms of merit transfer. The second part of the sect's objection is based on a critique of the way *mizuko kuyō* is enacted, which is described as artificial, exploitative, and morally degraded. Merit transfer is seen most prominently in connection with the Buddhist funerals and ancestral rites of sects other than Jōdo Shinshū.

In contrast with the importance given merit transfer in other sects, according to Jōdo Shinshū, humanity's salvation will be brought about by the *nenbutsu,* a phrase hailing Amida, the principal Buddha revered by the sect, and by Amida's grace. Therefore, there is no need to provide ritual in the hope of salvation, because salvation is already assured. The priesthood is not empowered to offer a ritual above and beyond this understanding, and the pretense of such an ability is no more than a promise to work magic. Thus, no human death is ritualized through merit transfer, and this includes all those categories of deaths elsewhere treated as *mizuko.*

A childhood death, stillbirth, miscarriage, and abortion are all treated in the same manner as any human death in Jōdo Shinshū. A fetus is recognized as fully human from the moment of conception (and thus abortion is wrong), and if a fetus should die, regardless of the circumstances, it is ritualized on the same model, though on a smaller scale, than adult deaths. This means that there is neither need nor justification for singling out a special category of death for special treatment.

The second part of Jōdo Shinshū's objection to *mizuko kuyō* sees it as a debased, magical practice drawing on a historical belief in folk religion that unsettled spirits maliciously attack the living, either as punishment or to make their plight known to those with a duty to provide ritual for them. The "attacks" (*tatari*) come in multiple forms, sickness, strife, and economic misfortune being the ones most frequently mentioned. This belief in *tatari* is entirely groundless in Jōdo Shinshū's view, and the job of genuine religionists is not to exploit the fear of *tatari*, but instead to educate people as to its superstitious nature and to lead them to conceptualize human life in terms of Amida's teaching.

Although the motive of misguided clients seeking *mizuko kuyō* can be traced to folk traditions concerning *tatari*, Jōdo Shinshū points out *mizuko kuyō*'s recency as a matter of religious concern. Jōdo Shinshū especially emphasizes the fabricated nature of the practice as proof of its artificiality, noting that its present, commercialized form was invented in the 1970s by Hashimoto Tetsuma, founding priest of Shiunzan Jizōji and right-wing activist (*Nyonin ōjō*, p. 74). *Mizuko kuyō* represents a callous exploitation of the fear and regret of those who have experienced abortion, entirely exploitative in nature, unfairly placing all guilt or responsibility for abortion on women. *Mizuko kuyō* is a vulgar, commoditized parasitism, taking advantage of religious naiveté. Its practitioners are morally corrupt, because they exploit and profit from the confused emotions surrounding abortion, profiting from women's fears that abortion is wrong, but never, themselves, taking a position against it.

While the central administration of Jōdo Shinshū has elaborated a consistent doctrinal response to *mizuko kuyō*, the sect's parishioners nevertheless request these rites, and the parish priests confronted with these situations understandably ask for guidance. Priests obviously would prefer not to deny their parishioners' sincere desire for ritual or to turn them away coldly. The sect magazine *Shinshū* has presented model conversations for priests to use in handling requests. These instruct priests to accede to parishioners' requests for sutra recitation, but only after a consultation with the priest. At the consultation, the priest should instruct the client that she (it is assumed that women will be the main clients) has committed two kinds of sins: first, she has killed a child, and second, by thinking that that child would work a spirit attack upon her, she has turned it into a devil (*akuma*). Imagining that she can now apologize by purchasing a ritual will not wipe out sin. Instead, only sincere repentance can save the *mizuko*.[25]

Other sects have not publicly promulgated a position on *mizuko kuyō*, but priests have occasionally reported their individual views or described the way they respond to parishioners' requests for these rites. Frequently their views show a strong influence from popular treatments in the tabloids. For example, a priest of the Nichiren sect described *mizuko* as floating like jellyfish, white or gray in color, moving purposelessly in a deep darkness, giving off a rotten smell. They have no will, a description which seems to deny their capacity to work spirit attacks. Here we can see that the lack of canonical basis for *any* description of *mizuko* becomes a license for the exercise of fantasy among the priesthood as much as for the readers of the tabloids, and that the jellyfish image, a shapeless form floating in liquid, derives directly from the imagistic possibilities provided by fetal photography. Another Nichiren priest described them as shivering with cold, always hovering in their parents' vicinity. A Shingon priest described *mizuko* as an impure existence between this world and the spirit world, working spirit attacks in order to awaken their parents to perform rites for them.[26]

When these same priests were asked how *mizuko kuyō* should be performed, the Nichiren priests advised that clients go to specialists in *mizuko kuyō*, rather than to their parish temples, whether the specialist be an ordained Buddhist priest or a spiritualist. In any case, they should also come to the home temple and pray at its installation for those without relations to ritualize them, asking those souls to welcome *mizuko* among them. This formulation construes *mizuko* as one subtype of those "without relations" (*muen*), but seems also to imply that parish priests and their temples should not deign to perform these rites. Clients should perform *kuyō* at least three times. The Shingon priest had no distinctive prescription for how to perform *kuyō*, saying merely that clients should pray before the domestic Buddhist altar, make offerings there and to the temple, and occasionally have the priests pray for them, also going on regular grave visits, participating in ancestral memorial rites, and praying for the *mizuko*'s purification. Except for the last item, this bland description, completely devoid of sectarian coloration, would also serve as a reasonable answer to the question, "What are the duties of a Buddhist parishioner?"[27] All these formulations have an ad hoc character strongly suggesting that priests are very much on their own in the struggle to respond to parishioners requesting *mizuko kuyō*, and that they get as much guidance from the tabloids as from their sect headquarters.

That being the case, we should not imagine that unanimity reigns within each sect, but, instead, as the differing responses of the two Nichiren priests above suggest, that there may be wide variety within a single sect, and that there may be little communication even among priests of the same sect in the same town. An example of two Sōtō priests in the town of Yukuhashi, described at length in chapter 5, makes this clear. It is also fair to conclude that the shared Tendai origins of Morita Guyō and Miura Dōmyō seem to have affected their practice of *mizuko kuyō* very little.

A final example of sectarian variety comes from the Rinzai sect of Zen. The Myōshinji subsect of Rinzai published a survey of its priests' views on karma in 1989 that included useful information on their practice of *mizuko kuyō*. First, it was determined that 33 percent of the subsect's 443 survey respondents practice *mizuko kuyō*, while most do not, a finding even lower than those of national surveys discussed in chapter 2, and lower than this study's findings in its four field sites. Some of the priests elaborated on their responses, saying variously that they perform it only upon request (i.e., they do not specialize in it or advertise it), that the laypeople concerned should perform rites without priestly mediation, and that *mizuko* do not really cause spirit attacks, because their souls are originally pure and innocent. By contrast, their erstwhile parents should repent for their evil deeds.[28] These responses are so much at cross-purposes that it appears that this subsect has not even clarified which of the issues raised by *mizuko kuyō* it is most important to address. This inconsistency is probably more the rule than the exception.

Conclusion

This chapter has shown how spiritualists promote *mizuko kuyō*, adopting fetocentric ideology that is frequently misogynist, and often targeting people in their fifties and older. Clients seem to seek in ritual a way to resolve their feelings once and for all. By contrast, spiritualists seek to adapt *mizuko kuyō* so that it is not a one-time-only, cash transaction, but instead the occasion for a long-lasting, multifaceted relationship between themselves, their temples, and the clients. Where the spiritualists succeed, they are sometimes able to regularize their followings and their incomes based on rites that may begin with *mizuko kuyō* but include many others as well. In the next chapter, we examine *mizuko kuyō* in the parish temples of four locales, showing how an ideology actively promoted by spiritualists is becoming institutionalized in Japanese religions.

Several themes we encountered earlier are repeated here. It is clear, for example, that Japan's premodern history of abortion and infanticide have been mythologized in the thought of contemporary spiritualists such as Morita Guyō. Characterizing premodern life as having moral purity and material impoverishment sets the stage for an "economic hardship" justification of abortion, provided that regret and repentance are in evidence. In contrast with this recognition of economic hardship, one crucial element of contemporary Japan's "common sense" about abortion, the Callous Man, is absent. In his place is a heightened demonization of female sexuality, especially the sexuality of young women, and a readiness to blame them exclusively for all their own problems, and everyone else's as well, in rhetoric of menopausal and ghostly symptomology familiar to us from its appearance in the tabloids. Finally, in the shadowy presence in Bentenshū of fascist icon Sasagawa Ryōichi, we see a persistent association of the misogyny of abortion opposition and *mizuko kuyō* with the more antediluvian and unreconstructed elements of Japan's right wing.

In contrast with spiritualists, the Buddhist priesthood as a whole has been passive and reactive, receiving no guidance from sectarian headquarters except in the case of Jōdo Shinshū, and depending upon the spiritualists and the tabloids as a result. Only the Jōdo sect, from which Saint Yūten came, has a firm premodern precedent for *mizuko kuyō,* and of course no sect has a canonical warrant. That being the case, parish priests rely upon their own resources in dealing with parishioners who request these rites, and it is little wonder that their responses are so varied and lacking in intellectual sophistication. This may be the price of remaining uninvolved in ethical debate for the sake of preserving Olympian remove, along with being overtaken by the more aggressive entrepreneurship of spiritualists.

CHAPTER 5

Mizuko Kuyō in Four Locales

The purpose of this chapter is to examine the practice of *mizuko kuyō* in four distinct areas of Japan in order to discover significant regional differences. Patterns of sectarian variation in the practice of *mizuko kuyō* by Buddhist temples are discussed in the appendix. This chapter mainly focuses on Buddhist parish temples, but it also discusses *mizuko kuyō* in Shintō shrines, and in Shugendō temples (which are generally affiliated with but not identical in their practice to Shingon or Tendai Buddhist temples). In this chapter, we examine parish temples that have recently come to practice *mizuko kuyō* in addition to an annual liturgical calendar mainly revolving around funerals, ancestral memorials, and such sect-specific observances as the anniversary of the sect founder's death. In these temples, and also in shrines and Shugendō establishments, the inception of *mizuko kuyō,* a new practice lacking canonical warrant and colored by faddish, unsavory associations with tabloid publicity and abortion, represents the culmination of a decision-making process, the nature of which differs in each locale. In these religious institutions, we can see the character of older men's and women's involvement in *mizuko kuyō,* people whose experience of abortion is much less recent than the younger women to whom the tabloids are mainly addressed, and who figure prominently among the clients of spiritualists. It is not that younger women are absent as clients for *mizuko kuyō* at parish temples, but they usually come as outsiders. In contrast, older women (and men) tend to prevail on their usual parish temples not only to perform a single memorial service, but also to make such memorials part of the ongoing, routine ritual of the temple. The

ritual then becomes so embedded in the temple's practices that all parishioners are asked to pay for the construction of statues and other ritual equipment dedicated to *mizuko kuyō,* regardless of their experience
of abortion—or lack of it.

That ordinary parish temples, Shintō shrines, and Shugendō temples
should, since 1975, have commenced *mizuko kuyō* at all is remarkable,
given the inherent conservatism of Japanese religious institutions. As
we will see, the practice has in fact met with considerable resistance and
opposition, especially from the Jōdo Shinshū sect, Japan's largest sect of
Buddhism. Almost nowhere, it would seem, has the acceptance of *mizuko kuyō* been straightforward or unproblematic, nor can we take it as
a given that, once established, *mizuko kuyō* will be performed in perpetuity. As we shall see, the experience of some communities with *mizuko
kuyō* has so soured them that local people vow to wash their hands of the
whole business. There, it seems likely that the statues erected at such
expense, and, undoubtedly, after long discussion and difficult decisions,
may be turned over to other uses before long. While we can see in these
four field sites that religious concerns originally voiced by women have
found widespread institutional expression, it may be that future generations of both sexes will produce a different ritualization of sexual and
reproductive experience, one not necessarily driven by a fear of fetal
spirit attacks, and that the *mizuko kuyō* installations we see in religious
institutions now may bear different labels twenty years from now.

Description, Goals, and Methods of the Field Study

I carried out the field study at each site as follows. First, I
obtained a listing of the temples in each locale from national temple directories. I cross-checked this list with the telephone directory.[1] I placed
a telephone call to each temple to determine whether it offers *mizuko
kuyō* and to what sect it is affiliated. In most cases the person answering
the call was the wife or mother of the resident priest. She was usually
willing to answer further queries, such as whether *mizuko kuyō* is offered to nonparishioners as well as parishioners and with what frequency it is performed. In cases where the particular temple does *not*
perform *mizuko kuyō,* the woman would frequently volunteer information about what local temples *do* perform it. Having called all the

temples, I could calculate what proportion of a locale's temples offer *mizuko kuyō* and with what sectarian distribution. On that basis, and on the basis of the receptivity (or lack of it) to the telephone inquiry, I selected six to seven temples in each area for on-site observation. I traveled with a research assistant to each of these temples, documenting the nature of *mizuko kuyō* practice at each one. I documented the physical facilities of the practice with sketches and photographs. In many cases, priests, worshippers and *mizuko kuyō,* clients were present, and my contact with them taught me something about participants' motivation and orientation. Following observation at each of the four sites, I visited temples and shrines in larger adjacent cities in order to sample variations on *mizuko kuyō* available to residents of the four field site areas within two hours by train travel.

The physical facilities for *mizuko kuyō* at many temples make it possible to calculate the nature and extent of religious activity. For example, a common devotional practice is to have the temple priest write a *sotoba* (or *tōba*) for the souls of the clients' *mizuko.* This device derives from the Indian stupa and is used elsewhere in Japanese religious life as a memorialization of the ancestors. People place a thin stick of wood (available in a variety of sizes and prices) before the family grave at the spring and autumn equinoxes and at the summer festival, *obon.* The field study was carried out during the *obon* season, meaning that many new *tōba* had recently been placed at the *mizuko kuyō* facility. The *tōba* are inscribed with phrases, which differ by sect, expressing hope for the *mizuko*'s salvation. The devotee's name is also inscribed, which made it possible for me to calculate the distribution by sex of clients for *mizuko kuyō.* In some cases, the dedication of *tōba* was done not only by individuals, but also by stem-family groups, such as "for the *mizuko* of the Tanaka *ie,*" by groups of unrelated persons, such as a corporation, and by the women's group of the particular temple.

Tōba are typically placed before a statue of Jizō or Kannon. In such a case, the facility as a whole then consists of the statue, a fountain of water to pour over the statue (*aka mizu*), a rack for *tōba,* sometimes a rack for devotional candles, an incense box, and usually an offering box. In some cases, the statue, the fountain, and the racks bear further inscriptions of the date of their dedication and the names of those who gave money for their construction and installation. The recorded names yield further information about the breakdown by sex and family groupings of persons supporting *mizuko kuyō.* In most temples observed in this study, the number of *tōba* placed before a *mizuko kuyō* statue of Jizō or Kannon numbered 100 or fewer, and it was thus feasible to record the details of their dedication. In some cases, however, there might be several hundred, or their placement might be inaccessible, in which case precise calculation was impossible.

Another type of physical facility for *mizuko kuyō,* sometimes seen in combination with that just described, is an installation of stone or metal statues of Jizō or Kannon, each inscribed with the donors' names. These again make it possible to determine the distribution of patronage of *mizuko kuyō* by sex and groupings of people. A large-scale facility of this type may have a thousand statues or more, and in such cases the limitations of the study's resources of money and time did not allow for precise calculations. Far more common, however, is a grouping of 100 statues or fewer. In those cases, the desired calculation could be made, except when statues were placed such that the dedicatory inscription was obscured by a row of statues in front of or behind the one being examined.

At each temple I visited, the placement of the *mizuko kuyō* facility within the larger precincts was identified as reflecting the relation of *mizuko* spirits to the Buddha(s) and Buddhist deities enshrined in the main hall, on the one hand, and to the ancestral spirits identified with gravesites, on the other. In all cases, I observed a clear spatial separation between the main hall and the graveyard. Although, in the abstract, the *mizuko* would appear to be a subtype of the dead, the consistent location of *mizuko kuyō* facilities apart from the graveyard indicates that they are conceptualized differently from the ancestors. Similarly, the spatial disjunction of *mizuko* from Buddhas and Bodhisattvas indicates another distinctive conceptualization. I observed a variety of spatial arrangements, as Plans 2 through 7 illustrate.

Choice of Field Sites

Previous studies of *mizuko kuyō* have neither noticed the local variation nor treated the practice as arising from the history and social relations of a specific locale. By contrast, this study takes regional variation as one subject of inquiry and interprets *mizuko kuyō* as requiring both local and macro levels of explanation.

Mizuko kuyō shows considerable regional variation in the timing of its inception, the proportion of the total number of local temples that

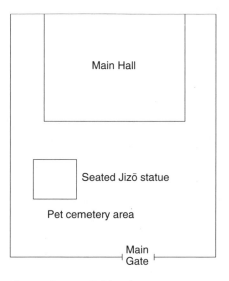

Plan 2. Ryūgenji (Tōno)

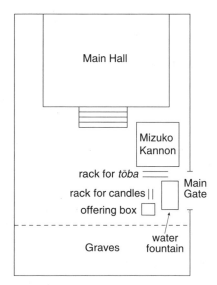

Plan 3. Chōanji (Tsuyama)

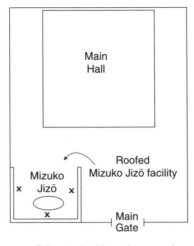

Graves located outside and behind the temple precincts

Main Hall

Roofed Mizuko Jizō facility

Mizuko Jizō

x: *Tōba* stacked in racks around three walls; over 1,000 total

Plan 4. Hōsenji (Yukuhashi)

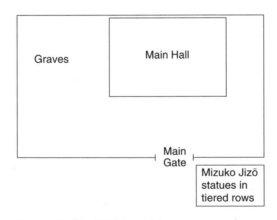

Graves

Main Hall

Main Gate

Mizuko Jizō statues in tiered rows

Plan 5. Saifukuji (Yukuhashi)

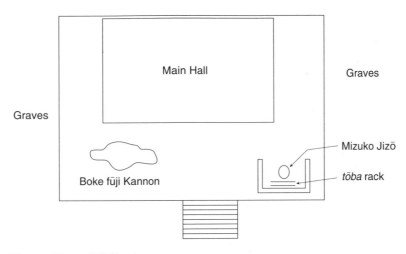

Plan 6. Myōonji (Miura)

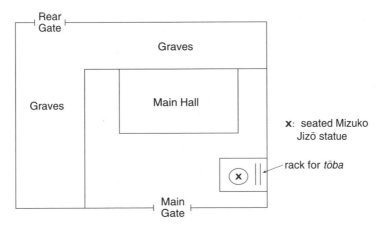

Plan 7. Honzuiji (Miura)

perform it, its sectarian distribution, the proportion of participation by men and stem-family groups, the age of participants, and the relation of participants to the sponsoring institution and its surrounding community. In some areas, *mizuko kuyō* was instituted in the 1970s, while in others it did not appear until the mid- or late 1980s. Some areas show a skewed distribution of temples offering *mizuko kuyō* by sect, while others do not. In some areas or particular temples, it is common to find only individuals as sponsors of *mizuko kuyō*, while in other areas stem-family groups are much more prominent. In some places, people in middle age or older are the chief clients, far overshadowing younger persons. Men are hardly found as sponsors at all in some places, while in others they may far outnumber women. In some cases, *mizuko kuyō* becomes the basis for an ongoing relation between the temple and the individual requesting these rites, while in others the sponsor is never seen again. Sometimes the sponsor has recently experienced abortion, while in others the sponsor or sponsoring group has either no personal experience of abortion, or several decades have passed between an experience of miscarriage, stillbirth, abortion, or a child's death and performance of *mizuko kuyō*.

I chose this study's four field sites with the following considerations in mind. First, most previously published studies of *mizuko kuyō*, insofar as they have any ethnographic basis, are based principally upon observation of temples in and around metropolitan Tokyo. This study identifies four sites representing different areas of Japan outside large, metropolitan areas. A second consideration was whether the character of religious life in and the history of the area prior to the inception of *mizuko kuyō* are well documented, making it possible to determine how *mizuko kuyō* relates to the area's traditional religious practice, and to gauge the degree of change brought about by its inception. All four sites have been the object of study in the past. See Map 1. Tsuyama and Tōno have been the object of classic works; Yanagita Kunio's *Tōno monogatari* is a founding text of Japanese folklore. *Mimasaka no minzoku* by Yanagita's student Wakamori Tarō covers Tsuyama's folkloric history and is, if anything, more thorough than Yanagita's work. *Tōno monogatari* spawned a number of subsequent works on the traditions of Tōno. It is thus possible to determine with certainty whether any basis for *mizuko kuyō* existed in Tōno's recent history, and to gauge the extent of religious change. Miura's and Yukuhashi's religious histories have not been as extensively documented as those of the other two sites, but accounts in local and prefectural histories, as well as other works, are available. A search for a variety of historical sources revealed no trace of traditional religious practices resembling *mizuko kuyō* in any of these sites. In none of them does it predate the 1970s.

Besides representing four distinct geographical areas, I chose sites as representing different historical patterns of settlement. Tōno is a fairly remote, mountainous area, in which agriculture, stoneworking, and forestry provide major forms of subsistence. Yukuhashi has become in-

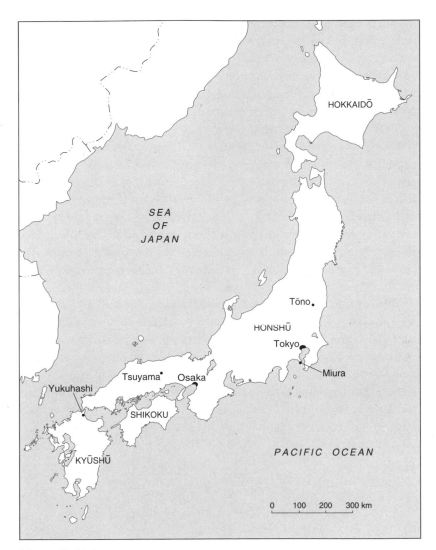

Map 1. Field sites

dustrialized in the twentieth century, and in the vicinity there are major chemical, petroleum refining, and steel manufacturing industries whose national center is the nearby city Kokura. These industries coexist with agriculture and coastal fishing on a small scale. Because Kokura, a major port and industrial center, is located twenty minutes by express train from Yukuhashi, it is quite feasible to commute there for employment from Yukuhashi. Like Yukuhashi, Miura is located within commuting distance of two major cities, Yokohama and Yokosuka. The commuting population in this case, however, represents not so much the influx of rural people to the city as people spilling over from metropolitan areas in search of affordable housing. Those who have resided longest in Miura work in agriculture (more truck gardening than paddy fields), coastal fishing, and more recently, tourism.

Tsuyama is a former castle town, meaning that during the Edo period a *daimyō* resided in the local castle and administered the domain from that site. Typical of the religious organization of castle towns is the requirement for each Buddhist sect to construct temples there, creating within the town a "temple district" (*tera machi*), where a large number of temples have been built in a very concentrated area. Tsuyama's history as a castle town means that it shows a wider distribution of sects than the other three sites, where more skewed patterns are found. Rice agriculture, service industries, and tile manufacturing provide Tsuyama's contemporary economic base.

While these four sites are sufficiently representative of distinctive geographical areas to suggest the extent of variation in *mizuko kuyō,* they should not be taken as comprehensive in sum. Economic resources permitted research at only four sites, but each one yielded such strikingly new forms of ritual and varied patterns of sectarian involvement that there is every reason to believe that more sites would have revealed even more variation. This study can at best point the way for more comprehensive studies, ideally undertaken by a team of researchers, to document *mizuko kuyō* more completely.

Local- and Macro-Level Interpretations

The fact that *mizuko kuyō* did not exist in an institutionalized, commoditized form before the 1970s means that its adoption constitutes a break with traditional temple practice, which had to be overcome—at the local level—temple by temple. Given the inherent conservatism of religious institutions, initiating a new practice requiring substantial cash outlay would undoubtedly necessitate marshaling strong reasons in favor of the change, reasons sufficient to convince parishioners to commit resources. In many cases, the initial proposal to commence *mizuko kuyō* at a certain temple has originated not with its priest and parishioners, but with local stonemasonry firms or an advertising campaign by merchants of Buddhist statuary, approaching a temple with a proposal for constructing an installation for *mizuko kuyō*. In such a case, a temple may end up erecting a *mizuko kuyō* facility even though the parishioners have not shown any particular desire for one, simply in the hope of generating revenue for the temple. Either the priest or lay leaders called *sōdai* may be the main force calling for the new practice. The initiation of *mizuko kuyō* at a particular temple may also originate in a contract for the temple to perform rites on behalf of a gynecological clinic or hospital on a regular basis for aborted fetuses and the souls of animals used in experiments. In other cases, a temple may first provide mausoleum services for abortion remains, later offering *mizuko kuyō* as an outgrowth of the original disposal service. More straightforwardly, the temple priest may seek to increase income from *kitō* or *kuyō* rites of all kinds, and thus institute *mizuko kuyō* as one of several types of ritual offered by the temple, sometimes making these known through advertising in the telephone directory or by direct mail advertising campaigns. In all these cases, the association of *mizuko kuyō* with abortion is muted, and the practice may come into being without a strong basis in parishioners' religious beliefs concerning *mizuko*.

Why would an area with millennia of religious history suddenly in the 1970s or 1980s adopt—across sectarian boundaries—a practice previously unknown there? This is a question that finds only a partial answer in terms of the postwar rise in abortion or the generally declining levels of economic support for Buddhist temples. These macro-level factors cannot, one could argue, come into play unless and until particular religious institutions decide to allocate some proportion of their resources to the construction of expensive facilities. Probably the majority of Buddhist temples in the country do *not* perform *mizuko kuyō* and in many cases have made decisions *not* to erect costly facilities. Their decision to remain aloof from *mizuko kuyō*, as this study will show, may be based on the following reasons:

1. a clearly stated policy of sectarian opposition to *mizuko kuyō* in Jōdo Shinshū, the largest sect of Japanese Buddhism;
2. dislike of the practice by priest or parishioners, based on any of the following beliefs:
    a. *mizuko* are a fabricated superstition having no actual existence;
    b. *mizuko kuyō* represents an exploitative practice improper to genuine religionists;
    c. *mizuko kuyō* represents a cheap vulgarization of Buddhist practice and lacks any legitimacy;

d. temples should not allow themselves to be used for the provision of cheap, emotional pap for those who have committed abortion without ever considering its real significance;

3. unwillingness or inability to commit the funds for construction of the facilities;

4. fear that straightforward promotion of *mizuko kuyō* will cause local people to identify the temple with that single practice, leading to the temple's disparagement in the community as cheap, money-grubbing, and willing to participate in a practice marginalized and stigmatized by more "proper" temples.

Local Trends in *Mizuko Kuyō*

Of 157 institutions surveyed in this study, 69 (or 44 percent) perform *mizuko kuyō*, while 72 (or 46 percent) clearly do not, and the remaining 16 (or 10 percent) have no clear policy, as Table 17 shows (of these 157 institutions, 148 were Buddhist temples). This finding accords closely with those of the national surveys discussed in chapter 2, which found that 43 percent of the temples surveyed across the country perform *mizuko kuyō*. These overall averages are closely approximated by the statistics for Tsuyama, Yukuhashi, and Miura, in spite of their differing patterns of temple distribution by sect. Tōno's performance, as noted above, is unusually high. These figures suggest that some factors transcend sectarian differences and call for explanation in terms of the circumstances specific to the separate locales. Since Tōno is the exception to the overall average, let us examine it first.

Tōno

Tōno, where there are *kappa* under every bridge and *kami* in every tree, and where anyone over sixty can recite at least a hundred folktales from memory. The name Tōno evokes an image of the great founder of Japanese folklore studies, Yanagita Kunio (1875–1962), traveling through the wooded hills and hand-tilled paddies on a borrowed horse to interview elderly storytellers and document the spirits of the crossroads in 1908 and 1909, or furiously copying down the area's folktales as they spilled by the hundreds from the lips of his main

Table 17. *Performance of* mizuko kuyō, *by field site*
(includes temples, shrines, new religions, and Shugendō sites)

	Tsuyama	Yukuhashi	Miura	Tōno	Overall
Number of institutions surveyed	57	52	37	11	157
Performs *mizuko kuyō*	25 (44%)	22 (42%)	15 (40%)	7 (64%)	69 (44%)
Does not perform *mizuko kuyō*	26 (46%)	27 (52%)	18 (49%)	1 (9%)	72 (46%)
Policy unclear	6 (10%)	3 (6%)	4 (11%)	3 (27%)	16 (10%)

informant, Sasaki Kiyoshi.[2] *Tōno monogatari* (Tales of Tōno), the book Yanagita first published in 1910, a collection of area tales, songs, and folk traditions, is widely regarded as a distillation of the traditional communal folk ways of a Japan not yet sullied by industrialization, a Japan whose spiritual life was more concerned with the doings of *kami* than with the "real world." Tōno conjures up a rural hamlet captured in amber, a living museum of a simpler time, much as if Berea, Kentucky, or some remote Appalachian hamlet of 1910 could be imagined without rickets and pellagra, a happy Sleepy Hollow. Tōno's population in the summer of 1994 was 7,326.

The urge to pop this roseate balloon, this impossibly pretty picture, is irresistible, of course, and Yanagita's romanticism has spawned numerous studies identifying all of Tōno's failings. Here, too, infanticide was rife in the Edo period, it is claimed, and the poor sold their daughters into prostitution and abandoned the old to die during famines. Untouched by modern history? What about the "Hawaiian Village" theme park and health spa? What about the new bus service and tourist courses, to say nothing of all the trucks and cars Tōno people now own? And the town museum is nothing more than a self-serving monument to the place's pretense of purity.[3] Purists predictably rebut the cynics in defense of Tōno's reputation.[4] The heated exchange contests Tōno's image as the nation's quintessential *furusato,* or "old homeplace."

There is no indication in Yanagita's work of any parallel to *mizuko kuyō.* There are scattered references to the spirits of children, water spirits, and child deities, but the following story seems to be the only item that could possibly provide any basis in local thought for the acceptance of contemporary ideas about *mizuko*. Although Yanagita includes the word in the title, "Thoughts on *Mizuko*," the story itself does not use the term, and *mizuko* does not appear as an entry in Yanagita's lexicon of Tōno, titled *Tōno monogatari shūi*.

This is a story I heard directly from the wife of a friend of Sasaki. This woman's first labor was so difficult that she was about to die. She, herself, however, was filled with the feeling that she was going someplace in a great hurry. As she was hastening along a road, she entered a vast, bright room. She was about to pass into the next room, so she threw open the sliding doors. Just then, the room filled with innumerable babies all around her, preventing her from going forward. When she tried to return the way she had come, however, the babies immediately made way. She went back and forth like this several times, until she heard someone calling her name. Then she returned the way she had come. When she regained consciousness, she was being held by a neighbor, and everyone was making a great uproar around her.[5]

This story recounts one woman's vision of the passage to the world of the dead. The spirits of babies appear in order to prevent her death in childbirth and to return her to the land of the living, where she eventually gives birth. The story seems to presuppose an existence in limbo for the spirits of babies, but there is no association with abortion. If this narrative vaguely supports the *mizuko* notion, however, another Tōno tradition leads in a different direction. Recorded as item 245 in Yanagita's lexicon, the local explanation of the vernacular term for rebirth, *umarekawari*, is as follows: "They say that it is common for people to be reborn. Last year in Kamigō Village a child was born with a closed fist. When the hand did not open for a long time, the family forced it open, and what should they find but a scrap of paper saying that this child was the reborn old man Tajiri Tarō of Kami-kita. When the Tajiri family heard about it, they said that old Tarō had died less than a year before, and they were delighted that he had been reborn so soon."[6] Whereas the contemporary *mizuko* idea presupposes the existence of myriad fetal spirits anxiously awaiting birth, this older story merely suggests that the dead are speedily reborn, leaving no cause for worry in the human world. It might be possible to reconcile these notions, but there is no precedent here for the idea of vengeful fetal spirits. We can conclude that the basis in earlier folk traditions of the Tōno area to support contemporary *mizuko kuyō* is thin at best, virtually nonexistent.

There are eleven temples presently operating in Tōno, of which seven perform *mizuko kuyō*.[7] See Map 2. Three of these seven show no sign of

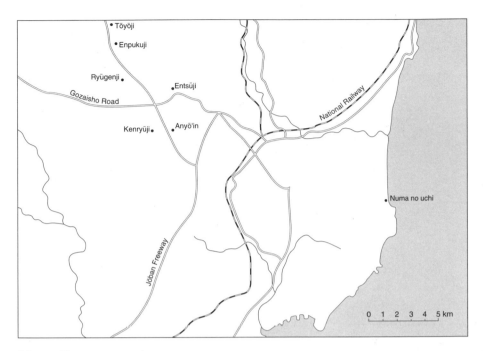

Map 2. Tōno area temples

any devotional activity. All three belong to the Shingon sect; two of them, Anyō'in and Ryūgenji, have a recognizable *mizuko kuyō* installation, with a statue of Jizō. The third temple, Tōyōji, affirms that rites are available, but there is no installation in the precincts.

In the two temples showing no recent activity, the oldest inscription for any of the statuary is at Anyō'in, dated 1976, having been dedicated by twenty named individuals, of whom four are women. The inscription lists a monetary amount by each name. It is reasonable to regard the twenty names as those people representing the parishioner households (*ie*) of the temple, who have contributed to the statue-building project by *ie*-units. The women are probably widowed heads-of-household who are named for that reason, rather than because they (or any of the men, for that matter) have any personal experience of *mizuko*. While it is possible that there may have been cultic activity at Anyō'in's *mizuko kuyō* facility at some time between 1976 and 1994, it would seem to have died out entirely by late 1994.

The situation at Ryūgenji indicates, if anything, an even shallower base of support for *mizuko kuyō* (see Plan 2). Ryūgenji's unattended

Figure 13. *Mizuko kuyō* installation of Ryūgenji (Tōno)

statue of Jizō is located in line with a small area dedicated to *kuyō* for deceased animal pets. See Figure 13. Its dedicatory inscription lists the donors for the statue as one male stonemason and one stonemasonry firm. The question naturally occurring to anyone visiting Ryūgenji is, "Why has the temple put up this statue if no one is interested in attending it?" Because we observed Ryūgenji shortly after the *obon* season, there was a greater likelihood at that time of the year than at any other that offerings and *tōba* would be placed before the statue. Their complete absence indicates that *mizuko kuyō* exists at Ryūgenji in name only. As an active practice it either never existed, or it died out in less than twenty years.

There is an intimate connection in Tōno between stoneworking and the installation of *mizuko kuyō* facilities in the temples of the area. The area is dotted with small firms providing stone for construction purposes, for use in gardens, and for carving a variety of religious statuary, including the Jizō and Kannon statues used in *mizuko kuyō*. Stonemasonry is a major industry of the area, and it probably provides employment to some of the families who are parishioners of Tōno temples.

It would be difficult for a temple to resist an appeal from parishioners involved in stoneworking to erect a *mizuko kuyō* facility, especially if, as at Ryūgenji, the stoneworkers or their companies donated the statue outright. Alternatively, it would be most welcome to stoneworker-parishioners to receive a priest's request to construct such a statue on the understanding, as seems to have been the case at Anyō'in, that parishioners would contribute to the project by household units. Either way, whether the initiative originated with a priest or stoneworker-parishioners, it could proceed with or without a sudden reorientation of the religious lives of any of the parties. The present desertion of the facilities indicates that no such reorientation has occurred.

The hypothesis that *mizuko kuyō* as it exists in Tōno today may have originated to a large extent with area stoneworkers finds confirmation at a coastal site located about twenty minutes from Tōno by car, called Numa no Uchi Sainokawara, or the Sainokawara of Numa no Uchi. Numa no Uchi is a small harbor for coastal fishing boats. On the south side of the harbor are two caves facing the beach. One of these, the area's original ritual site, is now in disuse. It extends about twenty meters into the hillside, with only one opening facing the sea. During the Edo period it was used as a Sainokawara, or symbolic replica of that part of the afterworld inhabited by the souls of dead children, the miscarried, aborted, and stillborn, and protected by Jizō. People, especially the mothers or would-be mothers of these "children," would go to the cave and pile up stones in a five-story pagoda. This private, devotional act was performed entirely without priestly mediation and expressed the hope that the souls of the "children" would be carried out to sea with the tide to the other world, later to be reborn in this one. A statue of Jizō had been installed in the cave at some point, but no one knows exactly when, or when this cave fell into disuse. The symbolism of the site was recently destroyed entirely by the placement between the caves and the sea of a retaining wall of concrete blocks to prevent beach erosion.

The second cave has newly been outfitted as a *mizuko kuyō* site. See Figure 14. It differs from the original site in that in addition to an opening on the ocean side, it also has a small opening on the landward side. It would have been disqualified as a ritual site in premodern times, when the symbolism depended on the idea that the tide would carry the souls *away*, out to sea. An opening toward the land leaves open the possibility that those souls would continue to linger among the living, exactly the opposite of the desired effect of the informal rites carried out in the original cave.

Figure 14. *Mizuko kuyō* installation at the new cave (Numa no Uchi Sainokawara)

A stone stele records how this second cave was transformed into a *mizuko kuyō* site:

This place originated hundreds of years ago as a Sainokawara, a sacred place to pacify and comfort the souls of *mizuko* and young children. In 1985, the president of Fukushima Stoneworks [Fukushima Sekizai], Takahagi Katsushige, came here, saying that he wished to set up a new, great sacred site for *mizuko kuyō*. At his own expense and through his own resources, he constructed this dignified sacred place. It has contributed greatly to the development of Numa no Uchi, as is widely known.

This stele has been erected to inform future generations of his great contribution.

June 1985   Numa no Uchi Ward

Local people interviewed during observation at Numa no Uchi relate the events leading up to the opening of the new cave as a *mizuko kuyō* site rather differently. Around 1980, through a deal struck between the mayor of Numa no Uchi and the president of Fukushima Stoneworks, the Jizō statue was moved from the original cave to the new one, and local people were encouraged to pile up stones in groups of five there, like the old practice. A piece of land adjacent to the cave's land-ward entrance was paved over to make a parking lot, and local tour companies were encouraged to put Numa no Uchi on their routes of local tourist sites. The mayor then prevailed upon every household in Numa no Uchi to contribute ¥30,000 (about U.S.$300) to erect smaller Jizō statues to accompany the large Jizō from the old cave. The mayor accompanied his request with a special incentive—any household fail-ing to contribute to the project would henceforth be branded "misers" (*ketchi*), so virtually everybody coughed up in the end. Adding insult to injury, it was specified that only statuary constructed by Fukushima Stoneworks could be placed in the cave. Thus the total expense to the president of Fukushima Stoneworks was whatever it cost to move the old statue to the new cave and to pave the parking lot (about 100 square meters). The rest of the cost of the site's construction was borne—un-der duress, according to one elderly fisherman—entirely by local people.

Also, according to this informant, local people became so disgrun-tled with the whole idea of *mizuko kuyō* as a result of this experience that none of them participate any longer. They also fear that they may be subject to spirit attacks (*tatari*) from the spirits of the old cave for disrupting it to build the new one. In fact, when the president of Fuku-shima Stoneworks died, his death was widely attributed to the *tatari* of the *mizuko*. As if all this were not enough, the tourism to Numa no Uchi that has resulted from building the new site has been minimal and yields virtually no income to the area. Parking is free, and the only place in the vicinity to buy anything is a bait shop. It is widely believed that the only people benefiting from the venture were the deceased presi-dent of Fukushima Stoneworks and the mayor, who is thought to have received a hefty kickback on the smaller Jizō statues.

The example of this site makes clear that it is possible to plan and ex-ecute the construction of a *mizuko kuyō* site without regard to the reli-gious sentiments of those called upon to finance and generally support the project, purely as a scheme to enhance revenue. The site remains, however, after the original economic transaction, more or less unre-lated to the religious lives of local people. As one person interviewed at Numa no Uchi put it, the site only survives now through the attentions of sentimental, middle-aged housewives trucked in from someplace else by the bus companies.

In response to his remarks, one woman so trucked in spoke up. She had overheard him discussing the fabricated nature of the site and said, "History is a constructed thing anyway" (*rekishi wa tsukuru mon da-*

kara). Her implication was that the artificiality of the site was in no way an obstacle to her devotion. So saying, she disappeared into the cave to place incense before each of the statues erected at such expense and with such reluctance by local people. In other words, she values the emotions and activities of her devotions for *mizuko* in and of themselves and rejects the idea that these are at all undermined by the facts of the site's origins.

This interchange encapsulated something essential about the nature of *mizuko kuyō*. Many of the people involved in it do not do so by choice. They find their temples or their towns promoting it and themselves called upon to support the practice on the basis of their membership in relevant groups, not on the basis of religious conviction. The practice's recency and obviously fabricated nature invalidate it in the eyes of many, though they are not in a position to tear down statues once they have been consecrated. In many places, therefore, *mizuko kuyō* persists with virtually no local support. Instead, Japan's wonderful transportation system of highways, trains, buses, taxis, and private cars delivers outsiders even to such remote places as Numa no Uchi and the temples of Tōno. Those outsider pilgrims may choose to perform *mizuko kuyō* there precisely *because* the area is so remote, and there is such a small chance that their participation in *mizuko kuyō* will ever become known to the members of their family or home communities. By ignoring the origins of any particular *mizuko kuyō* site, these outsider pilgrims are able to concentrate on their own beliefs and feelings about *mizuko,* and to see their religious devotion as pure and sincere.

Tsuyama

Mizuko kuyō in Tsuyama is found in Buddhist temples, a Shintō shrine, and a Shugendō temple. Tsuyama is also the location of Jionji, discussed in detail in chapter 4, operated by priest-spiritualist Morita Guyō. Tsuyama thus shows more ritual variation in the performance of *mizuko kuyō* than any other site. Its population in 1994 was 89,572.

The folk life of Tsuyama up to the 1970s offered little in the way of traditions onto which *mizuko kuyō* could easily be grafted. The town itself is located in a small, low-lying plain of rice fields. This plain is ringed with mountains, several of which are major sites of western Japan's Shugendō, such as Hōki Taisen in Tottori Prefecture and Ushiroyama in eastern Okayama. The headquarters of one of the smaller

Shugendō sects, Kojima Goryūshugen, is located in southern Okayama. Shugendō and associated beliefs about mountains thus influence Tsuyama strongly. The area's folk religion is characterized by notable cults of fox possession and belief in an imaginary possessing spirit called *tobyō,* which is something like a snake with legs. Tendai and Shingon are the strongest sects of Buddhism there. Among the new religions, the Shintō group Kurozumikyō (founded in 1814) is deeply entrenched in pockets of the area, which in the early nineteenth century gave rise to important disciples of the founder Kurozumi Munetada. But with the exception of Kurozumikyō, no other new religions show significant strength there, nor does Christianity, though it was an important social movement here in the early Meiji period.[8]

The practice of *mizuko kuyō* in Tsuyama seems to be directly affected by the location of religious institutions. See Map 3. The shrine and temples located outside the temple district are "free" to perform *mizuko kuyō* in novel ways and on a large scale. By contrast, temples within the temple district show much greater conformity in such matters as the placement of their *mizuko kuyō* statuary (to the right of the entrance to the main hall, away from graves, regardless of the sect) and type of ritual (*tōba* placement in all cases). The proximity of temples in the temple district creates a possibility for mutual monitoring that does not exist where temples are not so densely situated.

My telephone survey revealed that within the temple district, there is a significant group of temples (nine) that will perform *mizuko kuyō* only for their parishioners. An equal number of temples said that they will perform rites on request for parishioners and nonparishioners. One temple-district temple reported that *mizuko kuyō* is performed there for both parishioners and nonparishioners, and also that most of its *mizuko kuyō* clients come from outside Tsuyama. One temple performs *mizuko kuyō* in fulfillment of a contract it maintains with a local hospital to perform rites for abortion and stillbirth remains.

A number of responses to the telephone survey suggested that temples view *mizuko kuyō* critically. Four respondents said that their temple does not perform *mizuko kuyō,* because the priest dislikes it. Another admitted that the rites are performed, but qualified that information by saying, "But we are not *mizuko kuyō* professionals." Similarly, one respondent quickly added, "But we don't do it for profit." Several temples said that they do not offer *mizuko kuyō,* but they refer requests for it to one of two temple-district temples offering the rites—Chōanji (Sōtō) or Aizenji (Shingon). See Figure 15.

Chōanji and Aizenji are not the only temple-district temples where

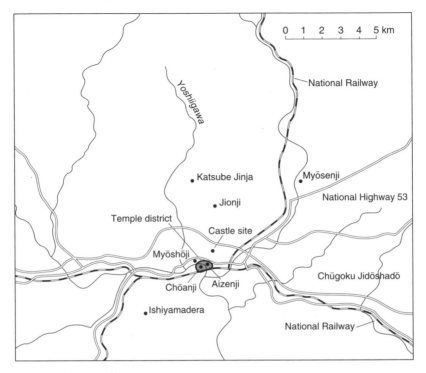

Map 3. Tsuyama City

mizuko kuyō is performed, but they share an important element: they have both hung out signs advertising *mizuko kuyō*. Several telephone respondents from other temples commented on these signs negatively, as if to say, "The very idea—imagine hanging out a shingle." The signs themselves are small wooden plaques by the front gate, visually unobtrusive. It is the association of the signs with advertising, rather than their appearance, which local people find inappropriate to a "proper" temple. Their attitude is not unlike that which an old, prestigious firm of attorneys might take to the personal injury lawyers who advertise on television, labeling them "ambulance chasers." The "proper temples" in Tsuyama repeatedly associate the practice of *mizuko kuyō* with the expression *kane-mōke*, "moneygrubbing." Thus, in Tsuyama there is a strong critique of *mizuko kuyō*, probably enhanced by the proximity of temples in the temple district and the atmosphere of mutual surveillance that prevails among these temples as a result.

Mizuko kuyō does not, in fact, appear to provide a major source of revenue for the temples in the temple district. Five temples said they

Figure 15. *Mizuko kuyō* installation, with Kannon statue (Chōanji, Tsuyama)

had never had a request for *mizuko kuyō,* and another five said that they receive fewer than five requests per year. Chōanji, Aizenji (both mentioned above), and Myōshōji (Nichiren) are the temple-district temples that offer *mizuko kuyō* on the largest scale in the district, but altogether their *mizuko kuyō* facilities had only fifteen *tōba* when I visited, some going back at least a year, and nearly all were of small, inexpensive sizes. Aizenji had in addition a grouping of about 150 small statues of Jizō, but as these were only four to six inches in height, it is unlikely that the temple receives abundant revenue from their sale, even in combination with other ritual fees.

Observation at Tsuyama temples, and, indeed, at all four field sites in this survey, revealed significant rates of male participation, a feature of *mizuko kuyō* in provincial areas that is not noted in existing literature. Because *mizuko kuyō* is not organized by anything resembling a membership basis, however, it is difficult to estimate with confidence the rate of male sponsorship. The only available method is to calculate the proportions of male and female names on the statues and *tōba* found at each separate temple's *mizuko kuyō* facility. While there was no realistic alternative to this method for the present survey, in many cases the numbers concerned are so small that they provide only a dubious basis from which to generalize, say, about the nationwide character of the practice. Small though these numbers may be, however, they nevertheless give important indexes of the strength of the cult at a given site and its relative support by each sex.

Analyzing the fifteen *tōba* observed in the temples of Tsuyama's temple district, we note that they have been dedicated by the following categories of persons:

Individual women	6	(40%)
Individual men	4	(27%)
Ie-groups	2	(13%)
Groups of unrelated women	2	(13%)
Anonymous	1	(7%)

We can see that individual women are the most frequent sponsors of *mizuko kuyō*, but individual men are nearly as numerous, followed by groups of unrelated women, the latter a phenomenon restricted to Myō-shōji, a Nichiren temple where the Women's Group had dedicated *tōba*. Myōshōji was also the sole temple in this area where *tōba* for *mizuko* had been dedicated by *ie*-groups.[9] Noting that individual men account for 27 percent of the total, we can assume that men are also represented in the *ie*-groups, and thus conclude that their total representation here may be on the order of 30 percent.

In addition to the temples of the temple district, several other Tsuyama institutions offering *mizuko kuyō* contribute to our understanding of the site's overall pattern. The shrine, the Katsube Jinja, will be dealt with in a later section addressing *mizuko kuyō* at shrines, while Ishiyamadera (Tendai) will be discussed in a section examining *mizuko kuyō* at Shugendō temples. Myōsenji, a Nichiren temple, illustrates the

importance of a temple's location near a major national route of transportation, and it appears to realize significant revenue from *mizuko kuyō*.

Myōsenji is located near the superhighway called the Chūgoku
Jidōshadō, which runs from Osaka to Hiroshima. The Tsuyama exit can
be reached in about two hours from Osaka, making a day trip easily
possible. Myōsenji is located at the area's furthest remove from the
temple district. This temple has its own parishioners, but several facts indicate that other sources of revenue may provide a more significant income. Placed on a hill in an agricultural area, Myōsenji has been able, as
no other nearby temple has been, to rebuild completely in recent years,
including a massive parking lot and long, covered passages leading
through a complex of several buildings.

The temple has a graveyard for its parishioners, but it also performs
a variety of ancestral and *mizuko kuyō* rites for people who come to the
temple by car. According to the priest, many of these ritual sponsors
have no access to their family's temple, so they find it convenient to
have the priest of Myōsenji write a *tōba* and then leave it behind a stone
pillar at the far end of Myōsenji's parking lot. When I visited, between
150 and 200 large, recently dedicated *tōba* had been placed there. This
was the only installation in which *tōba* for ancestors and *mizuko* were
observed to have been placed together.

It would appear that Myōsenji's new prosperity has come through
the entrepreneurship of its energetic priest. Now about forty, he took
over from his father what was then a rather sleepy, remote temple serving a small group of traditional adherents. This priest said that there are
many people who feel the desire to perform rites for deceased parents,
relatives, and *mizuko,* but who are stymied by not being active parishioners in the temple to which their family is affiliated. This loss of connection with the home temple can come about in many ways. The person may have moved away from the area where the temple is, or *never*
lived in proximity to it, therefore lacking any personal history of connection to it. Strife within a family can also contribute to a fragile connection to a temple. Similarly, women who have experienced divorce
may lack any clear status within either the temple of the natal family or
the ex-husband's family. When people in these circumstances feel the
desire to perform ceremonies for their deceased relatives or *mizuko,* they
must seek a temple where being a parishioner is not a prerequisite. This
is where Myōsenji comes in. Knowledge about an obliging temple probably spreads mostly by word of mouth, and the superhighway's proximity makes it possible to draw in clients from as far away as Osaka,

Okayama, Hiroshima, and Shimane, giving Myōsenji a considerably wider catchment area than the temples in the temple district.

Myōsenji's practice of *mizuko kuyō* differs in another significant respect from that of the temples in the temple district. Whereas temple-district temples are concerned with the distinction between offering *mizuko kuyō* to nonparishioners as well as parishioners, it is highly unlikely that any of them would ever offer ancestral rites to nonparishioners, because the rationale for temple performance of those rites is so intimately bound up with the temple's custodianship of graves and the consequent link between parishioner and temple based on the performance of funerals. From the temple's perspective, providing any of these rites presupposes an ongoing relationship in which parishioners contribute to the temple's support over generations. From the parishioners' perspective, supporting the temple on a regular basis means that they can depend on the temple for funeral and ancestral rites whenever the need arises. The standing of the temple and its parishioners is built on this ongoing exchange and also upon the exclusion from it of outsiders. Taking in miscellaneous street traffic in ritual does not enhance the temple's prestige in local society, but instead undermines it, suggesting commercialization and commoditization in a relationship from which these traits should be absent.

Myōsenji offers funeral and ancestral rites to its own parishioners on the customary basis just described. In addition, it offers ritual in the form of writing *tōba* for ancestral spirits on the same basis as its casual trade in *mizuko kuyō*. Myōsenji does not require its customers for either type of ritual to establish a long-term relationship with the temple, though it is possible that some people initially contacting Myōsenji in this way would visit the temple again. The pillar at the end of the parking lot is not identifiable as a facility for either ancestral rites or *mizuko kuyō,* and this lack of clear definition allows it to be used for both.

Mizuko kuyō at Myōsenji is mostly requested by nonparishioners who come from outside Tsuyama, according to its priest. This means that the appearance of *mizuko kuyō* on a large scale during the last ten years or so cannot be taken as a natural outgrowth of the religious sentiments of the temple's parishioners. Instead, it is highly likely that the priest's decision to commence offering both *mizuko kuyō* and ancestral rites to outsiders represented a strategy of economic survival for a temple whose prospects, based on its remote location from Tsuyama and the area's agricultural economy, were not very promising. In the absence of some means to increase revenue beyond the support of parishioners, this temple might even have had to close its doors. *Mizuko kuyō* and the detachment of many people, especially in the cities, from traditional temple affiliations thus offered an opportunity for commercialization that evidently has paid off.

Yukuhashi

Mizuko kuyō in Yukuhashi is performed at 42 percent of the area's fifty-two temples. The population of the town in 1994 was 68,113. A search of folkloric materials and religious histories of the area revealed no earlier traces of anything like these contemporary observances. Of the temples now involved in *mizuko kuyō*, Jōdo-sect temples provide rites on the largest scale (in the sense of serving more clients). Jōdo Shinshū temples provide rites without a visible facility in the precincts, as does one Sōtō temple, following a pattern seen also in Miura. A second Sōtō temple's priest is highly critical of *mizuko kuyō*, in part because these rites distract attention from more serious issues, such as Buddhism's involvement in discrimination against the *burakumin*, or outcaste groups. Two Shugendō sites, described in a later section, provide *mizuko kuyō*, though the priest in charge of one of them reports that there have been virtually no requests for *mizuko kuyō* in the last five years, following an earlier period of higher interest in the practice.

In addition to this distinctive mix of sectarian variety, Yukuhashi shows a geographical bifurcation in its practice of *mizuko kuyō*, with a coastal temple, Hōsenji, offering *mizuko kuyō* on a much larger scale than any of the inland temples, and with a different type of rite. See Map 4. This section will focus on the crosscutting factors of sect affiliation and geographical location, along with Sōtō critique of *mizuko kuyō*.

Jōdo Shinshū objects to *mizuko kuyō*, as discussed in chapter 4. Nevertheless, in Yukuhashi and Miura, nearly 20 percent of the Jōdo Shinshū temples report that they do offer the rites, although none of them have erected the usual statuary and offering sites. This suggests that the temples are aware of the sect's prohibition on *mizuko kuyō*, and that they take pains not to advertise their practice so openly that it could come to the attention of their sect headquarters. When so requested, however, they will perform *mizuko kuyō*.

Jōdo temples' practice of *mizuko kuyō* reveals a distinctive geographical bifurcation. See Map 4. Hōsenji has a form of the practice seen only

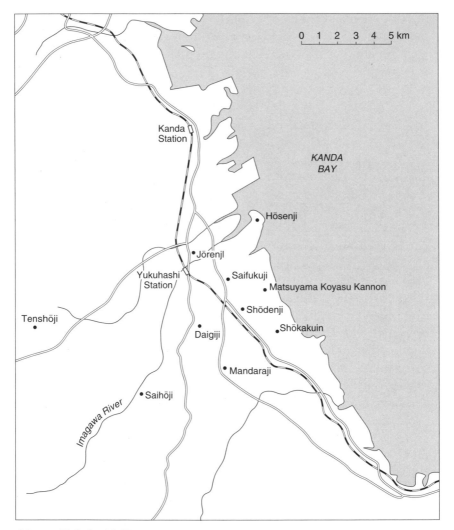

Map 4. Yukuhashi City

on the coastal fringe of Yukuhashi. This temple is located on Minoshima, which is now connected to the mainland by a small stretch of landfill, having previously been separated as an island. Minoshima retains its earlier character as a small fishing hamlet, but in addition, the hilly, forested interior has been made into a park, and a public beach has been created. The park and beach thus provide a spot for local tourists, and while it is unlikely that people would come from a great distance, there is evidently a seasonal traffic of people from nearby areas in Kyūshū. It is likely that at least some of the clients for *mizuko kuyō* at Hōsenji come from outside Yukuhashi, because it is difficult to imagine that all the temple's brisk business in these rites originates locally. Hōsenji offers *mizuko kuyō* on the largest scale to be seen in Yukuhashi, receiving about thirty requests per month. The *mizuko kuyō* facility houses a statue of Jizō and is located on the left and immediately inside the temple gate, clearly separated from the main hall and from graves. See Figure 16. Clients have the priest write a *tōba* and place it in racks around the three inside walls. The *tōba*, in several sizes, from thin wood shavings to substantial boards, number more than one thousand.

The inland Jōdo temples of Yukuhashi show a different form of *mizuko kuyō* than Hōsenji, with the physical facilities for these rites placed outside the temple precinct, a pattern represented by Saifukuji and Mandaraji. At Saifukuji, the *mizuko kuyō* facility is located outside the main gate, to its right. It is composed of a stair-stepped installation of eighty-eight seated statues of Jizō. See Figure 17. The statues are placed in such a way that the donors' names for only the first row of statues can be read; those higher up are obscured by the ones below. The donors' names on the first row of statues show that one woman donated three statues, suggesting a custom of donating one statue per *mizuko*. Not all the statues were donated by individuals, however; some were donated by *ie*-units. The *mizuko kuyō* facility appears to be Saifukuji's newest construction, and otherwise it shows no conspicuous evidence of other commoditized ritual forms or recent grave construction on a large scale.

Mandaraji, another inland Yukuhashi Jōdo temple, is like Saifukuji in locating its *mizuko kuyō* facility outside the temple precinct. It is located behind the precinct, on a hill above the graveyard. See Figure 18. The forty-six Jizō statues that comprise it are new, probably built in the last ten years. A plaque bears this poem:

Hopelessly piling up stones, no one can walk over Sainokawara.
The children's eyes brim with tears at the pain of the stones.
Jizō's lullaby, holding these children, so bewildered, not knowing what to do.
The water is cold, and the darkness of Sainokawara is so deep that you can't tell left from right.
Taking these confused children by the hand, Jizō makes them all pure.
Rain pelts down on Sainokawara.
As they break into tears, Jizō comforts these bewildered children.

Figure 16. *Mizuko kuyō* installation at Hōsenji (Yukuhashi)

The donors of the Jizō statues are recorded and the statues placed so that all of them can be read. The statues have been donated by thirty-six individual women, six individual men, three *ie*-units, and one married couple. See Figure 19. This mixture of donation forms probably indicates a variety of orientations toward *mizuko kuyō*.

One striking element is the rate of male participation. We have no way of knowing how many men are represented by the three *ie*-donors, but if we suppose even a minimum of one per *ie* and add those three to the six individual male donors and the husband from the married

Figure 17. *Mizuko kuyō* installation at Saifukuji (Yukuhashi)

Figure 18. *Mizuko kuyō* installation at Mandaraji (Yukuhashi)

Figure 19. *Mizuko kuyō* installation at Mandaraji (Yukuhashi), showing a statue donated by a corporation

couple, we have a total of ten male donors, about 22 percent of the total number of statue donors for this temple.

Unlike Saifukuji (and Hōsenji), Mandaraji has a recently constructed bell tower, and new graves have been built on a lavish scale. *Mizuko kuyō* may well have provided one source of recent revenue allowing Mandaraji to build on a scale unmatched by other area temples of the sect.

Two Yukuhashi Sōtō temples illustrate a stark contrast in the attitudes within a single sect and the material circumstances surrounding *mizuko kuyō.* Daigiji was originally established as a branch temple of Tenshōji. Daigiji does not perform *mizuko kuyō;* Tenshōji does.

Reverend Takai Ryūichi, the priest at Daigiji, is about seventy years of age and succeeded his father as the resident priest. His longest period of residence away from the temple occurred when he was a student at Komazawa University, which is affiliated with the Sōtō sect, just after the end of World War II. The experience has given him a commitment to a correct historical understanding of Sōtō's position in society, he said, leading to a similar approach to Buddhism as a whole.

He said that he does not perform *mizuko kuyō,* because it goes against his principles. He preferred not to discuss his reasons more specifically, however, probably because his remarks might in that case have been taken as implied criticism of those temples that do. Rather than answering the question more directly, he began to talk about Buddhism's role in perpetuating discrimination against the *burakumin,* descendants of slaughterers, tanners, and leather-workers, who formed a distinct "outcaste" group during the Edo period. Taking out Daigiji's temple registers (*kakochō*), usually kept in a safe, he pointed out that he had affixed a stamp to each one, warning, "Forbidden to Read" (*etsuran kinshi*). He explained that by searching through temple records such as these, it is possible to identify living persons as being descended from *burakumin.* If that fact becomes known, they may be discriminated against in marriage and employment. Because of a custom of investigating personal background in this way, Buddhist temples that allow their records to be used for this purpose comply in perpetuating this unfair and ugly discrimination. The priest spoke passionately, and I noted that in the entrance foyer he had put up a large poster calling on Buddhists of good conscience to examine their hearts and root out the spirit of discrimination. His implication seemed to be that when the society of living people is beset with problems like this, and when it can be seen that Buddhism historically has facilitated class discrimination against *burakumin,* it is better to focus on these problems rather than becoming preoccupied with spirits lacking any canonical basis.

Tenshōji shows a very different approach to *mizuko kuyō* from Daigiji. When initially contacted by telephone, the priest was very reluctant to reveal to what sect the temple belonged. Overhearing my research assistant's difficulty in getting an answer to such a straightforward question, I said from across the room, "*Kitōshi deshō* [He must be a prayer healer]." I had not intended this remark to be audible over the telephone, but apparently it was, and the priest then said, "*Sō iū koto*

[That's about the size of it]" and hung up, having also said that he does perform *mizuko kuyō*. Undecided about whether to go to Tenshōji, we set out for Daigiji. Besides the conversation about *mizuko kuyō*, we were also in search of the temple records of my assistant's ancestors, one of whom, Suemoto Matsujirō, had been an acolyte at a Yukuhashi Sōtō temple, though we didn't yet know which one. The Daigiji priest said that there had been no Suemotos among the acolytes at Daigiji in his youth, but that there might have been at Tenshōji. This was our first clue that Tenshōji is a Sōtō temple. The Daigiji priest called Tenshōji to ask if there were any Suemotos among its parishioners, saying in an aside to us that Tenshōji's temple registers had long ago been lost in a fire.

Arriving in a torrential downpour after a long drive, we found a very different kind of temple from Daigiji. Whereas Daigiji has a small group of parishioners, a modest graveyard, and a small precinct showing no recent building, Tenshōji has recently rebuilt one of its main buildings, and the *tatami* mats of the whole complex have recently been replaced. The furnishings and much of the golden altar equipment of the main hall are new and gleam brilliantly.

Although the priest was dressed in priestly garb (in *samui*), he no longer shaved his head. Although Daigiji's priest thought that Tenshōji lost its registers in a fire, the priest showed us a great basket of them, looking through them with us until we found the right Suemotos and evidence that Matsujirō had been an acolyte at Tenshōji around 1890. It was made clear to us that the priest expected to be paid for our use of the registers. Putting this together with the earlier conversation at Daigiji concerning illegitimate use of the registers to perpetuate discrimination, we hypothesized that the Tenshōji priest prefers to have the Daigiji priest think that Tenshōji no longer possesses registers and hence could not allow itself to be used in that way. On the contrary, however, Tenshōji displays the registers for a fee.

Returning to the ancestor search, we concluded that Suemoto Matsujirō must have been from a parishioner family of Tenshōji, so we inquired if the temple had a family grave where his ancestors might have been buried. The priest then revealed that Tenshōji had never had a graveyard, and that its parishioners were all buried in their respective village graveyards. This means, then, that Tenshōji does not have "automatic income" flowing from the performance of funerals, memorials, and grave-site sales. Even if the temple performs such rites in some cases, it does not have such strong control over these matters as would be the case, for example, at Daigiji, where the graves are on-site.

From these miscellaneous hints, we were able to assemble a picture of *mizuko kuyō* at Tenshōji. A Sōtō priest who will say over the telephone that he is a *kitōshi* is living a very different life from the priest at Daigiji, who expressed no interest in commoditizing ritual, and whose entire orientation toward the priesthood involves reestablishing the rectitude of Buddhist practice. The Tenshōji priest may lack the luxury to be so principled, because he does not have the same sort of link with his parishioners. He evidently makes himself and the temple available for a variety of rituals-for-fees, of which *mizuko kuyō* may be only one item on a much longer menu. That he would grow out his hair, deceive another priest, and call himself a prayer healer suggests that he has stepped away from the priesthood. Economic necessity may have facilitated or necessitated this move. The ten-mile separation of Tenshōji from Daigiji allows him to avoid confrontation, and I think that Daigiji has little idea of Tenshōji's transformation, or its performance of *mizuko kuyō*. The contrasting situation at these two temples indicates on the one hand a temple's reluctance to perform rites of questionable character and significance, and, on the other, its appropriation of *mizuko kuyō* along with other fee-based *kitō* and *kuyō* rites as an economic strategy.

Miura

Miura's population in 1994 was 53,280. Forty percent of Miura's thirty-seven temples currently offer *mizuko kuyō*, though the area's religious history reveals no earlier basis for the practice. Contrary to what this figure might suggest, however, is a tendency to offer it in a hidden form, without publicizing its availability and without erecting a worship facility in or near the temple precincts. I have noted this tendency before in discussing *mizuko kuyō* at Jōdo Shinshū temples in Yukuhashi. Miura replicates that pattern for Jōdo Shinshū, and, in addition, it is found in a Sōtō and a Nichiren temple. To offer *mizuko kuyō* only, in effect, on the basis of a private consultation, leaving no trace in the temple precincts, suggests either a reluctance or an economic inability to erect the customary ritual facility, or, perhaps, a lingering sense that *mizuko kuyō* is not quite proper, that its associations with abortion are unsavory.

Tending in the opposite direction, toward an interpretation suggesting that *mizuko kuyō* has become an accepted and established part of

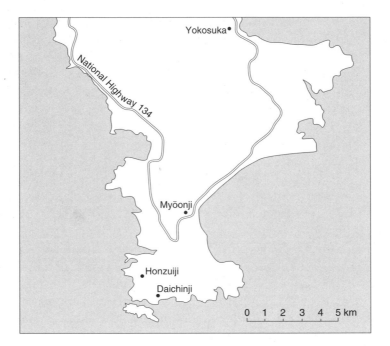

Map 5. Miura City

the ritual life of another group of temples, is a high rate of male participation, and we can see, as in Tōno, a conspicuous trend toward *ie*-
units' sponsorship of these rites. This section concentrates on temples in
which men are a significant portion of the clientele for *mizuko kuyō*.

First, let us consider the Shingon temple Myōonji. See Map 5. This
temple has at its front gate a large, colored, and illustrated sign advertising its attractions and services. The grounds to the rear of the building are evidently an attractive spot for viewing flowers in spring. A wide
variety of *kitō* and *kuyō* rites are available, as well as ancestral rites. Grave
sites are available for sale. The type of *kitō* most visibly advertised with
a ritual site in the precincts is not *mizuko kuyō* but *boke fūji*, rites to prevent senility. A monumental statue of Kannon and an old couple clinging to the Bodhisattva occupies a large space immediately to the left of
the steps leading up to the main hall. The *mizuko kuyō* facility, much
smaller by comparison, is to the right just inside the front gate. The *mizuko kuyō* site contains ten *tōba*, all donated by men. It may be that the
price is out of reach for women. Each *kitō* or *kuyō* rite costs ¥100,000
(about U.S.$1,000) per spirit. Thus, the ten *tōba* represent a sum of
$10,000 in revenue for Myōonji.

Figure 20. *Mizuko kuyō* installation at Honzuiji (Miura)

Honzuiji, a Sōtō temple, suggests a different significance for male participation. Here the *mizuko kuyō* installation consists of a seated Jizō statue with a rack for *tōba*. See Figure 20. One hundred twenty *tōba* had been placed there, of which sixteen had been dedicated in 1994. Of these, seven (44 percent) had been donated by women, and nine (56 percent) by men. Thus, at both Myōonji and Honzuiji, men are the majority of clients for *mizuko kuyō*.

While making these observations at Honzuiji, I was able to see the way in which parishioners carry out the customary summer grave visit, which may bear on the character of *mizuko kuyō* sponsored by men at this temple. A man in his fifties entered the temple grounds by the main gate, pausing to bow before an assemblage of sacred stones near the gate. He next approached the *mizuko kuyō* facility, offered incense before it, and bowed briefly. He proceeded to a position in line with the steps leading up to the main hall, bowed there, and then entered the grave area, where he picked up a water bucket and brush to clean the grave. In other words, the grave visit was preceded by brief obeisance at each of several spots marked off as sacred space, which now include a *mizuko kuyō* facility. This worshipper may take no more notice of the details of this *mizuko kuyō* facility than of the worn-away characters on sacred stones placed near the temple gate. Far less can we conclude that this man has any involvement with abortion. His behavior is entirely comprehensible without assuming that he has any personal interest in *mizuko.*

The practice of *mizuko kuyō* in Miura shows a geographical bifurcation between coastal and inland temples, reminiscent of Yukuhashi. In Miura it is also a coastal temple, located close to tourist sites, that seems to do the greatest volume of business in *mizuko kuyō.* This Rinzai temple, Daichinji, is located near the harbor at the peninsula's tip, where earlier it probably served the local population engaged in coastal fishing. While preserving its character as a fishing town, the area also hosts a small tourist trade supported by rail and road transportation that make possible easy day trips from Tokyo, Yokohama, and Yokosuka.

Daichinji seems to have taken a variety of steps to ensure its survival during the area's economic transformation. It operates a large nursery school next door to the temple precincts, and it has two *mizuko kuyō* facilities. The first of these is a small, covered shed on the left inside the main gate, and the second is a statue of Kannon. The shed contains eight statues of Jizō. On the shelves in the wall behind the statues were placed four *ihai* for *mizuko,* small spirit tablets bearing a simple posthumous name. Also on the shelf was a small box, wrapped in brocade, of cremation remains, evidently of a fetus aborted after four months of pregnancy, for which national law requires cremation or burial. See Figure 21.

The Kannon installation contained thirty-two *tōba,* of which twenty-seven (84 percent) had been dedicated by *ie*-groups, four (13 percent) by individual men, and one (3 percent) by an individual woman. It seems reasonable to suppose that the *ie* dedications have been made by parishioners, and that the individual dedications have been made by people without an ongoing connection to the temple.

MALE PARTICIPATION

Miura temples show a high rate of male participation in *mizuko kuyō.* At Honzuiji and Daichinji, male donors are in the majority, and at Myōonji they monopolize the practice entirely. Sponsorship of *mizuko kuyō* by *ie*-units suggests that the practice is gradually becoming an established part of Japanese religious life, and that here, at least, *mizuko kuyō* is gradually losing its *sub rosa* quality and becoming

Figure 21. *Mizuko kuyō* installation at Daichinji (Miura), showing cremation remains in brocade-wrapped box

an unexceptional religious observance. The behavior of the man worshipping at Honzuiji strongly suggests that this is the case. *Ie*-sponsorship of *mizuko kuyō* lends a very public face to the practice and acts to legitimate it. The elasticity of definitions of *mizuko* diffuses the association with abortion. The more *mizuko kuyō* becomes established at unexceptional temples with unexceptional parishioners, the thinner and less definite its associations with guilt and secrecy become.

It is entirely possible that a man, acting alone and as a single individual, may wish to memorialize an experience of abortion and seek out a Miura temple at which to do so, without forming any long-lasting tie to the temple, a pattern of atomistic ritual action we have seen in the other three field sites, though with women as the predominant actors. Miura's proximity to Tokyo, Yokosuka, and Yokohama makes this scenario entirely plausible not only for men living in Miura, but for men from nearby cities also. However, in none of the Miura temples I visited, with the exception of Daichinji, were there any nonparishioner-sponsored rites in significant proportion. Also, I have never observed a man sponsoring *mizuko kuyō* except when accompanied by a woman; men may, of course, act independently and alone, but observation suggests that this pattern is rare. I believe that it may be limited to small-scale rites such as the purchase of a simple ceremony and a small *tōba*, not resulting in an ongoing tie to the temple.

The more likely explanation for male participation in *mizuko kuyō* at Miura temples, especially where, as at Myōonji, a large capital outlay is required, is that the man is acting in the capacity of head of a parishioner *ie*. That would mean that the man's parents are deceased, and thus he is most likely fifty years of age or older. It means also that he is acting as the *ie*'s representative to the temple, and if the temple elders have assessed each *ie* for *mizuko kuyō*, the separate heads may pay the assessment as a matter of fulfilling their parishioner duty to support the temple, rather than because they have any interest in, anxiety about, or experience of abortion. In fact, a mature male parishioner is highly *unlikely* to put the *ie* name to an idiosyncratic practice, but instead will probably seek assurance that other men in his position are doing likewise, and act on the collective decision rather than his personal beliefs.

Male participation as named heads of *ie* is also a proxy for interest in *mizuko kuyō* among older women, the wives and female relatives of *ie* heads. It may be women's insistence upon ritualizing a difficult and long-ago experience that eventually pressures temple priests, elders, and male parishioners in control of significant economic resources to commence *mizuko kuyō* at parish temples in Miura.

Mizuko Kuyō at Shrines

Mizuko kuyō appeared first in a Buddhist form. Only very recently has it begun to appear at shrines in a Shintō form. The shrine forms of *mizuko kuyō* seem to be entirely distinct from the Buddhist forms and designed within each shrine separately, without reference to the practice of other shrines. Unlike Buddhist temples, shrines have no graves, and, generally speaking, they maintain so great a premium on purity that they refrain from any observances connected with death or blood. Thus, people in mourning and (traditionally) pregnant women (from the time of tying on the *iwata obi* until the lifting of birth pollution about a month after childbirth) abstained from worshipping at shrines. Except in a tiny number of shrines, meat of any kind is excluded from the food offerings placed before altars of the *kami*. Priests undergo systematic purifications and abstinences before approaching the altars of the *kami*. Because of the importance of purity, the appropriation of the *mizuko* cult, albeit under euphemistic names, is both highly unusual and unexpected. A considerable effort to reconcile the expectation of purity with *mizuko*'s significance as the embodiment of moral and physical pollution is inevitably required, and Shintō offers few resources for such an attempt. I made observations at three shrines, one in Okayama (the Kibitsu Shrine), one in Tsuyama (the Katsube Shrine), and one in Kyoto (the Ichihime Shrine). Of these, the Ichihime Shrine specializes in rites concerning women and displays signs and flags advertising that fact, bearing such inscriptions such as "*Nyonin yaku yoke*," meaning, "Removal of Women's Misfortunes." While the Ichihime Shrine is located in central Kyoto, the Kibitsu Shrine and the Katsube Shrine are located in rural settings on the outskirts of their respective cities. All three are accessible by public transportation, though the Kibitsu Shrine undoubtedly receives far more visitors than the other two.

THE KIBITSU SHRINE

The Kibitsu Shrine is large, ancient, and very prestigious. It held the high rank of National Shrine of the Middle Rank (*kanpei chūsha*) from 1914 until the dissolution of this state ranking system after 1945. Established in mythological times, supposedly in the reign of Emperor Sujin, it is mentioned in such ancient texts as the *Kojiki* (712) and the *Engi-shiki* (927). Historically, it held a large estate commanding the ancient province of Kibi, comprising the territories of Bizen, Bitchū, and Bingo. Its priesthood was highly influential in the provincial society of western Japan, being composed of more than sixty households, of whom the Kayo and Fujii lines were the most prominent. Until the Meiji period, the shrine was served regularly by more than eighty priests. The shrine was particularly associated with *on'yōdō*, the philosophy and divinatory practices based on *yin* and *yang*, acting as a base of transmission for this tradition. One of the shrine's distinctive ritual practices is divination employing a huge cauldron. Fired by two *miko* at New Year's, the cauldron can be made to emit a sound like the bellow of cattle in response to a client's questions, interpreted as a kind of oracle. In contemporary times, it has become one of a small number of shrines perpetuating *bugaku,* a type of masked, sacred dance performed as entertainment for the *kami.* Although doubtless no shrine is impervious to change, the Kibitsu Shrine has not frequently initiated new ritual forms. Within this century, its only new installation has been a subsidiary shrine for ancestors (*sōreisha*), and next to it a second subsidiary shrine for *chigo,* the term this shrine uses for souls of the aborted, miscarried, and stillborn. In other words, those souls ritualized elsewhere as *mizuko* are called *chigo* here, and the ritual site places them with ancestral spirits.[10]

Chigo, sometimes translated "divine child," originally referred to a child who acts as the receptacle or embodiment of the *kami*'s presence during communal festivals (*matsuri*). The term does not specify age or sex, and different shrines employ prepubescent boys or girls. The *chigo* is chosen from among shrine parishioners and supporters, undergoing a period of purification before the festival. *Chigo* are lavishly attired in silk robes of many layers, after the fashion of the medieval period, with stylized makeup to whiten their faces and rouge their cheeks. They generally ride a horse in a festival procession, and it is understood that the *kami* enters into them when they mount the horse. Following the *kami*'s progress around the shrine's territory, the *chigo* may perform divinations or deliver oracles, assisted by adult priests.[11]

The Kibitsu Shrine's appropriation of the term *chigo* for *mizuko* is euphemistic, allowing all concerned to sidestep any association with abortion and to focus instead upon the connotations of purity and divinity that flow from the term *chigo*'s provenance. These associations are heightened by the placement of the *chigo-sha* (the subsidiary shrine for *chigo*) immediately adjacent to the ancestral shrine. The area allotted to these two subsidiary shrines is completed by a small, motorized waterwheel, which preserves the aquatic associations of *mizuko,* and which has further connotations in a shrine context of something's being purified by being carried away on water. Shrine workers at the main hall of the Kibitsu Shrine report that the *chigo-sha* is mainly visited by heterosexual couples, without priestly mediation. Their devotions consist mainly of individual prayers, with offerings of flowers, children's foods, and toys.

In addition to these private observances, however, the shrine offers a

special *kitō* for *chigo* at the spring and autumn equinoxes. Those desiring *kitō* for their own *chigo* purchase from the shrine a small, wooden
kokeshi doll about three inches high. *Kokeshi,* originally a folk toy most
characteristic of northern Japan, are dolls usually made from a single
piece of wood for the body, sometimes with a second piece of wood
carved for the head, but having no movable arms or legs, generally cut
to represent a child in *kimono.* Frequently, the head is disproportionately large, leaving the maker ample space to paint in a face with ink
and bright-colored paints. *Kokeshi* have usually been regarded as toys
appropriate for girls, and most *kokeshi* represent girls, though boy *kokeshi* are not unknown. At the Kibitsu Shrine, the client receives a *kokeshi* with no markings of any kind. The client is supposed to draw on a
face and clothing in the style desired. A priest then prays over these and
deposits them in a chamber under the *chigo* shrine, but still above
ground. Anyone who has *chigo kitō* performed is registered by the
shrine, and announcements of each subsequent equinoctial rite are
thereafter sent by mail.

The symbolism of this rite is linked to the shrine's history. Because
the shrine was originally founded as the liturgical center of the Kibi
clan, its deities are the divinized ancestors of the clan, apotheosized as
the tutelary gods of the Kibi area.[12] Having been founded as a clan
shrine and enshrining deified ancestors create an association with the
pure, benign, tutelary associations of the dead who have become ancestors. It is in this connection that *chigo/mizuko* can be brought into a
connection with the shrine and yet avoid the association with abortion.
The placement of the *chigo-sha* immediately adjacent to the ancestor
shrine, with the further connection to running water, suggests these
overlapping readings:

1. The souls of *chigo/mizuko* will be purified by water and protected
   by the ancestors.

2. The *chigo/mizuko* will be transformed to pure, benign, and protective ancestral spirits through the *kitō* offered by the shrine.

3. Having taken on the protective function of ancestors, *chigo/
   mizuko* will protect those who have ritualized them.

THE ICHIHIME SHRINE

Founded in 795 as the shrine of the old city marketplace,
this small, urban shrine offers *mizuko kuyō* as part of its contemporary
specialization in "dispelling women's misfortunes" (*nyonin yaku yoke*),

advertised on large signs posted along major roads nearby. Since there is no longer a central market held in that part of the city, the shrine has probably had to accept a secondary identity to ensure its survival, and *mizuko kuyō* is merely one item on a longer list of novel offerings particularly appealing to women, especially young women.

The female associations of the shrine can be traced to the five female *kami* it enshrines,[13] along with the Buddhist goddess Benzaiten, a protector of women. Otherwise largely unknown and not otherwise the object of widespread popular devotion, the shrine's five main goddesses are direct descendants of the sun goddess Amaterasu.[14] The shrine's function as protector of the marketplace guarantees its adherents the benefits of success in business. Among those rites directed especially to women are those ensuring conception, celebrating menarche, and ensuring safe childbirth; the shrine also offers water to be used at a birth, and *mizuko kuyō*. Other benefits advertised include improving health, dispelling negative influence (*yaku yoke*), granting love and a good marriage, and a very novel one called "Lucky Chance" (*rakki chansu*).

Following a more widespread practice of memorial services for such items of daily use as needles, the Ichihime Shrine has erected a large stainless steel sculpture of credit cards and encourages its adherents to bring old plastic cards to be purified with water from a well on the premises. Closely allied with this practice, for which an annual festival is held on September 9, is the shrine's distribution of protective talismans in the form of a plastic card (*happī kādo*) to be carried on the person.

Mizuko kuyō at this shrine is conducted principally through private devotions at one of the subsidiary shrines in the precinct. As one of so many observances at the Ichihime Shrine, *mizuko kuyō* does not seem to have a particular prominence there, nor to be an unusual revenue source, but exists instead in a routinized form, "naturalized" by the shrine's major concern with women.

THE KATSUBE SHRINE

Located a mile or so north of Tsuyama's outskirts, the Katsube Shrine is easy to overlook—blink and you've missed it. I only suspected that it might offer *mizuko kuyō* because it had purchased a listing in the telephone book under "temples," which I learned is sometimes a code for a shrine offering these rites. Known to no registry of Shintō shrines, the Katsube Shrine probably originated as a tutelary shrine of a hamlet of the same name. It has a tottery stone *torii,* and a small main shrine at the end of an avenue ten meters or so in length, a

Figure 22. Rites for aborted fetuses, called *hiruko,* at the Katsube Shrine (Tsuyama)

building on stilts, about three meters to a side. Flanking the right side of the avenue are five subsidiary shrines on cement pillars, perhaps half a meter per side and one meter high. The one closest to the *torii* has been designated as the *yashiro* for *hiruko* (a placement corresponding to the placement of Tsuyama temple *mizuko* facilities, just inside the main gate and to the right). See Figure 22.

Hiruko means "Leech Child," deriving from chapter 3 of book I of the mythological compendium, the *Kojiki* (712). In this myth, the primal brother-sister *kami,* Izanagi and Izanami, perform a rite of "marriage" to solemnize their mission of procreation, by which they will give birth to the Japanese islands and other *kami*. They are to circumambulate the Heavenly Pillar in opposite directions, connecting the heavens and the human world. When they meet halfway around, they are to exchange compliments and then proceed to the heavenly mission—sexual intercourse. Their first attempt is a failure, however; Izanami gives birth to the Leech Child, which must be floated away and abandoned. Subsequent interrogation reveals that the cause of the failure was that Izanami, the female, spoke first. When they try again and Izanagi pronounces his compliments first, their offspring are viable. The name that the priest of the Katsube Shrine has given *mizuko* to rid them of their Buddhist associations is "Leech Child." Appropriation of the term *hiruko* also imports clear associations of male dominance and the aquatic imagery of *mizuko*.

The priest, elderly and seriously handicapped with spinal disease, reported that he receives five or six requests per year for Leech Child Purification (*hiruko barai*), most of which are from outsiders, rather than people connected to the shrine in an ongoing way. The ritual he has composed consists of reciting the Great Purification Prayer (*Ōharai norito*) and a shorter prayer of his own composition. He explained how he places small wooden plaques wrapped in inscribed paper in the shrine for each spirit. Of the several subsidiary shrines in the precinct, the Leech Child shrine was the only one with any offerings before it—a tomato and a wilted gladiola. It is clear that the shrine receives no significant revenue from these rites.

In spite of my initial surprise that any form of *mizuko kuyō* could be possible at shrines, two of the three shrines described here have found rubrics that make it possible within Shintō terminology: *chigo* and *hiruko*. In the first case, at the Kibitsu Shrine, an extension of the meaning of a term in wide circulation is the key, while in the second, the Katsube Shrine, a word from mythic tradition probably not well known among the general population is made to serve. In the Ichihime Shrine, the shrine's preexisting focus on women makes it possible to appropriate the term *mizuko kuyō* without modification.

Mizuko Kuyō in Shugendō Temples and Sites

Many rural temples associated with Shugendō have in their precincts small hills serving as miniature representations of the mountains they revere and where their followers travel as pilgrims to perform ascetic rites. These miniature mountains can be natural or artificial. Statues representing Buddhist deities associated with Shugendō, such as the Fudō and Zao Gongen, are placed on the miniature mountain to illustrate visibly the Shugendō idea of mountains as the home of the gods. In the two temples associated with Shugendō observed in this study, statues of Jizō and Kannon had been added to the array of divinities on their miniature mountains.

At Ishiyamadera outside Tsuyama, a Shugendō temple linked to the Tendai sect, the miniature mountain is a large outcropping of rock. See Figure 23. There are no separate *mizuko kuyō* facilities apart from this. People desiring *mizuko kuyō* can have a small statue of Kannon dedicated in the name of their *mizuko* to take home and place in their Buddhist altar. If circumstances prevent them from doing this, the temple will take care of the statue for them.

Shōkakuin, a Yukuhashi Shingon-affiliated Shugendō temple, has a miniature mountain, beside which a waterfall has been created for purifications and austerities. See Figure 24. Besides numerous statues of Fudō and other mountain deities, several small, seated Jizō statues had been put, apparently by individual believers, not permanently attached to the mountain. These Jizō carried no donor identification, and were of rough concrete, probably quite inexpensive.

Mizuko kuyō at both Ishiyamadera and Shōkakuin is one of many types of rites and practices available at these temples, not enjoying any particular prominence among them, and certainly not the main one. It is unlikely that *mizuko kuyō* provides a conspicuous source of revenue in either case.

The Matsuyama Koyasu Kannon is located in a rural area south of Yukuhashi. Lacking a consecrated object of worship, it could not be called a temple, but is instead a ritual site now claimed by a Jōdo temple called Shōdenji, located about a mile away from it. Reached by a fifteen-minute walk through rice fields and forest, the site is located at the top of a small but steep hill, and a wooden stairway has smoothed what must have been a muddy track to the top.

It would appear that this place became a ritual site because it is the highest spot in the immediate vicinity, and that it has taken on a different character in various ages. Although presently claimed by a Jōdo temple, there were Tengu masks and other Shugendō gear in the small prayer building, and signs advertising the site as a meeting place for confraternities revering Kōbō Daishi. None of these materials bear any relation to the Jōdo sect. The spot on the site where *mizuko kuyō* would be carried out is an open shed that houses about seventy-five

Figure 23. Miniature mountain installation at Ishiyamadera
(Tsuyama), where *mizuko kuyō* can also be performed

very small statues of Jizō, evidently placed there by individual devotees.
None bear dedicatory inscriptions of any kind. There were no signs at
the site of any recent visitation. By telephone, the priest of Shōdenji
said that five or six years earlier there had been an upsurge of interest in
mizuko kuyō, but that there is virtually none now. Those seeking *mizuko kuyō* in the late 1980s were mainly older women in the area.

   That *mizuko kuyō* in a Shugendō form should have been created at
all is remarkable, given the masculinist tone of its ascetic emphasis and

Figure 24. Miniature mountain installation at Shōkakuin
(Yukuhashi), where *mizuko kuyō* can also be performed

its exclusion of women until the postwar era. Within the contemporary
religious scene, Shugendō as a whole is maintaining a small number of
traditional adherents, though these are mainly men in their fifties and
older. Like Japanese Buddhism and Shintō, Shugendō has had difficulty
maintaining its institutional base and its numbers. The postwar entrance
of women has undoubtedly helped slow its decline, and it seems likely
that women would provide an important voice within Shugendō for
the creation of *mizuko kuyō*. This does not, however, preclude male

sponsorship of such rites. It is likely that if figures were available, male participation would contribute the same proportion of support as at other rural religious institutions, which is to say between 20 and 30 percent. Because none of the temples practiced *mizuko kuyō* in a way that allows for identification of patrons by sex, however, this estimate remains speculative.

Conclusion

This chapter has surveyed four field sites in order to identify major factors that affect and color the practice of *mizuko kuyō*. Those factors which have emerged with most clarity can be listed as follows. The importance of spatial distinctions at two levels was observed clearly. Within any temple, *mizuko* facilities are spatially separated from the Buddhas and the ancestors (all sites). Within a community, a bifurcation of *mizuko kuyō* practice was identified: between temples inside and outside a temple district (Tsuyama), and between coastal and inland temples (Yukuhashi, Miura, Tōno).

In all sites a critical discourse opposed to *mizuko kuyō* modulates its practice. At least four bases for criticism arise in various circumstances: (1) because local people may be pressured into supporting it economically without a corresponding change in their beliefs (Tōno temples and Numa no Uchi Sainokawara); (2) because its association with abortion is distasteful (all sites); (3) because it is seen as distracting attention from issues more pressing for Buddhism (Yukuhashi, Daigiji); (4) because of Jōdo Shinshū's various objections (Tsuyama, Yukuhashi, Miura).

Some religious institutions seek to use *mizuko kuyō* as an economic strategy. Usually this attempt is made in combination with a variety of other fee-based rites, as at these temples: (1) Tsuyama: Myōsenji; (2) Yukuhashi: Tenshōji; (3) Miura: Myōonji; (4) Tōno: Numa no Uchi Sainokawara. *Mizuko kuyō* does not, however, always yield conspicuous revenue; this is the case in Tsuyama's temple-district temples. Furthermore, *mizuko kuyō* can be overshadowed by other commoditized rites, as in these cases: (1) Pet *kuyō*: Miura (Enjūji, a Nichiren temple not discussed above); (2) *Boke fūji*: Miura (Myōonji). Concern about pets and senility is another recent trend in Buddhist temples, and a temple that becomes known for either one of these rites may attract as much business on that basis as for *mizuko kuyō*.

The most powerful promoters of a rationale for *mizuko kuyō* are spiritualists and independent religious entrepreneurs such as Morita Guyō of Jionji in Tsuyama, discussed in chapter 4. The attitude of ordinary parish temples is, by comparison, passive and reactive, though priests are gratified by the income. Temples most likely to perform *mizuko kuyō* probably share one or more of the following characteristics: (1) they lack a customary group of parishioners (Jionji, Tsuyama); (2) they are not Jōdo Shinshū; (3) they are located in one or more of the following ways: (a) on the coast; (b) outside a sphere of mutual surveillance by other temples; (c) far from their sect's headquarters; (d) near a major transportation route facilitating visits from clients residing outside the immediate area. Their priests are likely to share one or more of the following characteristics: (1) youth (by the standards of today's priesthood, this means being under sixty or so); (2) specialization in *kitō* (Jionji, Tsuyama; Tenshōji, Yukuhashi); (3) an entrepreneurial spirit (Myōsenji, Tsuyama; Tenshōji, Yukuhashi).

Mizuko kuyō can provide a basis for ongoing relations between client and temple, but this is not inevitably the case. The practice can end in a one-time, cash-on-the-barrelhead transaction, augment an existing parishioner relationship, or forge a relation where none existed before. In the last case, the client may continue to maintain parishioner status in some other temple. The formation of a perduring relation with the temple will probably depend on the client's forming a personal bond with the ritualist, who will probably be a prayer healer offering general spiritual counsel.

Mizuko kuyō can exist apart from the religious lives of the people in whose parish temples it is established. This is true at Tōno temples, because of stoneworkers' influence, in Tsuyama among Myōsenji parishioners, and in Miura at Honzuiji, where it assumes a customary character. Within a given community, *mizuko kuyō*'s tendency to exist apart from the residents' religious lives is closely linked to a strong tendency for clients to come from outside the community, seeking to have *mizuko kuyō* performed secretly, and, if possible, anonymously. This is true at the following temples: in Tōno at Numa no Uchi Sainokawara; in Tsuyama at Myōsenji; in Yukuhashi at Hōsenji; and in Miura at Daichinji.

The participation in *mizuko kuyō* of men and *ie*-groups indicates a growing acceptance, legitimation, and routinization of the practice. This can be seen everywhere, to varying degrees. This gradual incorporation coexists with strong, cross-sectarian critique of *mizuko kuyō*. That this study and the national surveys introduced in chapter 2 should tally so precisely at 44 and 43 percent, respectively, of temples performing *mi-*

zuko kuyō attests both to the strength of criticism against the practice and to the determination of its supporters.

These findings call for qualifications of existing literature. Previous studies have not recorded or analyzed the significant rates of male and *ie* participation, the strong critique of *mizuko kuyō,* nor the increasing routinization of the practice. Furthermore, existing literature suggests a concentration in Tendai and Shingon temples; this study finds high rates of performance also in the Nichiren, Sōtō, and Jōdo sects.

Even to create a comprehensive description of *mizuko kuyō* in rural Japan is no small feat. There are striking yet highly contradictory features of the phenomenon that must be accounted for. It is a cultic phenomenon—a type of ritual which within the short space of twenty years has appeared in all the major types of Japanese religious institutions, having Buddhist, Shintō, Shugendō, new religions, and prayer healer forms. The institutional boundaries which have proven so impervious to "crossovers" for most of Japanese religious history have been breached so conspicuously by a ritual form principally patronized by women, a group systematically excluded from leadership in most of these institutions. The rapidity and breadth of *mizuko kuyō*'s spread might incline one to predict that it would prove to be a phenomenon of great strength, but other features of it seem to lead toward a different assessment.

Expensive installations of Buddhist statuary have sprung up across the nation for *mizuko kuyō,* and each of these represents a heavy financial investment on the part of a temple and its parishioner households. At each temple, those favoring the initiation of a new ritual form (never seen there before and bearing unsavory associations with abortion) had to persuade the rest that their temple would not be dishonored. They had to persuade fellow parishioners and sometimes the priest as well that *mizuko kuyō* carried sufficient religious significance that the temple should provide it even if it had no textual basis and no previous existence in Japanese Buddhism. And yet, in many areas, these same installations, erected at such expense and running against inherent resistance, have fallen into disuse within twenty years. Not only that, in some of the same locales, such as the Sainokawara at Numa no Uchi, money-making schemes built on *mizuko kuyō* have failed conspicuously and easily, turning whole communities against the practice.

In rural society, the patrons of *mizuko kuyō* are mainly people in their late fifties and older, predominantly women, but with a considerable proportion of men, on average around 30 percent. Those Japanese

Table 18. *Rates of abortion and contraceptive use over the reproductive lives of those born from 1920 to 1940*

Year	1945	1950	1955	1960	1965	1970	1975	1990
Rate of contraceptive use (percentage)[1]		19.5	33.6	42.3 (1961)	55.5	52.6	60.5	57.9
Ratio of abortions to live births[2]		20.9	67.6	66.2	46.2	37.8	35.3	37.4 (1989)
Age if born in 1920	25	30	35	40	45			
Age if born in 1925	20	25	30	35	40	45		
Age if born in 1930		20	25	30	35	40	45	
Age if born in 1935			20	25	30	35	40	
Age if born in 1940				20	25	30	35	

[1]SOURCE: Mainichi Shinbunsha Jinkō Mondai Chōsakai, ed., *Kiroku: Nihon no jinkō, Shōsan e no kiseki* (Tokyo: Mainichi Shinbunsha, 1992), p. 54, table 1.

[2]SOURCE: Ibid., p. 337, table 24.

people who were between fifty-five and seventy-five in 1995 were born between 1920 and 1940. See Table 18. This group was of reproductive age between 1940 and 1975, precisely the period of Japan's highest rates of abortion. Compared with live births, abortion was the outcome of 40 percent to 67.6 percent of all pregnancies. This was also the period in which Japan's overall pattern of fertility came into conformity with that typical of Western societies. In other words, the age group most prominent as sponsors of *mizuko kuyō* in parish temples is identical with the cohort responsible for Japan's historic demographic transition. Rural women have shown consistently higher rates of abortion than those in the cities. This outcome reflects differential patterns of contraceptive availability on the one hand, and, probably, more entrenched attitudes about male sexual prerogatives on the other, leading to women's less favorable position in negotiating contraception with men.

The women and men who practice *mizuko kuyō* in rural Japan today have experienced abortion at its highest rates. Though abortion has been legally available to them for their entire reproductive lives, contraception only came to be practiced by a majority of couples slowly. In the immediate postwar years, it was not widely available at prices people could afford. The oldest cohort among those born between 1920 and 1940 lived through years when abortion was more readily procured than contraception. For none of this period, nor today, is contraception by female-controlled methods widely practiced. This means that many born between 1920 and 1940 adopted abortion as a substitute for contraception, not as one choice among alternatives, but as the only way out when faced with a pregnancy when raising a child was impossible.

There is no doubt that, in a society whose religious institutions were virtually silent on reproductive issues until the 1970s, the combination of physical pain, spiritual questioning, and highly ambivalent emotions about abortion, even many years after the fact, made a ready and vulnerable market for ideas about the unassuaged wrath of aborted fetuses. *Ogamiya* and assorted religionists promoting these ideas in their own practice and through print and broadcast media opened old wounds as they spread their message. Since the cohort born between 1920 and 1940 were already mature members of communities, already stalwart supporters of temples and shrines, they turned to those institutions to provide suitable, dignified rites. As we have seen, many religious institutions answered this call, though not without their own ambivalence and critique.

Once the sense of unease and unfinished business was assuaged by *mizuko kuyō* rites, however, their patrons were satisfied. Their normal relations with temples and shrines continued, but there was no cause for a continued outpouring of feeling. In this way, the *mizuko kuyō* installations fell into disuse or came to be tended in a routinized way, incorporated into liturgical routine. Patronage by men and by *ie*-groups further legitimated the practice and further erased its exceptional, faddish, and sexualized meanings. In rural society, the statues and buildings erected for *mizuko kuyō* seem likely to remain for the future as monuments to the desire of a distinctive age cohort to ritualize an unresolved experience. The most likely sequel is a reconsecration of them to the religious aspirations of succeeding generations.

Conclusion

Japan has a long history of ritualizing reproductive life, through which it developed distinctive characterizations of abortion. Within that longer history, *mizuko kuyō* represents a major departure. It is a distinctively contemporary phenomenon. *Mizuko kuyō* arose in the 1970s, not as an unmediated expression of popular sentiment about abortion, but as the product of an intense media advertising campaign by entrepreneurial religionists. The media blitz rested upon a fetishization of visual images of the fetus made possible by such contemporary technologies as fetal photography. Outsized, lurid images of the full-term fetus, detached from the female body, turned head-up and snarling, were created through the interpretive lens of fetocentric rhetoric that construed any termination of pregnancy as an act of homicide by a woman, for which she would be punished by fetal "spirit attacks." *Mizuko kuyō* was advanced as the "answer" to a "problem" created mostly by those purveying the rites in question.

The media blitz immediately generated intense controversy, and *mizuko kuyō* has been the object of widespread criticism and disparagement from its inception. It has been attractive to no more than 15 to 20 percent of abortion recipients, even at the height of its marketing campaign. The majority of religious institutions that have ever been surveyed reject *mizuko kuyō*. It is repudiated by the largest sect of Japanese Buddhism, Jōdo Shinshū, and by many priests of all sects for a broad variety of reasons. Indeed, since the idea of *mizuko* is absent from the Buddhist canons, and since, therefore, the canons provide no authorization for ritualizing any such spirits, widespread rejection of *mizuko kuyō* is hardly surprising. Criticism of *mizuko kuyō* among the Buddhist priesthood is widespread, and chapter 1's examination of Saint Yūten's self-proclaimed eccentricity in directing rites of merit transfer to fetuses shows that his example, from the Jōdo sect, is virtually the sole premodern "precedent" for *mizuko kuyō*. The text's insistence on its own idiosyncrasy strongly suggests that the "precedent" is weak and shallow.

Saint Yūten's legends are nevertheless an important storehouse of the Edo period's "common sense" about abortion. The age's distinctive characterizations of abortion were bifurcated. The first type addressed abortion and infanticide together, as the final resort of the peasantry in situations of extreme economic hardship. Abortion and infanticide carried out for these reasons were regarded as simultaneously sad, pitiable, and unavoidable. Except for periodic pronouncements against these practices and child abandonment, Edo-period religious institutions generally remained aloof from any connection with reproductive life. Certainly, no commercialized, transsectarian ritual form arose, nor was fetocentric rhetoric used for a wholesale stigmatization of one sex. The Edo period's second characterization of abortion addressed the question of its arising from an illicit pursuit of sexual pleasure, and it produced two long-lived stock characters, the Callous Man and the Foolish Woman. Abortions carried out to terminate pregnancies conceived between these characters were criticized, and stereotyped tales predicted that the Callous Man would give the Foolish Woman abortifacients so lethal that she herself would die, along with the fetus. Even in this case, however, no commercialization of ritual emerged, nor did fetocentric rhetoric necessarily provide the principal basis for the critique. The Callous Man and the Foolish Woman were censured in roughly equal measure. The age did not, in any case, attempt to reach a single, absolute moral position on abortion apart from the circumstances leading to it. There was a pervasive understanding that abortion was rooted in sexual and social relations over which no individual could have full control, and therefore it would be wrong to force any single individual to bear full responsibility.

When we examine *mizuko kuyō* in practice, we find that it departs from Japanese characterizations of abortion from the Edo period until the 1970s most strikingly in making the Callous Man invisible. The misogyny of *mizuko kuyō* derives in large part from the use of fetocentric rhetoric to stigmatize the nonreproductive sexual activity of women uniquely, shielding their male partners from any responsibility.

Edo-period conceptualizations of both pregnancy and abortion rested upon a unity of the fetus and the maternal body. While religious institutions did not address reproductive life much, pregnancy and first childbirth were nevertheless extensively ritualized in folk religious life. The midwife played a central role, conducting a soul, through the maternal body, into social life in the community. In this conceptualization, the oneness of the woman and the fetus was such a powerful motif that any separation of the two, any pretense that the fetus's existence was independent from—far less opposed to—that of the mother, was virtually inconceivable. The idea of wrathful fetuses, the hallmark of *mizuko kuyō*, could scarcely exist. The view that the fetus is a part of the maternal body until it is born is reflected even in contemporary legal interpretation of the Eugenics Protection Law. The understanding that the fetus is not a legal person, and that therefore it is not properly the subject of human rights, underlay the Ministry of Justice's rejection of Seichō no Ie's unsuccessful attempt to overturn the economic hardship clause.

That this basic conception of the unity of the fetus and the maternal body could have endured the deritualization of pregnancy and childbirth that occurred over the modern period, as well as contemporary *mizuko kuyō*'s attempted popularization of fetocentrism, is eloquent testimony to its strength. The medicalization of pregnancy and childbirth that accompanied their deritualization substituted a biologically based account of intrauterine fetal development for the former folk-religious understanding about the transit of the soul and Buddhist ideas of rebirth. Early Meiji provisions of criminal law divided the foregoing continuum, linking abortion and infanticide in popular thought, unambiguously aligning infanticide and homicide. Abortion was criminalized and its practice made more difficult, but it remained in a different category from homicide and infanticide. Throughout the prewar decades, an ideology of motherhood gained state approval and indirectly supported abortion's criminalization, and the later criminalization of contraception, both of which remained in place until the end of World War II, in service to a pronatalist social policy.

After postwar amendments to the Eugenics Protection Law legalized abortion for reasons of economic hardship, many Japanese women terminated pregnancies through abortion. While the available statistics are far from perfect, even official estimates suggest a ratio of abortions to live births of between 40 and 67 percent, and all commentators believe that the actual ratio was significantly higher in the early postwar years. Analysis of popular media interpretations of abortion in the newspaper advice columns (*jinsei annai*) shows that the Edo period's bifurcated characterizations of abortion have lived on in modern dress. Especially in the early postwar years of food shortages and massive repatriation of military personnel and colonists, and before the widespread diffusion of contraceptive devices, abortion was the major means of family limitation. Recognition of abortion's inevitability and inescapability was reflected in widespread tolerance for it. The sympathetic portrayal of abortion offered to women in such circumstances by the advice columns was presented as the voice of realism. A continuum linking contraception, abortion, and sterilization emerged, and women were urged to control their fertility by any available means, not waiting until they could convince their husbands that they had a right to do so. At the same time, when the advice columns interpreted a pregnancy as conceived between a Callous Man and a Foolish Woman, writers would not hesitate to urge the woman to renounce all illusions about the man, about the pregnancy, and terminate the relationship. Protestations about a "child conceived in love" or the woman's desire to demonstrate her selfless devotion to the man by raising his illegitimate child were disdained as deluded egotism. Abortion was presented as preferable by far to burdening a child with the stigma of illegitimacy. Such Foolish Women were told in no uncertain terms to "get a life." Furthermore, the advice writers poured scorn and contempt upon the Callous Men who had impregnated these women, calling the men selfish, egotistical, and despoilers of women. These popular portrayals of abortion were effectively unchallenged by the religious world (except for Seichō no Ie) until the 1970s.

The ethos of the religious world from 1945 to the 1970s was expansive and optimistic. Freed from restrictions imposed on religious bodies under the prewar state, the early postwar period saw a great proliferation of new religious groups and the more gradual recovery of older ones. New religions generally downplayed older traditions in which the clergy reigned preeminent, establishing instead many important roles for laypeople. Women have been prominent in many of these associations, as founders and grassroots organizers. New religions shared a view that individuals could attain worldly happiness and spiritual perfection through their own efforts. The paths prescribed for adherents varied widely, but shared a general orientation seeking a harmonious accord between the self and the body, other people, the natural world, and a supernatural world regarded as benevolently inclined toward humanity. People conceptualized the population of the supernatural world with great variety, frequently reserving a special place for ancestral spirits who could provide protection and spiritual strength. Ritual in daily life often took the form of observances to maintain a flow of benefice from the other world by expressions of faith and sincerity through prayer and offerings. Some new religions envisioned that ancestors' protective benevolence could be breached through neglect of such rites. As a minor theme, the idea emerged that such spirits could cause damage to their descendents in order to make the latter reinstate the rites and rededicate themselves to the attitudes the rites symbolized (gratitude, sincerity, filial piety, diligence, and others). Overall, however, self-determination was the dominant theme, and the notion that life was determined by chance, fate, or malevolent spirits was alien to the religious ethos of the postwar decades up until the 1970s. Thus, *mizuko kuyō,* based directly upon the idea of menacing fetal spirits, would have been quite out of place, and it did not emerge until later.

Following the oil shocks of the mid-1970s and the end of the high economic growth that had begun in 1955, the ethos of the religious world changed. A new generation of religions emerged, in which fate, chance, and spirits regarded as not necessarily benevolent toward humanity played increasingly larger roles. An "occult boom" saw the popularization of astrology and many other practices aiming to divine the will of supernatural beings and forces otherwise inaccessible to humanity. While self-determination remained an important theme, the idea that life could be determined by forces beyond the reach of individual faith and devotion began to overtake it. Youth of both sexes were prominent in post-1970s religious life, overshadowing the "modal members" of earlier associations—married, middle-aged housewives. *Mizuko kuyō*'s emphasis on spirit wrath is entirely consonant with this new ethos, which, by comparison with the early postwar years, is pessimistic and fatalistic. *Mizuko kuyō* shares with the occult boom another distinctively contemporary characteristic—its transmission through and dependence upon the industries of popular culture, rather than transmission through proselytization, which was a widespread characteristic of religions flourishing through the early postwar decades. *Mizuko kuyō*'s stress on guilt and fear, its fatalism and pessimism, and its dependence upon the media, especially upon tabloids marketed to young, unmarried women, establish its place in the post-1970s religious world.

The embeddedness of much post-1970s religious life in popular culture facilitated increased commercialization through media channels of many religious practices, including *mizuko kuyō.* Books and magazines on religion had, of course, been widely available before, but the prospect of marketing religion to young, affluent customers was newly created by the "occult boom." Publishers foresaw a new market, and the "need" for both publications and religious ritual was eagerly created by entrepreneurial religionists of all kinds, but especially by spiritualists and prayer healers. These were the circumstances in which *mizuko kuyō* was originally marketed.

By the 1970s, significant changes had occurred in the practice of abortion. The diffusion of contraceptive devices had proceeded to the point that contraception was universally available at prices people could readily afford. Abortion no longer substituted for contraception. Furthermore, the standard of living had risen enough to impinge on the economic hardship clause of the Eugenics Protection Law. When Seichō no Ie launched its campaign to abolish the economic hardship clause, it could claim that the extreme hardship of the early postwar years was a thing of the past, and that no one needed to terminate a pregnancy on that basis. The religion backed up its claims with fetocentric rhetoric very consonant with that adopted by purveyors of *mizuko kuyō.* Dependent upon the continued practice of abortion for their own livelihood, however, the latter did not join Seichō no Ie's abortion opposition.

The eight texts presented in chapter 3 provide insight into the changed meaning of economic hardship, as well as revealing how the meanings of abortion can differ for women and men. Six of the eight texts were originally written to refute Seichō no Ie's claims that the economic hardship clause is no longer necessary; all of them show dramatically both the continued need for legalized abortion and abortion's many meanings in contemporary sexual culture. Popular rejection of Seichō no Ie's fetocentrism is mirrored in the critique surrounding *mizuko kuyō.*

Among other things, *mizuko kuyō* represents an economic strategy on the part of entrepreneurial religionists. We have seen how spiritualists attempt to popularize *mizuko kuyō* in order to use it as the basis on which to establish an ongoing relation with clients, on the model of a Buddhist temple supported by traditional parishioners. Clients would support a spiritualist by regular payments for ritual. In order for spiritualists to appropriate *mizuko kuyō* in this way, however, clients must believe that the *mizuko* can never be finally put to rest, and that clients' culpability in abortion can never be completely expunged. In *mizuko kuyō* the attempt to convince clients of their eternal guilt is underwritten by dire predictions that women who fail to perform the rites will suffer the physical symptoms and emotional problems associated in Japan with menopause. In other words, they will lose their sexual attractiveness to men.

Most clients, however, seek a resolution to their feelings that would not result in an ongoing relation to a spiritualist. Young women, especially, frequently seek out a religionist whom they can approach anonymously, in some location far from their homes, on a one-time-only basis. This means that virtually no religionist can rely exclusively on *mizuko kuyō* for a livelihood.

Older clients for *mizuko kuyō* frequently seek to have rites performed by a parish temple with which their family is already affiliated. The Buddhist priesthood remains highly critical of entrepreneurial spiritualists' commercialization of *mizuko kuyō,* and even where *mizuko kuyō* has been established in ordinary parish temples, it usually falls into a category of minor rites such as pet memorials and rites to prevent or cure senility. *Mizuko kuyō*'s economic contribution to such temples is usually far overshadowed by funerals and ancestral memorial rites. When it assumes a larger role, it is generally because the temple is unable, for some reason, to sustain itself by traditional means.

When parish temples adopt *mizuko kuyō,* the practice can be incorporated in a form based on assessments levied on each parishioner household, on the basis of their parish membership, rather than on the basis of individual religious belief. This means that *mizuko kuyō* can be established more in the hope of economic return rather than on a foundation of universal support. This means also that *mizuko kuyō* can be established and practiced in parish temples by people who have no personal experience of abortion. In extreme cases, it can be established through coercion, and, as a result, people can turn against it. Even in such circumstances, however, the practice can be sustained at a low level by outsiders with no ongoing relation to the temple, if the priest does not oppose it.

In rural Japan, *mizuko kuyō* is practiced most by that generation born between 1920 and 1940, that is, by those who were of reproductive age when Japan's rate of abortion was highest. Among this group, male participation stands at between 20 to 30 percent. These rural supporters of *mizuko kuyō* are drawn from that cohort of Japan's population who brought Japan's birthrate down at an unparalleled speed, principally through abortion. These people thus bore the brunt of a major social change, ritualizing their experience long after the fact.

Observation at rural temples suggests, however, that the "boom" for *mizuko kuyō* is over, that statues erected for the purpose receive scant attention now, and that interest is decreasing.

The situation of *mizuko kuyō* in Japan today suggests that fetocentric rhetoric is rejected by the majority, even in the religious world. This is a hopeful conclusion, one pointing also to the majority's rejection of the fatalism and misogyny upon which the practice rests, a disdain for the use of fetishized images of the fetus to intimidate, a repudiation of religion's use to stigmatize and damn. This finding further suggests a reason to hope that pessimism and fatalism in Japan's religious world can be displaced by a more expansive and optimistic outlook.

Appendix: Sectarian Patterns in *Mizuko Kuyō*

The role of a temple's sectarian affiliation in determining whether it will offer *mizuko kuyō* for sale is a complex matter. Factors bearing on that question include not only the receptivity of priest and parishioners to the idea of *mizuko kuyō* itself, and the necessity of committing economic resources to construction of a facility for its practice (statues and associated liturgical gear), but also questions of the relations between sects in a given area, and, at another level, a sect administration's view of *mizuko kuyō*.

To what extent does the distribution of temples seen in the four field sites of this study differ from the representation of major sects in Japan as a whole? This question bears directly upon how much this study's results might be generalized to predict the extent to which *mizuko kuyō* is practiced nationally, the degree to which one might see the survey's results as representative of the larger phenomenon. While a significant skewing of sectarian distribution can be seen in the four field sites considered individually, when viewed collectively, the overall picture conforms in rough outline to the national distribution, as can be seen in Table A.1.

The three largest sects of Japanese Buddhism are Jōdo Shinshū, Sōtō, and Shingon, as measured by number of temples, accounting for roughly 29, 20, and 17 percent of the total number of temples in the country, respectively. The number of temples maintained by a particular sect can be taken as a reading of the number of believers. Indeed, given that official statistics on religious affiliation published by the Ministry of Education's Bureau of Culture are based on self-reporting by

Table A.1. *Field site temples by sect, compared with national sectarian distribution*

Sect	Total number of sectarian temples, all field sites	Percentage of sectarian temples, all field sites	Sect's percentage of all temples in Japan (total = 74,659)
Shingon	21	14.2	17
Tendai	12	8.1	6
Nichiren	18	12.2	9
Sōtō	14	9.5	20
Rinzai	14	9.5	8
Jōdo	30	20.1	11
Jōdo Shinshū	39	26.4	29
Total	148	100	100

SOURCE: Bunkachō, *Shūkyō nenkan, Heisei 4-nenban* (Tokyo: Gyōsei shuppan, 1993). This table omits temples of minor Buddhist sects not represented in the four field sites.

religious organizations, the number of temples reported may be a more reliable indicator than a sect's self-reported membership estimates. The latter are often reported in numbers such as "100,000," suggesting at best a "guesstimate." The number of temples, by contrast, is much less subject to rough estimation.[1] Table A.1 compares the percentage of temples of each sect represented in the survey to that sect's proportion of all Buddhist temples in Japan.[2] It will be seen that the Sōtō sect is somewhat underrepresented in the survey, while the Jōdo sect is somewhat overrepresented. The other major sects of Japanese Buddhism are represented in the survey in proportions deviating from their national distribution by less than 4 percent. Thus, the distribution of temples by sect in the survey roughly mirrors that found nationwide, taken as an aggregate.

The sectarian distribution of temples in each field site, however, is much less even, as seen in Table A.2. Tsuyama shows the most even pattern, deriving from its settlement as a castle town and the resulting concentration of temples in the temple district. The site is most notable for the underrepresentation of Jōdo Shinshū and Sōtō, and a considerable overrepresentation of Tendai. Tendai temples were not present in any of the other three field sites. Yukuhashi shows a contrasting concentration of Jōdo and Jōdo Shinshū. Miura shows a large concentration of Jōdo, Jōdo Shinshū, Rinzai, and Nichiren temples, with a corresponding underrepresentation of Sōtō and Shingon. Finally, in Tōno, Shingon and Sōtō have the largest number of temples, while Jōdo and Jōdo Shinshū are completely absent.

These various patterns of sectarian distribution of temples reflect historical patterns, such as the phenomenon discussed above of temple districts formed in castle towns, and the tendency for a sect to flourish in an area where its founder was active or in which disciples undertook major proselytization campaigns. While the factors just named help to account for why a sect may be overrepresented in a particular place, other historical factors may account for underrepresentation. The Nichiren, Jōdo Shinshū, and (to a lesser extent) Jōdo sects promote an exclusive orientation holding that theirs is the only path to salvation and that the alternatives offered by other sects are at best mistaken. By contrast, a more inclusive attitude is found in Shingon, Tendai, and the Zen schools. The exclusive attitude characterizing Nichiren, Jōdo Shinshū, and Jōdo is linked to patterns of temples that sought to blanket an area and exclude competing sects, though they rarely succeeded entirely. Also, at various points in Japan's premodern history, campaigns of persecution were leveled at branches of the Nichiren and Pure Land lines. During the Edo period, the *daimyō* of Okayama, Mito, and Owari pursued a policy promoting Shintō at Buddhism's expense, seeking opportunities to close or amalgamate temples. Similarly, in the early Meiji period, a movement called *haibutsukishaku* (roughly, "movement to destroy Buddhism") resulted in the destruction of numerous temples, but with wide regional disparity and a variety of results for different sects.

Let us consider Tsuyama first, referring to Table A.2. The concentration of temples in the temple district creates a situation unique to this site. If a temple in the temple district initiates *mizuko kuyō,* that fact is immediately known by the priests and parishioners of all the other temples located there, because they are all in unusual proximity to each other. This means that temples know that a decision to erect statues and commence a new, commercialized ritual will precipitate commentary and critique. In other words, the temples' proximity probably enhances the inherent conservatism of religious institutions, inhibiting any inclination to innovate, undoubtedly making many temples reluctant to start performing *mizuko kuyō.*

This trend is illustrated by the performance of Shingon in Tsuyama, as contrasted with its bearing in the other three sites. Only in Tsuyama do we find Shingon temples that do *not* perform *mizuko kuyō.* In all the

Table A.2. *Frequency of* mizuko kuyō *performance at Buddhist temples, by field site and sect*

Field site/sect[1]	Number of temples	Number offering *mizuko kuyō*	Number not offering *mizuko kuyō*	No clear policy; unknown
All temples surveyed	148 (100%)	64 (43%)	72 (49%)	12 (8%)
All temples surveyed, by sect				
Shingon	21 (100%)	17 (81%)	3 (14%)	1 (5%)
Tendai	12 (100%)	5 (42%)	6 (50%)	1 (8%)
Nichiren	18 (100%)	13 (72%)	5 (28%)	0 (0%)
Rinzai	14 (100%)	3 (21%)	8 (58%)	3 (21%)
Sōtō	14 (100%)	7 (50%)	5 (36%)	2 (14%)
Jōdo	30 (100%)	14 (47%)	12 (40%)	4 (13%)
Jōdo Shinshū	39 (100%)	5 (13%)	33 (85%)	1 (2%)
Field Sites				
Tsuyama	52 (100%)	22 (42%)	26 (50%)	4 (8%)
Sectarian breakdown:				
Shingon	13	9	3	1
Tendai	12	5	6	1
Nichiren	9	5	4	0
Rinzai	6	2	3	1
Sōtō	2	1	1	0
Jōdo	3	0	2	1
Jōdo Shinshū	7	0	7	0
Yukuhashi	49 (100%)	20 (41%)	27 (55%)	2 (4%)
Sectarian breakdown:				
Shingon	2	2	0	0
Tendai	0	0	0	0
Nichiren	2	2	0	0
Rinzai	0	0	0	0
Sōtō	4	2	2	0
Jōdo	17	10	6	1
Jōdo Shinshū	24	4	19	1
Miura	36 (100%)	15 (42%)	18 (50%)	3 (8%)
Sectarian breakdown:				
Shingon	1	1	0	0
Tendai	0	0	0	0
Nichiren	6	5	1	0
Rinzai	7	1	5	1
Sōtō	4	3	1	0
Jōdo	10	4	4	2
Jōdo Shinshū	8	1	7	0

Table A.2. *(continued)*

Field site sect[1]	Number of temples	Number offering *mizuko kuyō*	Number not offering *mizuko kuyō*	No clear policy; unknown
Tōno	11 (100%)	7 (64%)	1 (9%)	3 (27%)
Sectarian breakdown:				
Shingon	5	5	0	0
Tendai	0	0	0	0
Nichiren	1	1	0	0
Rinzai	1	0	0	1
Sōtō	4	1	1	2
Jōdo	0	0	0	0
Jōdo Shinshū	0	0	0	0

[1]Does not include new religions, non-Buddhist institutions, or Buddhist temples present in field sites but not presently operating.

other sites, all the Shingon temples provide these rites in some form. The same factor may be operating in Nichiren temples in Tsuyama, where the proportion of this sect's temples providing *mizuko kuyō* is almost the same as those that do not, whereas all of them do in Yukuhashi and Tōno, and only one Nichiren temple in Miura does not. Similarly, Tsuyama is the only site where Jōdo Shinshū's prohibition on *mizuko kuyō* is enacted to the letter.

By contrast with the Tsuyama temples located in the temple district, the two temples in the area offering *mizuko kuyō* on the largest scale and with the greatest degree of innovations in ritual form are located at a considerable distance from the district. Jionji (Tendai), discussed in chapter 4, and Myōsenji (Nichiren) are the most conspicuous purveyors of *mizuko kuyō* in Tsuyama at this time, and the scale of observance of the rites seen in the temple district pales by comparison.

Yukuhashi shows a much more skewed distribution of Buddhist temples by sect, with forty-one of forty-nine temples held by Jōdo Shinshū and Jōdo, overwhelming the number of other sects' temples. Here we find the highest number of Jōdo Shinshū temples offering *mizuko kuyō*. In the area of rites offered to nonparishioners, there is a sense in which Jōdo and Jōdo Shinshū are in competition with each other in Yukuhashi, and this may account, in part, for the willingness of some Jōdo Shinshū priests to provide *mizuko kuyō*. It should be noted, however, that in no Jōdo Shinshū temple observed in this survey did we see any of the characteristic paraphernalia of statuary and other equipment typical of *mizuko kuyō*. The practice takes the form of individual consultation, no doubt to avoid criticism for violation of sect policy. It may be more possible for Jōdo Shinshū temples at a distance from the sect's Kyoto headquarters to evade a requirement for conformity than for those located as close as Tsuyama.

Table A.2 shows that in Miura, the temples of the Nichiren and Sōtō sects perform *mizuko kuyō* at rates above their averages in the four sites taken collectively. It is also only in this site that a Rinzai temple, Daichinji, proved to be the area's largest provider of *mizuko kuyō*. The one Jōdo Shinshū temple in Miura that provides *mizuko kuyō* is located in the vicinity of Daichinji and, like it, is both surrounded by the residences of the area's coastal fishing population and located near tourist sites. By contrast, Miura has the survey's only Nichiren temple that offers *mizuko kuyō* without the customary statuary and other visible signs.

Tōno offers the most extreme distribution of *mizuko kuyō* services seen by sect, in that *all* of the temples of two sects, Shingon and Nichiren, offer the rites. Overall, 64 percent of the area's temples perform *mizuko kuyō* in some form, a significantly higher proportion than that observed elsewhere. However, this is an instance in which statistics conceal a different reality.

Tōno was originally chosen as a research site because it is, on the face of it, so unlikely an area to have initiated a novel practice. It is a deeply conservative agricultural area, rather remote from major cities, and not noted for its acceptance of religious change. It is the last place one would expect to find *mizuko kuyō*, but contrary to this expectation is the rate of 64 percent. How are we to account for this?

The absence in Tōno of Jōdo Shinshū temples probably facilitates the area's high overall rate of performance of *mizuko kuyō*. That is, there is no representation in Tōno of a sectarian opposition to *mizuko kuyō* on doctrinal grounds.

Observation at those Tōno temples which perform *mizuko kuyō* proved that while all but one of these temples have installed ritual facilities with statuary and the like, in several cases they showed no sign of *any* devotional activity. There were no offerings or *tōba*, and their flower vases were empty. The dedicatory inscriptions on the installations make it clear that *mizuko kuyō* was initiated in Tōno around 1975. Three of Tōno's five Shingon temples, all of which offer *mizuko kuyō*, nevertheless show no sign of any activity. One of these is the survey's only Shingon temple lacking the customary statuary and other ritual paraphernalia.

Notes

Preface

1. Rosalind Petchesky, *Abortion and Woman's Choice* (London: Verso, 1984); Kristin Luker, *Taking Chances: Abortion and the Decision Not to Contracept* (Berkeley and Los Angeles: University of California Press, 1975); idem, *Abortion and the Politics of Motherhood* (Berkeley and Los Angeles: University of California Press, 1984).

2. Rickie Solinger, *Wake Up Little Susie: Single Pregnancy and Race Before Roe v. Wade* (London: Routledge, 1992); Ellen Messer and Kathryn E. May, *Back Rooms: Voices from the Illegal Abortion Era* (Buffalo, N.Y.: Prometheus Books, 1994); Nancy Howell Lee, *The Search for an Abortionist* (Chicago: University of Chicago Press, 1969); Rita Townsend and Ann Perkins, *Bitter Fruit: Women's Experiences of Unplanned Pregnancy, Abortion, and Adoption* (Alameda, California: Hunter House, 1991); James C. Mohr, *Abortion in America: The Origins and Evolution of National Policy, 1800–1900* (Oxford: Oxford University Press, 1978); Laurel Thatcher Ulrich, *A Midwife's Tale: The Life of Martha Ballard, Based on Her Diary, 1785–1812* (New York: Vintage Books, 1990).

3. Judith A. Allen, *Sex and Secrets: Crimes Involving Australian Women Since 1880* (Oxford: Oxford University Press, 1990).

Introduction

1. Helen Hardacre, *Kurozumikyō and the New Religions of Japan* (Princeton: Princeton University Press, 1986), pp. 151–52.

2. Petchesky, *Abortion and Woman's Choice,* pp. 338–39.

3. George Devereux, "A Typological Study of Abortion in 350 Primitive, Ancient, and Pre-Industrial Societies," in *Abortion in America,* ed. Harold Rosen (Boston: Beacon Press, 1967), p. 98.

4. Quoted in Petchesky, *Abortion and Woman's Choice*, p. xii.

5. Osada Hideo's response to questioning, "Proceedings of the Budget Committee at the House of Councillors," no. 13 (April 2, 1970), 12; quoted in Kozy Kazuko Amemiya, "The Road to Pro-Choice Ideology in Japan: A Social History of the Contest Between the State and Individuals Over Abortion" (Ph.D. diss., University of California, San Diego, 1993), pp. 270–71.

6. *Liquid Life: Abortion and Buddhism in Japan* by William R. LaFleur (Princeton: Princeton University Press, 1992) is the most comprehensive of the scholarly studies of *mizuko kuyō*. This rich and evocative study seeks to provide an account of *mizuko kuyō* through its historical and contemporary religious associations, stressing the cult's continuity in general terms with such historic elements of Japanese religious history as the cult of Jizō and belief in spirit vengeance. A shorter study by Bardwell Smith, "Buddhism and Abortion in Contemporary Japan: *Mizuko kuyō* and the Confrontation with Death," *Japanese Journal of Religious Studies* 15 (1988): 3–24, provides general remarks and observations on the practice in terms of its providing a ritual means for dealing with abortion. An earlier work by Anne P. Brooks, "*Mizuko kuyō* and Japanese Buddhism," *Japanese Journal of Religious Studies* 8 (1981): 119–47, provided the first widely circulating study of the practice. A study based on surveys at Kyoto temples by Bardwell Smith and Elizabeth Harrison is forthcoming in English; a summary of its findings in Japanese is currently available in Rinzaishū Myōshinjiha Kyōka Center, *Gō no setsu ni kansuru honpa sōryō no ishiki to sono jittai*, Kenkyū Hōkoku 1 (Kyoto: Rinzaishū Myōshinjiha Kyōka Center, 1989), pp. 58–59, 159–66. Zwi Werblowsky's study of votive plaques dedicated to *mizuko* at a Tokyo temple is available in "*Mizuko kuyō*: Notulae on the Most Important 'New Religion' of Japan," *Japanese Journal of Religious Studies* 18 (1991): 295–334.

7. Buddhological studies of *mizuko kuyō* are mainly critical of the practice and see it as an illegitimate adaptation of the cult of the Bodhisattva Jizō; these sources are discussed in detail in chapter 1. A distinct category of Buddhological studies consists of those works deriving from the Jōdo Shinshū sect, which denies the validity of *mizuko kuyō* and prohibits its priests from performing it; these sources are discussed at length in chapter 4.

8. A group of scholars at Kyoto University, headed by Takahashi Saburō, has collected the most comprehensive data: "Mizuko kuyō ni kansuru tokei chōsa shiryō" (Kyoto Daigaku Kyōyōbu Shakaigaku Kyōshitsu, 1992); this study remains unpublished, but its results have been summarized in published form in Shinden Mitsuko, "Mizuko kuyō ni kansuru tokei chōsa shiryō," *Ryūkoku Daigaku Shakaigakubu Gakkai Kiyō* 2 (1991): 46–60. See also Kamihara Kazuko et al., "Nihonjin no shūkyō ishiki ni kansuru kyōdō kenkyū no hōkoku, oyobi ronbun," *Tōkyō Kōgei Daigaku Kōgakubu Kiyō* 8 (1985): 77–114; and, idem, "Nihonjin no shūkyō ishiki ni kansuru kyōdō kenkyū no hōkoku," *Tōkyō Kōgei Daigaku Kōgakubu Kiyō* 10 (1987): 22–54. See also the study by Rinzaishū Myōshinjiha mentioned in note 6, for miscellaneous data on the practice of *mizuko kuyō* in the Rinzai sect.

9. The ethnographic work of geographer Morikuri Shigekazu belongs in this category; see his "Mizuko kuyō no hassei to genjō," *Kokuritsu rekishi min-*

zoku hakubutsukan kenkyū hōkoku 57 (1994): 95–127. Since the completion of the present study, he has also published a monograph on the subject that includes an interesting investigation of tabloid advertising about *mizuko kuyō: Fushigidani no kodomotachi* (Tokyo: Shinjinbutsu ōraisha, 1995). A shorter study by Miyata Noboru, linking the contemporary phenomenon to Edo-period uses of the term *mizuko*, is available in *Kokoro naoshi wa naze hayaru* (Tokyo: Shōgakkan, 1993), pp. 80–88. Dōzen Mineo, specialist in the folklore of Okayama Prefecture, has written a highly critical study of the practice of *mizuko kuyō* throughout western Japan: *Akago, mabiki no shūzoku* (Okayama: Nihon bunkyō shuppan KK, 1989). See also Shimizu Kunihiko, "Shōwa 45 nen (1970) izen kara no mizuko kuyō," *Saikō minzokugaku* 148 (1994): 21–25, and Tano Noboru, *Ōsaka no Jizō-san* (Tokyo: Keizuisha, 1994), pp. 147–58.

10. One of the better studies of this kind is Hoshino Eiki and Takeda Dōshō, "*Mizuko kuyō* and Abortion in Contemporary Japan," in *Religion and Society in Modern Japan: Selected Readings,* ed. Mark Mullins et al. (Berkeley, Calif.: Asian Humanities Press, 1993), pp. 171–90. Hoshino and Takeda emphasize the influence upon *mizuko kuyō* of changing concepts of responsibility for abortion, from a collective focus to one centered uniquely upon individual women.

11. A number of studies criticizing *mizuko kuyō* are introduced in chapters 2 and 4; in addition to them, see the following works by Takahashi Man: "Mizuko kuyō to josei no iyashi," *Sei no porifonī* (Tokyo: Sekai shisōsha, 1990), pp. 284–94, and "Fuan no shakai ni motomeru shūkyō," *Gendai shakaigaku* 13 (1987): 41–57. See also Akitsu Shō, "Mizuko kuyō no enshutsu de boro mōke no shūkyōya-tachi," *Seikai ōrai* (June 1987): 236–45, and Takahashi Yoshinori, "Zaisekikan to sono keimetsu, mizuko kuyō chōsa kara," *Soshiorogī* 32 (1987): 93–97. A special issue of a journal dedicated to eradicating discrimination against *burakumin* was devoted to the significance of *mizuko kuyō* as a support for discrimination: *Sabetsu to tatakau bunka* 12 (spring 1984).

12. See, for example, Edwin O. Reischauer and John K. Fairbank, *East Asia, the Modern Transformation* (Boston: Houghton Mifflin, 1960); Marius B. Jansen, ed., *Changing Japanese Attitudes Toward Modernization,* Studies in the Modernization of Japan, no. 1 (Princeton: Princeton University Press, 1965); Ronald P. Dore, ed., *Aspects of Social Change in Modern Japan,* Studies in the Modernization of Japan, no. 3 (Princeton: Princeton University Press, 1967).

13. Earlier works of this kind included the work of E. H. Norman and John Dower; see John W. Dower, ed., *Origins of the Modern Japanese State: Selected Writings of E. H. Norman* (New York: Random House, 1975); John W. Dower, *Japan in War and Peace: Selected Essays* (New York: New Press, 1993).

14. See Hiroshi Wagatsuma and George DeVos, *Heritage of Endurance: Family Patterns and Delinquency Formation in Urban Japan* (Berkeley and Los Angeles: University of California Press, 1983); George DeVos, ed., *Japan's Invisible Race: Caste in Culture and Personality* (Berkeley and Los Angeles: University of California Press, 1966); Joyce Lebra, Joy Paulson, and Elizabeth Powers, eds., *Women in Changing Japan* (Boulder, Colo.: Westview, 1976); Takie Lebra, *Japanese Women: Constraint and Fulfillment* (Honolulu: University of Hawaii Press, 1984); Susan J. Pharr, *Losing Face: Status Politics in Japan* (Berkeley and

Los Angeles: University of California Press, 1990); idem, *Political Women in Japan: The Search for a Place in Political Life* (Berkeley and Los Angeles: University of California Press, 1981).

15. The People's History school is mainly associated with Irokawa Daikichi; see his "Freedom and the Concept of People's Rights," *Japan Quarterly* 14 (1967): 175–83, and *The Culture of the Meiji Period,* ed. and trans. Marius Jansen (Princeton: Princeton University Press, 1985). For an introduction to the People's History school, see Carol Gluck, "The People in History: Recent Trends in Japanese Historiography," *Journal of Asian Studies* 38 (1978): 25–50.

16. For example, see Victor Koschmann and Tetsuo Najita, eds., *Conflict in Japanese History: The Neglected Tradition* (Princeton: Princeton University Press, 1982); Ellis Krauss, Thomas Rohlen, and Patricia Steinhoff, eds., *Conflict in Japan* (Honolulu: University of Hawaii Press, 1984).

17. Ross Mouer and Yoshio Sugimoto, *Images of Japanese Society: A Study in the Social Construction of Reality* (New York: KPI, 1986).

18. Ian Reader and George Tanabe, eds. *Conflict and Religion in Japan,* special issue of *Japanese Journal of Religious Studies* 21 (June–September 1994).

19. Iwao Sumiko, *The Japanese Woman: Traditional Image and Changing Reality* (New York: Free Press, 1993).

1. Reproductive Ritualization Before *Mizuko Kuyō*

1. See Kamata Hisako, "Sanba—sono fujoteki seikaku ni tsuite," *Seijō bungei* 42 (1966): 47–60.

2. Matsuoka Etsuko, *Shussan no bunka jinruigaku* (Tokyo: Kaimeisha, 1985), p. 23.

3. Aoyagi Machiko, "Kihisareta sei," in *Ie to josei, kurashi no bunkashi* (Tokyo: Shōgakkan, 1985), 10:420 ff.

4. Kamata, "Sanba."

5. In a variation on this practice from Yamanashi Prefecture, known also in southern Kyūshū, the woman's natal family provided this meal, with the implication that they were putting the husband's family on notice that they would not tolerate the termination of the pregnancy by abortion; see Miyata, *Kokoro naoshi,* p. 87.

6. Takagi Seiichi, "Ninshin oyobi shussan ni kansuru zokushin," *Minzokugaku* 1 (1929): 49–53; Tachibana Shōichi, "Ninshin, shussan, ikuji ni kansuru zokushin," *Minzokugaku* 1 (1929): 351–53.

7. Tachibana, "Ninshin," 351–53.

8. Ijima Yoshiharu, "Kodomo no hakken to jidō yūgi no sekai," in *Ie to josei,* p. 241.

9. Kamata, "Sanba," 52–53.

10. Nagata Tsuneko, "Ubugami shinkō ni okeru ishi—Aichi-ken Mikawa chihō no jirei ni tsuite," *Josei to keiken* 8 (1983): 19–22; Kamata, "Sanba," 53.

11. Nagata, "Ubugami shinkō ni okeru ishi," 20.

12. Kamata, "Sanba," 57.

13. Nomura Keiko, "Osan no kamisama oboegaki," *Josei to keiken* 7 (1982): 9–12.

14. Tsuboi Hirofumi, "Murashakai to tsūka girei," in *Mura to murabito* (Tokyo: Shōgakkan, 1984), 8:455–506.

15. Kobayashi Norihiro, "Shussan no shūzoku ni mirareru juryoku," *Inaji* 27 (1983): 6.

16. Tone Takashiro, "Minzokushakai ni okeru shussan kūkan ninshiki no chiikisei," *Josei to keiken* 7 (1982): 57–61.

17. Aoyagi, "Kihisareta sei," pp. 420 ff. In Kumage County, Yamaguchi Prefecture, childlessness was believed to be a punishment for a woman's husband's killing birds, indicating a rare, veiled recognition of male infertility.

18. Tone, "Minzokushakai ni okeru shussan," 58–61.

19. See Susan B. Hanley and Kōzō Yamamura, *Economics and Demographic Change in Preindustrial Japan, 1600–1868* (Princeton: Princeton University Press, 1977).

20. Aoyagi, "Kihisareta sei," pp. 429–39.

21. Fujime Yuki, "Aru sanba no shisseki," *Nihonshi kenkyū* 366 (1993): 99; Ochiai Emiko, "Aru sanba no Nihon kindai," in *Seido toshite no onna—sei, san, kazoku no hikaku shakaishi* (Tokyo: Heibonsha, 1990).

22. Chiba Tokuji and Ōtsu Tadao, *Mabiki to mizuko* (Tokyo: Nōsan gyōson bunka kyōkai, 1983).

23. Ijima, "Kodomo no hakken," pp. 246–49.

24. Artifacts such as votive tablets from Buddhist temples depicting the sufferings in hell of people who commit abortion and infanticide are known, but have not been found in such numbers or been so widely distributed as to suggest a major campaign of stigmatization and sanction. One recent study examines numerous artifacts cited as evidence of premodern *mizuko kuyō* to deny this interpretation: Shimizu, "Shōwa 45 nen izen kara no mizuko kuyō," 21–25. Shimizu shows, for example, that the "*mizuko kuyō*" at the Tokyo temple Ekōin was actually erected to memorialize those who died with no relatives to perform rites for them in fires of the Meireki era (1655–1658), and had no relation whatsoever to reproductive practice. In this way, he accounts for virtually all the so-called evidence of premodern *mizuko kuyō* that originated in and around Edo and Osaka. In any case, most such "evidence" results from the didactic control measures of social elites, rather than reflecting popular sentiment.

25. John Henry Wigmore, ed., *Law and Justice in Tokugawa Japan: Materials for the History of Japanese Law and Justice under the Tokugawa Shogunate, 1603–1867* (Tokyo: University of Tokyo Press, 1967), 7:15–44.

26. Takemi Momoko, "'Menstruation Sutra' Belief in Japan," *Japanese Journal of Religious Studies* 10 (1983): 229–48.

27. Ono Yasuhiro, "Nagare kanjō kara mizuko kuyō e," *Dentō to gendai* 75 (1987): 18–25. In Ibaragi Prefecture, these rites were known as *kawa segaki*, "feeding the hungry ghosts of the river."

28. Ishikawa Rikizan, "Kirigami densho to kinsei Sōtō-shū," in *Minshū shūkyō no kōzō to keifu*, ed. Tamamuro Fumio (Tokyo: Yūzankaku, 1995), pp. 310–18.

29. Miyata, *Kokoro naoshi*, p. 86. For a survey of water imagery in Japanese religions that may inform the contemporary *mizuko* idea, see LaFleur, *Liquid Life*, pp. 22–26.

30. Wigmore, *Law and Justice in Tokugawa Japan*, 15–44.

31. Ijima, "Kodomo no hakken," pp. 264–67.

32. Yoritomi Motohiro, *Shomin no hotoke* (Tokyo: NHK, 1984), p. 158.

33. The three main Jizō sutras are: *Jizō hongankyō* (T 13, no. 412), *Daijō daijitsu Jizō jūrinkyō* (T 13, no. 411), *Senzatsu zen'aku gōhōkyō* (T 19, no. 839).

34. Yoritomi, *Shomin no hotoke,* pp. 97–113; Hayami Tasuku, *Bosatsu, Bukkyō nyūmon* (Tokyo: Tōkyō bijutsu, 1982), pp. 148–52.

35. For example, there was the illustrated scroll *Yata jizō engi emaki* and the miracle tale *Jizō bosatsu reigenki.*

36. Yoritomi, *Shomin no hotoke,* pp. 115–18.

37. Hayami, *Bosatsu,* p. 164; Yoritomi, *Shomin no hotoke,* pp. 147–48.

38. Manabe Kōsai, *Jizō bosatsu no kenkyū* (Kyoto: Sanmitsudō, 1960), pp. 98–222.

39. Ibid., pp. 205, 208.

40. Ibid., p. 214. Another study concludes that there are no premodern precedents for any association between Jizō and the idea of fetal wrath; see Tano, *Ōsaka no Jizō-san.*

41. Ibid., p. 209.

42. The following study presents a comparison of the several versions of this story: Kuretsukasa Yukiko, "Yūten shōnin no ichi daiki o chūshin to suru Kasane setsuwa no kenkyū," *Ocha no mizu daigaku kokubun* 43 (1970).

43. Takada Minoru, *Edo no akuryō baraishi* (Tokyo: Chikuma shobō, 1994), pp. 245–59.

44. Ibid., pp. 260–67.

45. The *Tokugawa jikki* (completed 1849), the official history of the Tokugawa house, established that Katsura Shōin became a patron of Yūten based on the fame he had achieved at Haniyū as an exorcist; see Takada, *Edo no akuryō baraishi,* p. 150.

46. Ibid., pp. 215 ff.

47. James McClain and John M. Merriman, "Edo and Paris: Cities and Power," in *Edo and Paris: Urban Life and the State in the Early Modern Era,* ed. James McClain and John M. Merriman (Ithaca: Cornell University Press, 1994), p. 17.

48. Jurgis Elisonas, "Notorious Places: A Brief Excursion into the Narrative Topography of Early Edo," in McClain and Merriman, *Edo and Paris,* pp. 265–67.

49. Quoted in Takada, *Edo no akuryō baraishi,* pp. 208–12.

50. Sekiyama Kazuo, *Sekkyō no rekishiteki kenkyū* (Kyoto: Hōzōkan, 1973), p. 307.

51. Ibid., p. 310.

52. Ibid., p. 307.

53. Takada, *Edo no akuryō baraishi,* p. 337.

54. Takada (ibid., pp. 24–25) says that the following passage from *Kishinron* (composed 1688–1704) was based in part on what Arai Hakuseki knew of Yūten's role in the Haniyū Village exorcisms, made known in the 1690 "Tale of Salvation for Spirits of the Dead."

55. Matsumura Akira et al., eds., *Arai Hakuseki,* vol. 35, *Nihonshisō taikei* (Tokyo: Iwanami shoten, 1975), pp. 159–60.

56. Samuel Hideo Yamashita, *Master Sorai's Responsals: An Annotated Translation of Sorai Sensei Tōmonsho* (Honolulu: University of Hawaii Press, 1994), p. 72.

57. Fujii Masao et al., eds., *Bukkyō sōsai daijiten* (Tokyo: Yūzankaku, 1980), pp. 57–60.

58. Nakamura Hajime, "Kitō," in *Bukkyōgo daijiten*, 3 vols. (Tokyo: Tōkyō shoseki, 1975), 1:205–6.

59. The word *mizuko* does not appear.

60. Ihara Saikaku, *Kōshoku ichidai no onna: The Life of an Amorous Woman and Other Writings*, ed. and trans. Ivan Morris (Norfolk, Conn.: New Directions, 1963). See also Takada, *Edo no akuryō baraishi*, p. 224.

61. Sekiyama, *Sekkyō no rekishiteki kenkyū*, pp. 271–72.

62. Takada, *Edo no akuryō baraishi*, pp. 215 ff.

63. Ibid., pp. 219–27.

64. Morikuri, "Mizuko kuyō no hassei to genjō," 98.

65. Miyata, *Kokoro naoshi*, pp. 83–84.

66. Hoshino and Takeda, "*Mizuko kuyō* and Abortion in Contemporary Japan," p. 175.

67. Ibid., p. 232.

68. David I. Kertzer, *Sacrificed for Honor: Infant Abandonment and the Politics of Reproductive Control* (Boston: Beacon, 1993).

69. Takada, *Edo no akuryō baraishi*, pp. 99, 117–18.

70. Murakami Shigeyoshi, "Tenrikyō no shinwa to minshū kyūzai," in *Minshū to shakai* (Tokyo: Shunbunsha, 1988), 10:194–98.

71. Ibid., pp. 198–202.

72. Tenrikyō Kyōkai Honbu, *Tenrikyō kyōsoden* (Tenri: Tenrikyō Dōyūkai, 1956), p. 1.

73. Murakami, "Tenrikyō no shinwa," p. 203.

74. Shimazono Susumu, "Kamigakari kara tasuke made," *Komazawa daigaku bukkyōgakubu ronshū* 8 (1977): 210.

75. Tenrikyō Kyōkai Honbu, *Kyōsoden*, pp. 262–64.

76. Yoshimura Noriko, "Josei no seikatsu to shussan kankō no henbō," *Kikan jinruigaku* 14 (1983); Matsuoka, *Shussan no bunka jinruigaku*.

77. Shima Kazuharu, *Sanba monogatari* (Tokyo: Kenkyūkan, 1981); Ueno Terumasa, "Shussan o meguru ishiki henka to josei no kenri," in *Nihon josei seikatsushi*, ed. Joseishi sōgō kenkyūkai (Tokyo: Tōkyō Daigaku shuppankai, 1990); Ochiai, "Aru sanba"; Fujime Yuki, "Senkanki Nihon no sanji chōsetsu undō to sono shisō," *Rekishi hyōron* 430 (1986): 79–100.

78. I am grateful to Tiana Norgren of Columbia University for useful consultations on the history of laws governing abortion and related matters, and for use of her unpublished translations of them.

79. Fujime, "Senkanki,"; Ishizaki Shōko, "Seishoku no jiyū to sanji chōsetsu undō," *Rekishi hyōron* 503 (1992): 92–107; Ichibangase Yasuko, *Nihon fujin mondai shiryō shūsei*, vol. 6, *Hoken, fukushi* (Tokyo: Domesu shuppan, 1978), chaps. 1–2.

80. See Fujime, "Aru sanba no shisseki."

81. Idem, "Aru sanba no shisseki" and "Senkanki"; Ishizaki, "Seishoku no jiyū"; Katō Shidzue, *A Fight for Women's Happiness: Pioneering the Family*

Planning Movement in Japan, JOICFP Document Series no. 11 (Tokyo: Japanese Organization for International Cooperation in Family Planning, 1984).

82. Tenrikyō Kyōkai Honbu, *Kyōsoden,* pp. 76, 262–64; Tenshōkōtai Jingūkyō, *Seisho* (Tabuse, Yamaguchi Prefecture: Tenshōkōtai Jingūkyō, 1952), 1:385.

83. Deborah Jane Hacker Oakley, "The Development of Population Policy in Japan, 1945–1952, and American Participation" (Ph.D. diss., University of Michigan, 1977).

84. Obayashi Michiko, *Josanpu no sengo* (Tokyo: Keisho shobō, 1989); for more on midwives in Japan's natural childbirth movement, see Matsuoka Etsuko, "Bunka to shussan—Nihon no shizen bunben undō o chūshin to-shite," *Minzokugaku kenkyū* 47 (1983): 356–81; Kōseishō 50 nenshi henshū iinkai, *Kōseishō 50 nenshi* (Tokyo: Kōsei mondai kenkyūkai, 1990).

85. Katō Kōichi, *Keikaku bunben* (Tokyo: Shindan to chiryōsha, 1988).

2. The Practice of *Mizuko Kuyō* and the Changing Nature of Abortion

1. A recent dissertation on SCAP's role in population policy identifies surprising reasons for neutrality in this area, having more to do with geopolitics than demographers' concerns. SCAP wished to minimize the Soviet role in the Occupation and not to encourage the growth of Japan's Communist Party. Since the Soviet Union's own policy was legal abortion and promotion of birth control, SCAP wanted to avoid creating Soviet sympathizers through fertility control. Second, the Nuremburg War Crimes Trials were proceeding, charging Germans with crimes against humanity and genocide, in part through forced sterilizations. In order to forestall a countercharge that occupying forces sought to commit genocide in Germany by controlling births, the Occupation in Germany permitted no birth control. Added to these considerations was a stream of pontifical invective against birth control, calling it "a greater disaster in Japan than the atomic bomb." These three factors combined to make neutrality the safest course for the Occupation in Japan, according to Oakley, "Development of Population Policy in Japan" (Ph.D. diss., University of Michigan, 1977), pp. 176–78, 209.

2. Kitaoka Jitsui, quoted in ibid., p. 6.

3. Katō, S., *A Fight for Women's Happiness,* p. 96.

4. Fumiko Amano, "Family Planning Movement in Japan," *Contemporary Japan* 23 (1955). Other American commentators have tended to confirm SCAP's neutrality, as did demographer Irene Taeuber and members of the 1948 Rockefeller Mission on Public Health in the Far East.

5. Kōseishō 50 nenshi henshū iinkai, *Kōseishō 50 nenshi,* pp. 716–18.

6. Tatsuo Honda, *Population Problems in Post War Japan* (Tokyo: The Institute of Population Problems, Welfare Ministry, 1957), pp. 13, 14, 18 n. 3; Robert Hodge and Ogawa Naohiro, *Fertility Change in Contemporary Japan* (Chicago: University of Chicago Press, 1991), p. 45.

7. See Andrew Gordon, "Conclusion," in *Postwar Japan as History,* ed. Andrew Gordon (Berkeley and Los Angeles: University of California Press, 1993).

8. Hardacre, *Kurozumikyō and the New Religions of Japan,* chap. 1.

9. The periodization of postwar religious life adopted here matches the account in Inoue Nobutaka et al., eds., *Shinshūkyō jiten* (Tokyo: Kōbundō, 1990), pp. 32–39.

10. While scholars recognize the reality of the "boom," not all are happy with this journalistic way of stating the matter. Inoue Nobutaka objects because the founding, expansion, routinization, and "fossilization" of religions is a regular feature of Japanese religious history, and thus the present state of affairs hardly comes out of the blue, but is to be expected. What is new here, he would say, is journalism's attention to religion, not rises and falls in religion's vitality. See Inoue Nobutaka, *Shinshūkyō no kaidoku* (Tokyo: Chikuma shobō, 1992), p. 160.

11. Shimazono Susumu, *Gendai kyūsai shūkyōron* (Tokyo: Seikyūsha, 1992), pp. 221–22.

12. Inoue et al., *Shinshūkyō jiten;* Nihon Hōsō Kyōkai, ed. *Gendai Nihonjin no ishiki kōzō* (Tokyo: Nihon Hōsō shuppan kyōkai, 1985), pp. 108–19.

13. Nishiyama Shigeru, "Reijutsuteki shinshūkyō no taitō to futatsu no kindaika," in *Kindaika to shūkyō būmu,* ed. Kokugakuin Daigaku Nihon Bunka Kenkyūjo (Tokyo: Dōbō shuppan, 1990), pp. 93–98.

14. The term "new-new religion" (*shin-shin shūkyō*) was originally coined by Taishō University sociologist of religions Nishiyama Shigeru, who has since repudiated it in favor of the adjective *reijutsuteki,* "concerning the manipulation of spirits"; see ibid., p. 69.

15. Numata Ken'ya, *Gendai Nihonjin no shinshūkyō* (Tokyo: Sōgensha, 1988).

16. On contemporary urban shamanism in Japan, see the following: Ōishi Kōichi, *Nihon no reinōryokusha* (Tokyo: Nihon bungeisha, 1983); Ōishi Kōichi, *Kiseki no reinōryokusha* (Tokyo: Nihon bungeisha, 1984); Asahi Shinbun Shakaibu, *Gendai no chiisa na kamigami* (Tokyo: Asahi Shinbun Shakaibu, 1984); Fujita Shōichi, *Ogamiyasan, reinōkitōshi no sekai* (Tokyo: Kōbundō, 1990); Maeda Atsushi, "Machi no reinōsha to shinjatachi," *Shisō no kagaku* 374 (1983); Maeda Hiroshi, *Nihon no reinōsha* (Tokyo: Kabushikigaisha koa, 1986); Ōishi Kōichi, *Nihon no reinōryokusha* (Tokyo: Nihon bungeisha, 1983); idem, *Kiseki no reinōryokusha* (Tokyo: Nihon bungeisha, 1984); Satō Noriaki, "Toshi shāmanizumu," in *Ronshū: Nihon Bukkyōshi—Taishō, Shōwa* (Tokyo: Yūzankaku, 1988); Shiromizu Hiroko, "Henka ējento to shite no shinshūkyō no reinōryokusha—S-Kyōdan no jirei," in *Hendōki no ningen to shūkyō,* ed. Morioka Kiyomi (Tokyo: Miraisha, 1978); Shūkyō Shakaigaku no Kai, *Ikoma no kamigami, gendai toshi no minzoku shūkyō* (Tokyo: Sōgensha, 1986); Sugeno Kuniharu, ed., *Kami no rei no koe o tsugeru hitobito—unmei ni hikari o ateru kiseki no reinōsha sanjūnin* (Tokyo: Shuppan kagaku sōgō kenkyūjo, 1986); Watanabe Masako, "Shinshūkyō shūdan no hassei katei—Hamamatsu-shi no Jiseikai ni okeru kyōso tanjō o megutte," in *Toshi shakai no shūkyō—Hamamatsu-shi ni okeru shūkyō hendō no shōsō,* ed. Tamaru Noriyoshi (Tokyo: Tōkyō Daigaku Shūkyōgaku Kenkyūshitsu, 1981).

17. Oakley, "Development of Population Policy," fig. 7, p. 187. Japan was spared the religious rancor characterizing debate over the meaning of condoms (disease preventative or contraceptive?) that occurred in the United States; see Joshua Gamson, "Rubber Wars: Struggle Over the Condom in the United States," in *American Sexual Politics: Sex, Gender, and Race Since the Civil*

War, ed. John C. Tout and M. S. Tantillo (Chicago: The University of Chicago Press, 1993), pp. 322–31.

18. Katō, S., *A Fight for Women's Happiness,* pp. 94 ff; Amano, "Family Planning," pp. 5 ff.

19. The Mainichi newspaper began a valuable biennial survey in 1950; see Honda, *Population Problems,* pp. 1 ff.

20. Katō, S., *A Fight for Women's Happiness,* p. 99.

21. Few studies of advice columns have been written, and most of these rather uncritically use them as direct reflections of social reality. A selection of translations from *jinsei annai* was published by John and Asako McKinstry (*Jinsei annai: Life's Guide,* Armonk, N.Y.: M. E. Sharpe, 1991), but without extensive analysis. A dissertation on the long-running series "Can This Marriage Be Saved?" shows how mythical images of the family are constructed; see Sandra O. Harrigan, "Marriage and Family: Myth, Media, Behavior" (Ph.D. diss., Columbia University Teachers College, 1989). A study by Christian Bringreve uses a Dutch advice column to chart changing social values in "On Modern Relationships: The Commandments of the New Freedom," *Netherlands Journal of Sociology* 18 (1982): 47–56.

22. Most letters on contraception and abortion have been written and responded to by women. This is the case in all the letters cited in this chapter.

23. Readers should not be understood as passive recipients of response writers' judgments, but as active participants in the construction of meaning. Studies of television and "women's fiction" have been especially influential in developing this perspective. See Dorothy Hobson, *"Crossroads": The Drama of a Soap Opera* (London: Methuen, 1982). David Morley shows how viewers of television use dramatic content in their interactions; see *Family Television: Cultural Power and Domestic Leisure* (London: Comedia, 1986). This study assumes that there is an analogy between television viewing and newspaper reading with respect to soap opera, family drama, and the advice columns, such that insights gained from film studies' discussions of spectatorship can, with qualifications, be applied to readership of *jinsei annai.* Influential studies have shown how film, print media, and advertising exist in a common "image context." See Susan Ohmer, "Female Spectatorships and Women's Magazines: Hollywood, *Good Housekeeping,* and World War II," *The Velvet Light Trap* 25 (1990): 53–68, and Michael Renov, "Advertising / Photojournalism / Cinema: The Shifting Rhetoric of Forties Female Representation," *Quarterly Review of Film and Video* 11 (1989): 1–21.

24. In pointing out the overdetermined character of *jinsei annai* letters on abortion, I do not maintain that negotiations cease between readers and text, but that the moralistic attempt of the response is to channel readers toward accepting the answer's logic. For a typology of readers' decoding of texts, see Stuart Hall, "Encoding/Decodings," in *Culture, Media, Language,* ed. Stuart Hall et al. (Birmingham, England: Centre for Contemporary Cultural Studies, 1980). It would, in any case, be erroneous to presume a homogenous readership of *jinsei annai.* The readership of advice columns seems likely to be clearly gendered and predominantly female, again following the analogy of television soap operas. See Judith Mayne, *Cinema and Spectatorship* (London: Routledge, 1993), p. 44.

25. In this, they share much with such moralizing filmmaking as quasi documentaries on venereal disease. See Annette Kuhn, *The Power of the Image: Essays on Representation and Sexuality* (London: Routledge and Kegan Paul, 1985), chap. 5.

26. Yomiuri shinbunsha fujinbu, *Nihonjin no jinsei annai* (Tokyo: Heibonsha, 1988), pp. 136–37.

27. Ibid., pp. 136–37.

28. Hodge and Ogawa, *Fertility Change in Contemporary Japan*, p. 47. Honda estimated that, "Of the births controlled [in 1955], nearly two-thirds are by abortions, and those by contraception account for only one-third of the figure." *Population Problems*, p. 19. By 1950, the birthrate declined from 34.3 (in 1947) to 28.3.

29. Katō, S., *A Fight for Women's Happiness*, p. 103.

30. Cited in Irene Taeuber and Marshall Balfour, "The Control of Fertility in Japan" (Office of Population Research, Princeton University), unpublished paper, pp. 13–17.

31. Ibid.

32. P. Pommerenke, quoted in Paul Gebhard et al., *Pregnancy, Birth, and Abortion* (Westport, Conn.: Greenwood, 1958), p. 219 n. 20.

33. Gebhard et al., *Pregnancy, Birth, and Abortion*, p. 219.

34. Amano, *Family Planning*, pp. 9, 11; Nakagawa Kiyoshi, "Toshi nichijō seikatsu no naka no sengo," in *Toshi to minshū*, ed. Narita Ryūichi (Tokyo: Yoshikawa Kōbunkan, 1993).

35. Nakagawa, "Toshi nichijō," pp. 272, 275–79. Between 1953 and 1964, the number of reported abortions was on average more than 50 percent of live births, a trend that began earlier in the cities and was stronger there than in rural areas.

36. Quoted in ibid., p. 282.

37. Yomiuri shinbun, *Jinsei annai*, pp. 123–24.

38. See also the letter published October 13, 1950 (ibid., pp. 132–33) for a response in a similar tone.

39. Different estimates of contraceptive use at this time are as high as 70 percent. See Nakagawa, "Toshi nichijō," p. 279.

40. Mainichi Shinbun Jinkō Mondai Chōsakai, ed., *Kiroku: Nihon no jinkō, shōsan e no kiseki* (Tokyo: Mainichi Shinbunsha, 1992); see also Hodge and Ogawa, *Fertility Change in Contemporary Japan*, pp. 54–58.

41. Nakagawa, "Toshi nichijō," pp. 275–76.

42. For example, a letter published January 30, 1964, tells a woman made pregnant by a married man to have an abortion rather than bear an illegitimate child (Yomiuri shinbun, *Jinsei annai*, pp. 334–35), much like the 1956 case translated in full (see chapter 2). See also pp. 335–36 and 345–46.

43. According to available statistics, Japan's rate and ratio of abortion are considerably less than those seen in Eastern Europe and the former Soviet Union, and roughly comparable with those of the United States, Italy, Germany, and Sweden. See S. K. Henshaw and J. Van Vort, eds., *Abortion Factbook: 1992 Edition* (New York: Alan Guttmacher Institute, 1992), p. 78, table 2.

44. Hodge and Ogawa, *Fertility Change in Contemporary Japan*, p. 48;

see also Hoshino and Takeda, "*Mizuko kuyō* and Abortion in Contemporary Japan," pp. 171–90, especially p. 180, chart 2.

45. Hodge and Ogawa, *Fertility Change in Contemporary Japan*, p. 102.

46. Yomiuri shinbun, *Jinsei annai*, pp. 635–36.

47. Matsuda Michiko, "Taiji o taisetsu ni," *Shirohata* (August 1978): 62–65.

48. This theme is expounded in a collection of forty testimonies: Kusumoto Kamino, ed., *Ryūsanji yo—yasuraka ni* (Tokyo: Nihon kyōbunsha, 1984).

49. Taniguchi Teruko, "Chūzetsuji no gen'ei o mite," *Shirohata* (September 1978): 84–87.

50. Inoue, *Shinshūkyō jiten*, pp. 196 (graph 3), 561, 564–70. Seichō no Ie tracts opposing abortion have been reproduced in Samuel Coleman, *Family Planning in Japanese Society: Traditional Birth Control in a Modern Urban Culture* (Princeton: Princeton University Press, 1983), and its antiabortion activism (and a spectrum of reactions to it) is discussed in LaFleur, *Liquid Life*, chap. 10.

51. Seichō no Ie's appropriation of the abortion issue closely resembles the use of the issue by the New Right in the United States, that is, as a symbol of all democratic and progressive social changes they seek to overturn. "Public discourse and debate have seemed obsessively preoccupied by women and fetuses . . . [including] a mass-based crusade against liberal abortion and all that the practice marked: teenage sex, nonmarital sex, nonreproductive sex, hedonism, careerism, women's work force participation, the denigration of 'traditional' gender identities, and the dissolution of the nuclear family. . . . Abortion became not only the symbol of the general malaise that was slowly but persistently destroying the social body, . . . but [also] the ideological centerpiece of the New Right's campaign to revitalize the country politically and rehabilitate it morally." Valerie Hartouni, "Containing Women: Reproductive Discourse in the 1980s," in *Technoculture*, ed. Constance Penley and Andrew Ross (Minneapolis: University of Minnesota Press, 1991), p. 33.

52. Katō, S., *A Fight for Women's Happiness*, p. 109.

53. Mary Ellen Brown defines trash as follows: "First, trash connotes that which ought to be discarded, a sort of instant garbage; second, it connotes cheapness, shoddiness, the overflow of the capitalist commodity system. Third, it connotes a superficial glitter designed to appeal to those whose tastes are illformed according to the dominant perspective. . . . Fourth, trash is excessive: it has more vulgarity, more tastelessness, more offensiveness than is necessary for its function as a cheap commodity," "Soap Opera and Women's Culture: Politics and the Popular," in *Doing Research on Women's Communication: Perspectives on Theory and Method*, ed. Kathryn Carter and Carole Spitzack (Norwood, N.J.: Ablex, 1989), pp. 161–90, quoted in S. Elizabeth Bird, *For Enquiring Minds: A Cultural Study of Supermarket Tabloids* (Knoxville: University of Tennessee Press, 1992), p. 107.

54. *Mizuko* articles in the tabloids have an indeterminate quality that resembles the media production in the United States of the rock star Madonna. Her allure is sustained in part by the refusal to confirm fully any single reading of her, making her a magnet for a wide variety of consumers. See Lisa Frank and Paul Smith, eds., *Madonnarama: Essays on Sex and Popular Culture* (Pittsburgh: Cleis, 1993).

55. Frederic Jameson, "Postmodernism, or the Cultural Logic of Late Capitalism," *New Left Review* 146 (1984): 53–92.

56. Bird, *For Enquiring Minds*, p. 2.

57. "Watakushi wa 300,000 no mizuko no sakebi-goe o kiki, sono hahatachi no namida o mitekita," *Josei 7* (16 May 1973): 191–93.

58. "Bōsō daichi no mizuko kuyō," *Shūkan josei* (15 August 1976): 122–23.

59. For a comprehensive study of tabloid articles on *mizuko kuyō*, see Morikuri, *Fushigidani no kodomotachi*.

60. "Zendai mibun no mizuko Jizō būmu no kyoten," *Shūkan gendai* (10 September 1980): 186–87.

61. "Jisha meguri," *Young Lady* (11 November 1980): 134–35.

62. "Kaze no yō ni," *Shūkan gendai* (16 October 1993): 68–69; see also "Natsu no gokuyō," *Heibon Punch* (8 August 1985). In fact, however, the national association of OB-GYNs performs *mizuko kuyō* annually, as Margaret Lock notes in *Encounters With Aging: Mythologies of Menopause in Japan and North America* (Berkeley and Los Angeles: University of California Press, 1993), p. 277. I would like to thank Tiana Norgren for useful information on this topic.

63. "Onna-gokoro ga sukuwareru mizuko-dera," *Shūkan josei* (16 June 1981): 40–45. This article notes Hashimoto's old age; born in 1890, he was too elderly to play so strong a role in promoting *mizuko kuyō* as the younger Miura Dōmyō, though Hashimoto's temple is a major center for the rites.

64. "Mizuko būmu ni keikoku suru," *Shūkan Post* (17 December 1982): 207–9.

65. "Totsuzen watakushi o osotta mizuko rei no tatari," *Young Lady* (23 July 1985): 145–48 (the first of a three-part series); "Joshi chūkōsei ni dai ryūkō: mizuko no tataribanashi," *Josei jishin* (4 November 1982): 193–95.

66. The timing of these articles illustrates a tendency toward their publication in bulk around the time of *obon*.

67. "Totsuzen watakushi o osotta," 145–48.

68. "Yurushite akachan, soshite yasuraka ni nemutte," *Young Lady* (3 August 1985): 155–60; "Mō, hitori de kurushimanakute ii," *Young Lady* (27 August 1985): 169–71.

69. Ironic readings of television soap operas and tabloids are analyzed in the following studies: Ien Ang, *Watching "Dallas": Soap Opera and the Melodramatic Imagination* (London: Methuen, 1985); Walter Ong, *Orality and Literacy: The Technologizing of the World* (London: Methuen, 1982), pp. 22, 45; Harold Schecter, *The Bosom Serpent: Folklore and Popular Art* (Iowa City: University of Iowa Press, 1988).

70. Hall, "Encoding/Decodings."

71. This hypothesis accords with the findings of the following studies: Annette Kuhn, "Women's Genres," *Screen* 25 (1984): 18–28; Tania Modleski, *Loving With a Vengence: Mass-Produced Fantasies for Women* (London: Methuen, 1982); Ang, *Watching "Dallas."*

72. Bird, *For Enquiring Minds*, p. 122.

73. Brown, "Soap Opera and Women's Culture," pp. 156–57.

74. Bird, *For Enquiring Minds*, p. 160. But see Meagan Morris's critique of these theories of multiple possibilities of readings as the "ethnographer's

mask," a disguise for a bourgeois attempt to police a genre associated with the "lower orders" without requiring the exposure of this ruse. "Banality in Cultural Studies," *Discourse* 10 (1988): 3–29.

75. Lock, *Encounters With Aging.* By contrast with North American women, "hot flashes" are apparently much less prominent in Japanese women's experience of menopause. For an association between menopausal symptoms and abortion, see p. 162.

76. See Rosalind Petchesky, "Foetal Images: The Power of Visual Culture in the Politics of Reproduction," in *Reproductive Technologies: Gender, Motherhood and Medicine,* ed. Michele Stanworth (Minneapolis: University of Minnesota Press, 1987), p. 61, and Carole Stabile, "Shooting the Mother: Fetal Images and the Politics of Disappearance," *Camera Obscura* 28 (January 1992): 183, for a discussion of these two presentations of fetal photography and their cultural significance.

77. Petchesky, "Foetal Images," pp. 61–63.

78. Renov, "Advertising / Photojournalism / Cinema," 16. See also Ray B. Brown, ed., *Objects of Special Devotion: Fetishes and Fetishism in Popular Culture* (Bowling Green, Ohio: Bowling Green University Popular Press, 1982). Renov discusses a technique of 1940s advertising in which male babies were shown as being many times the size of their mothers, humiliating them in various ways.

79. Takahashi Saburō. "Mizuko kuyō ni kansuru tōkei chōsa shiryō," Kyoto: Daigaku Kyōyōbu Shakaigaku Kyōshitsu, 1992.

80. Ibid. The same survey reports that of 681 Kyoto temples surveyed in 1991, 63 percent do not perform *mizuko kuyō,* while 36 percent do.

81. Ibid.

82. Ibid.

83. Kamihara et al., "Nihonjin no shūkyō ishiki," 1–38, especially 29.

84. Ibid.

85. Ibid., 59.

86. Ibid., 22–54.

3. Abortion in Contemporary Sexual Culture

1. Richard G. Parker, Gilbert Herdt, and M. Carballo, "Sexual Culture, HIV Transmission, and AIDS Research," *Journal of Sex Research* 28 (1991): 79; see also Richard Parker, *Bodies, Pleasures, and Passions: Sexual Culture in Contemporary Brazil* (New York: Beacon, 1993).

2. Gilbert Herdt and Robert J. Stoller, *Intimate Communications: Erotics and the Study of Culture* (New York: Columbia University Press, 1990), p. 53.

3. Lock, *Encounters With Aging;* Melvin Konner and Marjorie Shostak, "Timing and Management of Birth Among the !Kung: Biocultural Interaction in Reproductive Adaptation," *Cultural Anthropology* 2 (1987): 11–28; Timothy Buckley and A. Gottlieb, eds., *Blood Magic: The Anthropology of Menstruation* (Berkeley and Los Angeles: University of California Press, 1988); K. Dettwyler, "More Than Nutrition: Breastfeeding in Urban Mali," *Medical Anthropology*

Quarterly 2 (1988): 172–83; A. Millard, "The Place of the Clock in Pediatric Advice: Rationales, Cultural Themes, and Impediments to Breastfeeding," *Social Science and Medicine* 31 (1990): 211–21.

4. See Elizabeth Grosz, *Volatile Bodies* (Bloomington: Indiana University Press, 1994); idem, "Contemporary Theories of Power and Subjectivity," in *Feminist Knowledge,* ed. Sneja Gunew (London: Routledge, 1990), pp. 59–120; idem, "Notes Towards a Corporeal Feminism," *Australian Feminist Studies* 5 (1987): 1–16.

5. Christine Gilmartin et al., eds. *Engendering China: Women, Culture, and the State* (Cambridge: Harvard University Press, 1994); Jeffrey Weeks, *Sex, Politics and Society: The Regulation of Sexuality Since 1800* (London: Longman, 1981); Robert Padgug, "Sexual Matters: On Conceptualising Sexuality in History," *Radical History Review* 20 (1979): 3–23; Lilian Faderman, *Odd Girls and Twilight Lovers: A History of Lesbian Life in Twentieth-Century America* (New York: Columbia University Press, 1991); D. L. Davis and R. G. Whitten, "The Cross-Cultural Study of Human Sexuality," *Annual Review of Anthropology* 16 (1987): 69–98; R. Parker, *Bodies, Pleasures, and Passions;* Gilbert Herdt, *Guardians of the Flute* (New York: McGraw-Hill, 1981); Andrea Sankar, "Sisters and Brothers, Lovers and Enemies: Marriage Resistance in Southern Kwangtung [Hong Kong, 1865–1935]," *Journal of Homosexuality* 11 (1985): 69–81; John D'Emilio and Estelle Freedman, *Intimate Matters: A History of Sexuality in America* (New York: Harper and Row, 1988).

6. Nancy Cott, *The Bonds of Womanhood: 'Woman's Sphere' in New England, 1780–1835* (New Haven: Yale University Press, 1977); Carol Smith-Rosenberg, *Disorderly Conduct: Visions of Gender in Victorian America* (New York: Oxford University Press, 1985); Brett Harvey, *The Fifties: A Woman's Oral History* (New York: Harper Perennial, 1993); J. A. Mangen and James Walvin, eds., *Manliness and Morality: Middle-Class Masculinity in Britain and America, 1800–1940* (New York: St. Martin's, 1987); Peter Middleton, *The Inward Gaze: Masculinity and Subjectivity in Modern Culture* (London: Routledge, 1992); David Gilmore, *Manhood in the Making: Cultural Concepts of Masculinity* (New Haven: Yale University Press, 1990); Anthony Rotundo, *American Manhood: Transformations in Masculinity from the Revolution to the Modern Era* (New York: Basic Books, 1993); Michael Kimmel, "Invisible Masculinity," *Society* 30 (1993): 28–35.

7. Petchesky, *Abortion and Woman's Choice;* Luker, *Taking Chances;* Caroline Bledsoe, "The Politics of AIDS, Condoms, and Heterosexual Relations," in *Births and Power: Social Change and the Politics of Reproduction,* ed. A. Handwerker (Boulder, Colo.: Westview, 1990), pp. 197–223; Ronald Wetherington, "Culture and Reproduction: An Anthropological Critique of Demographic Transition Theory," *American Anthropologist* 89 (1987): 5–6; Barbara Leigh, "Reasons for Having and Avoiding Sex: Gender, Sexual Orientation and Relationship to Sexual Behavior," *The Journal of Sex Research* 26 (1989): 199–209; Nancy Netting, "Sexuality in Youth Culture: Identity and Change," *Adolescence* 27 (1992): 961–76.

8. Nihon Kazoku Renmei, ed., *Kanashimi o sabakemasu ka? Chūzetsu kinshi e no hanmon* (Tokyo: Ningen no kagakusha, 1983).

9. See Petchesky, *Abortion and Woman's Choice;* Luker, *Taking Chances;* and Arthur Shostak and Gary McLouth, *Men and Abortion: Lessons, Losses, and Love* (New York: Praeger, 1984).

10. Nihon Kazoku Renmei, *Kanashimi o sabakemasu ka?,* pp. 28–31.

11. Ibid., pp. 75–78.

12. Ibid., pp. 21–24.

13. Ibid., pp. 45–49.

14. Mary S. Calderone, ed., *Abortion in the United States* (New York: Hoeber-Harper, 1958), p. 62; Gebhard et al., *Pregnancy, Birth, and Abortion,* p. 213.

15. Sekidō Tetsuya, "Dokushin dansei kara mita chūzetsu," in *Onna, ninshin, chūzetsu* (Tokyo: Yukkasha, 1984): 114–22.

16. Ibid.

17. See Shostak and McLouth, *Men and Abortion,* passim.

18. Sekidō, "Dokushin dansei kara mita chūzetsu," pp. 118–22.

19. A number of modern novels take up the theme of women's self-sacrificing devotion to worthless men: Dazai Osamu, *Shayō* (Tokyo: Shinchōsha, 1950); Endō Shūsaku, *Watashi ga suteta onna* (Tokyo: Kōdansha bunko, 1972). More rare is the occasional reversal of this motif, that is, men who sacrifice themselves for women who are callous to them, as in the adopted husband who blinds himself to prove his love for his wife who has been blinded, a classic of masochistic literature: Tanizaki Jun'ichirō, *Shunkinshō* (Tokyo: Shinchō bunko, 1953).

20. Both Nakano and Itabashi are neighborhoods in Tokyo.

21. Nihon Kazoku Renmei, *Kanashimi o sabakemasu ka?,* pp. 40–45. The text calls the woman "I-ko," here changed to "Reiko" to prevent confusion.

22. This dislike of contraceptive devices by both sexes has been repeatedly cited as a reason for unplanned pregnancies, as the following interview exchanges with women (Luker, *Taking Chances,* p. 50) make clear:

Interviewer: What did you think about using contraceptive foam?

Response: Well, the foam is such a bitch to use. Especially for him because it just gets all over the place.

. . .

Interviewer: How did you decide not to use your diaphragm?

Response: God, I used to get so turned off putting it inside me, so I tried to get him to help do it, like they say in those marriage manuals, and it just turned us *both* off.

23. Nihon Kazoku Renmei, *Kanashimi o sabakemasu ka?,* pp. 32–40.

4. The Practitioners of Mizuko Kuyō

1. Fujita Shōichi, *Ogamiyasan: reinōkitōshi no sekai* (Tokyo: Kōbundō, 1990), pp. 196–200.

2. *Ogamiya* perform rites for fees and they do not necessarily form an ongoing relation with their clients, though a healing or other successful ritual performance can sometimes form the basis for a longer association.

3. Shōzaki Ryōsei, *Omikuji* (Koshigaya-shi, Saitama Prefecture: Kadokurabō, 1993), pp. 126–30.

4. The groups here assumed to be unrelated are persons with different surnames; the possibility nevertheless exists that groupings bearing different surnames, such as a married woman and her married daughter, might have dedicated a statue together.

5. The husband and one son have received *tokudo*, the first stage of ordination.

6. The temple is registered as an independent temple, not as a Tendai temple, because, according to Morita, the other Tendai temples in the area refused to recognize Jionji as legitimate.

7. Tamamuro Fumio, ed., "Enman'in," in *Nihon meisatsu daijiten* (Tokyo: Yūzankaku, 1992), pp. 68–69.

8. Interview with Vice-Abbot Miura Kōdō, August 1994.

9. Miura Dōmyō, *The Forgotten Child: An Ancient Eastern Answer to a Modern Problem* (Henley-on-Thames: Aiden Ellis, 1983).

10. Fujii Masao, ed., *Bukkyō girei jiten* (Tokyo: Tokyodō shuppan, 1977), pp. 82–84.

11. Ibid., pp. 112–14.

12. Miura Dōmyō, "Shōkuyō no shikata" (Ōtsu: Enman'in, n.d.), p. 37.

13. This expression about karma is probably related to the idea of "women's karma" expounded earlier by Morita Guyō. The notion is that women's bodies are inherently impure and that women's spiritual progress consequently is forever blocked, mired in physicality in a way that men's is not.

14. This account of Bentenshū's founder, history, and practice is drawn from Inoue et al., *Shinshūkyō jiten*, pp. 375–76, 418–19, 440–41, 773, 839.

15. Ōmori was certified as a Shingon "proselytizer" (*fukyōshi*) in 1940.

16. Ōmori attributed great importance to the proper conduct of rites for ancestors, but this is the only connection that can be identified between her thought and the cult of *mizuko* adopted after her death.

17. Yumiyama Tatsuya, "Bentenshū ni okeru kyūzairon no tenkai, toku ni mizuko kuyō ni kanrensasete," *Shūkyōgaku nenpō* 24 (1994): 95.

18. Ibid., pp. 95–96.

19. Ibid., p. 98.

20. Bentenshū, "Mizuko no rei ni yasuragi o," n.d.

21. Helen Hardacre, "Response of Buddhism and Shinto to the Issue of Brain Death and Organ Transplant," *Cambridge Quarterly of Healthcare Ethics* 3 (1994): 585–601.

22. *Bukkyō Times*, 15 April 1985.

23. Kyōgaku Honbu, ed., *Nyonin ōjō*, Kyōgaku shirīzu 1 (Kyoto: Honganji shuppanbu, 1988).

24. The interview took place on August 12, 1994.

25. Ikeda Yūtai, "Mizuko kuyō o megutte, shin'i ketsudan ni ikiru," *Shinshū* (April 1982): 20–24.

26. Kitazuka Mitsunori, *Shinshū to mizuko kuyō* (Tokyo: Nagata bunshodō, 1982), pp. 30–34.

27. Ibid., pp. 34–45.

28. Rinzaishū Myōshinjiha kyōka Center, *Gō no setsu*, pp. 57, 125.

5. *Mizuko Kuyō* in Four Locales

1. Because temple directories are not updated as frequently as telephone directories, the former inevitably contain listings of temples that have actually gone out of business. It is a safe assumption in Japan today that no temple that lacks a telephone is a functioning institution.

2. Sasaki Kiyoshi (1886–1933) later became a renowned folklorist himself, publishing several collections of folktales. Some consider him to be the Grimm of Japan.

3. A good example of critical studies of Tōno is Iwamoto Yoshiteru, *Mō hitotsu no Tōno monogatari* (Tokyo: Tōsui shobō, 1983).

4. See Kikuchi Teruo, *Tōno monogatari o aruku* (Tokyo: Dentō to gendai sha, 1983).

5. Yanagita Kunio, *Tōno monogatari* (Tokyo: Kyōdō kenkyūsha, 1936), pp. 155–56, story 159.

6. Yanagita Kunio, *Tōno monogatari shūi* (Tokyo: Kyōdō kenkyūsha, 1936), pp. 344–45.

7. This study surveys only temples located within Tōno Town itself; the area Yanagita surveyed included the town, but also extended to the surrounding area, north to Mt. Hachine.

8. On the religious history and folklore of Tsuyama, see Wakamori Tarō, ed., *Mimasaka no minzoku* (Tokyo: Yoshikawa Kōbunkan, 1963).

9. The priest at Myōshōji gave the most emphatically affirmative response I received in the temple district to the question of whether the temple performs *mizuko kuyō*. He exclaimed, "Tōzen deshō!", meaning "Of course we do!"

10. The Kibitsu Shrine flourished during the ancient period, when its founders, the Kibi clan, ruled the area semi-autonomously, under a land grant from the court. Emperor Go-Shirakawa made it the seat of his Department of Divinity (Jingikan), but during the Kamakura period, its holdings were transferred to the temple Ninnaji. As a result, many subtemples (*shasōji*) were placed within the shrine precinct and many Buddhist elements were introduced. Its holdings shrank during the Tokugawa era, but it held a shōgunal land grant (*shuinjo*) for 160 *koku* of rice annually. Its *monzen machi* hosted an important market, as well as teahouses and inns. There was a theater within the shrine precinct, and a prostitute population. It was by all accounts a flourishing spot along the San'yōdō highway until the Meiji Restoration. See "Kibitsu Jinja," *Kokushi Daijiten*, 4:196, and "Kibitsu Jinja," *Shintō Daijiten*, 2:427–28.

11. "Chigo," *Kokushi Daijiten*, 9:399. During the medieval period, *chigo* came to be applied to all those serving at shrines. The term was further extended to boys in the service of warrior households and temple acolytes. Another usage of the term refers to young male partners in the institutionalized, pedophilic practices of monastic and warrior society.

12. The shrine deities are Okibitsuhiko no mikoto, Chihayahime no mikoto, Yamato tohimono sohime no mikoto, Hikosasukatawake no mikoto, Yamato tohiwakayahime no mikoto, Hikonema no mikoto, Wakahiko Takekibitsuhiko mikoto, Mitowake no mikoto, and Nakahiko no mikoto.

13. The five *kami* are: Tagirihime no mikoto, Ichikishimahime no mikoto,

Tagitsuhime no mikoto, Kami oichihime no mikoto, and Shitateruhime no mikoto.

14. They are her descendants by the rite of *ukei,* when she and the male *kami* Susanoo produced children by chewing up and spitting out each other's emblems.

Appendix

1. Bunkachō, *Shūkyō nenkan, Heisei 4-nenban* (Tokyo: Gyōsei shuppan, 1993).

2. Some of the smaller sects of Japanese Buddhism, such as Jishū, Ōbaku, Hosso, and a few others, are not represented in the survey.

Selected Bibliography

Akitsu Shō. "Mizuko kuyō no enshutsu de boro mōke no shūkyōya-tachi." *Seikai ōrai* (June 1987): 236–45.

Amano, Fumiko. "Family Planning Movement in Japan." *Contemporary Japan* 23 (1955): 1–13.

Ang, Ien. *Watching "Dallas": Soap Opera and the Melodramatic Imagination.* London: Methuen, 1985.

Aoyagi Machiko. "Kihisareta sei." In *Ie to josei, kurashi no bunkashi.* Vol. 10. Tokyo: Shōgakkan, 1985.

———. *Kiseki o yobu hyōban no reinōsha.* Tokyo: Rironsha, 1987.

Asahi Shinbun Shakaibu. *Gendai no chiisa na kamigami.* Tokyo: Asahi Shinbun Shakaibu, 1984.

Bentenshū. *Mizuko no rei ni yasuragi o.* Pamphlet, n.d.

Bird, Elizabeth. *For Enquiring Minds: A Cultural Study of Supermarket Tabloids.* Knoxville: University of Tennessee Press, 1992.

Bledsoe, Caroline. "The Politics of AIDS, Condoms, and Heterosexual Relations." In *Births and Power: Social Change and the Politics of Reproduction,* edited by A. Handwerker, 197–223. Boulder, Colo.: Westview, 1990.

Bringreve, Christian. "On Modern Relationships: The Commandments of the New Freedom." *Netherlands Journal of Sociology* 18 (1982): 47–56.

Brooks, Anne P. "*Mizuko kuyō* and Japanese Buddhism." *Japanese Journal of Religious Studies* 8 (1981): 119–47.

Brown, Ray B., ed. *Objects of Special Devotion: Fetishes and Fetishism in Popular Culture.* Bowling Green, Ohio: Bowling Green University Popular Press, 1982.

Buckley, Timothy, and A. Gottlieb, eds. *Blood Magic: The Anthropology of Menstruation.* Berkeley: University of California Press, 1988.

Bunkachō. *Shūkyō nenkan, Heisei 4-nenban.* Tokyo: Gyōsei shuppan, 1993.

Calderone, Mary S., ed. *Abortion in the United States.* New York: Hoeber-Harper, 1958.

Chiba Tokuji and Ōtsu Tadao. *Mabiki to mizuko*. Tokyo: Nōsan gyōson bunka kyōkai, 1983.

Coleman, Samuel J. *Family Planning in Japanese Society: Traditional Birth Control in a Modern Urban Culture*. Princeton: Princeton University Press, 1983.

Cott, Nancy. *The Bonds of Womanhood: 'Woman's Sphere' in New England, 1780–1835*. New Haven: Yale University Press, 1977.

Davis, D. L., and R. G. Whitten. "The Cross-Cultural Study of Human Sexuality." *Annual Review of Anthropology* 16 (1987): 69–98.

Dazai Osamu. *Shayō*. Tokyo: Shinchōsha, 1950.

D'Emilio, John, and Estelle Freedman. *Intimate Matters: A History of Sexuality in America*. New York: Harper and Row, 1988.

Dettwyler, K. "More Than Nutrition: Breastfeeding in Urban Mali." *Medical Anthropology Quarterly* 2 (1988): 172–83.

Dōzen Mineo. *Akago, mabiki no shūzoku*. Okayama: Nihon bunkyō shuppan KK, 1989.

Elisonas, Jurgis. "Notorious Places: A Brief Excursion into the Narrative Topography of Early Edo." In *Edo and Paris: Urban Life and the State in the Early Modern Era*, edited by James McClain and John M. Merriman, 253–91. Ithaca: Cornell University Press, 1994.

Endō Shūsaku. *Watashi ga suteta onna*. Tokyo: Kōdansha bunko, 1972.

Faderman, Lilian. *Odd Girls and Twilight Lovers: A History of Lesbian Life in Twentieth-Century America*. New York: Columbia University Press, 1991.

Frank, Lisa, and Paul Smith, eds. *Madonnarama: Essays on Sex and Popular Culture*. Pittsburgh: Cleis, 1993.

Fujii Masao, ed. *Bukkyō girei jiten*. Tokyo: Tokyodō shuppan, 1977.

Fujii Masao et al., eds. *Bukkyō sōsai daijiten*. Tokyo: Yūzankaku, 1980.

Fujime Yuki. "Aru sanba no shisseki." *Nihonshi kenkyū* 366 (1993): 90–112.

———. "Senkanki Nihon no sanji chōsetsu undō to sono shisō." *Rekishi hyōron* 430 (1986): 79–100.

Fujita Shōichi. "Machi no reinōsha to shinjatachi." *Shisō no kagaku* 37 (1983): 58–64.

———. *Ogamiyasan: reinōkitōshi no sekai*. Tokyo: Kōbundō, 1990.

Gamson, Joshua. "Rubber Wars: Struggle Over the Condom in the United States." In *American Sexual Politics: Sex, Gender, and Race Since the Civil War*, edited by John C. Tout and Maura Shaw Tantillo, 322–31. Chicago: University of Chicago Press, 1993.

Gebhard, Paul H., Wardel B. Pomeroy, Clyde E. Martin, and Cornelia V. Christenson. *Pregnancy, Birth, and Abortion*. Westport, Conn.: Greenwood, 1958.

Gilmartin, Christine, et al., eds. *Engendering China: Women, Culture, and the State*. Cambridge: Harvard University Press, 1994.

Gilmore, David. *Manhood in the Making: Cultural Concepts of Masculinity*. New Haven: Yale University Press, 1990.

Gordon, Andrew, ed. *Postwar Japan as History*. Berkeley and Los Angeles: University of California Press, 1993.

Grosz, Elizabeth. "Notes Towards a Corporeal Feminism." *Australian Feminist Studies* 5 (1987): 1–16.

————. *Volatile Bodies.* Bloomington: Indiana University Press, 1994.

Hall, Stuart. "Encoding/Decodings." In *Culture, Media, Language,* edited by Stuart Hall et al., 128–38. Birmingham, England: Centre for Contemporary Cultural Studies, 1980.

Hanley, Susan, and Kōzō Yamamura. *Economics and Demographic Change in Preindustrial Japan, 1600–1868.* Princeton: Princeton University Press, 1977.

Hardacre, Helen. *Kurozumikyō and the New Religions of Japan.* Princeton: Princeton University Press, 1986.

————. "Response of Buddhism and Shinto to the Issue of Brain Death and Organ Transplant." *Cambridge Quarterly of Healthcare Ethics* 3 (1994): 585–601.

————. *Shintō and the State, 1868–1988.* Princeton: Princeton University Press, 1989.

Harrigan, Sandra Oliver. "Marriage and Family: Myth, Media, Behavior." Ph.D. diss., Columbia University Teachers College, 1989.

Hartouni, Valerie. "Containing Women: Reproductive Discourse in the 1980s." In *Technoculture,* edited by Constance Penley and Andrew Ross, 27–56. Minneapolis: University of Minnesota Press, 1991.

Harvey, Brett. *The Fifties: A Woman's Oral History.* New York: Harper Perennial, 1993.

Hayami Tasuku. *Bosatsu, Bukkyō nyūmon.* Tokyo: Tōkyō bijutsu, 1982.

Heibon Punch.

"Natsu no gokuyō." 8 August 1985.

Henshaw, Stanley K., and Jennifer Van Vort, eds. *Abortion Factbook: 1992 Edition.* New York: Alan Guttmacher Institute, 1992.

Herdt, Gilbert. *Guardians of the Flute.* New York: McGraw-Hill, 1981.

Herdt, Gilbert, and Robert J. Stoller. *Intimate Communications: Erotics and the Study of Culture.* New York: Columbia University Press, 1990.

Hobson, Dorothy. *"Crossroads": The Drama of a Soap Opera.* London: Methuen, 1982.

Hodge, Robert, and Ogawa Naohiro. *Fertility Change in Contemporary Japan.* Chicago: University of Chicago Press, 1991.

Honda, Tatsuo. *Population Problems in Post War Japan.* Tokyo: The Institute of Population Problems, Welfare Ministry, 1957.

Hoshino Eiki and Takeda Dōshō. "*Mizuko Kuyō* and Abortion in Contemporary Japan." In *Religion and Society in Modern Japan: Selected Readings,* edited by Mark Mullins, Shimazono Susumu, and Paul Swanson, 171–90. Berkeley, Calif.: Asian Humanities Press, 1993.

Ichibangase Yasuko. *Hoken, fukushi.* Vol. 6 of *Nihon fujin mondai shiryō shūsei.* Tokyo: Domesu shuppan, 1978.

Ihara Saikaku. *Kōshoku ichidai no onna: The Life of an Amorous Woman and Other Writings.* Edited and translated by Ivan Morris. Norfolk, Conn.: New Directions, 1963.

Ijima Yoshiharu. "Kodomo no hakken to jidō yūgi no sekai." In *Ie to josei, kurashi no bunkashi.* Vol. 10. Tokyo: Shōgakkan, 1985.

Ikeda Yūtai. "Mizuko kuyō o megutte, shin'i ketsudan ni ikiru." *Shinshū* (April 1982): 20–24.

Inoue Nobutaka et al., eds. *Shinshūkyō jiten.* Tokyo: Kōbundō, 1990.

————. *Shinshūkyō no kaidoku*. Tokyo: Chikuma shobō, 1992.

Ishikawa Rikizan. "Kirigami denshō to kinsei Sōtō-shū." In *Minshū shūkyō no kōzō to keifu*, edited by Tamamuro Fumio, 298–322. Tokyo: Yūzankaku, 1995.

Ishizaki Shōko. "Seishoku no jiyū to sanji chōsetsu undō." *Rekishi hyōron* 503 (1992): 92–107.

Iwamoto Yoshiteru. *Mō hitotsu no Tōno monogatari*. Tokyo: Tōsui shobō, 1983.

Jameson, Frederic. "Postmodernism, or the Cultural Logic of Late Capitalism." *New Left Review* 146 (1984): 53–92.

Josei jishin.
"Joshi chūkōsei ni dai ryūkō: mizuko no tataribanashi." 4 November 1982, 193–95.

Josei 7.
"Watakushi wa 300,000 no mizuko no sakebi-goe o kiki, sono haha-tachi no namida o mitekita." 16 May 1973, 191–93.

Kamata Hisako. "Sanba—sono fujoteki seikaku ni tsuite." *Seijō bungei* 42 (1966): 47–60.

Kamihara Kazuko et al. "Nihonjin no shūkyō ishiki ni kansuru kyōdō kenkyū no hōkoku." *Tōkyō Kōgei Daigaku Kōgakubu Kiyō* 10 (1987): 22–54.

————. "Nihonjin no shūkyō ishiki ni kansuru kyōdō kenkyū no hōkoku, oyobi ronbun." *Tōkyō Kōgei Daigaku Kōgakubu Kiyō* 8 (1985): 77–114.

Katō Kōichi. *Keikaku bunben*. Tokyo: Shindan to chiryōsha, 1988.

Katō, Shidzue. *A Fight for Women's Happiness: Pioneering the Family Planning Movement in Japan*. JOICFP Document Series 11. Tokyo: Japanese Organization for International Cooperation in Family Planning, 1984.

Kertzer, David I. *Sacrificed for Honor: Infant Abandonment and the Politics of Reproductive Control*. Boston: Beacon, 1993.

Kikuchi Teruo. *Tōno monogatari o aruku*. Tokyo: Dentō to gendai sha, 1983.

Kimmel, Michael. "Invisible Masculinity." *Society* 30 (1993): 28–35.

Kitazuka Mitsunori. *Shinshū to mizuko kuyō*. Tokyo: Nagata bunshodō, 1982.

Kobayashi Norihiro. "Shussan no shūzoku ni mirareru juryoku." *Inaji* 27 (1983): 5–8.

Konner, Melvin, and Marjorie Shostak. "Timing and Management of Birth Among the !Kung: Biocultural Interaction in Reproductive Adaptation." *Cultural Anthropology* 2 (1987): 11–28.

Kōseishō 50 nenshi henshū iinkai. *Kōseishō 50 nenshi*. Tokyo: Kōsei mondai kenkyūkai, 1990.

Kuhn, Annette. *The Power of the Image: Essays on Representation and Sexuality*. London: Routledge and Kegan Paul, 1985.

————. "Women's Genres." *Screen* 25 (1984): 18–28.

Kuretsukasa Yukiko. "Yūten shōnin no ichi daiki o chūshin to suru Kasane setsuwa no kenkyū." *Ocha no mizu daigaku kokubun* 43 (1970).

Kusumoto Kamino, ed. *Ryūsanji yo—yasuraka ni*. Tokyo: Nihon kyōbunsha, 1984.

Kyōgaku Honbu, ed. *Nyonin ōjō*. Kyōgaku shirīzu 1. Kyoto: Honganji shuppanbu, 1988.

LaFleur, William. *Liquid Life: Abortion and Buddhism in Japan*. Princeton: Princeton University Press, 1992.

Leigh, Barbara. "Reasons for Having and Avoiding Sex: Gender, Sexual Orientation and Relationship to Sexual Behavior." *The Journal of Sex Research* 26 (1989): 199–209.

Lock, Margaret. *Encounters With Aging: Mythologies of Menopause in Japan and North America*. Berkeley and Los Angeles: University of California Press, 1993.

Luker, Kristin. *Taking Chances: Abortion and the Decision Not to Contracept*. Berkeley and Los Angeles: University of California Press, 1975.

Maeda Hiroshi. *Nihon no reinōsha*. Tokyo: Kabushikigaisha koa, 1986.

Mainichi Shinbun Jinkō Mondai Chōsakai, ed. *Kiroku: Nihon no jinkō*. Tokyo: Mainichi Shinbunsha, 1992.

Manabe Kōsai. *Jizō bosatsu no kenkyū*. Kyoto: Sanmitsudō, 1960.

Mangen, J. A., and James Walvin, eds. *Manliness and Morality: Middle-Class Masculinity in Britain and America, 1800–1940*. New York: St. Martin's, 1987.

Matsuda Michiko. "Taiji o taisetsu ni." *Shirohata* (August 1978): 62–65.

Matsumura Akira et al., eds. *Arai Hakuseki*. Vol. 35 of *Nihonshisō taikei*. Tokyo: Iwanami shoten, 1975.

Matsuoka Etsuko. "Bunka to shussan—Nihon no shizen bunben undō o chūshin toshite." *Minzokugaku kenkyū* 47 (1983): 356–81.

———. *Shussan no bunka jinruigaku*. Tokyo: Kaimeisha, 1985.

Mayne, Judith. *Cinema and Spectatorship*. London: Routledge, 1993.

McClain, James, and John M. Merriman. "Edo and Paris: Cities and Power." In *Edo and Paris: Urban Life and the State in the Early Modern Era*, edited by James McClain and John M. Merriman, 3–38. Ithaca: Cornell University Press, 1994.

McKinstry, John, and Asako McKinstry. *Jinsei annai: Life's Guide*. Armonk, N.Y.: M. E. Sharpe, 1991.

McLaren, Angus, and Arlene McLaren. *The Bedroom and the State*. Toronto: McClelland and Stewart, 1986.

Middleton, Peter. *The Inward Gaze: Masculinity and Subjectivity in Modern Culture*. London: Routledge, 1992.

Millard, A. "The Place of the Clock in Pediatric Advice: Rationales, Cultural Themes, and Impediments to Breastfeeding." *Social Science and Medicine* 31 (1990): 211–21.

Miura Dōmyō. *The Forgotten Child: An Ancient Eastern Answer to a Modern Problem*. Henley-on-Thames: Aiden Ellis, 1983.

Miyata Noboru. *Kokoro naoshi wa naze hayaru*. Tokyo: Shōgakkan, 1993.

Modleski, Tania. *Loving With a Vengeance: Mass-Produced Fantasies for Women*. London: Methuen, 1982.

Morikuri Shigekazu. "Mizuko kuyō no hassei to genjō." *Kokuritsu rekishi minzoku hakubutsukan kenkyū hōkoku* 57 (1994): 1–95.

Morley, David. *Family Television: Cultural Power and Domestic Leisure*. London: Comedia, 1986.

Morris, Meagan. "Banality in Cultural Studies." *Discourse* 10 (1988): 3–29.

Murakami Shigeyoshi. "Tenrikyō no shinwa to minshū kyūzai." In *Minshū to shakai*. Vol. 10. Tokyo: Shunbunsha, 1988.

Nagata Tsuneko. "Ubugami shinkō ni okeru ishi—Aichi-ken Mikawa chihō no jirei ni tsuite." *Josei to keiken* 8 (1983): 19–22.

Nakagawa Kiyoshi. "Toshi nichijō seikatsu no naka no sengo." In *Toshi to minshū*, edited by Narita Ryūichi, 263–90. Tokyo: Yoshikawa Kōbunkan, 1993.

Nakamura Hajime. *Bukkyōgo daijiten.* 3 vols. Tokyo: Tōkyō shoseki, 1975.

Netting, Nancy. "Sexuality in Youth Culture: Identity and Change." *Adolescence* 27 (1992): 961–76.

Nihon Kazoku Renmei, ed. *Kanashimi o sabakemasu ka? Chūzetsu kinshi e no hanmon.* Tokyo: Ningen no kagakusha, 1983.

Nomura Keiko. "Osan no kamisama oboegaki." *Josei to keiken* 7 (1982).

Oakley, Deborah Jane Hacker. "The Development of Population Policy in Japan, 1945–1952, and American Participation." Ph.D. diss., University of Michigan, 1977.

Obayashi Michiko. *Josanpu no sengo.* Tokyo: Keisō shobō, 1989.

Ochiai Emiko. "Aru sanba no Nihon kindai." In *Seido toshite no onna—sei, san, kazoku no hikaku shakaishi*, 258–322. Tokyo: Heibonsha, 1990.

Ohmer, Susan. "Female Spectatorships and Women's Magazines: Hollywood, *Good Housekeeping*, and World War II." *The Velvet Light Trap* 25 (1990): 53–68.

Ōishi Kōichi. *Kiseki no reinōryokusha.* Tokyo: Nihon bungeisha, 1984.

———. *Nihon no reinōryokusha.* Tokyo: Nihon bungeisha, 1983.

———. *Zenkoku reinō, fushigi mappu.* Tokyo: Taka shobō, 1987.

Ong, Walter. *Orality and Literacy: The Technologizing of the World.* London: Methuen, 1982.

Ono Yasuhiro. "Nagare kanjō kara mizuko kuyō e." *Dentō to gendai* 75 (1987): 18–25.

Padgug, Robert. "Sexual Matters: On Conceptualising Sexuality in History." *Radical History Review* 20 (1979): 3–23.

Parker, Richard. *Bodies, Pleasures, and Passions: Sexual Culture in Contemporary Brazil.* New York: Beacon, 1993.

Parker, Richard, Gilbert Herdt, and M. Carballo. "Sexual Culture, HIV Transmission, and AIDS Research." *Journal of Sex Research* 28 (1991): 77–98.

Petchesky, Rosalind. *Abortion and Woman's Choice.* London: Verso, 1984.

———. "Foetal Images: The Power of Visual Culture in the Politics of Reproduction." In *Reproductive Technologies: Gender, Motherhood and Medicine*, edited by Michele Stanworth, 57–80. Minneapolis: University of Minnesota Press, 1978.

Renov, Michael. "Advertising / Photojournalism / Cinema: The Shifting Rhetoric of Forties Female Representation." *Quarterly Review of Film and Video* 11 (1989): 1–21.

Rinzaishū Myōshinjiha Kyōka Center. *Gō no setsu ni kansuru honpa sōryō no ishiki to sono jittai.* Kenkyū Hōkoku 1. Kyoto: Rinzaishū Myōshinjiha Kyōka Center, 1989.

Rotundo, Anthony. *American Manhood: Transformations in Masculinity from the Revolution to the Modern Era.* New York: Basic Books, 1993.

Sankar, Andrea. "Sisters and Brothers, Lovers and Enemies: Marriage Resistance in Southern Kwangtung [Hong Kong, 1865–1935]." *Journal of Homosexuality* 11 (1985): 69–81.

Satō Noriaki. "Toshi shamanizumu." In *Ronshū: Nihon Bukkyōshi—Taishō, Shōwa,* 267–92. Tokyo: Yūzankaku, 1988.

Schecter, Harold. *The Bosom Serpent: Folklore and Popular Art.* Iowa City: University of Iowa Press, 1988.

Sekidō Tetsuya. "Dokushin dansei kara mita chūzetsu." In *Onna, ninshin, chūzetsu,* 114–22. Shirīzu: Ima o ikiru 9. Tokyo: Yukkasha, 1984.

Sekiyama Kazuo. *Sekkyō no rekishiteki kenkyū.* Kyoto: Hōzōkan, 1973.

Shima Kazuharu. *Sanba monogatari.* Tokyo: Kenkyūkan, 1981.

Shimazono Susumu. *Gendai kyūsai shūkyōron.* Tokyo: Seikyūsha, 1992.

———. "Kamigakari kara tasuke made." *Komazawa Daigaku bukkyōgakubu ronshū* 8 (1977): 209–26.

Shimizu Kunihiko. "Shōwa 45 nen izen kara no mizuko kuyō." *Saikō minzokugaku* 148 (1994): 21–25.

Shinden Mitsuko. "Mizuko kuyō ni kansuru tōkei chōsa shiryō." *Ryūkoku Daigaku Shakaigakubu Gakkai Kiyō* 2 (1991): 46–60.

Shiramizu Hiroko. "Henka ējento to shite no shinshūkyō no reinōryokusha—S-Kyōdan no jirei." In *Hendōki no ningen to shūkyō,* edited by Morioka Kiyomi, 71–95. Tokyo: Miraisha, 1978.

Shostak, Arthur, and Gary McLouth. *Men and Abortion: Lessons, Losses, and Love.* New York: Praeger, 1984.

Shōzaki Ryōsei. *Omikuji.* Koshigaya-shi, Saitama Prefecture: Kadokurabō, 1993.

Shūkan gendai.
"Kaze no yō ni." 16 October 1993, 68–69.
"Zendai mibun no mizuko Jizō būmu no kyoten." 10 September 1980, 186–87.

Shūkan josei.
"Bōsō daichi no mizuko kuyō." 15 August 1976, 122–23.
"Onna-gokoro ga sukuwareru mizuko-dera." 16 June, 1981: 40–45.

Shūkan Post.
"Mizuko būmu ni keikoku suru." 17 December 1982, 207–9.

Shūkyō Shakaigaku no Kai. *Ikoma no kamigami, gendai toshi no minzoku shūkyō.* Tokyo: Sōgensha, 1986.

Smith, Bardwell. "Buddhism and Abortion in Contemporary Japan: *Mizuko kuyō* and the Confrontation With Death." *Japanese Journal of Religious Studies* 15 (1988): 3–24.

Smith-Rosenberg, Carol. *Disorderly Conduct: Visions of Gender in Victorian America.* New York: Oxford University Press, 1985.

Sono, Ayako. *Watcher from the Shore.* Translated by Edward Putzar. Tokyo: Kōdansha International, 1990.

Stabile, Carole. "Shooting the Mother: Fetal Images and the Politics of Disappearance." *Camera Obscura* 28 (January 1992): 179–205.

Sugeno Kuniharu, ed. *Kami no rei no koe o tsugeru hitobito—unmei ni hikari o ateru kiseki no reinōsha sanjūnin.* Tokyo: Shuppan kagaku sōgō kenkyūjo, 1986.

Tachibana Shōichi. "Ninshin, shussan, ikuji ni kansuru zokushin." *Minzoku-gaku* 1 (1929): 351–53.

Taeuber, Irene, and Marshall Balfour. "The Control of Fertility in Japan." Office of Population Research, Princeton University, n.d.

Takada Minoru. *Edo no akuryō baraishi*. Tokyo: Chikuma shobō, 1994.

Takagi Seiichi. "Ninshin oyobi shussan ni kansuru zokushin." *Minzokugaku* 1 (1929): 49–53.

Takahashi, Man. "Fuan no shakai ni motomeru shūkyō." *Gendai shakaigaku* 13 (1987): 41–57.

———. "Mizuko kuyō to josei no iyashi." *Sei no porifonī*. Tokyo: Sekai no shisōsha, 1990.

Takahashi Saburō et al. "Mizuko kuyō ni kansuru tōkei chōsa shiryō." Unpublished survey. Kyoto Daigaku Kyōyōbu Shakaigaku Kyōshitsu, 1992.

Takahashi Yoshinori. "Zaisekikan to sono keimetsu, mizuko kuyō chōsa kara." *Soshiorogī* 32 (1987): 93–97.

Takemi Momoko. "'Menstruation Sutra' Belief in Japan." *Japanese Journal of Religious Studies* 10 (1983): 229–48.

Tamamuro Fumio, ed. *Nihon meisatsu daijiten*. Tokyo: Yūzankaku, 1992.

Taniguchi Teruko. "Chūzetsuji no gen'ei o mite." *Shirohata* (September 1978): 84–87.

Tanizaki Jun'ichirō. *Shunkinshō*. Tokyo: Shinchō bunko, 1953.

Tano Noboru. *Ōsaka no Jizō-san*. Tokyo: Keizuisha, 1994.

Tenrikyō Kyōkai Honbu. *Tenrikyō kyōsoden*. Tenri: Tenrikyō Dōyūkai, 1956.

———. *Tenrikyō kyōsoden oitsuwahen*. Tenri: Tenrikyō Dōyūkai, 1976.

Tenshōkōtai Jingūkyō. *Seisho*. 2 vols. Tabuse, Yamaguchi Prefecture: Tenshōkōtai Jingūkyō, 1952.

Tone Takashiro. "Minzokushakai ni okeru shussan kūkan ninshiki no chiiki-sei." *Josei to keiken* 7 (1982).

Tsuboi Hirofumi. "Murashakai to tsūka girei." In *Mura to murabito*. Vol. 8. Tokyo: Shōgakkan, 1984.

Ueno Terumasa. "Shussan o meguru ishiki henka to josei no kenri." In *Nihon josei seikatsushi*, edited by Joseishi Sōgō Kenkyūkai, vol. 5, 101–31. Tokyo: Tōkyō Daigaku shuppankai, 1990.

Wakamori Tarō, ed. *Mimasaka no minzoku*. Tokyo: Yoshikawa Kōbunkan, 1963.

Watanabe Masako. "Shinshūkyō shūdan no hassei katei—Hamamatsu-shi no Jiseikai ni okeru kyōso tanjō o megutte." In *Toshi shakai no shūkyō—Hamamatsu-shi ni okeru shūkyō hendō no shōsō*, edited by Tamaru Noriyoshi, 103–27. Tōkyō: Tokyo Daigaku Shūkyōgaku Kenkyūshitsu, 1981.

Weeks, Jeffrey. *Sex, Politics and Society: The Regulation of Sexuality Since 1800*. London: Longman, 1981.

Werblowsky, Zwi. "*Mizuko kuyō*: Notulae on the Most Important 'New Religion' of Japan." *Japanese Journal of Religious Studies* 18 (1991): 295–334.

Wetherington, Ronald. "Culture and Reproduction: An Anthropological Critique of Demographic Transition Theory." *American Anthropologist* 89 (1987): 5–6.

Wigmore, John Henry, ed. *Law and Justice in Tokugawa Japan: Materials for the History of Japanese Law and Justice under the Tokugawa Shogunate, 1603–1867*. 9 vols. Tokyo: University of Tokyo Press, 1967.

Yamashita, Samuel Hideo. *Master Sorai's Responsals: An Annotated Translation of Sorai Sensei Tōmonsho.* Honolulu: University of Hawaii Press, 1994.

Yanagita Kunio. *Tōno monogatari.* Tokyo: Kyōdō kenkyūsha, 1936.

———. *Tōno monogatari shūi.* Tokyo: Kyōdō kenkyūsha, 1936.

Yomiuri shinbunsha fujinbu. *Nihonjin no jinsei annai.* Tokyo: Heibonsha, 1988.

Yoritomi Motohiro. *Shomin no hotoke.* Tokyo: NHK, 1984.

Yoshimura Noriko. "Josei no seikatsu to shussan kankō no henbō." *Kikan jinruigaku* 14 (1983): 84–140.

Young Lady.

"Jisha meguri." 11 November 1980, 134–35.

"Mō, hitori de kurushimanakute ii." 27 August 1985, 169–71.

"Totsuzen watakushi o osotta mizuko rei no tatari." 23 July 1985, 145–48.

"Yurushite akachan, soshite yasuraka ni nemutte." 3 August 1985, 155–60.

Yumiyama Tatsuya. "Bentenshū ni okeru kyūzairon no tenkai, toku ni mizuko kuyō ni kanrensasete." *Shūkyōgaku nenpō* 24 (1994): 87–99.

Selected Character List

Agon-shū 阿含宗

aijō yue no onaka no ko
　　愛情故のお腹の子

Aizenji 愛染寺

akago 赤子

akamizu 閼伽水

akuma 悪魔

Anyō'in 安養院

Arai Hakuseki 新井白石

Asahi Geinō 朝日芸能

Bashō 芭蕉

bekka 別火

Bentenshū 弁天宗

Benzaiten 弁財天

Bodaiji 菩提寺

boke fūji ぼけ封じ

Bukkyō terefon sōdan
　　仏教テレフォン相談

bunraku 文楽

burakumin 部落民

butsudan 仏壇

chigo 稚児

chigosha 稚児社

chō, machi 町

Chōanji 長安寺

Daigiji 大儀寺

daikokubashira 大黒柱

Daisōjō 大僧上

denmayaku 伝馬役

eisei 衛生

ekō 回向

Enman'in 円滿院

Enman'in Daijōkai 円滿院大乗会

Enma-ō 閻魔王

Ennin 円仁

Fudō, Fudō Myōō 不動, 不動明王

Fujin Kōron 婦人公論

fujō 不淨

Funakoshi Toshiko 船越利子

furusato 古郷

futari de umu 二人で産む

gaki 餓鬼

gō 業

Hashimoto Tetsuma 橋本徹馬

hatsu miyamairi 初宮参り

Heibon Punch 平凡パンチ

hinoe uma 丙午

Hiratsuka Raichō 平塚雷鳥

hiruko 蛭子

hiruko barai 蛭子祓い

Honzuiji 本瑞寺

Hōsenji 法泉寺

hosshin　発心

hōwa　法話

Ichihime Jinja　市姫神社

ihai　位牌

Ishihara Shintarō　石原慎太郎

Ishiyama-dera　石山寺

iwata obi　岩田帯

Izanagi no Mikoto　伊弉諾尊

Izanami no Mikoto　伊弉冉尊

Jikaku Daishi　慈覚大師

jinkakusha　人格者

jinsei annai　人生案内

Jionji　慈恩寺

Jizō　地蔵

Jizō bon　地蔵盆

Jizō Hongan kyō　地蔵本願経

Jizō wasan　地蔵和讃

Jōdo　浄土

Jōdo Shinshū　浄土真宗

Jōdo Shinshū Kyōgaku Kenkyūjo
　浄土真宗教学研究所

josanpu　助産婦

Josei 7　女性7

jūshoku　住職

kaesu　返す

kagura　神楽

Kakehashi Jitsuen　掛橋実円

kakochō　過去帳

kami　神

kami no uchi　神の内

kanashibari　金縛り

Kannon　観音

Kappa　河童

Katō (Ishimoto) Shizue
　加藤(石本)シズエ

Katsube Jinja　勝部神社

kencha　献茶

kenka　献花

kenkō　献香

kentō　献灯

ki　気

Kibitsu Jinja　吉備津神社

kigan　祈願

Kishinron　鬼神論

Kitamura Sayo　北村さよ

kitō　祈祷

kitōshi　祈祷師

ko, ji, shi　子

Kōbō Daishi　弘法大師

Kojima Goryūshugen
　小島五流修験

kokeshi　こけし

Konjaku monogatari　今昔物語

Konkōkyō　金光教

korosu　殺す

Kuroda Minoru　黒田みのる

Kurozumikyō　黒住教

Kurozumi Munetada　黒住宗忠

kuyō　供養

kyōfu sangyō　恐怖産業

mabiki　間引き

Mahikari (Sūkyō Mahikari Kyōdan)
　真光(崇教真光教団)

Mandaraji　曼陀羅寺

manga　漫画

mappō　末法

Matsuyama Koyasu Kannon
　松山子安観音

miai　見合い

minshūshi　民衆史

Miura Dōmyō　三浦道明

Miura-shi　三浦市

Miyo　みよ

mizuko　水子

mizuko daihōyō　水子大法要

mizuko Jizō　水子地蔵

mizuko Kannon　水子観音

mizuko kuyō　水子供養

mizuko no reishō　水子の霊障

mizuko sōrei　水子総霊

mokugyo　木魚

monzeki　門跡

Morita Guyō　森田愚幼

muen　無縁

muenbotoke　無縁仏

mushi no yosa　虫の良さ

Myō-on　妙音
Myōonji　妙音寺
Myōsenji　妙宣寺
Myōshōji　妙勝寺
nagare kanjō　流れ灌頂
Nakabashi　中橋
Nakaoka Tetsuya　中岡鉄也
Nakayama Miki　中山みき
Namu Tenriō no Mikoto
　　南無天理王命
nanushi　名主
Narita Fudō　成田不動
nenbutsu　念仏
nenbutsu odori　念仏踊り
Nichiren　日蓮
Nihon Reikōgaku Kenkyūkai
　　日本霊交学研究会
ninpu　妊婦
Numa no Uchi Sainokawara
　　沼の内賽の河原
nyonin wa tsumifukashi
　　女人は罪深し
nyonin yaku yoke　女人厄除け
obi　帯
obiya　帯屋
obiyayurushi　帯屋許し
ogamiya　拝み屋
ogamu　拝む
Ogino Kyūsaku　荻野久作
Ogyū Sorai　荻生徂徠
Ōharai norito　大祓い祝詞
Oharu　おはる
oku ka, kaesu ka　置くか，返すか
omikuji　おみくじ
Ōmori Chiben　大森智弁
Ōmotokyō　大本教
oni　鬼
onna no gō　女の業
onna no kenri　女の権利
onryō　怨霊
Osorezan　恐山
Ōta Tenrei　大田典礼
Ōtsu-e　大津絵

Reiyūkai Kyōdan　霊友会教団
Risshōkōseikai　立正佼成会
Ryūgenji　滝元寺
Saifukuji　西福寺
Sainokawara　賽の河原
sanba　産婆
sanya　産屋
Sasagawa Ryōichi　笹川良一
segaki-e　施餓鬼会
Seichō no Ie　生長の家
Seichō no Ie Seiji Rengō
　　生長の家政治連合
seishin no sekai　精神の世界
senzo kuyō　先祖供養
Shibahara Urako　柴原浦子
Shingon　真言
shin-shin shūkyō　新新宗教
Shintō　神道
shiryō　死霊
Shiryō gedatsu monogatari kikigaki
　　死霊解脱物語聞書
Shiunzan　紫雲山
shizenjin　自然人
Shōdenji　正伝寺
Shōkakuin　正覚院
Shufu no Tomo　主婦の友
Shugendō　修験道
Shūkan Gendai　週刊現代
Shūkan Post　週刊ポスト
Shūkan Sankei　週刊サンケイ
shūkyō hōjin　宗教法人
shūnen　執念
sōdai　総代
Sōka Gakkai　創価学会
Sono Ayako　曽野綾子
Sōtō　曹洞
sotoba　卒塔婆
suishi　水子
Suke　すけ
Taniguchi Masaharu　谷口雅春
tatari　たたり
teihatsu　剃髪
Tendai　天台

tengu　天狗

Tenrikyō　天理教

Tenshōji　天聖寺

Tenshōkōtai Jingūkyō
　天照皇大神宮教

tōba　塔婆

tokudo　得度

Tokugawa Tsunayoshi　徳川綱吉

Tōno-chō　遠野町

toriagebāsan　取り上げ婆さん

torihikibāsan　取り引き婆さん

torii　鳥居

Tōyōji　東陽寺

tsuizen kuyō　追善供養

tsumi　罪

tsumi no ishiki　罪の意識

Tsuyama-shi　津山市

ubugami　産神

umarekawari　生まれ変わり

umasete kureru　産ませてくれる

umazume　石女

umeyo, fuyaseyo　産めよ，増やせよ

uranai　占い

uranaishi　占師

wakashū　若衆

yaku yoke　厄除け

yamabushi　山伏

Yamamoto Sumika
　山本鈴美香

Yasukuni Jinja　靖国神社

Yoshi　よし

Yoshiwara　吉原

Yukuhashi-shi　行橋市

yūsei hogo hō　優生保護法

Yūten Shōnin　祐天上人

Yūten Shōnin daisōjō godenki
　祐天上人大僧正御伝記

Zaō Gongen　蔵王権現

zasu　座主

Zōjōji　増上寺

Index

Abortion: age of women undergoing, in 1955, 65; attitudes toward, 69, 71, 126–27; coerced, 70–71, 73; "common sense" approach, 14, 63, 101, 153, 169, 174, 196, 251; and context of relationship, 103, 126, 128, 148; and contraception, 25, 66, 67–68, 150, 256; cost of, 149; under Criminal Code of 1907, 49–50; criminal convictions of providers, 50; criminalized in Meiji, 21, 253; and desired family size, 152; doctors' earnings from, 77; and economic growth, 67; and economic hardship, 63, 65, 73, 98, 153, 196; in Edo period, 12, 20, 30, 43; among employed women, 112; and family problems, 88, 90, 126; first, from a man's perspective, 127–31, 132–33, 133–35, 137–40, 140–42, 152; of first pregnancy, 106, 125; and future ability to bear children, 113, 116; as gendered phenomenon, 11, 102; illegal, 57; and illicit affairs, 63–64, 66–67; legalization of, 3, 13, 21; meanings attached to, 104, 125; media portrayal of, 77, 130; and menopause symptoms, 88, 98; men's attitudes toward, 134, 148, 152–53; men's role in, 99, 132–33, 149, 152, 168–69; methods of, 65; moralizing on, 63; personal accounts of, 14, 104–53; politicization of, 104, 105; portrayal of, in advice columns, 14, 63–64, 253–54; prefered to illegitimacy, 67, 68, 72; in premodern Japan, xxi, 25, 196; regret for, 66, 70, 127, 148; religious considerations, 65, 127, 152; responsibility for, 267n10; and sexual pleasure, 14, 21, 150, 173, 174; stereotypical representations of, 64; studies of, xix–xx; sufferings in hell for, 269n24; teenage, 63, 71–73; unresolved feelings about, in older generation, 16, 78, 156; and women's autonomy, 103, 118, 119. *See also* Abortion rate

Abortion clinics: contracts with temple to perform rites, 207; in Edo period, 43; Planned Parenthood, 145–46, 148

Abortion rate: compared to Western countries, 275n43; highest point, 249, 257; from 1950 to 1989, 58; from 1953 to 1964, 275n35; from 1955 to 1975, 68; from 1955 to 1980, 110–11; 1976 to present, 71; in 1984, *83;* postwar, 253

Abortion remains, 207, 217

Advertising, 3, 79–80, 251, 267n9, 278n78; by temples and shrines, 93, 94, 207, 218, 240

Advice columns. See *Jinsei annai*

Afterbirth, disposal of, 24–25

Agon-shū, 60, 154, 190

Aizenji (Tsuyama), 217, *218,* 219

Akago (red child), 27

Aka mizu, 199

Alien, 91

Allen, Judith, *Sex and Secrets* by, xx

Amano, Fumiko, 56, 60

Amaterasu, 240, 283n14

American influence, 174

Amida. *See* Buddha Amida

Ancestor worship: in Bentenshū, 185; emphasized by spiritualists, 159; at Myō-senji, 221, 222; and parish temples, 157; in Shintō, 238

Ancestral spirits, 255

Compositor:	G&S Typesetters, Inc.
Text:	10/13 Galliard
Display:	Galliard
Printer:	Thomson-Shore, Inc.
Binder:	Thomson-Shore, Inc.